Operation Pedro Pan and the Exodus of Cuba's Children

OPERATION PEDRO PAN AND THE EXODUS OF CUBA'S CHILDREN

DEBORAH SHNOOKAL

University of Florida Press
Gainesville

Publication of this paperback edition made possible by a Sustaining the Humanities through the American Rescue Plan grant from the National Endowment for the Humanities.

Copyright 2020 by Deborah Shnookal
All rights reserved
Published in the United States of America

First cloth printing, 2020
First paperback printing, 2022

27 26 25 24 23 22   6 5 4 3 2 1

Library of Congress Cataloging-in-Publication Data
Names: Shnookal, Deborah, author.
Title: Operation Pedro Pan and the exodus of Cuba's children / Deborah Shnookal.
Description: Gainesville : University of Florida Press, 2020. | Includes bibliographical references and index.
Identifiers: LCCN 2019058809 (print) | LCCN 2019058810 (ebook) | ISBN 9781683401551 (hardback) | ISBN 9781683401827 (pdf) | ISBN 9781683402671 (pbk.)
Subjects: LCSH: Refugee children—Cuba. | Refugee children—United States. | Refugee children—Services for—United States.
Classification: LCC HV640.5.C9 S55 2020 (print) | LCC HV640.5.C9 (ebook) | DDC 362.7/7914089687291073—dc23
LC record available at https://lccn.loc.gov/2019058809
LC ebook record available at https://lccn.loc.gov/2019058810

| UF PRESS

UNIVERSITY
OF FLORIDA

University of Florida Press
2046 NE Waldo Road
Suite 2100
Gainesville, FL 32609
http://upress.ufl.edu

CONTENTS

List of Figures   vii

Acknowledgments   ix

List of Abbreviations   xi

Introduction   1

1. A Revolutionary Hurricane Sweeps Cuba   21
2. *Alfabeticemos!* Let's Teach Literacy! Learning the "Why" of the Revolution   63
3. The *Patria Potestad* Hoax   105
4. Operation Pedro Pan and the Children Who Could Fly   127
5. The Dark Side of Neverland   160
6. The Pedro Pan Paradox   197

   Conclusion: Ambassadors, Soldiers, or Spies?   213

   Notes   223

   Bibliography   285

   Index   305

FIGURES

0.1. Pedro Pan girls waiting at Miami airport   10
0.2. Literacy *brigadista* girls, 1961   19
1.1. "The youthful face of Cuba today"   23
1.2. Literacy *brigadistas*, 1961   27
1.3. "How they want to dress this Day of the Kings," 1961   29
1.4. "Avon calling for unity!"   37
1.5. Young *brigadista* and his pupil   41
1.6. "*Compañera* Domestic: Study!"   44
1.7. Nationalization of private schools: "Thanks Fidel!"   56
1.8. Battle of the billboards: "Will this child be a believer or an atheist?"   61
2.1. Vanquishing illiteracy and Uncle Sam   66
2.2. Recruitment advertisement for literacy campaign *brigadistas*   71
2.3. Report from the Conrado Benítez Brigades   78
2.4. Father's song to his *brigadista* son   88
2.5. Literacy *brigadistas* with giant pencils   93
2.6. The anti-Castro movement view of the literacy campaign   98
2.7. Literacy *brigadistas* celebrate the end of the campaign   102
3.1. "Hide the kid!"   107
3.2. Cuban press report of the discovery of fake *patria potestad* law   115
4.1. "Last one in . . ."   131
4.2. Fr. Bryan Walsh with Pedro Pans at St. Raphael's, Miami   156
5.1. Pedro Pans learn to salute the U.S. flag   189
6.1. Film poster for the 2017 documentary, *Elián*   205
6.2. Statue of José Martí and child, Havana   211

ACKNOWLEDGMENTS

This project has had a rather long gestation, and there are many people I wish to thank for their support.

First and foremost, I am grateful to the Pedro Pans and the literacy *brigadistas* who were most generous in sharing their stories with me.

I also must acknowledge the assistance I received from many others in Cuba and the United States, especially Mirta Muñiz; Jesús Arboleya; Fabián Escalante; José Buajasán; Ramón Torreira; Luisa Campos, director of the Museo de la Alfabetización (National Literacy Campaign Museum) in Havana; Prensa Latina photo archive (Havana); Ximena Valdivia (Barry University Library, Miami); Amanda Moreno (University of Miami Library); Irving Kessler and Jerry Nickel the librarian (Lourdes Casal Library, Center for Cuban Studies, New York); and Jon Elliston (former researcher at the National Security Archive, George Washington University, Washington, D.C.). A number of librarians at La Trobe University's Borchardt Library also facilitated my access to overseas materials from Australia.

The wonderfully supportive and stimulating environment of La Trobe University's Institute of Latin American Studies has offered me inspiration and encouragement over many years.

I would also like to thank Ralph Newmark and Heidi Zogbaum at La Trobe University, and also Lou-anne Barker and Christine Graunas, for their help in getting the final manuscript knocked into shape. My thanks also to Stephanye Hunter and the editorial team at the University of Florida Press for their enthusiasm about publishing this book.

Most importantly, I have sincerely appreciated the patience, advice, and encouragement from my wonderful dear friends and colleagues Barry Carr and the late Steve Niblo.

Finally, I should express my gratitude to my *compañero* David for supporting me when it was most needed on this and our longer journey and many adventures together.

ABBREVIATIONS

ACU	Agrupación Católica Universitaria / Catholic University Association
AJR	Asociación de Jóvenes Rebeldes / Association of Rebel Youth
CDR	Comité de Defensa de la Revolución / Committee for the Defense of the Revolution
CHC	Centro Hispano Católico / Catholic Hispanic Center (Miami)
CIA	Central Intelligence Agency
CIHSE	Centro de Investigaciones Históricas de la Seguridad del Estado / Center for Historical Investigations on State Security
CRC	Consejo Revolucionario Cubano / Cuban Revolutionary Council
CWB	Catholic Welfare Bureau
DHEW	Department of Health, Education, and Welfare
DRE	Directorio Revolucionario Estudiantil / Revolutionary Student Directorate
EIR	Escuelas de Instrucción Revolucionaria / Schools of Revolutionary Instruction
FAR	Fuerzas Armadas Revolucionarias / Revolutionary Armed Forces
FBI	Federal Bureau of Investigation
FEU	Federación de Estudiantes Universitarios / Federation of University Students
FMC	Federación de Mujeres Cubanas / Federation of Cuban Women
FRD	Frente Revolucionario Democrático / Revolutionary Democratic Front
HIAS	Hebrew Immigrant Aid Society
ICAIC	Instituto Cubano de Artes e Industrias Cinematográficas / Cuban Institute of Cinema Arts

INRA	Instituto Nacional de Reforma Agraria / National Institute of Agrarian Reform
INS	Immigration and Naturalization Service
MDC	Movimiento Democrático Cristiano / Democratic Christian Movement
MINED	Ministerio de Educación / Ministry of Education
MINFAR	Ministerio de las Fuerzas Armadas Revolucionarias / Ministry of the Revolutionary Armed Forces
MININT	Ministerio del Interior / Ministry of the Interior
MINREX	Ministerio de Relaciones Exteriores / Ministry of Foreign Relations
MNR	Milicias Nacionales Revolucionarias / Revolutionary National Militias
MRP	Movimiento Revolucionario del Pueblo / Revolutionary Movement of the People
MRR	Movimiento de Recuperación Revolucionario / Revolutionary Recovery Movement
NSC	National Security Council
OAS	Organization of American States
ORI	Organizaciones Revolucionarias Integradas / Integrated Revolutionary Organizations
PCC	Partido Comunista de Cuba / Cuban Communist Party
PSP	Partido Socialista Popular / Popular Socialist Party (Cuba's communist party prior to 1959)
PURS	Partido Unido de la Revolución Socialista de Cuba / United Party of the Socialist Revolution
UJC	Unión de Jóvenes Comunistas / Union of Communist Youth
UNEAC	Unión de Escritores y Artistas de Cuba / Cuban Union of Writers and Artists
UR	Unidad Revolucionaria / Revolutionary Unity
USIA	United States Information Agency

Introduction

In March 1962, the *Miami Herald* broke the dramatic story: eight thousand Cuban children had been "saved from Castro brainwashing."[1] Described as "[l]onely and often frightened without their parents," the young refugees had been cared for by church groups and local welfare agencies, funded by the U.S. government. Their flight from Cuba was reported to have been organized by a young Miami priest, Father Bryan O. Walsh, director of the modest Catholic Welfare Bureau.[2]

In what was quaintly dubbed Operation Pedro (or Peter) Pan, fourteen thousand Cuban children were airlifted to Miami over twenty-two months from December 1960 to October 1962. Although all the young "Pedro Pans" (as they were christened in the United States) were intensely aware of being caught up in the revolutionary hurricane that swept the island of Cuba after the 1959 revolution, few realized they were actually part of an organized effort to "rescue" them.[3] They left behind a country undergoing a profound social transformation that generated excitement and optimism in many Cubans and confusion, anger, and fear in others.

It was a "very scary time," remembered Alex López, who left as a twelve-year-old Pedro Pan in July 1962; his parents, like many others, believed they were acting in their son's best interests and that he would attend a prestigious, church-run U.S. boarding school.[4] "Ay! Dios mío!" said his mother, "I was so afraid that [the revolutionary government] was going to take my son from me . . ."[5] For Rosa Otero, "it was like a cloud that enveloped all of us. We actually never knew what was happening. The only thing they said was that we [children] had to go." Her parents told her that it was going to be like in biblical times, when King Herod gathered up the children for slaughter.[6]

"It [became] like a chain reaction," one exile recalled: "One mother would say, 'I'm sending my son [out of the country],' and the other one would say, 'Me, too!' Anyway, they thought it was only for a short time until the Americans got rid of Fidel Castro. I don't think they would have sent their children away if they had thought it was going to be for such a long time. But they [believed] it would only be for a few months and that the priests [in Miami] would take care of their children."[7]

Young Raquel, who remained in Cuba, watched in amazement as her school friends and neighbors "disappeared" to the North, "as if by magic." She realized her world was now "split in two irreconcilable halves: before and now, there [Miami] and here [Cuba], 'worms' and revolutionaries, traitors and patriots, Catholics and Communists. Both halves tugged at our hearts, dividing our emotions, our friends, our families, and above all else, forcing us to decide."[8]

What was behind this unprecedented mass exodus of Cuban children is still highly contested. In Cuba, even though no one was ever arrested or charged for having organized the evacuation scheme, the story is often recounted as one of a mass kidnapping of the nation's smallest citizens.[9] On the other hand, the story of Operation Pedro Pan has served ideologically to bolster Washington's belligerent policy toward revolutionary Cuba for well over half a century. When U.S. president Donald Trump announced in June 2017 that he was "canceling" his predecessor Barack Obama's Cuba policy, he made special mention of "Operation Peter Pan" as evidence of what he stressed was the "brutal nature of the Castro regime."[10] In doing so, President Trump was simply reiterating what has become the orthodox view of the "rescue" project in the United States: that organizers of the airlift simply responded to Cuban parents' desperation to prevent the "communist indoctrination" of their children and "defend" the Cuban family that was said to be under threat from the revolutionary government.[11]

Operation Pedro Pan and the Exodus of Cuba's Children interrogates both views and suggests that a multitude of complex factors drove the children's flight, unpacking the various renditions of this story generated on different sides of the Florida Straits as a tale of triumph or tragedy, rescue or kidnap, salvation or sacrifice. Furthermore, an examination of what propelled a generation of young Cubans on such divergent paths can offer a deeper understanding of the dynamics of the social revolution that unfolded on that Caribbean island after 1959, how it impacted individuals and families, and why they reacted and acted as they did.

When the Missile Crisis stopped all flights between Cuba and the United States in October 1962, several thousand Pedro Pans found themselves stranded and alone, and many had to wait years to be reunited with their parents. Some never saw one or both parents again. Although many former Pedro Pans have expressed their gratitude for having had the chance to "live the American dream," many of them experienced significant trauma and bear lasting emotional scars due to the abrupt and often prolonged separation from their families.

For those young Cubans who flew away with Operation Pedro Pan, and for those they left behind on the island, thousands of whom participated in the 1961 national literacy campaign, their experiences were clearly transcendental—especially as they occurred during the individual's most formative years. What makes this story particularly fascinating is that the Pedro Pans and the literacy *brigadistas* were the same cohort: classmates, cousins, friends, neighbors, sometimes even siblings. Thus, the options of Miami or the mountains symbolized, for that generation of young Cubans and for Cuba itself, far more than geographical locations.

Over the years, the story of the flight of the Pedro Pans became key to the ideological foundation or "creation myth" of the Cuban exile community—traded upon by aspiring political candidates and celebrities alike—in order to discredit Cuba's revolutionary project and inoculate others, especially in Latin America, who might consider a similar socialist experiment.[12] For Cuban émigrés in the United States, the story of Operation Pedro Pan became central to demonstrating that conditions in Castro's Cuba were so horrific that parents were driven to take desperate measures to protect their children.[13] Thus, any suggestion that factors other than humanitarian concerns were behind the exodus has been considered apostasy in Miami, and any mention of the trauma or abuse the children might have experienced in their lonely exile dismissed as "ingratitude."[14]

When the five-year-old Cuban boy Elián González was rescued at sea on Thanksgiving in November 1999, and then held by his Miami relatives against his father's wishes, the ensuing international custody battle evoked great bitterness and painful memories for many former Pedro Pans, who felt that they, too, had been regarded as trophies in a political game.[15] "This is not the first time," wrote a former Pedro Pan, Chicago professor María de los Angeles Torres, "that Cuba's destiny has been contested through children."[16] Another Pedro Pan pleaded with U.S. political leaders to "stop the forty-year practice of using Cuban children as proxies in their fight and start exploring ways to normalize relations between Cuba and the United States."[17]

The initial impetus for Operation Pedro Pan apparently arose in the lead-up to the April 1961 Bay of Pigs invasion from Cubans engaged in the struggle to halt the revolutionary process and overthrow Fidel Castro and his government. "I had made the decision to struggle for the liberation of Cuba," said one father, "and I wanted to ensure that [my children] did not become victims due to my conspiratorial activity."[18] But the fear of "communism" and its supposed threat to children and the family was how most Cuban parents explained their decision to send their children alone to Miami, Cold War propaganda emanating from the Vatican and the United States about the "red menace" having deeply penetrated the Cuban psyche. But an individual or a class's perceptions and experiences of such a profound revolutionary, transformative process as that unleashed on the island of Cuba in 1959 are not the same as, nor do they necessarily explain, what the revolution was all about and what the revolutionary leadership's intentions or goals might have been with regard to children, education, and the family. Moreover, as with all migration processes, a variety of push and pull factors was in play.[19]

The real story of Operation Pedro Pan is therefore far more than a simple Cold War conspiracy tale of intrigue and rescue as it has often been portrayed. The goal here is to unravel the threads of this story in order to expose its complexity and the many factors that lay behind the exodus of the Cuban children. Like the thousands of Latin American families displaced today by drug wars, gang violence, or poverty, Cuban parents were not only driven to find a way to safeguard their children from perceived or real threats. They, like millions of others across the globe today, were seeking a better life for their children, beckoned by and believing the welcoming words on New York's Statue of Liberty. Moreover, the border between Cuba and the United States had historically been very porous, with regular migration flows in both directions. The Pedro Pans arrived in a country that was neither far nor foreign to more prosperous Cuban families, and therefore the proposition of sending one's children to "the North" for a brief period was not as drastic or desperate an act as it may first appear, especially when special visas, free airfares, tuition, and board were all on offer. Operation Pedro Pan apparently presented an opportunity for a much-prized U.S. educational scholarship or *"beca,"* which had a "magnet effect" that undoubtedly influenced some, if not many, Cuban parents' decision.[20]

Significantly, about half the number of unaccompanied minors sent out of Cuba were claimed by family friends or relatives already living in the United States.[21] Many young Cubans from privileged families had already visited the United States as students, for summer camp, or on family vacations.[22] Therefore the prospect of a trip to the United States as a Pedro Pan, for many, seemed like just another holiday adventure. One young girl was surprised by her mother's tearfulness: "But *everyone's* going," she remembers pleading. Another Pedro Pan, whose cousins had studied in the United States, knew this was "something only rich people did. So we pretended that we, too, were rich and going overseas to study."[23]

Furthermore, Cuba's historical dependency on Washington to step in at times of political crisis encouraged passivity, if not paralysis, on the part of those who might otherwise have formed a coherent and cohesive brake on the deepening radicalization process of the revolution.[24] Although some parents of Pedro Pans were actively engaged in efforts to overthrow the revolutionary government—as were some Pedro Pans themselves—many other disaffected middle- and upper-class Cubans simply chose to place themselves or at least their children temporarily offshore until, as they believed would happen, the U.S. Marines stepped in to remove Fidel Castro and restore the former status quo.

Unlike the Central American and other migrant families, whose children were so brutally torn from their parents' arms in the name of President Trump's "zero-tolerance" policy toward undocumented entrants, Father Bryan Walsh, the young priest who ran a small staff at the Catholic Welfare Bureau in Miami, received the imprimatur of the State Department to sign visa waivers for as many Cuban children as their parents wanted to dispatch. Moreover, Cubans arriving on U.S. soil were deemed to be political refugees solely on the basis of their country of origin: "communist" Cuba.[25]

Thus, mythologizing Operation Pedro Pan came to feed not only the exile community's raison d'être or creation myth but flattered North Americans' self-image as refuge for those escaping tyranny and oppression. "It is a mark of the faith these parents [have] in the warm heart of the United States," observed the director of the Cuban Refugee Program, "that they sent their children alone ... to this country."[26] As Washington's hostility toward the new revolutionary government ramped up, the historical "ties of singular intimacy" between the two nations were rent asunder, forcing Cubans to choose which side they were on, like a bitter breakup within a family.[27]

Understanding the unique nature of this relationship helps explain a significant element behind parents' readiness to enroll their children in Operation Pedro Pan—a separation generally assumed to be brief, and certainly (at least not in the beginning) not viewed as a prelude to the emigration of the entire family. Moreover, underlying the escalating U.S.-Cuba conflict was not so much a Cold War dichotomy but Washington's inability to imagine Cuba as anything but a colony. Since the nineteenth century, North Americans had tended to regard Cubans as "children incapable of understanding their best interests."[28] Here the Peter Pan metaphor might be deployed to argue that Cuba itself represented the child who never grew up or would never grow up.

Occurring at the height of the Cold War and ninety miles off the Florida coast, the Cuban revolution's audacious rejection of Washington's dictates immediately sparked concerns about its political hue.[29] Indeed, after a brief encounter with the Cuban leader in April 1959, Vice President Richard Nixon was one of the first to conclude that Castro was either a communist or "incredibly naïve with regard to the communist threat," and he instantly became an ardent advocate of Castro's overthrow.[30]

Events in Cuba became a significant issue in the 1960 U.S. presidential election campaign, with Senator John F. Kennedy scoring points against his opponent, Richard Nixon, by saying he was not doing enough to get rid of Castro.[31] But Kennedy's accusations were simply electoral theatrics, as he had already been briefed about President Dwight D. Eisenhower's "regime change" program to overthrow the revolutionary government, approved by the president on 17 March 1960.[32]

The thousands of Cubans pouring into the then sleepy little town of Miami soon required a response from the U.S. government; and because the problem had received considerable publicity, the Eisenhower administration had to be seen as "doing something suitable . . . not necessarily related to the *actual needs* of the situation," but something, the State Department concluded, that would "reflect credit upon [our] response to the needs of these victims of Castro's oppression."[33] This set the tone for the Cuban refugee policy in the last months of the Eisenhower administration, a policy expanded by President Kennedy, who regarded the Cuban refugees as "victims of the Cold War and thus a national responsibility."[34] Fighting and winning the Cold War in Latin America became one of Kennedy's paramount concerns, an objective he described during his campaign as "a struggle for supremacy between two conflicting ideologies: Freedom under God versus ruthless, godless tyranny."[35]

Early on, Washington policymakers recognized that the portrayal of Cuban children as "helpless victims of terrorism" could be a particularly effective focus for propaganda in order "to make the world choose the anti-Castro side."[36] The plight of the Cuban children would subsequently feature prominently in the psychological warfare waged against the revolutionary government, and in the propaganda campaign to win popular support for Washington's covert war against Cuba and overcome domestic resistance to the U.S. "open door" policy for Cuban refugees.

As the pace of the revolutionary reforms quickened, so did the exodus of Cubans from the island, and as the revolution reached deeper and deeper into Cuban society, children and their parents often reacted quite differently to the changes. A Pedro Pan later reflected: "A revolution sweeps away all previous values. And [our parents] wanted us to be like them. They knew that if we stayed, we were going to be different. So that's why they sent us out of Cuba."[37]

Establishing a new sense of what it meant to be Cuban was a cornerstone of the new revolutionary project, which inevitably meant challenging not just the existential economic and political relationship between the two countries but also the overwhelming cultural influence of the United States. Explaining the need to "Cubanize" Cuba, Fidel Castro recalled, "we ourselves lived imbued with that type of complex of doubt, of resignation and where we undervalued the interest of our nationality before things foreign. We lived with the sensation that everything here was bad."[38] Almost overnight, recalled one young émigré, the United States "went from father figure to scapegoat."[39]

Above all, it was the 1961 national literacy campaign—a highly political as well as pedagogical exercise—coinciding as it did with the attempted invasion of the island at the Bay of Pigs by exiles, trained and armed by the United States, that marked an abrupt shift in how most Cubans saw themselves and their closest neighbor, dramatically underscoring the alternatives facing the Cuban people. Teenage Cubans, and some even younger, signed up in the thousands as *brigadistas* to emulate their revolutionary heroes by teaching literacy to their less fortunate compatriots in the mountains and villages across the island. It was soon evident to analysts in Washington that young Cubans were overwhelmingly behind Fidel and the revolution.[40]

Horror stories circulated about how children "were taught to view the revolution as their ultimate master, to tell on their parents if they were engaged in 'counterrevolutionary activities.'"[41] The former director of a Havana private school reported some young Cubans were resisting their parents' plans to send them to the United States. The young generation, he remarked, "is growing up in the Communist environment. . . . They are real fanatics; they are Communist fanatics," he despaired. Sometimes, he said, parents were afraid "to share any of their political ideas with their own children."[42]

Father Bryan O. Walsh, the Irish-born Miami priest responsible for the airlift (who was promoted to monsignor in 1962), was aware that some Cuban parents had become gravely concerned about their children when they began to join progovernment youth groups. Most affected, he said, were the families of "the small minority, generally of the middle class, who were practicing Catholics and those . . . who worked in foreign-owned businesses."[43] The "whole foundation of Pedro Pan," said Msgr. Walsh, "was the inalienable rights of the parents to decide the education of their children. . . . All Pedro Pan did was create a window of opportunity for Cuban parents to exercise their rights." The literacy campaign and the subsequent education reforms, he suggested, underscored the urgency of the rescue mission.[44] While he rejected any suggestion that Operation Pedro Pan was ever used as "propaganda" against the Cuban government or that it had any connection to the Central Intelligence Agency (CIA), Msgr. Walsh evidently relished his bit part in a Cold War drama, recalling the moment the child airlift began: "We were now sharing the worries of families we did not even know, hundreds of miles away, in a life and death struggle in the Cold War."[45]

There is, however, an aspect of the Cuban revolution that, to date, has been largely ignored by those writing about Operation Pedro Pan, probably because it is so obvious—or maybe because it gets in the way of preconceived arguments or frameworks. The Cuban revolution was, above all else, a revolution of the youth, by the youth, as well as for the youth, a fact most dramatically illustrated by the literacy campaign in which 100,000 young Cubans participated, leaving their comfortable homes in cities and towns to work as volunteer teachers in some of the most remote and underdeveloped parts of the island. What thousands of Cuban teenagers saw as an exciting adventure provoked a kind of moral panic among some parents who were concerned about preserving the propriety, piety, and obedience of their offspring—especially their daughters, who surprisingly were the majority of the literacy *brigadistas*—although they might have articulated different concerns.[46]

The 1961 literacy campaign is often identified as a significant, if not the most important, driving factor behind Operation Pedro Pan, which is undoubtedly the case, but not because of the Cold War trope that is usually rolled out: that it was, in essence, a mass indoctrination campaign and a conscious plan by the revolutionary government to place children beyond the influence and control of their parents. The literacy campaign did, however, introduce a new paradigm in mobilizing youth in the revolutionary social justice project.[47] And it gave young Cubans—as active participants—an identification with, a sense of responsibility for, and ownership of the revolution, a process from which some of their elders were feeling increasingly alienated or hostile.

The fact that the vast majority of Pedro Pans were teenagers—70 percent of them were boys over twelve—rather than young children (as the Pedro Pans are often portrayed), suggests that many of their parents were hoping to ensure their children's adherence to the "old ways" and circumvent their growing independence and political activism by removing them from revolutionary Cuba.[48] Recognizing this as one of the elements behind Operation Pedro Pan, of course, does not contain the same emotional power or dramatic effect as the image of frantic parents handing small children "into the arms of strangers" for the sake of their safety or indeed survival, as was the case in the *Kindertransport* of Jewish children out of Nazi-occupied Europe, to which Operation Pedro Pan is sometimes—inappropriately—compared.[49]

To regard Cuban youth solely as innocent victims swept up in the revolutionary hurricane rather than agents of and involved in the transformation of Cuba fits neatly with both the heroic rescue narrative and the argument that their parents were hoodwinked by CIA propaganda. The fact that more privileged Cuban parents committed to the preservation of the traditional patriarchal family were beginning to feel uncomfortable or unwelcome in the New Cuba under construction, and they were somewhat horrified to see their children become the people they "had warned them about" (as the 1960s slogan went).

Thus, Operation Pedro Pan can be viewed not only in the frameworks of a Cold War contest for the hearts and minds of the next generation and the breakdown in U.S.-Cuba relations from 1959 to 1961 that shattered a

Figure 0.1. Pedro Pan girls waiting to be collected at Miami airport. This photo was first published in Frances Stanley, *The New World Refugee . . . The Cuban Exodus* (USA: Church World Service, 1966).

historical relationship of patronage and protection. It can also be seen as a backlash to the challenge the Cuban revolution presented to traditional or conservative middle-class values, especially those concerning gender roles, racial discrimination, sexuality, and intrafamilial relationships. It was a revolution, which, in many ways, proved to be a harbinger of the youth revolt (in both its political and cultural expressions) that was to shake many parts of the world in the 1960s.[50] Apart from the self-reliance the Pedro Pans were forced to learn while they waited to be reunited with their parents, ironically, many if not most of the Pedro Pans were soon seduced by the teenage culture (or "youthquake" as it was dubbed by *Vogue* editor Diane Vreeland) they were exposed to in the United States, so that by the time their parents arrived they were no longer the children they had been, or whom their parents expected them to be, and families often found they were unable to take up where they had left off.

The Never-Ending Story of Operation Pedro Pan

I first learned about Operation Pedro Pan in the 1980s from Cuban American members of the Antonio Maceo Brigade who were living in New York, having been forced to leave Miami because of threats from exile terrorist groups opposed to any form of dialogue with the Cuban government.[51] As the daughter of a child migrant, and later as a foster parent myself, I was intrigued by the story, a story that provoked my empathy for members of those families that had been ripped apart some decades earlier—unnecessarily, as I came to conclude. At around the same time, voices were beginning to be raised against decades-long government policies in North America and Australia of the forced removal of indigenous children from their families, and I began to think that the Pedro Pan children might be considered another "stolen generation." My research convinced me this was not an accurate description of the Pedro Pan story. What then became my primary motivation to examine this episode in detail was a desire to understand what it reflected about U.S.-Cuba relations and the early years of the revolution in an effort to understand why the Cuban revolution did not collapse under the totally devastating conditions on the island in the 1990s, as was predicted almost universally.

Over nearly three decades of visiting Cuba as a researcher and editor, I was able to draw on a wide variety of contacts who facilitated my access to archives and individuals relevant to this project. I also kept notes on comments made in casual conversations that helped me appreciate the profound shake-up Cubans experienced in those early years of the revolution in their common assumptions, social mores and customs, and world view, especially among those from more privileged families who were more likely to identify with and aspire to North American value systems and culture.

I was also struck by comments made by Cubans of the same generation as the Pedro Pans that they, too, had left home in 1961, in their case, as teenage volunteers in the national literacy brigades. Former *brigadistas* would get carried away recounting where they went, the families they stayed with, and the hardships endured. Without exception, the impact of the literacy campaign on the individuals who participated as youthful *brigadistas* was life changing. It was often hard to get them back to my questions about what they remembered about the disappearance of their classmates and friends with Operation Pedro Pan.

This prompted me to further probe the social dynamics of what was taking place in revolutionary Cuba at the time, why some Cubans might have felt so uneasy or even threatened by changes affecting education, gender, race, and relations within the family, and how Cubans' identity as individuals and as a nation was radically transformed.

Remarkably few sources seem to exist in Cuba specifically about Operation Pedro Pan—the organized evacuation scheme—although the rumor campaign and the fake law that suggested the revolutionary government intended to eliminate parents' authority over their children is well documented. It was only during the international wrangle over Elián González that a Cuban book was published about the operation, describing the Pedro Pans as 14,000 *Eliáncitos* (little Eliáns).[52] This was a report prepared by two researchers who had been assigned a year or so earlier by the newly established Centro de Investigaciones Históricas de la Seguridad del Estado (Center for Historical Investigations on State Security, CIHSE), partly stimulated by my questions about what the Cuban government knew about Operation Pedro Pan at the time.[53] They examined evidence presented at the trials of individuals arrested for a range of CIA-backed counterrevolutionary activities but concluded that no one was ever sanctioned for their part in Operation Pedro Pan.[54] This included Ramón ("Mongo") Grau and his sister Leopoldina ("Polita"), key players in Operation Pedro Pan who later asserted they were jailed for assisting the evacuation scheme, but who, in reality, were charged and incarcerated for their part in assassination plots against leaders of the revolutionary government and other acts of terrorism.[55]

The lack of documentation in Cuba about Operation Pedro Pan does not necessarily prove that the children were successfully spirited off the island in secret but is more likely due to the fact that the departures of the children were not regarded at the time as particularly unusual, although the increasing numbers of unaccompanied children presenting for flights to Miami must have been noted by Cuban authorities. But although the children bore somewhat suspect paperwork for entering the United States, often just copies of the visa waiver letter signed by Fr. Bryan Walsh, they had passports and exit visas approved by their parents and Cuban immigration authorities.

Therefore, most of the evidence offered here—about how parents' anxieties were exacerbated and manipulated, how Cuban emigration was used as a political weapon against the revolutionary government, and how the Pedro Pan children, in particular, came to be deployed as part of Washington's covert war against Cuba—generally comes not from Cuban sources but from U.S. sources, such as the documents of the U.S. government and its agencies, as well as from the testimony of individuals directly involved in Operation Pedro Pan and the counterrevolutionary movement. These sources adequately demonstrate the political agendas animating the individuals and institutions that initiated or participated in the program and how the operation became so interlocked with the anti-Castro struggle as to be inseparable, at a time when the counterrevolution was increasingly run from the White House.

Operation Pedro Pan and the Exodus of Cuba's Children draws on a broad range of sources, including personal interviews conducted with Msgr. Walsh, with two former officials in Cuban state security, as well as with Armando Hart, Cuban minister for education at the time of the literacy campaign, and two other officials responsible for the publicity work of that campaign. The book includes interviews with several Pedro Pans and literacy *brigadistas,* some of whose siblings and classmates left with Operation Pedro Pan. But the primary focus here is on the circumstances that led to their departure, rather than the Pedro Pans' experiences in the United States, which have been presented in numerous published books, documentaries, plays, children's stories, academic studies, and memoirs—and even a recent musical—many of which are cited.

Interestingly, in their many published memoirs, most Pedro Pans have tended to speak on behalf of their parents, offering their own understanding of the motives behind their parents' decision rather than allowing their parents to speak for themselves.[56] But while many former Pedro Pans wonder whether they now, as parents themselves, would or could do the same, most (not all) have concluded that their parents acted in their best interests.[57] One Pedro Pan remained convinced his parents "did the right thing," saving him from what he said would have been "a horrible fate in Cuba," even though they were never reunited.[58]

Journalist Yvonne Conde's interest in Operation Pedro Pan was spurred by a need to understand her own experience as part of a program she, like many of the Pedro Pan children, knew nothing about at the time. She drew attention to the trauma and lasting pain experienced by the child refugees and their families because of the unexpectedly prolonged separation, even though she, like most Pedro Pan alumni she interviewed, approved of the choice their parents had made for them because, she argued, the Cuban school system subsequently instituted exactly what many feared—that the state would assume the primary role in the socialization of children.[59]

María de los Angeles Torres, who has offered the most comprehensive study published to date about Operation Pedro Pan, was similarly driven by a desire to understand her own and others' parents' motives for sending their children away—why their concern to protect their children's minds, in her view, overrode their concern for their offspring's emotional well-being. This led her to examine the political and philosophical underpinnings of the operation—how and why children became the focus of a contest between two nation-building projects: the Old and the New Cubas.[60]

Other researchers have also viewed Operation Pedro Pan through the lens of the politics of childhood.[61] There has often been a tendency, however, among many of those writing about the operation to portray the Pedro Pans as very young children, sometimes even as babies, despite the fact that the majority of the Pedro Pans were adolescents.[62] This reinforces the modern cultural construct of childhood that imagines children as innocent and vulnerable, in need of both protection and spiritual and moral guidance.[63] The Cuban researchers similarly described the "principal victims" of Operation Pedro Pan as "defenseless children" whose parents were "often deceived or cleverly confused by false rumors."[64] More recent studies have challenged this static view of childhood and show how a child's moral and cognitive development generally occurs between the ages of twelve to fourteen, meaning that a child "has a degree of self-determination and autonomy, and can be assisted into making choices rather than being the passive object of concern."[65] There is an obvious difference between the vulnerability, consciousness, motivation, and therefore the agency of a five-year-old child and a teenager of fifteen or sixteen.

As most Pedro Pans were generally from affluent, middle-class families their experience of childhood was clearly quite different from their compatriots from poor urban or rural families, some of them frankly admitting to being real "*bitongos*" (mama's boys).[66] But at the same time, a good number of the Pedro Pans were already quite politically active—some supporting and some opposing the revolutionary government—as Fr. Bryan Walsh himself noted.[67] It is, therefore, an oversimplification to reduce the Pedro Pans or their cohort that remained in Cuba to beings encased in innocence and inertia, pawns in a Cold War power play, blank slates on which governments could write what they chose. Many Pedro Pans actively lobbied their parents to send them to Miami, and the young literacy *brigadistas* were far from unwilling or naïve conscripts, as will be shown in chapter 2.

Peter or Pedro?

The continuing controversy surrounding the 1960–1962 airlift of Cuban children is evident in the fact that there is no agreement even about its name—known as Operation "Peter" Pan in Cuba, while in North America, it is referred to as "Pedro" Pan. One explanation offered was that calling the program "Peter" suggests U.S. involvement and CIA manipulation, whereas "Pedro" reinforces the argument that the impetus came from Cuba and that Cuban parents made their own decisions about what was best for their children.[68]

I chose to use Pedro rather than Peter for various reasons. In English-speaking countries, to describe a person as a "Peter Pan" is to say she (or usually he) is someone who (like Peter in J. M. Barrie's children's story) never grew up—or refused to grow up. That was definitely not the case with the young Cuban refugees who found they had to grow up all too quickly when they were separated from their parents for months and often years. Therefore, it is rather confusing and highly inappropriate to refer to the child refugees as "Peter Pans."

Furthermore, it seems best to refer to the operation as it has been known in the United States since the child "rescue" scheme was first made public in early 1962, initially described as "the underground railway in the sky" that was reported to be flying Cuban children to freedom.[69] Msgr. Walsh has explained the name was a kind of "code name," coined by a close friend, Miami broadcaster Ralph Renick, when the local media agreed to keep the story under wraps.[70] Early researchers usually only referred to the Cuban Children's Program, but more recently "Operation Pedro Pan" is the commonly used name applied to both the evacuation scheme and the foster care program established to care for the young refugees once they reached the United States. But it is important to recognize that, at least initially, these were two distinct programs. Moreover, only about half the unaccompanied Cuban minors arriving in Miami required foster care, the rest being claimed by family friends or relatives.

An additional element of confusion comes from the tendency, particularly in Cuba, to conflate Operation Pedro Pan with the propaganda campaign about the revolutionary government's alleged threat to parents' rights.[71] As explained in chapter 3, the exodus of the children was fueled by the CIA-inspired and -instigated hoax about *patria potestad*, but that may not have been its original intention.[72]

While some female Pedro Pans have chosen to call themselves "Wendy," after the eldest child of the Darling family whom Peter Pan taught to fly in the original children's story, I have opted to call all the young Cuban refugees "Pedro," regardless of their gender.[73]

A more significant issue arises, however, with determining exactly who is now considered to be a Pedro Pan, a much-coveted status due to the importance of the story of Operation Pedro Pan as the raison d'être of the Cuban émigré community, especially in Miami, where it bears both cachet and considerable credibility.[74] To be recognized officially as a Pedro Pan, one must have arrived at Miami airport between the dates of 26 December 1960 and 23 October 1962 as an unaccompanied minor, and have one's name and details noted in the logbook meticulously maintained by Jorge ("George") Guarch, an employee of the Catholic Welfare Bureau who monitored all the flights arriving from Cuba.[75] The Operation Pedro Pan Group, Inc., founded in 1991 by Ely Chovel as a support group and charity, set itself the task of locating all former Pedro Pans.[76] More recently the *Miami Herald* established a database for former Pedro Pans to register and keep in touch with one another.[77] Consequently, when Guarch's logbooks were passed on to Barry University in Miami, which now holds Msgr. Bryan Walsh's papers, some Cuban Americans discovered much to their surprise that they should regard themselves as Pedro Pans.[78] This is because Guarch noted the names of all unaccompanied children arriving from Cuba, not just those taken into the care of the Catholic Welfare Bureau or other agencies.

There is a question about whether and for how long Operation Pedro Pan continued after October 1962, but for the purpose of this study the "official" definition of a Pedro Pan has been accepted.

The first chapter examines the countervailing forces within Cuban society that were exposed as a revolutionary hurricane swept the island. It discusses the revolutionary government's policies with regard to youth and the family—such as measures related to child care, religious belief, education, racial integration, and gender equality.

Because the 1961 literacy campaign is frequently identified as a significant stimulus for Operation Pedro Pan, the second chapter takes a detailed look at how the battle for the hearts and minds of the next generation unfolded with the mobilization by the revolutionary government of 100,000 teenagers to teach literacy in the mountains and remote regions of Cuba.

The next chapter reviews the impact in Cuba of Cold War propaganda about communism and the family, the origins of the rumor campaign that the revolutionary government planned to eliminate *patria potestad* (parental authority) and make all children wards of the state, and why this scare campaign was so effective in convincing many Cubans to send their children out of the country.

Who initiated the airlift and how it was organized is considered in chapter 4. This chapter suggests parents had many and varied motives for sending their children to Miami and did not simply swallow CIA propaganda. It also explains why the program was conceived as being specifically for unaccompanied minors rather than to assist the emigration of family groups and the role of the Catholic church in the promotion and organization of the scheme.

In chapter 5, Operation Pedro Pan is shown to be both the result of, and ultimately an integral part of, the U.S. government's regime change project to undermine and overthrow the Cuban government, how it depended on counterrevolutionary networks that were intimately bound up with the CIA, and how the Pedro Pans were seen in Washington as potential ambassadors, soldiers, or spies.

The next chapter considers the apparent paradox that although Operation Pedro Pan is generally regarded in Cuba as a criminal act against the revolution, no one was ever charged or imprisoned for that crime. This chapter also discusses how the story of Operation Pedro Pan became central to the creation myth of the émigré community in the United States and how, ironically, in the 1999–2000 custody battle over the refugee child Elián González, a Cuban father's right of *patria potestad* was temporarily overturned by the toxic politics of the exile community in Miami.

* * *

The story of Operation Pedro Pan appears destined to be regularly revived in the ongoing discourse on the troubled relationship between Cuba and the United States, probably because it stirs such conflicted and conflicting memories on both sides. When Fidel Castro died in November 2016, former Pedro Pans jostled one another to get in front of the television cameras as they had done during the battle over little Elián González, in order to recount their personal, tragic tales of how the Cuban leader was responsible for their lost or stolen childhoods and their broken families. For Cubans on the island, however, Operation Pedro Pan is viewed as a painful example of Washington's dirty war against the revolution.

Operation Pedro Pan and the Exodus of Cuba's Children uses various lenses to expose what lay behind this most dramatic and still highly controversial episode of Cuban–U.S. history that so marked the generation of the revolution and subsequent generations on both sides of the Florida Straits. By rejecting more Manichean understandings of this history, a more complex picture is revealed of the initial years of the Cuban revolution, the international political forces at play in the rapidly deteriorating relationship between Washington and Havana, and how the transformation of the social structure and political culture on the island impacted individuals and their families.

Different classes, and very often different generations, responded in different ways to the envisioning of a new, sovereign, and more socially just Cuba. In this context, the U.S. government implemented an unprecedented policy of admitting unlimited numbers of Cuban children, while making it more difficult for their parents to obtain visas so that they might stay on the island and participate in the struggle to overturn the revolutionary government. This ultimately led to the unforeseen and unnecessary separation of families and the stranding of the young refugees in the United States, many for several years.

In stark contrast to the Trump administration's recent policy of separating children from their parents as a means of deterring illegal immigration from Central America and elsewhere, Operation Pedro Pan actually encouraged the dispatch of unaccompanied Cuban children to the United States in an effort to destabilize Cuban society and undermine the revolutionary government. It was organized through, and dependent on, the same counterrevolutionary networks that conducted terrorist, assassination, and sabotage operations as part of Washington's covert action program. The *patria potestad* hoax that propelled the exodus—the rumor campaign that Cuban

Figure 0.2. Literacy *brigadista* girls, 1961. Courtesy of Prensa Latina photo archive.

parents' authority over their children was about to be eliminated—was part of the psychological warfare program callously and cynically manipulating parents' insecurities and anxieties, and which often caused lasting damage to families and children's lives.

Fr. Bryan Walsh and leading figures in the Catholic church, if not the church as an institution, evidently were not simply motivated by a humanitarian concern about homeless Cuban minors in Miami but were also inspired by a Cold War political agenda. Thus, the organizers of the airlift can be seen as doing far more than just responding to Cuban parents' requests for assistance; they actively promoted the evacuation scheme and massively expanded it through the creation of a nationwide foster-care program for the young refugees in the United States, the Cuban Children's Program.

Furthermore, far from being a straightforward plan to "save" the children from "communist indoctrination," Operation Pedro Pan can be seen as an extension of the longstanding U.S. "civilizing mission" on the island to prepare a new generation of political and business leaders in the expected (imminent) post-Castro scenario in order to maintain Cuba as a client state, a status the revolutionary government was energetically repudiating in its stated objective of "Cubanizing" Cuba.

Finally, by setting aside the distorting lens of Cold War ideology, a picture emerges more clearly of the bold, humanist, national project that Cubans embarked upon in 1959, epitomized by the 1961 literacy campaign, in which the youth of that revolutionary generation no longer appear as pawns in a Cold War contest but as agents of the social revolution taking place, inspired by the new political culture that gave them a role and a voice, along with new social values.

By focusing on the episode of Operation Pedro Pan and the experiences of the Pedro Pans' peers who remained on the island and joined the 1961 literacy campaign, *Operation Pedro Pan and the Exodus of Cuba's Children* offers a fresh look at the first years of the Cuban revolution, and sheds new light on what Eduardo Galeano called "one of the most dazzling human adventures of the twentieth century," which has, despite all predictions, endured into the post-Castro twenty-first century.[79]

1

A Revolutionary Hurricane Sweeps Cuba

"The revolution begins now" announced Fidel Castro in Céspedes Park, Santiago de Cuba, in the early hours of 2 January 1959, after General Fulgencio Batista had fled the country twenty-four hours earlier.[1] The violence and terror of the Batista years, the injustice and degradation of over a century, had drawn the Cuban people together around the "moral imperative" for a New Cuba.[2] Some of those who had fought against Batista, particularly more privileged Cubans, might well have presumed that the "revolution" was now over. But to everyone in the cheering crowds who greeted the long-haired, unshaven, youthful rebels as they marched in a triumphal procession across the island in January 1959, the future seemed exciting, if not exhilarating.

"The generation which came to power [in 1959] was infused with its task: to propel the country into modernity," wrote Lisandro Otero: "They were prophets of the new era, [driven by] rapt romanticism, patriotic passion, and extreme utopian idealism. The Egyptian pyramids were built in stages. . . . The young people who assumed power [in Cuba] thought they were building a chain of pyramids that would cover the world in short order. The enormity of [the task] never daunted them."[3]

In the first euphoric days of 1959, most Cubans would have been unaware that a revolutionary hurricane was about to descend on the island, a revolutionary hurricane that became a thoroughgoing social revolution, leaving no individual untouched, and which accelerated as the revolution became politically ever more radical. Within months, especially after the announcement of the agrarian reform, the broad social and political alliance that had been established to overthrow the Batista regime started to unravel, and relations with the United States, Cuba's historic patron and protector, became strained as the revolutionary government adopted the explicit goal of economic and social transformation, the creation of a New Cuba that would fulfill José Martí's concept of national sovereignty based on real social justice.[4] A new, self-confident generation of Cubans now emerged "determined to pursue a destiny distinctly Cuban."[5]

As the last Latin American nation to throw off the colonial yoke in the nineteenth century, Cuba sought not just to attain economic independence and political sovereignty but to liberate itself from the cultural hegemony of the United States and create a new sense of what it meant to be Cuban.[6] Envisioning a New Cuba meant envisioning a "New Man," a New Cuban, which necessitated a process of political socialization or resocialization, the inculcation of new values and beliefs as well as new modes of behavior, and a conscious rejection of the past.[7]

Elizabeth Sutherland, a witness to the early years of the revolution, posed the question: "How can ways of thinking and behaving rooted in old economic relationships between people become altered to harmonize with new relationships? How do you change what is commonly called 'human nature'? . . . Can people who are themselves products of the old system direct the creation of a new consciousness?"[8]

The revolutionary leadership proposed that the Cuban people would learn these new revolutionary values of solidarity and unselfishness, and achieve a new sense of national identity or "*cubanidad*" as they themselves had: by participating in the process of making a revolution.[9] Shortly after the victorious insurrection, Ernesto (Che) Guevara recalled how the experience of the "communion with the people" had transformed the individual guerrilla's theories into "a fundamental part of our being." "Those suffering and loyal inhabitants of the Sierra Maestra," he wrote, "never suspected the role they played in forging our revolutionary ideology."[10] Fidel Castro argued that revolution is a "great teacher," an "extraordinary process of education."[11]

Reflecting on two years of the revolution in January 1961, Fidel Castro stated that a revolution is necessarily "a battle to the death between the future and the past. . . . The old order always refuses to die."[12] A decade later, during an extended visit to President Salvador Allende's Chile in 1971, Fidel explained how, in a revolutionary process, "the people learn things which, otherwise, it would take dozens of years to learn." The question is, he said,

Figure 1.1. "The youthful face of Cuba today." *Bohemia*, 4 June 1961. The original caption accompanying this photo read: "Yes, they are the same. It is that generation that appeared lost in frivolity and hedonism. Many believed that it would never be possible to incorporate them in tough, revolutionary work. But a miracle occurred. One day they abandoned their rock-and-roll records and headed off to the countryside. Today they are literacy teachers. They are *brigadistas*. This is the youthful face of Cuba today, looking to the future."

"Who will learn more and sooner? Who will develop more of an awareness faster? The exploiters or the exploited?"[13]

Educating the next generation became the most important focus of the revolutionary government's plans to create the new socialist society, and an integral aspect of this education was the creation of a new revolutionary consciousness.[14] Every state and its institutions "socialize individuals in ways supportive of the system and the status quo," Damián Fernández contended; accordingly, the new revolutionary government immediately initiated a range of programs, including the 1961 literacy campaign, "to transmit the values of the new society" it hoped to create.[15] "To build communism," wrote Che Guevara, "it is necessary, simultaneously with the new material foundations, to build the new man and woman."[16] This was precisely what the revolutionary government intended to do in order to transmit the values of the new society—a new *conciencia*.[17]

Participation became the decisive element in this process, not only because popular support was important to accomplish the fulfillment of economic and social transformation and defend national sovereignty, but also because of its key role in creating new values, norms, and behavior among Cuban citizens.[18] Mired in a Cold War mind-set, most policymakers in Washington and some Cubans presumed this talk of a "New Cuban" suggested a process of "brainwashing" or "indoctrination." Yet the Cuban revolutionary leadership's concept of a new participatory citizen could be considered not too far removed—albeit in a very different context—from President John F. Kennedy's famous challenge to North Americans: "Ask not what your country can do for you but what you can do for your country," a statement intended to inspire political engagement and a belief that every individual could make a difference in creating a better society.

Whether Cubans found the vision and challenge of this New Cuba unsettling or inspiring depended largely, although not entirely, on their age. Inevitably, the revolutionary transformation of the island focused on the youth, the generation that would create and inherit the New Cuba, the generation that would become the New Cuban men and women. An examination of aspects of the social revolution that was unleashed in 1959, especially the revolutionary government's policies with regard to youth, education, and the family—including such issues as child care, religious belief, racial integration, and gender equality—reveals why some sectors of the population might have been increasingly disturbed by these changes and consider them a challenge to "traditional" family values, and why individual Cubans acted and reacted in the ways that they did.

"The Youngest Revolution"

As the revolution was proclaimed to be "for the children," and educating the next generation became central to the revolutionary project to create the New Cuban, "Save the Children" arose as the battle cry of the anti-Castro opposition.[19] There may be a never-ending debate about the nature of the Cuban revolution—what drove its radicalization, the role played by various social sectors and the relative weight of the urban and rural struggles, and many other aspects of the revolution—but all contemporary observers commented on the youthful nature of the revolution.[20] It is therefore incontestable that the revolution was not just made *on behalf of* Cuba's children but largely made *by* young Cubans.

The political activism of Cuban youth, however, did not begin in 1959. Young Cubans were already highly politicized before January 1959, and historically, youth had been the catalyst for political change on the island. Since the university reform movement of 1923, students had seen their movement as extending "beyond the academic walls."[21] Cuban politics had traditionally been viewed in generational rather than class terms, the revolutionary movement that emerged in the 1950s being no exception.[22] The University of Havana, in particular, became a center of opposition to Batista, and the university was eventually closed in 1956, an action that "threw almost 18,000 students into the vortex of national politics."[23]

During the political protests prior to January 1959, youth became a special target of Batista's henchmen. The torture and murder of four young men in Santiago, whose bodies were left hanging from trees, provoked a large militant protest by women in January 1957.[24] Although the guerrilla war was, until August 1958, generally confined to the remote mountains of Oriente province, even before the rebels called for a "total war" against the regime in March 1958, urban areas had experienced strikes, bombings, assassinations, kidnappings, and sometimes shoot-outs on the streets.[25] On the night of 16 March 1958, over one hundred bombs exploded in Havana; *New York Times* journalist Ruby Hart Phillips wondered how these "school children" had obtained such enormous amounts of explosives.[26] "Since a revolution was needed," wrote Jean-Paul Sartre after visiting the island in 1960, "circumstances willed that youth should accomplish it. Only the young had enough anger and anguish to attempt it, enough integrity to succeed." Young Cubans, he decided, "had nothing to lose."[27]

Batista and his enforcers in the police and Military Intelligence Service responded with brutal repression and assassinations of student leaders, such as the cold-blooded murder of several young rebels following the 13 March 1957 assault on the Presidential Palace led by student leader José Antonio Echeverría. Among the thousands of young Cubans arrested, tortured, or killed, the July 26 Movement estimated that at least two hundred of its members had been murdered on the order of Police Chief Pilar García alone.[28] The Batista regime's vicious reprisals against young Cubans, Ruby Hart Phillips reported, had the opposite effect from that intended, as many decided they were safer in the hills fighting with the guerrillas than "remaining defenseless in towns and cities where they could be picked up by the authorities."[29]

High school students, too, were drawn into the maelstrom of the anti-Batista protest movement. By mid-March 1958, Ricardo Alarcón, a leader of the National Student Front, recalled schools across the island, including many private schools, were shut down through strike action by students.[30] The threats to Cuban youth were real, and countless numbers were killed or imprisoned. On arriving in Havana on 8 January 1959, Fidel Castro suggested that, with the inauguration of a new era of peace, Cuban mothers would be the happiest of all Cuban citizens, being either the mothers of Batista's soldiers or mothers of revolutionary activists.[31]

The "Kids" Take Charge

Bohemia published a special edition on 18 January 1959 to celebrate the victory, featuring on the front cover a remarkably fair-skinned and blond Cuban teenager with the headline: "This is our youth!" The caption read: "His name doesn't matter: he is the image and symbol of the new Cuban youth, of that heroic youth that, with his example and sacrifice has returned faith to an entire people. There are hundreds like him . . . in Fidel Castro's Rebel Army."[32]

Given that young Cubans were thus portrayed—and saw themselves—as the victors over Batista, it was inevitable they would lay claim to the revolution as their own and seek to shape it in their own image. In this, they received every encouragement from revolutionary leaders who believed that only the young were free of the cultural burden of the past.[33] Fidel Castro liked to invoke the spirit of José Martí, who had written: "Enthusiasm has never had gray hair."[34] So those who had already played an active part in bringing down a dictator were hardly likely to retreat from political life, and those who had not previously participated in the revolutionary movement were inspired to become involved in what seemed to be a new, exciting adventure. Children became obsessed with collecting relics of the war, such as bullets, berets, gun belts, and grenades. "For a boy like myself," wrote Pablo Medina, "whose dreams fed on the feats of warriors struggling against evil, the appearance of the triumphant bearded ones on the streets of my city was the ultimate confirmation that heroes existed beyond the pages of adventure novels."[35]

Figure 1.2. Literacy campaign *brigadistas*, 1961. Courtesy of Prensa Latina photo archive.

A former Pedro Pan commented it was "not hard to fathom how such a climate could make middle-class families worry about the direction of their children's future." Pointing to the 1961 literacy campaign, he wondered "if the real threat to parental rights lay not in a plan to form cadres in other socialist countries but, rather, in the lure of the revolutionary culture itself."[36]

The "generation gap" that was much discussed in the 1960s took a particular form in revolutionary Cuba. When he visited the island in 1960, the ideologue of the 1960s youth rebellion Jean-Paul Sartre remarked that "the kids" seemed to have taken over in Cuba. "The greatest scandal of the Cuban revolution," he wrote, "isn't that it expropriated the plantations but that it brought children to power."[37] That is certainly what Cuba looked like in 1959: Fidel Castro was just thirty-two, Che Guevara was thirty, Raúl Castro was twenty-seven, and Armando Hart, minister of education, at twenty-eight looked scarcely older than the high school students he mobilized in their thousands for the 1961 literacy campaign. The average age of those constituting the Council of Ministers was thirty-three, and the youngest minister in cabinet was Enrique Oltuski, who was just twenty-three.[38]

"Youth is happy because it is blind," wrote Cuba's national hero, José Martí, and "this blindness is its grandeur, and this inexperience its sublime confidence."[39] Because the revolutionary leaders looked to the new generations that would emerge "free of the original sin," and because they themselves were young, the government promoted a kind of "youth cult" that inevitably changed the relationship of power between parents and children.[40] While the first stirrings of the 1960s youth radicalization were beginning in North America with the Civil Rights movement, it seemed to have already exploded on a small Caribbean island. A woman who was nine years old at the time of the revolution recalled telling her parents: "Oh, you're just an old-timer. You don't know. This is going to be so cool."[41] Symptomatic of the rebellious spirit among youth was the public scandal about an altar boy who "verbally challenged" Bishop Alfredo Müller when he denigrated a priest who supported the revolution in defiance of the church hierarchy.[42] In New Cuba, it seemed as if the kids were no longer *under* control but rather now *in* control. Raúl Castro confessed as much in July 1960, saying "it is youth that is now running Cuba and, despite its inevitable mistakes, we can honestly say it is making a pretty good job of it."[43]

After the March 1960 explosion on the ship *La Coubre* that was bringing the Cuban government weapons from Europe—apparently an act of counterrevolutionary sabotage—children were organized to collect funds to buy arms with which the revolution could defend itself.[44] The mobilization of young Cubans for defense of the country was systematized with the formation of the Association of Rebel Youth (AJR) in October 1960.[45] A memo sent to CIA director Allen Dulles disparagingly described the AJR as a "significant arm of the Castroist political organization" composed of teenagers, "of the type that would be found in juvenile gangs, [that] are a terror to their parents, their schoolmates, and the general public. They have charge of indoctrination in schools and have been active in the formation of the [Committees for the Defense of the Revolution (CDRs)]."[46]

Fashioning itself as the descendant of the 1868, 1898, 1933, and 1953 revolutionary generations, the new government regarded involvement in the militias as "a unique socializing experience" for young Cubans and essential to the defense of the nation by an armed citizenry.[47] Fidel Castro insisted Cuban direct democracy would be achieved by arming the people.[48] Young children were organized in the *Patrolles Juveniles* (Junior Patrols) and Pioneers; cowboy suits were now replaced by olive green rebel uniforms, complete with a fake beard and toy rifle, as the outfit of choice of little children.[49] An advertisement in *El Mundo* suggested parents buy their boys and girls Rebel Army or militia uniforms for Three Kings' Day in January 1961 as well as traditional Spanish outfits.[50]

Figure 1.3. "How they want to dress this Day of the Kings." *El Mundo*, 5 January 1961. The Flogar department store had recently been bombed by anti-Castro arsonists after it was nationalized by the revolutionary government.

The Junior Patrols, the precursor of the AJR, were organized by the newly established national police as a way to channel the revolutionary enthusiasm of school-aged Cubans, and it featured prominently in the July 26 celebrations in 1959. The Red Cross and the fire brigade also offered training for children in various tasks of civil defense.[51] In response to escalating threats emanating from Washington, in the months prior to the U.S.-backed invasion at the Bay of Pigs in April 1961, President Osvaldo Dorticós told a national meeting of the newly formed AJR that, because the future belonged to the youth, their duty was to study, work, and defend the revolution from its enemies.[52] The U.S. media responded with horror: "Even 7-Year-Olds Spy for Castro Now."[53]

"It was indeed fitting," wrote Antoni Kapcia, "that the 1960s should be ushered in by an event that went on to contribute to later global radicalism but also foretold, in its early euphoria, the rebelliousness of that decade."[54] Following their first visit to Cuba in March 1960, two U.S. researchers commented: "In Cuba they are actually doing what young people all over the world are dreaming about and would like to do."[55] Within the patriarchal Cuban family, children had been expected to be obedient and respectful to their elders, so the new culture of youth encouraged by the revolutionary leadership must have alarmed many conservative-minded parents. One former Pedro Pan child, Ileana Fuentes, speculated that her parents' decision to send her away "wasn't so much about political oppression as it was about premature personal freedom."[56]

As the vast majority of Pedro Pans were teenagers, many of their parents might well have been motivated by a concern about their offspring's increasingly asserted (or potential) independence and political activity.[57] Some of those caring for the refugee children in Miami, including Fr. Walsh, remarked on their young charges' awareness of political issues and readiness to engage in political activity.[58] Not all young activists, however, supported the revolutionary government. The antigovernment Revolutionary Student Directorate (DRE) emphasized the important role of young Cubans as the "vanguard" of the national and international struggle against communism.[59] And quite a few former Pedro Pans still like to boast about their activities in the anti-Castro underground.[60]

Because young Cubans were already highly politicized, as the revolution reached deeper into Cuban society and politics became sharply polarized, some of them, particularly members of Catholic youth groups, most of which had actively supported the anti-Batista movement, now took the lead in opposing the new government. The church provided these groups an organizational and ideological framework for their anticommunist activities as well as a "doctrinal alternative to communism."[61]

By the start of the 1960 academic year, schools and universities once more became political battlefields, as they had been during the Batista years. Catholic students were among the most militant anticommunist activists, and led the protests against the visit of Soviet vice premier Anastas Mikoyan in February 1960. Antigovernment resistance by students at some of Havana's most prestigious Catholic colleges, as well as the November 1960 national student strike, were often organized with the imprimatur of their priests and teachers.

In the wake of the 1960 nationalizations of U.S. companies and growing hostility voiced from Washington, heated political discussions and even brawls occurred at private schools like Havana's elite Ruston Academy between Cuban and North American students, many of the latter group being children of U.S. business executives and staff at the U.S. embassy. When students at La Salle College were expelled for demonstrating their support for the revolutionary government in the tense days before the Bay of Pigs invasion, parents and students rallied to demand their reinstatement.[62] Antigovernment protests extended to the bombing in February 1961 of a private school in Havana, the Nobel Academy, causing significant damage and leaving several adolescents and a teacher seriously injured; two students, who had apparently been engaged in previous counterrevolutionary provocations, were charged with the crime.[63] Parents like hers, said Silvia Ríos, "were afraid their children would get involved against the revolution . . . and would be killed," so they sent her brother to the United States.[64] In fact, more than a few Pedro Pans had been involved in antigovernment activities, like Raquel Mendieta, who at fifteen joined an underground group and made hoax bomb threats from public phones while her young sister Ana kept a lookout. When her father, who was also an active oppositionist, learned what his daughters were doing, he immediately shipped them off to Miami.[65]

After years of social turmoil and political violence under Batista, the escalating U.S.-sponsored covert war and increasing terrorism perpetrated by counterrevolutionary forces naturally prompted parents to think about putting their children temporarily "out of harm's way"; moreover, because it was very common for wealthy Cubans to send their children to study in the United States, this was not in the least unusual.

"Save the Children!"

Despite the hysteria inflamed by anticommunist propaganda against the revolution emanating from Miami, the Cuban government actually took steps after 1959 to shore up the family unit rather than destroy it, reforms initially welcomed by the Catholic church.[66] Most of the measures undertaken after 1959 suggested the revolutionary government saw "nuclear families as an indicator of economic development and modernization," even though the nuclear family was "not historically the predominant family structure" in Cuba.[67] Fidel Castro repeatedly insisted that the goal was to give all Cuban children "stable, economically secure homes" so that they might "experience the common joys of childhood while learning a sense of responsibility."[68] In May 1960, the government initiated *"Operación Familia"* (Operation Family), which encouraged de facto couples to legalize their unions and register their children (at no cost) in an explicit effort to stabilize families by recognizing the rights of women and children and the responsibilities of parenthood.[69] Far from undermining the family, this move has been criticized occasionally for "normalizing patriarchy."[70] In fact, the requirement for parents to register their children, under Laws 797 and 884, meant that tens of thousands of Cubans actually established their legal rights over their children for the first time, as Minister of Justice Alfredo Yabur explained on television in December 1960, when the rumors began that the government was planning to eliminate *patria potestad*.[71]

Early on, Education Minister Armando Hart assured two researchers that the philosophy of the revolution was "strongly oriented toward, not away from, the individual family." The North Americans were actually disappointed to learn that the revolutionary government was, at that point, not in favor of a general system of boarding schools and that the housing policy was biased toward home ownership by individual family units rather than developing services that would lead to more communal living.[72] The potential for such programs, however, was limited both by economic constraints and the persistent belief among the Cuban population that domestic chores were women's work. The existence of extended family networks also lessened pressure on the state to socialize these tasks.

Both the early urban and agrarian reforms of 1959 and 1960 were based on titles being given to family units, which was another reason the government urged couples to formalize their unions. Some observers, like Oscar Lewis, suggested Cuban leaders were "conscious of the dangers of tampering with too many fundamentals at once, and the home, family, and machismo come as close to being basic as anything in Cuba."[73] Nevertheless, a decade before the revolution, some of the features of the traditional patriarchal Cuban family were beginning to be broken down.[74] Tony Mendoza, a young Cuban who had just graduated from high school in the United States, was more than happy to return there with his family after the revolution because

American girls appealed to him far more than Cuban girls, who, he said, "not only didn't drink or neck on dates but also brought along a chaperone."[75]

The emotional, child-centered political struggle that arose as the revolution turned toward socialism was largely fought by members of Cuba's more privileged classes and primarily reflected the concerns of those families. On the other hand, the revolutionary government was specifically addressing the problems faced by families of the urban and rural poor. Children in those families had a different experience of "childhood," usually being expected to work from a very young age, and were almost universally "neglected."[76] Che Guevara had been horrified by the particularly appalling health of children in the Sierra Maestra.[77] In many poor families, women were the breadwinners and heads of the household, while men were largely peripheral to the sustenance of the family and child rearing.[78] Girls could be sent off to work as domestic servants as young as eight years old and married at twelve. Oscar Lewis and his colleagues found the women they interviewed in some of Cuba's slums were not so bound by stereotypical feminine characteristics, such as "dependency and submissiveness," as suggested by the idealized (North American) model of a middle-class housewife that wealthy Cubans sought to emulate.[79] They acknowledged that the government was attempting to moderate the extreme differences in approaches to child rearing between the "pampering and indulgence among the children of the upper classes and the hardships, even cruelties, of life for children of the poor."[80]

In the early years of the revolution, the government prioritized care of those children without parents or family to care for them, such as orphans, abandoned infants, and children or teenagers found to be homeless as a result of social disruption, poverty, or the revolutionary war that had ended Batista's dictatorship.[81] Orphanages were closed and the children transferred to group homes; two luxurious estates owned by former Batista cronies were expropriated in 1959 and handed to the Ministry of Social Welfare to establish boarding schools for the four hundred street children who were a significant burden on the new government's resources.[82] This was one reason Fidel Castro ridiculed the rumor that the state was about to assume custody over the nation's children, saying this would have been impossible, even if it had been government policy, due to the financial cost it would have implied.[83] As it was, Celia Sánchez and Fidel Castro took quite a number of children into their own household.[84]

The rising antigovernment terrorism visited on the island created an atmosphere of uncertainty and anxiety. In the months leading up to the 1961 Bay of Pigs invasion, counterrevolutionary violence spread: cane fields were burned, factories sabotaged, and several of Havana's main department stores (including the famous El Encanto) were destroyed. But the greatest impact on the Cuban family in the early years of the revolution was the new political culture of a participatory citizenry that increasingly brought women and adolescents out from the confines of the home, thereby challenging traditional gender roles and the patriarchal family. This may well not have been foreseen or intended by the government that never directly attacked the concept of the nuclear family or promoted alternatives to it as the basic unit of social organization. Children were encouraged to participate along with their families in community activities such as planting the greenbelt around Havana and orchards in Pinar del Río; sometimes entire families went on camping trips for a week to plant trees, as Mirta Muñiz (a single mother) did with her young son.[85]

The line between private and public spheres, the individual and the collective, became increasingly blurred and politicized in the effort to create a new society and a New Cuban.[86] Thus, the rapid social changes inevitably placed great strain on Cuban families and individuals, and caught unawares those Cubans who imagined that the revolution would stop at their front doors. And as it turned out, for middle-class and other Habaneros, the revolution came *in* their front doors, in the form of about half a million *campesinos* (farmers or peasants). For the first celebration of 26 July after the overthrow of Batista in 1959, the government came up with the idea of welcoming to the capital thousands of Cubans from the provinces, many of the island's poorest and most marginalized citizens, many of them Afro-Cuban.[87] They arrived on buses and trains, and Havana families were encouraged to open their homes to their "country cousins" in a mass getting-to-know-you exercise designed explicitly to bring the "two Cubas" together.[88] This was meant to be "the grand narrative of the Revolution in the flesh," a communion of the very different sectors of the Cuban population that would be repeated again on a mass scale with the 1961 literacy campaign.[89]

Rebel Women

As the revolution came in the front door, women began to march out the back door. Now it was not just young Cubans who were exercising their newly acquired sense of independence: maids were demanding time off from their employers to attend self-improvement and literacy classes.[90] Former prostitutes were encouraged to seek alternative occupations, so that now a former "client" might find himself conveyed in a taxi driven by a "rehabilitated" sex worker.[91] A popular urban myth circulated describing the embarrassing predicament of a middle-class housewife who encounters her former maid as a now respectable bank teller.[92]

The government's call for women to come out of their *casas* into the *calle* provoked "apocalyptic" claims about the destruction of the family and fears that the new revolutionary women would be unable to protect the family from the state.[93] Established in August 1960, the Federation of Cuban Women (FMC) was the first of the new mass organizations created to encourage women to participate in various revolutionary projects, building on the foundation laid by the militant "maternalism" that had mobilized women in the struggle against Batista.[94] The unprecedented spectacle of militia women engaged in small arms training and parading in formation was highly disturbing for more conservative-minded Cubans, inspiring many negative remarks, such as "There go the prostitutes."[95]

Considered particularly outrageous was the example revolutionary leader Celia Sánchez offered young Cuban women by driving herself around Havana in a jeep, dressed in olive green fatigues, cigarette between her lips.[96] Many rebel leaders, like Raúl Castro and Vilma Espín (the latter wearing a pearl tiara), tried to set a good example with very public wedding ceremonies to legalize their unions.[97] Aleida March related in her memoir how, for the sake of propriety, she and Che Guevara had to maintain the fiction of separate bedrooms at La Cabaña fortress until Che's divorce from his former wife came through.[98]

Child-care centers (*círculos infantiles*) were established in early 1961 to facilitate the participation of women in the workforce and political life; the centers were also part of the government's plan for a system of early childhood education, which was virtually nonexistent before 1959.[99] Although José Martí had raised the idea of day care, especially for poorer families, all these initiatives were viewed by some opponents of the revolution as quite sinister—as apparent evidence of the government's move toward communism and the replacement of the family by the state.[100]

Nevertheless, the revolutionary government's attitude toward women's liberation was somewhat contradictory, tentative, and even "consensus-seeking."[101] Vilma Espín insisted the FMC began with "no preconceptions" but recognized it "had to change both woman's image of herself and society's image of women."[102] This was not "without its difficulties," said Espín. "A cultural tradition dating back centuries is not broken from one day to the next."[103] The FMC never talked in terms of women's individual liberation nor challenged the somewhat idealized and sentimentalized view of motherhood prevalent in Cuba. With the establishment of the new *Casas de Matrimonio* (or wedding palaces), weddings with all the trappings were now available to poorer couples, and daughters' *quinceañeras* continued to be celebrated lavishly by those who could afford it.[104] For their graduation ceremony, students at the Ana Betancourt schools for country girls were dressed in white like debutantes, with corsages on their shoulders.[105] On the other hand, it is worth remembering that the idea of a community development program focused on women, like the Ana Betancourt schools for *campesinos'* daughters, was remarkably advanced for its time. In these schools, the girls learned to read and write, to cut and sew, and about basic nutrition and hygiene; they then returned home with a sewing machine and were encouraged to teach ten others in their village.[106]

Significantly, both the teacher's manual for the literacy campaign materials and the *Manual de Capacitación Cívica,* which outlined the new revolutionary ideology, specifically addressed the question of racial discrimination, but neither explicitly took up the issue of women's liberation.[107] The mobilizations of the early years, beginning with the encouragement of women to join the militias, certainly undermined traditional views of femininity and masculinity, but stereotypical, sexist portrayals of women continued to appear in cartoons and government propaganda alongside exhortations for women to participate in the revolution.[108] One such example was an advertisement for Avon beauty products, headlined "Avon calling for unity," depicting a glamorous mulatta in militia uniform with the text "Avon calls on the noble heart of the women of Cuba to make this revolution their own."[109]

While the government encouraged women to work outside the home (which apparently met with some resistance from men and women, from both the working class and middle class), women were generally directed toward traditional female occupations, such as child care, teaching, and nursing. Moreover, many working-class and poor women saw their "liberation" as release from the need for outside employment in order to devote themselves to domestic tasks in their own homes. But despite the drive to

Figure 1.4. "Avon calling for unity!" An adaptation of the popular 1960s advertising jingle. *Bohemia*, 18 June 1961.

increase the numbers of women in the workforce, there was no corresponding government push to get men into the kitchen.[110]

Nevertheless, there was, as Oscar Lewis and his colleagues noted, a "tremendous distance between the subservient, dependent, apolitical, homebound model of the traditional Latin woman and the militant, independent, politicized, and community-minded model of the socialist woman" being promoted by the revolutionary government.[111] This "New Woman" apparently made some working-class émigré men most uncomfortable and was identified in one study as the "main source of their rage and a contributing factor to their total rejection of the revolution."[112]

Women were far more than passive beneficiaries of the revolution; like young Cubans, they became empowered in the process of participating in the revolutionary project, most demonstrably in the literacy campaign.[113] Even when rights are handed down from above, this can provide a space for women to organize around their own demands.[114] It is easy to imagine how shocked traditionally minded Cuban parents would have been at the prospect that their young daughters, who were not permitted to walk down the street without a chaperone, might want to disappear over the horizon to teach literacy in the furthest reaches of the island.[115] Apparently, some *campesinos*, too, were horrified to see the young *brigadista* girls arriving on their doorsteps wearing trousers, viewing them as Havana "libertines."[116]

The 1961 literacy campaign in many ways signaled the first confrontation between the revolution and the patriarchal Cuban family, clearly flouting established gender roles and expectations among both the urban middle class and the more tradition-bound peasantry. Underlying the horror or discomfort expressed about these new Cuban women, especially young women, was often a moralistic and conservative attitude toward sexuality. Opponents of the literacy campaign liked to warn parents of the potential for sexual activity among supposedly unsupervised *brigadistas*; one exile publication proposed that if 1961 was the "Year of Education," 1962 would be the "Year of Maternity."[117] A CIA information report also noted parents' concern about the risks, particularly for their daughters, implied in the literacy drive, and the potential for parents to lose control over their children's upbringing.[118] To some parents, the idea of sending their well-bred teenagers to the wild and evidently unsanitary countryside, where they might encounter or even engage in promiscuous sex, was yet another example of the threat posed by the new social order.[119] James Baker, director of the elite Ruston Academy in Havana, complained that the government was telling teenagers "sex is normal, it's like Conga—you should be satisfied."[120] Angst at challenges to established social norms clearly also reflected "racial specters," as white, middle-class parents were particularly anxious about potential "interracial unions" by their progeny.[121]

One Race, One Nation: Cuban

Racial integration, however, was fundamental to the process of creating the New Cuba, and this also suddenly brought the revolution home to many Cubans, which for some was a further unwelcome invasion of private space, personal relationships, and family life. On 22 March 1959, Fidel announced that henceforth all Cuban beaches and other public spaces would be open to all, regardless of skin color (although private facilities at those beaches were not included at first). Although racism and racial segregation in Cuba had not been sanctioned through legislation, as with the Jim Crow laws in the southern states of the United States, Langston Hughes described Cuba's "color line" as more flexible and "much more subtle."[122] Class divisions and hefty fees ensured racial segregation quite effectively in private schools, social clubs, employment, and housing.[123]

Some more prosperous white Cubans and even some workers regarded Fidel's speech as "an assault on their dearest values: family, decency, and religion." A rumor circulated that Fidel had invited black men to "invade the country's aristocratic sanctuaries [the private social clubs] to dance and revel with the vestal virgins who, up to that moment, had managed to avoid the terrible contact with black skin." Afro-Cubans, it was feared, might mistake "liberty for license."[124] So fast and furious was the reaction of some Cubans that a few days later Fidel felt obliged to clarify that the revolution would not "impose" anything on anyone and that people could dance with whomever they chose.[125]

Cuba's late achievement of independence in 1898 has often been attributed to an underlying fear of a rebellion of black slaves and former slaves. The racial composition of Cuba at the time of the revolution was quite distinct from most other Latin American countries in that nearly one-third of the population were black or mulatto.[126] The movement of the nineteenth century that lobbied for annexation to the United States was partly or largely motivated by a desire to unite with slaveholding states of the antebellum South in order to crush any potential uprising of black Cubans.[127]

The Haitian revolution of 1791–1804 had had an extraordinary impact on Cuba, and a "black fear" persisted among white Cubans into the twentieth century.[128] A sugar planter's daughter described her childhood terrors at stories of a black bogeyman who ate naughty children.[129] The standard racist stereotype was that all black men had an insatiable sexual desire for white women, and even paler-skinned men who lived with Afro-Cubans objected to their sisters or daughters marrying one.[130] So the shock for white Cubans steeped in these prejudices and anxieties is easily imaginable when they saw Afro-Cuban commander Juan Almeida, one of the key leaders of the July 26 Movement, act as judge in the July 1959 Miss Cuba beauty contest and present the prize to the winning white contestant. This apparently unsettling incident was considered significant enough to be reported to Washington by the U.S. embassy in Havana, because several months later, Almeida presided over Havana's Carnival Queen pageant.[131]

One woman candidly admitted to another parent that she was sending her children to the United States with Operation Pedro Pan because she did not want them "sitting next to a black kid in school."[132] That was indeed the predicament faced by children like Marta, a former student of the exclusive, and almost exclusively white, Ruston Academy.[133] The 1961 nationalization of the private schools effectively destroyed one of the key pillars of racism in Cuba, and the literacy campaign brought together Cubans of different social (and racial) backgrounds as never before.[134] This was of particular concern to some white parents who opposed their daughters participating in the literacy campaign in remote rural areas where their adult pupils would most likely be black or mulatto.

In general, however, desegregation was accomplished in revolutionary Cuba in a nonconfrontational manner in the name of *los sin nada* (the have-nots) rather than in racial terms, following José Martí's reasoning that there were no mulatto, black, or white Cubans—only Cubans.[135] Although the Cuban government never introduced any form of affirmative action program for Afro-Cubans, a new pride was observed among black Cubans.[136] This offended and even angered those white Cubans who expected their darker-skinned compatriots to "know their place"; some "very respectable white ladies" arriving in Miami complained how, all of a sudden, "blacks" had become quite "impossible."[137] Before departing as a Pedro Pan, Carlos Eire suffered the indignity of taunts from his Afro-Cuban maid, who told him he'd soon be doing her chores of sweeping the floor and taking out the trash.[138]

The revolution not only came in the front door but now moved in next door, to the dismay of some of Havana's wealthier and more prejudiced residents. With the urban reform of October 1960, Afro-Cubans and urban poor families moved into previously exclusive neighborhoods, declared "Frozen Zones" when large homes were abandoned by their wealthy owners when

Figure 1.5. Young literacy *brigadista* and his pupil. Courtesy of Prensa Latina photo archive.

they left for exile.[139] The scholarship children from the countryside reportedly upset the neighbors by playing in the streets, parks, and yards, picking fruit from private gardens, and marching around in formation, joyfully singing and shouting revolutionary slogans.[140] Alina Fernández described the girls who arrived from the countryside to study in Havana at the Ana Betancourt schools as "a plague." Most of them had no teeth, she said, "did not know how to use toilets, washed clothes in bathtubs, and cooked on fires in backyards."[141] In the movie *Memorias del subdesarrollo*, Sergio despairs that the capital now looked like an ugly provincial town.[142] When Fidel emphasized on May Day 1960 that the revolution was made to benefit "*los humildes*" (the humble), more privileged Cubans like Nicolás came to believe there would be no place for his family in the New Cuba.[143] "We found we were living in a country in which we were the enemy," remembered Ana Riewerts, a Pedro Pan whose father lost significant property holdings with the urban reform in October 1960.[144]

The urban reform affected many middle-class Cubans, who—up to that point—had generally applauded other social justice measures designed to benefit the majority of Cubans. Antonio Villaverde's mother called to congratulate her son after seeing him on television explaining the urban housing reform, but she was not so pleased when he told her his father would lose most of his properties.[145] Now, the families of Cuba's elite began to feel that their aspirations, their livelihoods, and their way of life were under assault; their exclusive social clubs were no longer the refuges they had been. The rich were not only losing their power and privileges, observed Alfred Padula, "but their servants as well."[146] With the increasing restrictions on the import of luxury goods and other economic constraints, including the embargo on most U.S. exports to Cuba imposed in October 1960, the standard of living of middle-class Cubans deteriorated markedly while it improved for the majority.

Nevertheless, it almost seemed easier for the revolutionary leadership to break the island's economic dependence on the United States and establish the material and political basis of a new, independent Cuba than to decolonize Cubans' minds. The theorist of the colonial revolution, Frantz Fanon, described decolonization as "a meeting of two forces, opposed to each other by their very nature . . . [that] never takes place unnoticed, for it influences individuals and modifies them fundamentally."[147] Louis Pérez comments: "The full dimension of the mental strain and psychological stress experienced in many thousands of households [in revolutionary Cuba] may never be known. These must be seen as deeply personal and traumatic confrontations for vast numbers who slowly and painfully arrived at the realization that the norms of their everyday lives, the values and moral codes that served as the basis of their being, were under assault."[148]

The cultural decolonization process that commenced in 1959 was, therefore, particularly wrenching for Cubans, largely because U.S. culture had penetrated Cuban life so deeply it was indistinguishable from what was considered Cuban.[149] By the 1920s, Terry's *Guide to Cuba* advised North American travelers: "[The] present-day Cuban is rapidly becoming Americanized (*americanizado*). Thousands act, think, talk and look like Americans, wear American clothes, ride in American autos; use American furniture and machinery; oftentimes send their children to American colleges; live for a time in the States themselves or expect to. . . . A great and growing army of them speak English . . . [and] unlike many other Latins, their ideals are American."[150]

U.S. journalist Elizabeth Sutherland commented that Cubans, like most colonized peoples, suffered from a "cultural inferiority complex" that was difficult to eradicate.[151] As Frantz Fanon explained, colonialism does not merely hold "a people in its grip and [empty] the native's brain of all form and content. By a perverted logic, it turns to the past of the oppressed people, and distorts, disfigures and destroys it."[152]

The reassertion of Cuba's own story and identity in the drive to create a new, united Cuban nation was at the heart of the education reforms and literacy campaign in revolutionary Cuba, frequently referred to as a "battle for culture." Cubans were now encouraged to read the works of José Martí and Spanish classics like *Don Quijote*.[153] This, inevitably, provoked a crisis of identity in those middle-class Cubans who had most effectively absorbed or aspired to North American culture, norms, and values. Some Cubans had even "imagined" they were actually living in the suburbs of North America.[154]

One of the most important functions of the state, explained Antonio Gramsci, "is to raise the great mass of the population to a particular cultural and moral level ... which corresponds to the needs of the productive forces of development, and hence to the interests of the ruling classes."[155] This only becomes evident, however, when a government or a nation sets out to alter or revolutionize the existing socioeconomic order or culture. Then, wrote Che Guevara, the new society in formation "has to compete fiercely with the past," making itself felt on the consciousness of individuals.[156]

Thus, as the political began to intersect sharply with the personal, individuals from all social classes experienced a shake-up in attitudes and relationships between neighbors; blacks, whites, and mulattoes; men and women; and parents and children. Suddenly, as one émigré explained, "a brutal change came into our lives. Our democratic, religious, and cultural institutions were crushed overnight. There was complete disunity in the Cuban family."[157] Inevitably, this sense of a world turned upside down led to some Cubans becoming anxious about the future facing their children.

Exile seemed "the obvious option" for those Cubans experiencing discomfort or disorientation in the New Cuba, especially for those "Americanized" Cubans who never regarded the United States as a foreign country.[158] "We are Cubanizing Cuba," said Fidel Castro, and with that pronouncement, snowflakes and Santa Claus were jettisoned from the first Christmas celebration in revolutionary Cuba.[159] At the time, the Catholic church did not see this as an attempt to remove Jesus from the celebration of Christmas, but the church soon found itself in a losing battle with the revolution on the moral or human dimension of the *patria*, the New Cuba.

Figure 1.6. "*Compañera* Domestic: Study! The Revolution will help you." *Verde Olivo*, 6 December 1961.

"Castro v. the Virgin"

On 3 January 1959, Archbishop Enrique Pérez Serantes issued a pastoral letter titled "Vida Nueva" (New Life), welcoming the new era in Cuba.[160] Although the Catholic hierarchy had had a somewhat ambiguous attitude toward Batista, it expected amicable relations with the new government and, in fact, hoped to increase its influence by expanding religious instruction in public schools, something that had been expressly prohibited in Cuba for decades.[161] The church sought to pressure the government by pointing to a survey that indicated nearly 90 percent of Cubans regarded themselves as Catholics, although significantly fewer than 10 percent practiced their religion.[162]

The church had experienced a kind of renaissance in the 1950s, and talk of "New Cubans" and "New Cuba" initially resonated with Cuban Catholics. Fidel consistently stated (at the time and over the succeeding decades) that there was no contradiction between the aims of religion and socialism, due to a "common concern for the humble, exploited and persecuted and the goal of brotherhood of humankind."[163]

Nevertheless, the revolutionary promise of moral redemption for the nation and its people seemed to supplant the church's role as the guardian of ethics and values.[164] In many ways, the revolution took the banner of social justice from the church, driving it on to the defensive in order to reassert its moral leadership and its authority to shape the minds and souls of the island's children and youth. Young Catholics had played an important role in the movement against Batista, in particular by publishing a report that exposed the glaring discrepancy between the two Cubas of the rich and poor, drawing attention to the appalling poverty in the countryside, and arguing agrarian reform was needed desperately.[165]

This report was frequently cited by Fidel Castro and other revolutionary leaders, and ironically, excerpts were published in the first edition of *Cuba Socialista* in December 1961.[166] The Cuban Catholic church was also, however, significantly influenced by the U.S. Catholic church. As early as January 1959, Cardinal Richard Cushing of Boston protested the alleged seizure of church property by the revolutionary government, a fact the Cuban church hierarchy felt obliged to deny.[167] Cuban church leaders also found it necessary to refute the charges made in Washington by the defecting pilot Pedro Díaz Lanz regarding religious persecution in revolutionary Cuba.[168]

The experience of the 1936–1939 Civil War in Spain was fresh in the memories of Cuban clergy (most of whom were of Spanish origin) and among Cubans generally, over one thousand of whom had volunteered to fight for the Spanish Republic.[169] When the newly formed revolutionary militias adopted some of the songs of the Spanish Republic, an immediate connection was made between the revolution and events in Spain, where convents were sacked and clergy assaulted or even killed, leading some Cubans to fear the same thing might happen in Cuba.[170]

The revolution unfortunately caught the Catholic church in Cuba in a period of transition, as it moved toward "Cubanization," after having been historically closely identified with Spanish colonialism, suffering from "a surfeit of foreign clergy" and an insufficient concern with social problems.[171] Its close ties with Franco's Spain were exposed in an incident in January 1960 when the Spanish ambassador, the Marquis de Lojendro, summoned the Spanish clergy on the island to alert them to Fidel Castro's "leftist militance."[172] Although not all the Spanish clergy in Cuba were Francoists (the most obvious exception being Basque Franciscan priests), such blatant political interference undoubtedly played a role in the Cuban leader's subsequent denunciation of some clergy as "falangists," that is, supporters of General Franco.[173] At a time when the world was sharply divided between Russian and U.S. poles, Rome had chosen to align itself with Washington, leaving the Catholic church also open to Fidel Castro's taunt of being "the Church of Washington."[174]

Although very few Cubans were adversely affected by the first agrarian reform of June 1959, the angry U.S. response and its rejection of the terms of the compensation offered reminded Cubans (most of whom had expected the United States to recognize the justice of the reform) that it was dangerous to cross their powerful and protective neighbor, a friendly nation that supposedly had always known what was in the best interests of the island and its people. Adjusting his step to synchronize with protests emanating from the North, the Bishop of Matanzas, Alberto Martín Villaverde (who had originally praised the reform) reminded the faithful of the immutable right to private property and alerted Cubans to his suspicions of communist influence behind the reform.[175] Archbishop Pérez Serantes quickly joined the chorus with a pastoral letter on 21 July 1959 on the same subject, pronouncing that those who drafted the agrarian reform appeared to "have drunk from the same fountain" as communists.[176] After a meeting of church leaders at Belén College in June 1959, clergy began to use their pulpits to criticize the direction of the revolution and the supposed threat to private property, which was declared to be "an absolute right" sanctified by the church.[177]

It has been suggested the tragedy of the Cuban church "was that its renaissance came a decade too late, the revolution a decade too soon."[178] Although the church had been moving toward more engagement with the poor, a policy the Second Vatican Council (1961–1965) would shortly adopt, in 1959 it was still functioning in accordance with the 1949 Vatican Decree on Communism and was acutely alert to any potential threat from "atheistic communism." It was, therefore, not likely to welcome a self-proclaimed Marxist revolution but unable to mobilize effective long-term opposition. Cuban Catholics soon became convinced that their duty was to oppose communism and defend the rights to private property and religious education.[179]

As the primary institution to pit itself against the hurricane of the Cuban revolution, the Catholic church confronted the revolutionary government, holding aloft the banner of anticommunism and representing, in the view of some scholars, the revolutionary government's "most vigorous opponent and its last competitor for control of the hearts and minds of the island's children."[180] Although Cubans were not known to be particularly devout—said to visit church only twice in their lives: for baptism and burial—the church had a cultural influence beyond the numbers seated in pews at Sunday mass.[181] Before the revolution, religion in Cuba had been generally regarded as women's business, but paradoxically, Sr. Miriam Strong remarked, "Castro [has sent] men to their knees."[182] Cuban children, too, were terrified by the "great ghost of the word 'communism,'" one young émigré recalled, and were encouraged by priests to believe it was their "religious duty" to resist their country's descent into "irreligious and atheistic" communism.[183]

The first open test of strength between the church and the revolution occurred at the November 1959 National Catholic Congress, a gigantic gathering that previously attracted only some thousands. José Buajasán, a former Catholic youth activist, recalled a priest standing beside him telling another person jubilantly: "Hey, we've got more people than Fidel!"[184] Fidel Castro and President Osvaldo Dorticós (a former member of the Popular Socialist [communist] Party) attended the rally, which closed with angry shouts of "Social Justice, Yes! Communism, No!"[185] Addressing thousands of students at Havana University a few days later, Fidel complained that the congress and even the Virgin of Charity (Cuba's patron saint) were being "used by vested interests to attack the Cuban Revolution."[186]

For Christian and more privileged Cubans keenly alert to the "communist menace," the arrival of Soviet vice premier Anastas Mikoyan a few months later in February 1960 confirmed their worst fears. Catholic students took the lead in organizing protests against the visit in what was one of the first instances of open opposition to the revolutionary government. The political polarization between the Old and New Cubas was thus increasingly portrayed both in Cuba and in the U.S. media as a battle between Christianity and "godless" communism.[187] Frequent clashes began to take place outside churches, especially between young government supporters and Catholic youth, amid shouts of "Cuba, Yes! Russia, No!"[188] By mid-1960, the polarization between the church and the revolution was complete, and clergy were beginning to move beyond words to engage in counterrevolutionary actions. In an interview in the late 1960s, the rector of Havana's San Carlos Seminary, Carlos Manuel de Céspedes, reflected on the climate of hostility that prevailed, blaming "well-off individuals who were feeling the pinch of the Revolution [who] tried to use the Church as the standard-bearer for their anticommunism." He expressed his suspicions that some of his fellow priests were actively supporting (and urging all Catholics to support) the counterrevolution and go into exile.[189]

Evidence of Cuban clergy's participation in the counterrevolutionary movement was frequently provided by leading anti-Castro activists, like Revolutionary Student Directorate (DRE) leader Reynold González, who, on his arrest in 1961, confirmed that members of the clergy had participated actively in the counterrevolution, and that the hierarchy had acted through the priests. González named the Catholic University Association (ACU) among other Catholic organizations he said had "served to prop up various [counterrevolutionary] movements."[190]

A year before Fidel Castro's pronouncement of the socialist character of the revolution, Archbishop Pérez Serantes issued a pastoral letter in May 1960, "Por Díos y por Cuba" (For God and for Cuba), stating there could be absolutely no compromise with communism. He warned that the communist enemy was now working to undermine all human values, the family, matrimony, and the "right to hold property," subverting "the very foundations of the entire social order."[191] Over 200,000 copies of this letter were distributed at churches and Catholic schools, an act the revolutionary government regarded as a provocation.

This was followed by the hierarchy's first collective pastoral letter of 7 August 1960 reminding Cubans that communism and Catholicism were "totally opposed to each other" and could never be reconciled. Specifically, communism was said to destroy family life by "driving women to leave their homes" and denying parents a choice in the education of their children.[192] The church hierarchy now not only expressed opposition to the changes but also encouraged Cuba's Catholics to actively resist the changes.[193] For the church, wrote Ruby Hart Phillips in 1960, "this is a fight for survival . . . not only in Cuba but in Latin America generally."[194]

In November 1960, Archbishop Pérez Serantes laid out the choice: "Rome or Moscow."[195] The reading and distribution of this pastoral letter at mass provoked scuffles in various Catholic churches and inspired the protests of students at Villanueva University.[196] By this time, it should be noted, Washington had already adopted, and was actively pursuing, a "regime change" program for Cuba.[197] Moreover, the propaganda value of the plight of children and the elderly as "helpless victims of terrorism" had already been identified as the "first and easiest" to exploit.[198]

Fidel Castro continued to denounce the attempt by the counterrevolution to "paint the Revolution as an enemy of religion," asking: "If, as Christ said, 'My kingdom is not of this world,' what are they doing meddling in the problems of this world? . . . They adapted to living with [Batista's] regime of colonialist and imperialist exploitation, and now they oppose a regime of social justice."[199]

By Easter 1961, the Cuban leader's language was angrier, calling the clergy a "plague of cassocked thugs and mercenary professors."[200] The Popular Socialist Party (PSP) leader Juan Marinello deeply offended many Catholics by warning them to stay out of politics and "to remain inside their temples adoring their images."[201] The final showdown with the hierarchy occurred in September 1961, when the outspoken Bishop Eduardo Boza Masvidal orchestrated a mass protest as part of the annual festival of the Virgin of Charity, described by *Newsweek* as the "biggest anti-Castro demonstration since Castro swept to power early in 1959."[202] The result was the deportation to Spain of Bishop Boza Masvidal along with 135 priests.[203]

Nevertheless, the intoxicating enthusiasm and irresistible appeal of the literacy campaign drew many believers in behind the government's moral crusade, even if they retained suspicions or even opposition to its radical course. A Christian émigré reassured this researcher: "Really everybody was happy to see the kids go [to teach literacy] . . . because there was great confidence in the revolution and the revolutionaries—at that time."[204] A very religious young woman admitted to Oscar Lewis that she had been hoping that "the Americans" would succeed with the Bay of Pigs invasion because she saw Cuba "drifting into communism"; but even so, she saw the literacy campaign as "a good thing," and she, too, wanted to join in.[205]

Thus, the year 1961 saw both the defeat of the U.S.-backed invasion and the revolution's definitive moral ascendancy over the church; while the militias defeated the invading exile brigade, the literacy campaign delivered the final moral blow. The church had been able to offer no alternative to Fidel Castro's revolution other than anticommunism. While Fidel repeatedly stated that the revolution was "olive green" not "red," the social program of the revolution brought real material benefits to the vast majority of Cuban families, and intensive political education succeeded in softening anticommunist sentiments among broad sectors of the population. All this laid the basis for the acceptance, if not enthusiastic support, for the pronouncement of the socialist goal of the revolution in April 1961.[206]

Young Cubans like María López Vigil, who left for Spain with her parents that year as a sixteen-year-old, still felt torn between their faith and the revolution, reflecting: "As part of the lower middle-class of Havana, we stood to gain from the changes the revolution was bringing. And as Christians we were sensitive to the social issues of our country. But the purity of the Catholic ideology that filled my house—and the rejection of Communism that was an essential element of that ideology—won out over the dazzling, seductive lights of the revolution and its banners of national dignity and social justice."[207]

The government conscientiously avoided persecuting the church so that the revolution could not be portrayed as against religion; this was more than a "strategic" consideration, Fidel said, but because "respect for religious belief" was a matter of "principle."[208] The church, however, chose to encourage the exodus from the island, hoping it would put international pressure on the Cuban government and remind international public opinion of the repression of religious belief occurring elsewhere in the socialist bloc. The exodus eventually included virtually the entire lay community and hierarchy of Cuba's Catholic church.[209]

During May and June of 1961, hundreds of clergy and lay Catholics left

Cuba voluntarily, apparently with the church's blessing; some were pressured to depart by their superiors, in order to leave parishes without priests as evidence of religious persecution on the island.[210] This, in reality, meant abandoning the field to the revolutionaries just at the moment when the government launched its greatest moral crusade, the literacy campaign, that would bring enlightenment and knowledge to the island's humblest citizens, a point not lost on many Cubans who opted to stay.

A former Catholic youth activist reflected that it was inevitable that the church and the revolutionary government would fall out over the education reforms because the elite religious schools were "powerful organizations [that were] sustained by the wealth and resources of the church—its farms, properties, and the contributions of the faithful."[211] Archbishop Pérez Serantes later lamented: "We loved our schools more than Jesus."[212] The Catholic church, however, not only lost its schools; with the government's nationalization of the Havana cemetery and urban reform measure, it also lost significant assets and income.[213]

Cuba: One Big School

If the "extent and quality of education are a key index of the state of society," then prerevolutionary Cuba "was a miserable failure," concluded two U.S. researchers in 1961.[214] Separate studies conducted in the 1950s had roundly condemned the state of public education in Cuba. Moreover, one of those surveys, a World Bank report, had found the Ministry of Education was "a principal focus of political patronage and of graft."[215] The Cuban education system was later described as "a fragmented microcosm faithfully reflecting the fragmented macrocosm of [Cuban] society at large."[216]

The government's goal was the democratization of education, the elimination of illiteracy, and the establishment of a free, secular, universal, nondiscriminatory education system as Fidel Castro had outlined at his 1953 trial. Every great social revolution of the modern era has sought to remake the education system according to its own vision, beginning with the French revolution of 1789.[217] The reform of a corrupt, dysfunctional, and discriminatory education system was always going to be a top priority for the new Cuban government. "Without preferential attention to the people's education," asserted Armando Hart, minister of education in 1959, "we could not expect the revolutionary purposes to be fulfilled."[218]

The education of Cuba's children had long been a contested site. During the first period of U.S. occupation of the island (1898–1902), the school system in Cuba was restructured to serve U.S. imperial interests and designs; many U.S. corporations sponsored the construction and operation of schools in Cuba in the expectation of a future benefit from the exposure of thousands of young Cubans to North American culture and values.[219] The "notion of mission" imbued nearly every aspect of U.S. involvement in Cuba, with special attention paid to education. This civilizing task was formulated in terms of "Americanization," a process in which Cuba's public school system was the key agent. Young Cubans subsequently studied from U.S. texts translated into Spanish, and they learned about the history of their own country as part of that of the United States from textbooks written by people from that country.[220] This was something Cuba's 1940 Constitution, one of the most progressive in the hemisphere at the time, had tried to correct, proposing all history and politics textbooks should be written by native-born Cubans.[221]

Young Cubans would benefit greatly from an American-style education, explained a U.S. public affairs officer in the early 1950s: "The indoctrination of Cuban children in the principles of democracy and the knowledge and understanding these children obtain of the United States while attending a school like Ruston [Academy] are perhaps the most effective means of shaping Cuban opinion in the future."[222]

The United States–run school in Havana, the Ruston Academy, epitomized this missionary spirit as its director Jim Baker explained: "My first experiences teaching in Ruston Academy made me appreciate more fully American democratic values and traditions and . . . I saw that by sharing these values with Cubans the school could contribute to the development of democracy in Cuba. Promoting this goal has been one of the dominant motivators of my life."[223]

Study in the United States, for a young Cuban, was even greater assurance of prestige, position, and prosperity, and prior to 1959, about 1,100 Cubans were enrolled each year in U.S. institutions of higher education.[224] This, then, was the promise Operation Pedro Pan offered to thousands of Cuban children, many of whose families might previously never have been able to afford such an opportunity.

The inequalities in prerevolutionary Cuba's education system both reflected and reproduced the class structure and social and economic inequality, as well as reinforced Cuba's cultural and technical dependence on the United States.[225] Thus, the success of the economic and cultural decolonization process in Cuba hinged on reform of the education system. Little wonder, therefore, that the new revolutionary leaders, with their vision of a New Cuba, planned to restructure education and revise textbooks to reflect Cuba's own story and Cuba's own needs, as flagged immediately by newly appointed minister for education Armando Hart.[226] The Cuban government announced that the education system would now inculcate the ideals of the revolution, civic responsibility, and nationalist sentiment from kindergarten to university, and that new texts and new teaching methods would be introduced.

Outlining the ideology and aims of education in revolutionary Cuba in 1960, Education Minister Hart argued that every society, even the most primitive, seeks to educate its next generation to perpetuate itself and its culture, an effort in which schooling is only one but a fundamental instrument. "Modern society is represented by the state," and therefore responsibility for education must be assumed by the state, he explained. The goal of education in a democratic society should be to "prepare each citizen to be able to think for themselves," he said, noting that liberty today is restricted "not only by force, brutality, and terror; other mechanisms of power exist that affect the way a man thinks, exercising a tyranny over him that is subtle but no less powerful or despotic"—repressive mechanisms that include not just schools and the education system but also the press, radio, cinema, television, and all other media.[227]

An early researcher into education in revolutionary Cuba admitted he was disturbed by the "avowedly Marxist content of Cuban education," but concluded that he did not regard the new system as "indoctrination" because the government had openly declared its intentions: "The effectiveness of the new teaching should be judged not only as politics on an island of the Cold War but as a 'package' solution to poverty, inequality and dependence.... That it is no soft sell is quite evident from the size of the educational effort. But neither is it indoctrination at gunpoint."[228]

Teachers began to depart from Cuba in large numbers and constituted the greatest number of professionals who left Cuba from 1959 to 1962. Prior to the revolution, nine thousand teachers were unemployed, but few of those would accept posts in rural schools.[229] Disaffected teachers arriving as refugees in Miami made great play of the revolutionary government's introduction of new texts and curricula into Cuban schools, stating only one kind of teaching was allowed now, "indoctrination" in communism, believing this is what U.S. citizens wanted to hear.[230] Ironically, due to the shortage of

Spanish-language materials in the United States, textbooks published by the new Cuban Ministry of Education brought by Pedro Pans were sometimes used in the Miami children's camps.[231]

The revolutionary government was now also questioning the traditionally close alignment of the Cuban and U.S. education systems, something seen as important by those who believed (or hoped) that the revolution would not last. And this change in educational philosophy did not pass unnoticed by the U.S. embassy in Havana.[232] For Cubans, the revolution was "all about history," but for North Americans, who had convinced themselves of the "beneficent purpose . . . from which [they] derived the moral authority to presume power over Cuba," this was "sheer effrontery."[233] Incredulous and perplexed, Washington could only react to the expressions of a newfound Cuban nationalism evident in these education reforms by seeing them as promoting a "hate campaign" against the United States, or in default mode: Cold War anticommunism.[234]

Fidel Castro's opponents now listed among his many "crimes" the conversion of Cuban schools "into centers of communist indoctrination" in which the souls of children were being "poisoned by the teachings of hatred and the art of spying, thus destroying their Christian principles and patriotic traditions."[235]

On 18 September 1959, the Council of Ministers approved Law 561 (the Education Reform Act) to create ten thousand new classrooms and train four thousand new teachers, who were asked to donate half of their nominal salaries to fund this massive expansion of education.[236] This was quite controversial, given the prevalence of graft and corruption in the teaching profession prior to the revolution; previously teachers were appointed for life, receiving their salaries whether or not they made an appearance in the classroom. The education reform (Law 680) of 23 December 1959 was a direct attack on the corruption and bureaucratism of the Ministry of Education in the effort to establish a fully integrated national system of free education—as the 1940 Constitution had proposed.[237] The government defended the measure, saying this would establish "truly democratic education without privilege and discrimination," while the Confederation of Catholic Schools saw it as a step toward the eventual nationalization of schools because private schools were now required to operate under the same guidelines as public schools.[238]

In announcing the initial education reforms, Education Minister Armando Hart had hinted that fewer private schools might be required if the quality of public education was improved.[239] This sparked some concern among Catholic and other private educators, especially when laws 76 and 367 established that private schools would be regulated according to the same standards as public schools, and that they would be subject to regular inspections by state officials and required to use the same texts approved by the Ministry of Education.[240] The announcement that all public schools would now be coeducational would have further disturbed some parents who desired sex-segregated, religious schooling for their children.[241] Before he left Cuba, José Miró Cardona (who had briefly served as prime minister in 1959) claimed that "the transformation of the elementary school system [was] turning the children against Christian principles [by giving] them a militia uniform and arms."[242]

From the first days of the revolution, the Catholic hierarchy lobbied hard to ensure parents' right to choose the education their children would receive, which meant, in effect, the government accepting the continued existence of elitist private schools. Many years later, Fidel Castro affirmed that the government originally had no intention of taking over the private schools.[243] But the director of three large Catholic colleges admitted at the time: "If the revolution proposes to make a society without privileged castes in which all Cubans have the same rights, there is no reason at all for the existence of the private school."[244]

The religious orders that ran schools and owners of other exclusive, private educational institutions, like James Baker's Ruston Academy, soon began to look for ways to relocate their schools. The prestigious Belén College reopened in Miami within a few months of the June 1961 nationalization, and La Salle College was ready to receive 260 former Cuban pupils in September 1961. The relocation of these and many other Cuban private schools undoubtedly acted as another pull factor for Operation Pedro Pan, as students often just followed their schools to Miami.[245] It was this matter of the future of Cuba's elite private schools that soon brought about the most serious confrontation between the church and the revolutionary government.

The End of Private Education

While the Cuban public school system retrogressed in the decade before the revolution, private schools experienced boom times and were considered some of the best in Latin America.[246] Parents, like Fidel Castro's, who could scrape together some cash sent their children to private schools.

Figure 1.7. "The latest disposition: nationalization of private schools. Thanks Fidel!" *Bohemia*, 4 June 1961.

Public schools, according to *Bohemia* in September 1956, were said to be "for the 'darkies' (*los negritos*) and the rabble (*la chusma*), who have no alternative."[247] Private schools thus bestowed class status (or aspirational class status) and promised success and economic security; being modeled on U.S. programs was their primary appeal, insofar as they equipped students with familiarity and skills required for employment in an environment dominated by U.S. culture and conventions.

In fact, the private schools symbolized more than anything else the U.S. dominance of the island, with English-language training at the core of their curriculum.[248] By the 1950s, many young Cubans graduating from Havana's elite, U.S.-run private schools apparently could not write in their mother tongue.[249] Attending schools such as the Ruston Academy in Havana was seen as the way to fast-track a Cuban student's access to a scholarship at a U.S. university.[250]

By early 1961 Cuba's private schools were beginning to collapse, having lost two-thirds of their enrollments and many of their staff with the exodus to Miami.[251] The active and outspoken resistance of church leaders to revolutionary reforms and the use of Catholic private schools as organizing centers made it inevitable that the government would close them down, especially as many of these schools and their teachers had refused to accept the government's instruction to cooperate with the literacy campaign and continued to operate as normal.[252]

In the aftermath of the failed Bay of Pigs invasion, on 1 May 1961 Fidel Castro announced the nationalization of the entire education system.

Accusing Catholic priests of conducting counterrevolutionary propaganda among students attending religious schools, he explained that those schools that have "maintained a patriotic and decent attitude with respect to the Revolution" would be compensated, and the teachers and employees of those schools would retain their jobs. Students would therefore be able to continue attending those same schools, but without the requirement to pay fees; religious instruction would be restricted to the churches by those priests "who do not carry out counterrevolutionary campaigns." Religion "is one thing and politics another," the Cuban leader said.[253]

The nationalization law itself (enacted 6 June 1961) used remarkably defensive language, emphasizing the government's commitment to a system of free, universal, nondiscriminatory education, a "unified integration of an education system [that would] respond to the cultural, technical and social needs" of Cuba.[254] Noting the dissemination of counterrevolutionary propaganda in institutions run by Catholic religious orders, the act restated Fidel's promise that the owners of those schools that had maintained a "patriotic attitude" would be compensated.[255] This is apparently what happened. The Jewish school in Havana, for example, received special government dispensation to continue operating.[256] In fact, Jewish children were permitted to take Hebrew classes, and the government provided a bus to transport them.[257] The school eventually closed in 1981, however, because most of Cuba's Jewish families, overwhelmingly small business owners, left the island when their businesses were nationalized.[258] Small numbers of Jewish children did arrive in the United States with Operation Pedro Pan, for whom responsibility was assumed by the Hebrew Immigrant Aid Society (HIAS).[259]

The formerly exclusive Villanueva University, which had catered to children of privileged families, was also taken over by the government; it was renamed for African revolutionary Patrice Lumumba and converted into a school for domestic servants, who were housed in abandoned mansions in nearby Miramar while they undertook three-month intensive courses in typing, shorthand, accounting, and mathematics.[260]

Student Exchanges with the Socialist Bloc

Coinciding with the first departures of Pedro Pans to Miami in the Year of Education (1961) was the commencement of student exchanges with socialist bloc countries, drawing howls from the U.S. media and the church, especially the more virulently anticommunist sectors that suggested this was clear evidence that Cuba was now a "Soviet satellite."[261] According to *U.S. News and World Report,* Fidel Castro's young son Fidelito was among those allegedly dispatched to the Soviet Union, a fact refuted by the Cuban government.[262]

The parents of María de los Angeles ("Candi") Sosa, a talented young singer, decided to send her to the United States when her name appeared on a list at her school of children awarded scholarships to further their music studies in the Soviet Union. Given the high standard of training for musicians in the Soviet Union, it might have been expected this would be regarded as a great privilege, but that was not how Candi's parents saw it.[263] Some parents feared the government had a plan to identify the island's "smartest children," in order to send them all to communist Russia.[264] While the dispatch of Cubans to the Soviet Union for training as technicians and other desperately needed skills provoked cries of outrage, scholarships offered by U.S. colleges to young Cuban refugees (along with young Hungarians) as part of a program to "aid foreign students in times of crisis" were evidently regarded as altruistic rather than inspired by any sinister motive.[265]

The *U.S. News and World Report* repeatedly warned that the minds of "innocents" were especially vulnerable: "Cuban officials concede that the older generations are too attached to the old ways of American traditions to be made over readily. Their goal is to concentrate on the young people and reshape them to the austere, harsh discipline of Communism. The indoctrination of youngsters is only beginning. It must have several years before it can begin to have long range effect."[266]

Carlos Eire felt he was most fortunate to have escaped from Cuba with Operation Pedro Pan, writing, "I was one of the lucky ones. Fidel couldn't obliterate me as he did the other children, slicing off their heads ever so slowly, and replacing them with fearful, slavish copies of his own."[267] Yvonne Conde also believed if she had stayed in Cuba she, too, "would have been subjected to constant indoctrination, [and] would have been a good little communist, at least for a while."[268] Utterly ludicrous, and shamelessly racist, reports appeared in the U.S. media about schools in revolutionary Cuba, such as the story published in the *Miami Herald* titled "African Savages Take Over Her School: A Cuban Girl Flees in Terror," which described the arrival of "big black men with rings in their noses," in a Matanzas school, said to be exchange students from Congo. "I was terrified," the teenage girl was reported as saying from the safety of Miami.[269]

By deciding to close all schools in April 1961 for the duration of the literacy campaign, the government was making a statement that, for the time being at least, the further education for those young Cubans fortunate to be in school was not as important as the effort to integrate illiterate citizens into the broader cultural and political life of the nation. Obviously, parents of Pedro Pans had a different view of the revolutionary government's priorities in allocating resources for education to those in greater need. Despite some suggestions to the contrary, Msgr. Walsh pointed out that the majority of Pedro Pans were from better-off families and had attended private schools in Cuba, which he said had become "the last refuge from indoctrination."[270] "They took over our schools," bemoaned one middle-class mother, "and our world collapsed."[271]

During the literacy campaign, elementary schoolchildren were served by a special activity program; but parents suspicious of, or hostile to, the government's education policy faced the dilemma of how to keep their teenagers occupied while schools were closed.[272] Moreover, once schools reopened in January 1962, all students were expected to enroll at public schools, which sometimes meant attending classes in the same buildings that had previously belonged to private schools, but without the obligation to pay fees. Anti-Castro forces urged families not to enroll their children in the newly nationalized schools, describing them as a "cemetery of souls."[273] The *Miami Herald* reported one Pedro Pan as saying: "My mother and father didn't want me to go to the school in Camagüey, [because] there is a picture of Khrushchev on the wall and they teach that communism is good."[274] One émigré journalist made the absurd allegation that, by destroying the patriarchal family, the revolutionary government left young Cubans with no other diversion but "free love."[275]

The story of "Iris" is probably typical of the Pedro Pans' privileged peer group. Describing herself as a *"cuña rica"* (rich kid) and "sort of like a society girl," she had attended the best private school her parents could find. After her school was closed, they refused to send her to the new "communist" schools. By 1962, all her (former) school friends had left or were getting their paperwork together in order to leave, which Iris described as the "fashionable" thing to do. Everyone "was talking about how [they would soon be] chewing gum and drinking Coke," she said, but her passport was lost, so her departure was delayed. Iris soon became an active "counterrevolutionary" after being disillusioned when her family's store and farms were "intervened" (expropriated) and their yacht seized. This activism involved writing slogans on poles in the streets, saying "Long live the *gusanos* [worms], *abajo los guayabitos* [down with the little mice]!"[276]

Although Iris had always gone to Catholic schools, she developed a new interest in religion and joined the Youth Catholics, who, she said, were engaging in some "really serious fights" with the Young Communists. While some revolutionary teenagers went to work on farms on Sundays "to help the revolution," others went to taunt their peers attending church, she recalled, "so if you walked around with your little veil on your head, then forget it!" She admitted her group was "pretty harmless," being composed of twelve-, thirteen-, and fourteen-year-olds; they mostly just played records, danced, told jokes, gossiped, and had fun, she said. As her friends left, she became bored, being one of "just a few leftover kids." Eventually she enrolled in a "communist" school, where she was confronted with all kinds of stimulating new ideas, such as Darwin's theory of evolution, which challenged her strict Catholic education. This experience she described as "exciting" and "expanding." As a teenager, she felt she had been "searching" and wanted to expand her horizons. "[For] us, it was exciting," she said, but for many parents, "it was like their world was ending."[277] Meanwhile, some parents concerned about the idleness of their children hired English-language tutors in preparation for their departure to the United States.[278]

* * *

The revolutionary project initiated in January 1959 was a process of economic and cultural transformation, an assertion of a vision of a New Cuba and a New Cuban. As such, it was an echo of the anticolonial revolutions that emerged in the postwar era. But in many ways, it also offered a foretaste of the youth social movements that would explode across the globe in the 1960s. Recoiling in horror at the questioning of their values and authority, more affluent Cubans articulated their anxieties and disorientation stirred by the revolutionary hurricane by iterating Cold War tropes about communism's threat to families and children's minds.

Thus, as some young Cubans began packing their bags for Miami, many of their peers set out to teach literacy in the countryside. More than an educational initiative, the literacy campaign became a kind of moral crusade, especially because it commenced at the precise moment of the Bay of Pigs

Figure 1.8. Battle of the billboards: "Will this child be a believer or an atheist?" vs. "Will this child be a patriot or a traitor?" *Newsweek*, 6 March 1961.

invasion. The dramatic defeat of the U.S.-backed exile invasion signaled for many that the revolution would not be halted so easily, and as it turned out, the debacle actually hastened "the demise of the Old Cuba the invaders had come to save."[279] It also accelerated the departures of the Pedro Pans.

One overprotected Pedro Pan teenager recalled with bitterness that his parents had prevented him from joining the Boy Scouts because it involved weekend camping expeditions away from home. Yet they sent him off alone to a foreign country where he found himself in an orphanage, only to be reunited with his family some five years later. "They sent the children away in order to save them. To save them from what?" he asked. The situation was "not the same as when the Jews were persecuted in Germany or the disappeared in Chile." He came to understand that middle-class parents like his were "completely terrified and ignorant about the changes taking place," and therefore afraid for their *"bitongos"* (mama's boys), which he candidly confessed he was.[280]

In drawing young Cubans into the literacy campaign, the new government encouraged them to see themselves as contributing to the revolutionary project. If parents believed they had to send their adolescent children to Miami in order to protect them from "communist indoctrination," their underlying fear was undoubtedly the challenge they imagined the revolution presented to existing social mores regarding the patriarchal family and race relations.

By 1961, the most fiercely contested battleground in revolutionary Cuba was the new generation of Cuban youth. In March, a billboard was erected in Havana featuring a photograph of a young boy, posing the question: "Will this child be a believer or an atheist?" "It depends on you. Pray for him and cooperate with the catechism" was the answer. Almost immediately, a second billboard appeared with a sketch of the same boy, stating "Will this child be a patriot or a traitor? It depends on you. Teach him the work of the revolution."[281] Learning the "work of the revolution" through the experience of teaching literacy to those less fortunate was at the very heart of the revolutionary project of creating New Cubans for a New Cuba.

So as thousands of young Cubans flew off to Miami with Operation Pedro Pan, another hundred thousand also left their homes, in this case as volunteers in the national literacy campaign that would take them to some of the most remote and underdeveloped parts of the island. The old social order was fast disappearing, and the choice for individual young Cubans and their families was becoming clear: Miami or the mountains, signifying far more than two points on a map.

2

Alfabeticemos! Let's Teach Literacy!

Learning the "Why" of the Revolution

The year 1961 proved to be decisive for the consolidation of the Cuban revolutionary project. It was the year in which the U.S.-backed invasion at the Bay of Pigs was defeated and the year of the national literacy campaign, both events that determined the pace and course of the revolution. Msgr. Walsh consistently argued it was the literacy campaign that convinced parents to send their children out of Cuba after they learned about the *brigadistas'* experiences, "the promiscuity, the lack of supervision, the indoctrination and all the rest." The literacy campaign, he insisted, "was what opened [parents'] eyes about what was happening in Cuba."[1] Jim Baker went as far as suggesting a special abortion clinic had to be established to cover up the "catastrophe" of girls returning pregnant from the literacy campaign.[2]

Why the literacy effort proved to be so controversial at the time and subsequently can only be understood by recognizing its explicit political context and nature—how it highlighted most dramatically the differences between the Old and the New Cubas—and, above all, the part played in the campaign by young Cubans. Antonio Villaverde, the former dean of La Salle University, remembered a social occasion in 1961 when a friend asked him about his sons. When he explained they were "away from home," the woman hugged him with great joy, saying her children, too, were now in Miami. Dr. Villaverde then had to explain that his boys were in the mountains as part of the literacy campaign. "I can still see the look of hate on her face," he recalled.[3]

The 1961 national literacy campaign came to symbolize the youthful spirit and humanist character of the revolution and New Cuba itself. Immediately after the insurrection, representatives of the new government toured the country asking the people what they needed beyond agrarian reform. "Doctors and teachers," was the response.[4] The purpose of the education reforms undertaken by the revolutionary government, as discussed in chapter 1, was to establish a more democratic, equitable system for the entire population, considering that education had been one of the most shamefully neglected and corrupt departments under the Batista regime, totally failing to meet the needs of the rural population in particular.[5] In fact, by 1958, Cuba's illiteracy rate was increasing.

Literacy work had already begun during the revolutionary war against Batista; an education department was set up within the Rebel Army; thirty-seven schools were established in liberated zones to teach illiterates among the troops and the local rural population, and the José Martí teacher training school was created.[6] A national literacy commission was set up in March 1959, and as thousands of teachers left the island, thousands of new ones were trained. Many teacher trainees were fast-tracked through their courses in order to fill teaching positions in rural areas. A volunteer teacher program began in April 1960 with an appeal for 1,000 young people to undergo an intensive three-month teacher training course. Between 4,000 and 5,000 applications were received, and 1,500 were accepted and 1,400 graduated at the end of August 1960.[7]

Addressing a group of volunteer teacher graduates on 29 August 1960, Fidel argued that a "school is not the building; a school is the communion between the teacher and the children" that can take place anywhere, even "under a tree."[8] The government built ten thousand new classrooms in the first two years of the revolution, with priority given to rural areas, and elementary school enrollment increased from 625,700 to over one million.[9] At a ceremony at Camp Columbia in September 1959, Fidel highlighted the symbolism of converting the former dictator Batista's military headquarters into a gigantic school complex.[10] A year later, addressing the United Nations General Assembly in September 1960, Fidel Castro announced that in the coming year "a great battle" to eliminate illiteracy would take place, with the ambitious goal of teaching every single illiterate person in the country to read and write. Ambitious it certainly was, but he assured his audience at the UN and Cubans listening at home that "Cuba will be the first country of Latin America that within a few months [would] be able to say that it does not have a single illiterate person."[11]

By designating 1961 the Year of Education, the revolutionary government planned to convert the entire island into one gigantic school: "Every tree, every home, every factory a school" was the campaign slogan adopted, explained the assistant director of propaganda for the campaign.[12] The literacy commission was reorganized under the presidency of Education Minister Armando Hart, with Mario Díaz as national coordinator, and efforts were stepped up to locate and register all those who could not read or write.[13] On 31 December 1960, Fidel Castro suggested that if not enough teachers and other adult literacy workers were available, the government would end the school year two months early and mobilize all students from sixth grade up to join what he called an "Education Army" to be sent to every corner of the country, "so that every illiterate who needs a teacher shall have one."[14]

At this time, Cuba had a potential professional teaching force of about 35,000 teachers and about 1,000,000 illiterates; to achieve the ratio of 4 pupils to 1 teacher, 250,000 teachers would be required.[15] So by the end of January, Fidel issued the call for 100,000 Cuban teenagers over the age of thirteen to participate in the literacy campaign: "With you," the Cuban leader said, "we will win this battle." By participating in this campaign as "missionaries of culture," young Cubans would "have something to be proud of their entire lives."[16]

The campaign atmosphere created around this "battle against illiteracy" succeeded in overcoming one of the greatest obstacles in any literacy drive—motivating those unable to read or write to come forward, overcome feelings of shame or lack of self-confidence, inspiring them to want to learn, and convincing them they could learn.[17] "Who says I'm too old to learn?" said seventy-eight-year-old Teodoro Izuaga. "I'm going to learn because Fidel and my fifty grandchildren want me to!"[18] Here, the energy and enthusiasm of the young *brigadistas* helped to create an almost irresistible momentum and overcame any resistance or hesitation on the part of illiterates.

New York Times journalist Herbert Matthews commented: "[The campaign was] revolutionary activity at its best. Thousands of youth who would never have left their cities or towns came into daily contact with peasants. All classes, white and black, experienced a communal life, a sort of social integration such as Cuba had never known." Moreover, he observed, the international attention—generally positive—gave Cubans a "sense of pride and enthusiasm [for] the Revolution in a critical year."[19]

Figure 2.1. Vanquishing illiteracy and Uncle Sam. *Bohemia*, 3 December 1961.

In this way, the literacy campaign would replicate the "communion with the people" experienced by the guerrillas during the revolutionary war, which, Che Guevara reflected, took them beyond theories and made them as individuals and as a group "feel in their bones" the need for a definitive change, and which entrenched the ideology of the revolution.[20] The goal of the campaign, veteran Cuban educationalist Mier Fables pointed out, "was always greater than to teach poor people how to read. . . . The dream," she said, "was to enable those two portions of the population who had been instrumental in the process of the revolution from the first to find a common bond, a common spirit, a common goal. The peasants discovered the word. The students discovered the poor. Together they all discovered their own *patria* [homeland]."[21]

Objectives of the Literacy Campaign

Although the national rate of illiteracy in Cuba of 23.6 percent was not as high as in many other Latin American countries, in rural areas of the island it was above 40 percent, thus representing one of the most graphic indicators of the imbalance in the development and cultural level between the cities and the countryside.[22]

The foundation of the campaign was the understanding that literacy was a universal human right, a matter of basic social justice. Campaign organizers saw illiteracy as a social phenomenon and, therefore, the challenge as establishing a new culture of education in Cuba. Although the literacy plan was extremely ambitious, it was also an achievable goal, given the linguistic homogeneity, geographic accessibility, and nature of the problem in Cuba.[23] In this sense, it showed the revolution could deliver almost immediately a personal material benefit to hundreds of thousands of Cuban citizens, along with other reforms that increased incomes and reduced rents and the costs of utilities.²⁴ "I don't know what Communism is," a *campesino* said, "but agrarian reform, free doctors and hospitals, and my chance to read and write is what the Revolution means to me."²⁵ As Fidel Castro told the first congress of the Cuban Communist Party (PCC), Cubans began to identify with the reality of socialism and communism even while they might have resisted the words themselves.²⁶

Raising the level of literacy and education generally in the population was therefore more than a strategic issue for the revolutionary government, but a matter of great moral importance. This concept of literacy as a human right was expressed most eloquently in the campaign slogan used on posters and other propaganda: *"Alfabetizar es hacer el hombre"* (To teach literacy is to humanize).²⁷ As its primary slogan, the campaign popularized José Martí's words: *"Ser cultos es el único modo de ser libre"* (To be educated is the only way to be free).²⁸ Education Minister Hart told the September 1961 National Literacy Congress that the revolution had given *campesinos* the treasure of land, had given the workers management of the factories, and would now guarantee the "patrimony of culture" to the entire Cuban people.²⁹

The profoundly humanist—even intimate—essence of the campaign was captured in a popular song written at the time by Eduardo Saborit titled *"Despertar"* (Awakening), in which a newly literate man describes his happiness in now being able to express in writing to his lover "all that [his] soul needed to say." On television in late January 1961, Education Minister Armando Hart spoke of the "sad yet somehow beautiful" scene that occurred when people rushed to greet the victorious Rebel Army soldiers and asked for their autographs, only to realize that many of them were unable to sign their names. It was necessary to tackle this problem as an urgent priority, he said, "because within this mass of illiterates is the revolutionary reserve of the country."³⁰ A significant sector of the Cuban population was *"dehumanized"* by having to sign documents or receipts with their thumbprints, apart from the fact that illiterate *campesinos* were easily exploited, explained a former literacy campaign organizer, and "for this reason we talk about the light of learning."³¹

The revolutionary leadership took as its guide in this campaign not the experiences of literacy teaching in Russia or China (about which they apparently knew very little) but the teachings of Cuba's great poet and independence fighter of the nineteenth century, José Martí. Thus, the literacy campaign proved to be "a Cuban struggle and a Cuban victory in almost all respects."[32] Martí had envisaged a troupe of "wandering teachers" that would bring enlightenment to the countryside. Peasants had no time to go to school, he wrote, so the school must come to them. Education would be a "new religion with its new priests," and farmers would be proselytized through "a campaign of gentleness and knowledge [by] a corps . . . of missionary teachers."[33] The Cuban 1961 literacy campaign paralleled the ideas Paolo Freire was developing at this time, later to be published in *The Pedagogy of the Oppressed* and his numerous other works, and this was no coincidence because Raúl Ferrer, the deputy coordinator of the campaign, was a personal friend of the Brazilian educator.[34]

The revolutionary government also regarded illiteracy as a major impediment to Cuba's urgent need for economic development. "Economically underdeveloped peoples," asserted Education Minister Armando Hart, "are culturally underdeveloped peoples."[35] Education was also seen as fundamental to the reconstruction of Cuban society generally, while it was also regarded as an essential "investment" in order to create the educated and technically trained workforce that agricultural reform and industrialization required.[36]

Veteran Cuban educationalist Fernando García Gutiérrez put it bluntly: "A country with millions of illiterates cannot develop." It was necessary to close schools for eight months, he said, "so that *everyone* would get into teaching. . . . [T]hose who were already in school could wait a year, but we felt that the illiterates *could not wait!*" An underdeveloped country like Cuba, he insisted, simply "couldn't wait years."[37] This was especially the case because Cuba lost thousands of professionals and technicians, along with departing U.S. personnel, in the postrevolutionary exodus to Miami—including as many as 50 percent of Cuba's doctors and teachers.[38]

Furthermore, the achievement of a basic level of literacy was the only way to incorporate a large sector of the population, the mass of peasants and most exploited urban workers—politically speaking, a very important sector for the revolution—into the political and cultural life of the country. How illiterate Cubans were to be taught was regarded as important as the achievement of literacy itself. By establishing a "direct dialogue that had never existed before between different social strata," organizer Raúl Ferrer explained, "participation became the crux of the pedagogy."[39]

Eventually, a teaching force of 271,000 was mobilized, plus another 30,000 Cubans acted as support workers in the literacy campaign.[40] The involvement of such a huge percentage of the population as teachers, learners, and others—estimated to be 1.25 million out of a population of 7 million—successfully extended the revolution, in terms of its support and participation, beyond the small guerrilla movement that had led the insurrection.[41] The "sheer magnitude of the effort," suggested an early researcher, "may have kindled further support and enthusiasm. Indeed, to have mobilized a teaching force of such size without developing any pride, loyalty, or sense of mission in itself would have been remarkable."[42] A Cuban teacher described the campaign as a "true movement of national fusion [in which] the entire populace could participate in the tasks of the revolution. The revolution no longer was a phenomenon reserved for a small group, zealous and active; it was converted into a true mass movement."[43]

The campaign was based on the idea that the people should teach the people, and that is more or less what happened; even small children taught their peers.[44] "We needed all the people in the wheel of one great task," said Raúl Ferrer, because "[we] had no choice. In the long run, almost every man and woman answered the call."[45] By participating in this extraordinarily ambitious national project, Cubans began to feel part of a single nation—an idea expressed simply in the letter written by a newly literate *campesino*: "I never really felt Cuban until I learned to read and write."[46] One of the "explicit objects of the literacy struggle," observed U.S. educator Jonathan Kozol, was "to build a sense of future solidarity between these two important segments of the Cuban population"—the city and the countryside.[47]

The literacy campaign would be "an experience from which everyone emerged with their views fundamentally changed," wrote Antoni Kapcia.

> The urban volunteers had their eyes opened to poverty and were inculcated early with the values of public service, self-sacrifice and solidarity, while the illiterate . . . were made rapidly aware of the real practical, as well as political benefits that the Revolution would bring them personally. . . . It was the first, but most massive, of the many mobilizations that created and confirmed a collective self-image of the Revolution as a *pueblo en marcha* ("a people on the march"), overcoming with subjective commitment the objective obstacles that underdevelopment and poverty had erected against full social integration and against educational progress.[48]

Around 120,000 People's Teachers were mobilized to teach locally, usually after work, and professional teachers continued to receive their regular salaries while teaching adults; for the final push of the campaign, professional teachers were compelled to participate, usually assigned to teach near where they lived.[49] But the national campaign would have been impossible to prosecute successfully without the participation of over 100,000 young *brigadistas*, a plan that had some obvious advantages: it did not disrupt production, which was seriously beginning to falter by this time, and it used the labor of energetic, enthusiastic volunteers with few ties. With limited budgetary resources, mobilizing this "people's force" was the only alternative for the revolutionary government to achieve its objective.[50]

Popular participation in the literacy effort began with media campaigns to encourage people to donate pencils, books, notebooks, and kerosene lamps. Mario Díaz, national coordinator of the campaign, said this was useful on three counts: a large amount of the necessary materials was collected, the campaign was publicized, and people began to become involved in the drive.[51] Youth leader Aldo Álvarez reported on television that in the first few months of 1961, students made fifty thousand blackboards at their schools to contribute to the campaign.[52]

For young Cubans, however, the campaign presented the opportunity to emulate their revolutionary heroes in a real and practical way, and this was its conscious intent. The mobilization of teenagers as literacy teachers, said Díaz, was designed not just to achieve the campaign's goals but also to have an "impact on the adolescents of the experience [who spent] a year living with the peasants in the countryside." Having their own uniform, flag, anthem, and emblem identified them as members of the "Education Army," a continuation of the rebel army, and presented "the best image" of the revolution. "That's how the peasants saw it," he said, "and it's what explains the enormous influence these youngsters had in the countryside."[53]

Moreover, the youthful "missionaries" would themselves learn, through their teaching experience, to understand the value of manual labor and the rigors of life in the countryside.[54] At a special family day on Mothers' Day (14 May 1961), held at the Varadero training camp for young literacy teachers, Fidel told departing *brigadistas:* "You are going to teach, but as you teach, you will also learn. You are going to learn much more than you can possibly teach. . . . Because while you teach them what you have learned in school, they will be teaching you what they have learned from the hard life that they have led. They will teach you the 'why' of the revolution better than any speech, better than any book."[55]

Figure 2.2. Recruitment advertisement for *brigadistas*: "While I prepare myself, I'm enjoying a vacation at Varadero." *Bohemia*, 18 June 1961.

Mobilization of the Conrado Benítez Brigades

That this would be no vacation was already clear after a counterrevolutionary group assassinated an eighteen-year-old Afro-Cuban youth, Conrado Benítez, on 5 January 1961 while he was teaching in the remote Escambray Mountains. He apparently showed the rebels his identity card as a volunteer teacher, which they took to be a "communist party" membership card.[56] "He was poor, he was black, he was a teacher. There you have three reasons for the agents of imperialism to assassinate him," stated Fidel, proposing that the new recruits to the literacy drive would bear his name and his image as members of the Conrado Benítez Brigades.[57]

Inevitably, the literacy campaign provoked some wildly conflicting responses. While the government insisted that the campaign was fundamentally about human dignity and giving equal educational opportunities to all, the U.S. media and the anti-Castro movement raged about its highly political nature, viewing it as a mass indoctrination effort of both the young literacy teachers and their pupils. Cuban teenagers were described by *Newsweek* as "Fidel's most fanatical followers," while their parents were said to be "less enthusiastic," worried about the unsanitary, primitive conditions under which their children would live in the rural regions. The "juvenile pedagogue," *Newsweek* reported, "must live with the family he is teaching and help cut sugar cane, drive cattle, fish, or do whatever else the family does for its living," so the "Year of Education will also be a year of indoctrination."[58]

"It was a wonderful scheme," Ruby Hart Phillips commented cynically. "The children were first indoctrinated with the 'ideals' of the revolution, which were Communist doctrine; then the peasants were to learn Communist doctrine with their letters." She concluded: "The parents of the children who had been frightened for months by rumors that the Castro regime would assume '*patria potestad*,' or paternal rights, over all children above the age of seven, viewed this Army of Education with alarm. It really was doing the same thing; that is, taking the children away from the influence of the parents to indoctrinate them with Communist ideas."[59]

By the time Yvonne Conde left Cuba as part of Operation Pedro Pan in August 1961, she asserted children faced the following options: "[I]f he or she were aged seven to thirteen, he or she would have to join the Union of Rebel Pioneers. Those twelve years of age or older had to go to the mountains to alphabetize the peasants and, upon turning thirteen, they had to join the Association of Rebel Youth (AJR). Refusal to participate equaled isolation, labelling oneself an outcast and therefore a counterrevolutionary. There were no gray areas in Cuba at the time."[60]

Some parents believed their children were being pressured into participating and suspected the literacy campaign as "little more than an attempt by the regime to separate their children from them and catechize the youngsters in Communism."[61] But coinciding as it did with the defeat of the 1961 U.S.-backed invasion, the literacy campaign became the revolution's greatest moral crusade. Certainly, the revolutionary government used this coincidence in their propaganda to contrast the moral and humanist aspect of the revolution to the violence, corruption, and backwardness of Old Cuba, represented by the invaders. "It would have been much easier if struggling against ignorance had been our only task," Fidel told *brigadistas* at the Varadero training camp. "But we have found ourselves confronting two great tasks: defending the revolution and the [homeland] from threats of aggression and, at the same time, doing battle against ignorance."[62]

National redemption now depended on every Cuban fulfilling his or her "duty."[63] This was certainly how the literacy campaign was promoted by the government, the moral weapon—social motivation—not compulsion or indoctrination proving to be highly effective in terms of encouraging illiterates to learn and young Cubans to teach.[64] "This is another army that imperialism won't be able to defeat," Mario Díaz told trainee *brigadistas* in Varadero, a week after the ill-fated U.S.-sponsored invasion at the Bay of Pigs.[65] The sheer number of young Cubans volunteering suggested the campaign inspired "a new hope for justice and dignity for the wretched of the earth."[66] Many were excited about "joining their peers in a brave, bold, and patriotic project . . . traveling to remote country areas in what would [often] be their first trip away from home."[67]

The idea that teenagers were forced to participate in the literacy campaign has been repeated often over the years. During the conflict over the Cuban child refugee Elián González in 2000, the *New York Times* repeated the story that, in the early years of the revolution, Cuban parents opted to send their children to the United States because their fears that the Castro government would remove children from their families, "indoctrinate them . . . that the state was more important than the family," were proven by the fact that the Cuban government "had taken many children out of urban schools and sent them to the countryside in a literacy campaign."[68]

Jonathan Kozol definitively rejected the idea that young Cubans were compelled to join the campaign, arguing the "ethical exhilaration" stimulated by the revolution was the primary factor motivating the young *brigadistas*. He pointed out that Cuba had not yet declared itself a "Marxist state" when the campaign was announced, and he contended that "those who misconceive the driving impulse as Marxist discipline and dogma . . . not only miss the motivation but . . . also ignore one of the main results [of the literacy drive]." It was the campaign itself, Kozol argued, that "turned 100,000 liberal, altruistic, and utopian kids into a rebel vanguard of committed or, at the very least, incipient socialists."[69]

The Cuban leaders were convinced that individual human beings made their own history and, in doing so, forged their own revolutionary spirit or *conciencia*. This, Che Guevara wrote, involved transforming a "love of living humanity" into "actual deeds, acts that serve as examples, as a moving force. . . . This is the way we educate our people."[70] This strategy proved highly effective in terms of achieving the goal of significantly reducing illiteracy and drawing a huge part of the population into the revolutionary project. "No amount of political indoctrination of the kind so often carried out, in tedious and didactic ways, by almost every nation in the modern world," Jonathan Kozol argued, "could possibly have generated loyalties, cut off old ties, and forged a consciousness of social justice as did the months these 95,000 Cuban youngsters dedicated to teaching reading to the poorest men and women of the land."[71]

The campaign organizers understood there was no way the goals of the literacy drive could be achieved in an apolitical manner, and the UNESCO Report on the campaign enthusiastically endorsed the literacy drive's overt political nature, commenting that as a "political event," its results "[could not] be perfectly understood without taking into consideration the social and cultural objectives."[72] As Brazilian educator Paolo Freire and Cuba's Raúl Ferrer, among many other educationalists, have concluded, there is no such thing as "neutral education" or "neutral literacy." "All learning is ideological in one way or another," Kozol asserted.[73]

With the revolution of 1959, Cubans had a chance to come to terms with their nation's history and, in particular, what had happened in 1898 when the United States stepped in to usurp Cuba's independence struggle against Spain. National sentiment was aroused by the revolutionary leadership to legitimize the revolution so that Cubans might recover their history and reclaim their historical agency.[74] Hence, controversially, the literacy campaign materials presented a different reading of Cuba's past and projected a vision of an alternative future, using what Paolo Freire called "active" words, discussing ideas such as agrarian reform, to which the learners could readily relate; the primer and teacher's manuals also developed themes of nationalism and internationalism, explaining the role of monopolies and capitalist exploitation. These texts, using remarkably little jargon, presented Cuba as a truly independent nation for the first time and armed the young *brigadistas* with the tools to teach literacy, while imparting the fundamental reasons why so many Cubans had been oppressed without land or education.[75]

The organizers of the literacy campaign openly defended the politically charged language of the texts: "[Others] do not dare to use the words we use," said Raúl Ferrer. "They do not dare to speak of land reform, to speak about the sick and the poor . . . the international corporations and the banks . . . they do not dare to put these words into the hands of the poor people. And, because they do not dare, therefore they fail—and they will always fail until they do!"[76]

But most U.S. observers could only see what was, to them, the Cuban government's constant harping about what had happened in 1898 as "anti-Americanism" and took umbrage at Cuba's challenge to their "established truths," especially because it appeared as if the Cubans were "impugning their motives."[77] On the other hand, Fidel Castro hardly needed to invent Cuba's long struggle for sovereignty and social justice because, after the revolution, the United States continually reminded Cubans of it.[78]

Those who defend "the neutrality of adult literacy programs are right in accusing us of political acts when we try to clarify reality," wrote Paolo Freire. "But they falsify the truth by denying their own efforts to mask reality." Moreover, as Raúl Ferrer insisted, there "is no way to [teach literacy] which is not political." For a person to feel they "can be the owner of the word," that is, achieve literacy, he said, "[that person must sense that he or she can also be] the owner of [their] own existence, of [their] toil, of the fruit of [their] own work. In order to sense that it can be within [one's] power to possess the *word*, [one] must believe . . . [it is possible to] gain the power to transform the *world* . . . to shape the world . . . to make it a more noble and more humane place to be."[79]

The UNESCO Report concluded that the very fact that the campaign "was itself a political event" was the secret of its success, but this was also the reason why it was so controversial.[80] One of the authors of the UNESCO Report later wrote: "When an illiterate adult [begins] to learn how to read and write, society itself [begins to] go to school. . . . The school opens its doors to life experiences, work problems, the tragedy of poverty. Society goes to school and learns to read and write; this process can release unknown forces."[81]

The Bay of Pigs invasion stimulated an even greater effort in the literacy campaign and an understanding of its political content among teachers and their pupils. A sixteen-year-old *brigadista* remarked that the attack made it easier to teach the first lesson in the primer on the Organization of American States and explain the conflict with the United States.[82] By 19 April 1961, when the invasion threat was defeated—an unexpectedly brief period of only a few days—recruitment of young volunteers as literacy teachers began in earnest. Within days, there were 7,220 youths in the Varadero training camp for *brigadistas*, and a week later 11,505 (6,040 girls and 5,465 boys) had already received their one-week's instruction.[83]

Not everything ran smoothly and, according to organizers, anxieties about separation from family, often for the first time, were manifest in a surprising number of the trainee *brigadistas*.[84] Nevertheless, by the last week of April, the first contingent of the Conrado Benítez Brigades departed for Oriente province, where the Sierra Maestra mountains are situated.[85] By the end of May, 26,000 *brigadistas* had already passed through Varadero and 60,000 had registered.[86] By the time the camp closed on 31 August 1961, 105,664 young Cubans (54,953 girls and 50,711 boys) had gone through the literacy-training course.[87]

This mobilization obviously required an extraordinary logistical effort with transport and communications, among many other challenges.[88] Given that the country was also beginning to feel the bite of the U.S. economic sanctions and an ongoing active campaign of sabotage and military aggression by counterrevolutionary groups, the resources committed to the literacy campaign are all the more remarkable. In fact, the Cuban government used the literacy campaign to significantly expand the nation's infrastructure, especially transport, communication, and public health, as well as education.[89] Coincident with the literacy campaign, for example, was a nationwide vaccination campaign against tuberculosis, cholera, and smallpox; the tuberculosis vaccine was administered in small portions of ice cream, which many rural children had never tasted before. Consequently, health workers had to be vigilant to ensure that children did not line up for multiple doses—once they got used to what one little girl described as the "burning sensation" of the ice cream on her tongue.[90]

Recruitment Propaganda

To understand why a young Cuban might have volunteered to teach literacy, it is necessary first to look at how these youths were recruited. Early in 1961, recruitment for the campaign began in schools and through neighborhood meetings, organized by the newly formed local block committees (Committees to Defend the Revolution, CDRs), the Federation of Cuban Women (FMC), and the AJR.[91] Former *brigadista* Mercedes Liriano Stuart recalled how, before schools were closed, the AJR went through the classrooms at her teacher training college in Havana urging students to join up to the pilot literacy programs.[92] The AJR prepared special guidelines for these meetings in the form of frequently asked questions and answers with which to reassure anxious parents about the supervision, safety, and security of their children. These included special emphasis on the supervision, care, and protection of girls.[93] Nevertheless, emotions often ran high at these meetings. Asteria Perdomo described the emotional scene at one of these community meetings where a young would-be *brigadista* convinced his somewhat overprotective mother to let him join up.[94] A shouting match between revolutionary students and "dissenters" from local Catholic schools broke out at another meeting in Holguín held to recruit volunteers for the literacy campaign.[95]

A total media blitz was launched to encourage youth to join up, involving a mobile radio station that traveled around the island interviewing *brigadistas*, peasants, and campaign organizers, encouraging a sense of popular participation. Newspapers also ran articles "from the front" in the "war against illiteracy," as well as a photo montage cartoon series, "Report from the Conrado Benítez Brigades," which featured a happy-faced cartoon lantern (a symbol of the campaign) and described the daily activities of the *brigadistas*. As the campaign developed, the newspapers published even more "Reports from the Education Army" and hundreds, if not thousands, of letters from *brigadistas* and newly literate Cubans. Short television ads continued throughout the campaign as a means of both encouraging greater participation from youth as well as adults, and to maintain the morale of both *brigadistas* and their parents, reinforcing the ideological message of the campaign. The campaign was, in effect, mythologized while it was still in progress.[96]

Recruitment propaganda for the Conrado Benítez Brigades had several features. First, there was a moral appeal invoking both humanist and

Figure 2.3. "Report from the Conrado Benítez Literacy Brigades." "Wherever there is an illiterate Cuban there is also a *brigadista*. The Army of Literacy Teachers is now on the march. And while they sow the flower of learning in our countryside, they join in the labor and struggle shoulder to shoulder together with the *campesino*. The *brigadista* and her pupil begin work early in the yard feeding the chickens. After sharing the housework in the morning, the *brigadista* and the *campesina* spend the afternoon prettying up the home. And when the hard work is done, they enjoy a quiet chat outside while they embroider. At the end of the day, when the men return from the fields, the yard becomes a classroom and the *brigadista* and her pupils review the lesson. And when [the *brigadistas*] return proud of what they have accomplished, they will be better men and better women... Better citizens for the homeland of tomorrow!" *Bohemia,* 18 June 1961.

patriotic sentiments. Recruitment ads for the literacy campaign published at the height of the recruitment period relied heavily on an emotional plea that a "peasant family is waiting for you." Appeals addressed to parents, teachers, and students pronounced: "To teach literacy is the most revolutionary task . . . [and it is] the duty of every student to join the Conrado Benítez Brigades to combat ignorance in the furthermost corners of our territory."[97] The obligation of "those who know more [is to] teach those who know less," so that every illiterate should have a teacher and that each teacher an illiterate was an idea popularized in the formula "QTATA²" (*Que todo analfabeto tiene alfabetizador / Que todo alfabetizador tenga analfabeto*; That every illiterate has a teacher / That every teacher has an illiterate pupil). This slogan was widely used in campaign propaganda—depicted as a double handshake: one white arm and one black arm, one black arm and one white arm, which the UNESCO Report saw as clearly expressing "the idea of human, social and racial integration."[98]

The campaign to convince illiterates to sign up for literacy classes relied on a similar moral appeal: that it was a revolutionary duty to educate oneself, but some material incentive was also offered. For example, a proposal was made (to come into effect from January 1962) that workers who refused to learn would not be eligible for wage increases or promotions. But compulsion was hardly necessary in the atmosphere of "well-publicized approval of all who studied and acclaim for those who succeeded."[99] The unique feature of the Cuban campaign was that it somehow motivated large numbers of illiterate adults to want to learn to read, despite the comparative lack of cohesive pedagogical policy and continued experimentation throughout the campaign.[100]

In many ways, the literacy campaign adopted many hallmarks of a capitalist advertising campaign. Certainly one of the idiosyncratic episodes of the campaign was the appearance of advertisements sponsored by Coca-Cola that read: "In the Year of Education. . . . Use the Pause that Refreshes to teach someone how to read and write."[101] Jonathan Kozol remarked this ad "may be . . . the only meeting-point in recent history of capitalist and socialist exhortations conveyed in the same words, presented by the same text, published in the same newspapers, and posted on the same huge signs along the road."[102] This may not have been such a surprising coincidence, however, because one of the leading propagandists for the literacy campaign, Mirta Muñiz, had previously worked for the U.S. advertising firm McCann-Erickson, which had the Coca-Cola account in Cuba.[103]

There can be no doubt that the momentum built up during the campaign, an atmosphere similar to that of a country at war—which in reality was the case—contributed to both the mass participation of the Cuban population as a whole and, especially, the participation of a very large percentage of eligible youth. An estimated 36.3 percent of all enrolled primary students and 46.7 percent of secondary students participated in the literacy campaign.[104] The constant use of the analogy with a military campaign gave the literacy campaign a spirit of excitement and urgency. It is obvious that young Cubans were far from being unwilling conscripts to the Education Army, and although they constituted less than half the teaching force mobilized, the *brigadistas* came to symbolize the spirit of the campaign and the campaign itself.

The militarism of the literacy campaign has been identified by some commentators as the beginning of the general militarization of Cuban youth.[105] But in defending Paolo Freire's statement, "Freedom is acquired by conquest, not by gift," Jonathan Kozol argued the military fervor of the campaign "helped to fire the passion of the literacy struggle" from the start: "The mood was militant, not tentative, resolute, not clever; keyed to victory, not keyed to interesting results.... They did not say, 'We hope to win' or 'We rather think that, with sufficient funds, we might.' Instead, they said, 'We *shall* [win].' And finally, after very real dangers of defeat, they did."[106]

After pilot literacy programs tested logistics, the effectiveness of the new primer, teaching methods, and the organization and motivation of groups of young volunteers, the second phase of the campaign began with the last day of the school year on 15 April 1961, the same day an air attack was launched against Cuba's air force as a prelude to the CIA-backed invasion. As the first group of Conrado Benítez *brigadistas* boarded buses and trucks departing for the Varadero training camp, they were mistaken for members of the militia because of their uniforms. A few of the teenagers became nervous when they overheard comments from passersby about how young they were to go off to fight and die! "What are we in for?" they asked themselves.[107]

As it turned out, during the attack at the Bay of Pigs, Varadero (which is not far across the island from the invasion site) did become the scene of off-shore provocations, and a pilot group of young literacy teachers was captured by the invading counterrevolutionary forces near Girón Beach, also being mistaken for members of the militia because of their uniforms.[108] A blackboard riddled with bullet holes displayed at the Museo de la Alfabetización (National Literacy Campaign Museum) in Havana bears eloquent testimony to the real dangers the *brigadistas* faced.

When asked whether the government ever considered postponing the campaign because of the invasion, Armando Hart responded definitively, "no."[109] What would have happened had the invasion become a long, drawn-out affair is not clear, however. It is interesting to note that despite their urgent pleas (especially by the young males) for weapons, the *brigadistas* were kept as much as possible out of the front lines during the attack. One *brigadista* later recalled that, at the time, they "didn't realize how much the literacy campaign would have been damaged had one of them been killed."[110] In fact, a couple of young literacy teachers were murdered during the campaign, including the horrific case of *brigadista* Manuel Asunce and his pupil Pedro Lantigua, whose mutilated bodies were hung from a tree side by side, mimicking the racist lynchings in the U.S. South.[111] When Fidel Castro discussed the brutal murders of Asunce and Lantigua, he said his greatest concern was the impact they might have on parents of *brigadistas*, "by spreading fear and panic," especially among mothers, and to "weaken and frustrate" the final effort of the literacy campaign. But to withdraw a single young *brigadista*, he said, would be an affront to the families of the victims and all other mothers as well as to the revolutionary concept of solidarity.[112]

In contrast to the armed exile invasion, the Cuban media reported a "new invasion of the Bay of Pigs" that took place a few months later, when 1,700 Conrado Benítez *brigadistas* wielding pencils and notebooks arrived on boats ready to teach literacy. Revolutionary leader Haydée Santamaría described the spectacle as "something marvelous to see . . . in the same place where those who tried to destroy us and threaten our peace dropped bombs." Photos accompanying these reports show young female *brigadistas* arriving on the shore in boats, bearing aloft the gigantic pencils that became a popular symbol of the campaign.[113]

Although initially only students of high school age (or older than thirteen) were accepted as *brigadistas*, this age was soon lowered to ten; and despite the many stories about girls being prevented from participating in the campaign by their parents, the fact that a majority (52 percent) of the Conrado Benítez *brigadistas* were girls or young women is truly astonishing.[114] Moreover, many of those confined to their homes did, nevertheless, participate as literacy teachers in their hometowns, local schools, or workplaces.[115]

It should be noted that the government made a special pledge to parents to watch over them, and the newly founded FMC played a particular role in monitoring accommodations and other problems young female *brigadistas* might encounter.[116]

Propaganda and news reports encouraged Cubans to think that the whole world was watching how they met this challenge. This was also emphasized in the last lesson of the literacy primer, "Cuba is not alone."[117] Announcing the planned mobilization of the Conrado Benítez Brigades, Fidel said Cuba's youth "are going to show all the peoples of Latin America what such a revolution can achieve."[118] The first principle of the *brigadista*'s identity card read: "We will bring honor to Cuba teaching the most isolated *campesinos* to read and write."[119] Addressing the AJR in March 1961, Fidel stressed that the literacy campaign would be a "lesson for Latin America, showing what all the dollars of imperialism haven't been able to do in a single Latin American country."[120]

René Mujica, who volunteered as a twelve-year-old, recalled: "[T]he enormous political idealism that the revolution generated . . . and the personality of Fidel inspired all of us, even young children, and motivated us to want to go out and help other people. . . . I felt that I had to do something for my country, even though I was very young. I felt that I had the responsibility and that I could do it."[121]

Participating in the campaign would be something to be proud of one's whole life, Fidel told trainee *brigadistas* at Varadero, and those returning will "feel that you have become more of a man or woman than you were when you left for the countryside." They would also feel like a "better citizen and a better revolutionary," and at the same time "be less demanding and more understanding of your parents," he said. At the same time, he warned that it would be "humiliating" later for those who opted to stay at home or those who succumbed to homesickness and quit.[122] Former *brigadistas* often say they wanted something to be proud of when they were older and also to show their parents they could do it.[123]

Clearly with an eye on what was expected, like many would-be *brigadistas*, sixteen-year-old Jorge Calderón Reinoso filled in his application form saying he wanted "to continue studying to serve my country and to assure my future," also mentioning that he wanted to make his parents "proud to have a son who has served the country and supports the Revolution."[124] Sergio Carles wrote a letter to Fidel Castro, as *brigadistas* were urged to do at the end of the campaign, explaining he had never been separated from his parents before, but that he recognized the "necessity for all young people to join the army of Conrado Benítez." Away from home from May to December 1961, he said he "returned home feeling grown-up and proud to have belonged to that Glorious Army, and I know my parents feel the same. Now my only desire is to continue studying so as to continue living for my country and the socialist revolution." Before closing, he added in not such an altruistic spirit: "I've already sent a telegram asking for a scholarship for a Technological School."[125]

Proving something to oneself and also to one's parents does appear to have been a strong motivating factor for many of these young Cubans. "Oscar's" father was not happy about his son living so far from home in a *"bohío* [hut] with dirty people"; as a *brigadista*, Oscar found the living conditions he encountered "even worse than [he] had thought possible." He said he wanted to quit many times over the first few weeks, writing, "I would have, too, except I had to prove to my father that I was right and he was wrong."[126] At only eleven years old, "Barbarita" described herself as a *"pantosa"* (scaredy-cat): "I was afraid of everything, spiders, frogs, everything." She said it was very hard for her, especially as her parents, both teachers, like many others, had told her she could not quit.[127]

Others were motivated by a Christian commitment to help those less fortunate than themselves. Among the frequent affirmations of a desire to support the "socialist revolution" in interviews and letters of *brigadistas* at the time, there are also expressions of religious sentiment, such as the poem written by *brigadista* Yolanda Domínguez Vizcay that is included in her file at the Museo de la Alfabetización in Havana:

> How sweet is the word *"brigadista"*
> Like the divine light that comes from the sun
> Like clear water that reflects the clear sky
> And great as everything created by God.
> You are so great, *brigadista*, so noble is your work
> It is the creation of days, it is the creation of God
> To sow seeds without expecting their fruit
> It is only a heroic act, of the Divine Pastor.[128]

Patria Silva described herself as a "Catholic socialist" at the time she joined the pilot literacy project in the Zapata swamp, where she was captured by the exile invasion force in April 1961; she was shocked to learn there were a couple of Catholic priests among the anti-Castro force. She accepted Fidel's proclamation of the socialist character of the revolution because, she said: "If that was what the revolution was achieving for the most humble, then I decided I was a socialist." She taught an old couple in their eighties and was extremely proud that they could sign their names when they eventually got married.[129]

Many of the *brigadistas*, most of whom were from urban and more affluent families, were no doubt motivated by a spirit of adventure and a chance to relive the revolutionary struggle in the mountains by Che and Fidel, rather than any consistent or well-developed Marxist convictions. Recruitment propaganda certainly encouraged this idea of youthful emulation through cartoons of *brigadistas* holding aloft the primer and teacher's manual and the gigantic pencils that were used to symbolize the campaign saying: "I, too, have my weapon."[130] Other exhortations to join the brigades emphasized that the literacy campaign was the next big battle to be fought against Uncle Sam.[131]

The overwhelming majority of *brigadistas* in their applications requested assignments in the Sierra Maestra where the revolutionary war had begun.[132] "Monica" remembered that all her friends applied for assignments in the Sierra, but her mother insisted she be assigned closer to home in Havana. In the end, she and her friend went to Pinar del Río. "We didn't want to be too near Havana. What would be the point of leaving home if I was going to have my relatives on top of me as usual?" she said.[133]

For many young Cubans, just to wear the uniform that was similar to the militia uniform their parents wore was enough. Those too young or not allowed to participate still anguish over the fact. "I so desperately wanted to go, just so that I could wear the uniform," said one woman who was only nine years old at the time.[134] After the campaign was over, another young woman boldly wrote to Fidel, explaining that she had wanted to be a *brigadista* like her brothers, but she had to stay home to care for their sick mother. She taught literacy in her neighborhood instead, but she wrote to Fidel on behalf of her classmates to propose that the *brigadista* uniform become their new school uniform.[135]

Self-interest or material incentives were not entirely absent from the recruitment propaganda; many appeals for young volunteers highlighted the chance for young Cubans to enjoy a week at the famous beach resort in Varadero, while undergoing their training as literacy teachers.[136] The hordes of happy teenagers overrunning the abandoned mansions of the rich had tremendous symbolic significance, which the government recognized as the best publicity for the campaign.[137] A range of parties and other recreational activities were part of the program at the Varadero camp, which were apparently strictly supervised. Monica described an atmosphere of "mild mass hysteria" among the girls, some of whom went silly over some good-looking lifeguards at the beach. "We'd talk of boys all day long," she said. One evening at a movie showing, the boys tore down a net that separated them from the girls in the auditorium and rushed at the girls, who were promptly marched out of the auditorium.[138]

Young Cubans may well have joined in the literacy teaching effort in the hope of a scholarship for 1962. María said her cousin wanted to become a doctor, so she joined the literacy campaign because she believed "it would be good for her future."[139] Although no recruitment propaganda made a direct link between participation in the literacy campaign and student scholarships, in fact, nearly three-quarters of Conrado Benítez *brigadistas* did receive scholarships for the year after the campaign.[140] Prior to the first intake of literacy *brigadistas*, the government had announced 10,000 new scholarships for secondary students.[141] At the end of the literacy campaign, the government offered special scholarships for fifteen- to twenty-five-year-olds to study art, dance, and music, but these were only available to *brigadistas*, and the scholarship application form required the student to indicate where he or she had taught literacy.[142]

It is difficult to ascertain how much the expectation of a scholarship influenced the decision to participate. Writing to Fidel Castro was part of the literacy test for illiterates, but it was not compulsory for *brigadistas*. Nevertheless, many thousands felt the need to write to Fidel relating their experiences and their views about many things in an often remarkably frank and intimate tone, and frequently at great length. These letters are kept at the Museo de la Alfabetización in Havana in hundreds of bound volumes, along with other documents (such as their application forms and final reports) that make up individual files on each *brigadista*. Some of the letters written by *brigadistas* to Fidel Castro after the literacy campaign make specific requests for scholarships, such as that from Nancy Urbino Pérez, who wrote that she was only thirteen but wanted a scholarship so that she could "prepare herself to continue helping the revolution."[143] Others sincerely thank Fidel for scholarships they have received: "I am very happy because I have a scholarship for Junior High School, although I never believed I could get a scholarship. My parents are very poor but are conscious of what the revolution is all about and its significance," wrote María Luisa Morena Díaz.[144] A most self-confident young woman, a former *brigadista*, had no qualms about explaining she had enlisted for the literacy campaign because she "knew how important it was for Cuba for our brothers the *campesinos* to know how to read and write." But she also mentioned that she hoped it would help her realize her dream of becoming an aviation pilot; she pleaded with Fidel that her fate was in his hands.[145]

The demand for, or interest expressed by *brigadistas* in scholarships, however, reflected the revolutionary government's promotion of the idea that education or *superación* (self-improvement) was a revolutionary duty for all Cubans, young and old. When the thousands of *brigadistas* gathered in Havana's Revolution Plaza at the end of the campaign on 22 December 1961 to celebrate the "victory over four-and-a-half centuries of ignorance," Fidel answered the *brigadistas* who were asking for their "next task" by saying that their duty was to study.[146] This reflected Cuba's desperate need for professionals and technicians to replace those who had left in the thousands. The 40,800 scholarships offered were very specific to Cuba's needs, as is clear from the list published at the end of the campaign. It might also reflect the general attitude toward education promoted by the government; youth who had just spent several months urging others to further their studies were not likely to consider dropping out of school themselves. A very common ambition among ex-*brigadistas* was to become qualified teachers, and many fulfilled this goal. The teaching profession definitely gained a new status in Cuba through the campaign.[147]

Although few ex-*brigadistas* readily admit it, peer pressure—not wanting to be left out of what looked like a real adventure—was undoubtedly a major factor drawing young Cubans into the literacy campaign. This often became a point of conflict between children and their parents. When thirteen-year-old Leonela Relys Díaz's friends signed up for the campaign, she was determined not to be left behind, but her parents would not agree. "So I signed [the form] myself" she said, "and when the time came, I got on the bus with nothing but the clothes I had on, and off I went."[148]

The Literacy Campaign and the Family

There is abundant evidence that permission to participate in the campaign was frequently a source of conflict between many parents and children—even those parents who supported the literacy effort wholeheartedly. Usually such disputes were settled amicably, by parents granting their consent or children agreeing to stay at home and teach in their neighborhood. Symptomatic of the patriarchal power relationship within Cuban families, "Olga," like many would-be *brigadistas*, successfully appealed to her father to let her join the literacy brigades over her mother's objections.[149] Similarly, María Masud's father ignored her mother's pleas not to send their children off to Miami with Operation Pedro Pan.[150]

The process of incorporation into the "Education Army" began with the completion of an application form that had to be signed by a parent or guardian. Organizers insist that no one was ever accepted without his or her parents' signature, although stories are common of children forging them. When interviewed, ex-*brigadista* Javier Salado was keen to display how he can still produce a perfect copy of his father's signature; his father was probably not the only anxious parent to turn up at the Varadero camp in search of a child who had disappeared from home after being overcome by revolutionary enthusiasm.[151]

Such attempts by teenagers to sidestep parental consent were inevitably discovered when a postcard was sent to the home of each *brigadista*, announcing their arrival at Varadero and in which dormitory they were housed. Immediately after a *brigadista* received an assignment or placement, another small postcard was sent to his or her parents with those details. *Brigadistas* were also given yet another card to be sent home once they arrived at their teaching posts.[152] When three thousand *brigadistas* left for Oriente province in late April, *Revolución* reported that the National Literacy Commission would officially inform parents of the exact location of their child, indicating which platoon, company, and brigade they were assigned to and in which peasant's home they were to stay.[153]

During the campaign, every effort was made to win the support of parents and involve them. A family festival was organized in Varadero for Mothers' Day, 14 May 1961, so that parents could see what their children were doing there and, according to the invitation published in the press, to encourage them to be proud of their children's readiness to "do their duty and fight imperialism by teaching literacy."[154] Parental pride in their *brigadista* children was immortalized in a popular song, "*Canción del padre del brigadista*," in which a father says he does not want a "cry-baby, cowardly, selfish son," but a "sharing and daring" one, a *brigadista*.[155]

As the campaign began, parents were invited to visit the pilot programs under way and advised that inexpensive excursion tickets were available for visits to their *brigadista* children.[156] This offer was reinforced through the

Figure 2.4. "Showing the way." Father's song to his *brigadista* son: "Go, my *brigadista* / to the most remote mountains / Go to baptize your boots with the soil and dew / Learn to cross rivers / overcome wilderness and swamp / bearing in your hand the light that you will share so well / You go to teach and to graduate / to graduate as a CUBAN." *Bohemia*, 21 May 1961.

regularly published photo montage cartoons "Reports from the Conrado Benítez Brigades"; one, for example, depicted the Sunday visit of a *brigadista*'s parents to the home of her "new *campesino* family." The mother assists by bringing flowers to plant in the garden, and the father helps out with various other tasks. Sometimes they bring along the girl's friends to inspire them about what she is doing.[157] Visits to *brigadistas* teaching in very remote areas, however, in reality were almost impossible.

Many of the reports from the front line of the literacy campaign show female *brigadistas* learning cooking, cleaning, child care, and other domestic duties. As a young female *brigadista* reported: "I learned to do lots of household tasks that a woman should know how to do. Moreover, I saw the work of people with no culture and with no livelihood. I am very grateful because, although they are very poor people, they all loved me like a daughter."[158]

Another *brigadista* wrote from Baracoa in the extreme east of the island about how difficult it was to be separated from her parents for such a long period of time, although she expressed her pride in being able to add her "small grain of sand [as a contribution to] our patriotic, democratic, and socialist revolution." As time passed and the studies of her eight pupils progressed, she said she understood how it had been worth exchanging her "beautiful clothes for the glorious uniform of a *brigadista*."[159]

Many, if not most, *brigadista* girls no doubt felt as "María" did: "The literacy struggle was the first time in my life, and I believe the first time in our history as well, that women were given an equal role with men in bringing monumental change."[160]

Many *brigadistas* assigned to remote locations had little communication with their families, many reporting they received only a couple of letters from their parents during the months they were away. Sometimes, at their Sunday gatherings, "Miguel" told Jonathan Kozol, they would "play a kind of game," reading each other their letters so that everyone could imagine they were receiving more news from home.[161]

Sometimes teenagers accompanied their parents to teach literacy (or vice versa).[162] Mario Díaz related the case of a mother and daughter who approached the campaign organizers, asking to be assigned to teach together: "'That's not a problem,' we said, 'you'll go together.' 'Fine, but we can't leave our dog alone for all that time . . .' Well, we found a nearby farm where the girl, the mother and the dog happily went off and were warmly received," Díaz recalled.[163]

On the other hand, Jesús Arboleya's father was a teacher in Havana who volunteered to go to Pinar del Río and wanted to take his teenage son with him. But the twelve-year-old, like most others, wanted to go to Oriente (the opposite end of the island) by himself—to be independent—and told his parents he would go anyway, even if they refused to sign the papers. He believed that he would never have been so bold to stand up to his parents at that age if it had not been for the revolution. He said he was inspired to be part of "something big, something important."[164]

At the end of the campaign, national coordinator Mario Díaz sent a letter of appreciation to all the parents of *brigadistas*, recognizing their sleepless nights worrying about their children and expressing the government's gratitude for their support that ensured the success of the campaign.[165] Those who argue that the literacy campaign was designed to separate children from the influence of their parents fail to take note of these government measures that reflect an almost excessive effort to address parents' concerns and anxieties. Moreover, they ignore the program of activities (*Plan Asistencial*) established for about half a million elementary schoolchildren while their schools were closed for the second half of 1961 and their teachers were mobilized for the final push of the literacy campaign. This program was largely run by the FMC and sought to *increase* parents' involvement in their children's education.[166]

The literacy campaign also involved bringing thousands of young Cubans from the countryside into Havana under various scholarship schemes. "Who will take the revolution into the homes of the peasants? Their own daughters," Fidel Castro said. The Ana Betancourt schools, first established in 1961 in the elegant Hotel Nacional and later in some of Havana's abandoned luxury mansions, trained twenty-one thousand young peasant women over two years in six-month courses in which they learned basic literacy, sewing skills, and modern nutrition and hygiene; some also acquired basic office skills.[167] Because country girls had previously come to the capital to pursue one profession only—prostitution—some fathers were highly suspicious of the program and turned up in Havana to retrieve them. There were reported attempts to disrupt the program by spreading rumors that the "Anitas," as the country girls were called, were being used as washerwomen for the militias, and fake telegrams were sent telling them not to return to Havana when they went home for a short break in their course.[168]

Most parents, however, were satisfied to see their daughters' achievements, especially as the first graduates returned home with sewing machines—an invaluable source of livelihood for themselves and their families—having also committed themselves to teaching ten others the skills they had learned in the city.[169] Some U.S. feminists criticized this and other programs for not challenging traditional female stereotypes, to which FMC leader Vilma Espín responded, "we started from where women were at to raise them to a new level" of both culture and skill.[170]

Learning the "Why" of the Revolution

The training in Varadero of the young literacy teachers was "short and intense" in the extreme, usually consisting of only one week's instruction in the use of the primer and a review of the teacher's manual. Given the youth of the volunteers and the complexity of their task, the program was remarkable. There was some technical training in the care of the all-important lantern because few *campesinos'* homes had electricity, and an attempt was made to orientate city-bred kids to life in the countryside without proper sanitation, let alone television and other comforts.[171] The lantern, hammock, and other bush-survival equipment included as part of the *brigadista*'s kit were meant to alert them about what to expect. But most were still shocked by what they encountered, like "Oscar," who said the *campesinos* "lived worse than the dogs in Havana. There wasn't that much to eat and everything you ate had bugs in it. They didn't even clean their cooking pot." Most of all, he remembered "the dirt—dirt everywhere."[172]

A key by-product of the literacy campaign was, in fact, the public health campaign that accompanied it, following the experience of earlier volunteer teacher programs that had also involved the construction of houses, latrines, and other services.[173] This public health campaign was designed to guarantee medical attention for the *brigadistas* as well as to provide services for the population of the remote rural communities.[174] The young literacy teachers took with them a manual on basic health and hygiene, including how to construct a sanitary latrine and how to avoid dysentery, intestinal parasites, and other diseases rife among the population in remote areas.[175]

It is, of course, open to speculation how much a teenager was capable of absorbing about community health issues and then transmitting to their hosts in rural villages. The surveys that *brigadistas* were expected to complete about the social and health conditions in the place where they were teaching were extraordinarily detailed; but no doubt most of them did their best.[176] Campaign organizers said some urban families helped to improve the facilities in the homes where their children were staying; the extension of postal services throughout the island during the campaign was another benefit to remote communities.[177] Thus, the results of the campaign were far greater than the number of Cubans achieving literacy; it also brought social services to previously neglected areas.[178]

The relationship of the *brigadista* to the illiterate person was the linchpin of the campaign, and this was the primary focus of the training, as Raúl Ferrer (poet, educationalist, and deputy director of the National Literacy Campaign) explained: "The goal for us was to instruct the *brigadistas* not to try to imitate the condescending manner of the kinds of teachers they had known in public schools before the revolution. This was one-half the job of preparation."[179] The relationship between the *brigadista* and the peasant was extolled in thousands of ways throughout the campaign, synthesized in the poem by the popular contemporary bard El Indio Naborí, "*Campesino to a Brigadista*": "I will learn from your primer, and you will learn from the land."[180]

Although ignorance was continually condemned by government leaders as a "vice," a "defect and a dishonor for any citizen," the youthful teachers were urged to be sympathetic and understanding with their pupils.[181] *Brigadista* identity cards instructed the young literacy teachers to "cordially and respectfully [integrate themselves] into the life and customs of our humble peasants . . . [and] cultivate comradeship on the basis of revolutionary fraternity and common work, with the firm convictions of men free of prejudice."[182] The *brigadistas* were urged to show respect, "not falsified flattery," to their *campesino* pupils.[183] This was the main point also emphasized in the teacher's manual, *Alfabeticemos,* which reminded them that "the work of literacy teaching is the common task of both teacher and [learner]."[184] As popular educationalists like Paolo Freire argued, the only successful literacy teacher is "one who relates most effectively with the illiterate at a personal level."[185] The secret of the success of the Cuban literacy effort campaign, according to the UNESCO Report, was the human relationships established, "those intellectual, sentimental and psychological chain reactions, which arise when relations are established between one human being and another."[186]

For the *brigadistas,* participation in the literacy campaign became "akin to a revolutionary rite of passage," wrote Richard Fagen, "their first opportunity to prove they were full-fledged revolutionaries." Most *brigadistas* and their pupils poured heart and soul into developing intimate and continuing

Figure 2.5. Literacy *brigadistas* with the giant pencils that became a symbol of the campaign. Courtesy of Prensa Latina photo archive.

human relationships that crossed lines of class and age.[187] Virtually every ex-*brigadista* interviewed in this research readily agreed that the experience of the literacy campaign was one of the most important events in their lives. Many are still in touch with their "other families" and have often taken their own children to visit. While interviewing contemporaries of the Pedro Pans in Cuba, it was impossible to avoid a discussion of the literacy campaign; and once started on the topic, my respondents would be hard to divert back to questions about the children who left with Operation Pedro Pan. With shining eyes, former *brigadistas* would describe where they went, the families they stayed with, and the hardships endured. Without exception, the experience of the literacy campaign for the individuals who participated as youthful *brigadistas* was transformative.

"I left home, too, in 1961," Jesús Arboleya remarked proudly. "Those kids who went to Miami often felt abandoned by their parents. But *I* was the one abandoning *my* parents when I went to the Sierra as a Conrado Benítez *brigadista*. And believe me, the conditions we faced in the mountains were far worse!"[188] "Miguel" was assigned to a village beyond Bayamo in Oriente province. The shack he was to live in, he recalled, "was so small that I could not hang my hammock in the single room. There was a mother, a father and two little girls, all in that tiny space." So he proposed they build a bigger house "before we settled down to read and write." And that is what they did—in two weeks. "It was a solid piece of work," he said proudly, "my first attempt in the construction industry!"[189]

Expressing herself poetically, Nilka Georgina Cuevas Durán described her first impressions:

> It was a beautiful morning when I first encountered the peasants in the area where I was assigned to teach, a place called Alegría [Happiness]. But the only happy thing about the place was its name . . . due to the peasants' living conditions. There were twelve *brigadistas* in my group, including my sister, who later became the leader of the group. We met and decided to change things. . . . We asked the local authorities for paint, sanitary latrines, and paintbrushes. We began to paint each house, we made gardens to beautify them, and finally we provided latrines for every house. What joy—then the place really lived up to its name.[190]

Nereyda Matos Martínez offered a similar moving account of her first impressions as a *brigadista*:

> I arrived at Antilla on 24 August, where I was taken to the house of an FMC member. They prepared a bath, food, and a bed for me there. The next day they took me to the Antillita Study Center, where I spent the night in a humble home, sleeping in a hammock for the first time. . . . My other impressions were those of seeing the children going barefoot, with no clothes; I had to go with the owner of the house to gather wood with which to cook, and [I realized] how far they had to carry water. But one of the greatest things was the extraordinary affection with which they treated me—not just the family I stayed with—but all the neighbors, too. The day of my departure was very emotional and unforgettable for me—to see everyone crying and asking me when I would return or when they could come and see me.[191]

Letters from young *brigadistas* like Julio Urrutia Vásquez tend to adopt a more boastful, macho style: "Like the *brigadista* that I am I want to tell you about the four months that I lived with the *campesinos*: I saw how they had to work so hard in a life of privation and lack of culture. The food was not good, but I always did my chores. If the revolution demands that I make another sacrifice, I will go, because I know that good revolutionaries never falter. So tell me what I can do next."[192]

Such bravado was not confined to boys alone. Ana Mirta Trijillo Reyes wrote: "We were teaching in a very poor area, and when it rained our boots got stuck in the mud and the roads were impassable. But this was no obstacle for us, and we took not one step backward nor flinched when we had to give imperialism the final push. So I am able to say with great pride that by 31 December [1961] there will not be a single illiterate person in Cuba."[193]

Comments about the poor quality and paucity of food are ever present in the teenage *brigadistas'* letters and recollections, which makes all the more amusing a *brigadista's* letter published in *Bohemia* saying she was getting so fat from life in the country that the uniform she received in Varadero no longer fit her![194] It would appear that their youthful spirit and adaptiveness usually saw them through. Cándida Rosa Orizondo Crespo commented how "surprisingly, we fitted into rural life relatively easily, in conditions we had only heard about, although it wasn't easy to assume the customs and traditions of our pupils. But the freshness of our youth served to attenuate the differences, as well as the honesty and almost naivety of the peasants."[195]

A sense of achievement and growing up is also evident among the *brigadistas*. Lidia Catalina Totman commented on how differently she was treated in the house where she stayed as a teacher, whereas at home, in spite of being sixteen, she felt she was "seen as a kid." "Only the literacy campaign," she said, "showed me that I was not a useless young girl. I felt responsible, and that helped me a lot in the task of teaching. . . . Those peasants loved me a lot, and I felt much better there than at home."[196]

That the *brigadistas* took their tasks very seriously cannot be doubted, as illustrated in another letter to Fidel Castro written at the end of the campaign: "I am writing to inform you of my life in the countryside. I found myself in a very poor household, and the little that they had for their children they shared with me, for which I am very grateful, as they really were not in a position to support a *brigadista*. They were ignorant of some of the works of the Revolution, and I opened their eyes to the Revolution, reading them magazines, newspapers, and books that had some of your speeches. They were happy with the work of the Revolution and each day loved Fidel more."[197]

René Mujica admitted his age and inexperience were initially impediments to his relationship with an old man he was trying to teach: "He was a very stubborn man who had a tremendous resistance to learning. He didn't see the need for it. He reasoned that he had been pretty well off so far without reading and writing.... It was difficult for me to relate to him as a teacher because I was only twelve years old. He was an old man with a lot of experience—he had seen many things in his life that I had no idea about. It was a conflicting relationship from the beginning."[198]

Some *brigadistas* adopt a rather superior tone in their letters to Fidel, describing how the people in the countryside "knew nothing about the Revolution and now feel happy because they can read your speeches in the newspapers."[199] But often *brigadistas* found teaching their elders, or sometimes just convincing them to learn, was not as easy as expected: "At first the *campesinos* didn't readily accept us. We had to prepare ourselves and them, explaining that we were going to teach them how to read and write and that it was important for the revolution to achieve this, for our people to become cultured as Martí said. But this wasn't so easy."[200]

Many young literacy teachers like Raúl Fernández also mention the difficulty their pupils had using a delicate tool like a pencil, an "insignificant stick of wood," after decades of hard physical labor: "We had to take their hands, guide them, until they gained confidence.... As they learned to write each word, or letter, they would feel proud and have more interest to keep working. After a while we began to see that they would go into the fields with their workbooks. During their breaks, you would often see them [practicing] writing. This was proof of their motivation."[201]

Sometimes it was more than a matter of just convincing the peasants of the necessity to learn, as fifteen-year-old "Oscar" recalled: "In those days there were still quite a few people who weren't sure about the Revolution. [My] first family thought Fidel was Jesus Christ, but in the third family I [taught] the parents were against the Revolution. The woman kept saying, 'They will just want the children to speak against their parents.'"[202]

Oscar tried to use the primer, *Venceremos*, to teach a particularly difficult student, "but I found I had to explain too much to him." Eventually, he said he gave up and taught the old man how to read "the way my maternal grandmother taught me—except without the shoe!"[203] Resistance to learning among elderly citizens was countered by the publicity given to pupils like 106-year-old María de la Cruz Sentmanat, who had been born a slave and was convinced "no one is too old to learn."[204]

Failing or defective eyesight was another problem, but those who needed them were given spectacles.[205] Nilka had a sixty-five-year-old pupil named

Alberto, who really wanted to learn but had difficulty because of his poor vision. "He became disheartened watching the progress of others," she recalled; she still remembers his smile and tears rolling down his cheeks when he received a pair of glasses.[206] In case a recipient failed to get the message, the eyeglass cases displayed the slogan: *"Viva nuestra revolución socialista!"* (Long live our Socialist Revolution).[207] Migdalia Martínez Pino had an old Haitian man in her class of ten whom she succeeded in teaching only how to write his name, on account of his age, poor eyesight, and language. Nevertheless, she said, the campaign provided him with a pair of spectacles, of which he was immensely proud.[208]

Occasionally *brigadistas* found themselves in a politically hostile environment, where their presence and their mission was resented, if not actively opposed. One old *campesino* told a young *brigadista* he did not want to learn and "certainly not [from] a woman!"[209] Another *brigadista* discovered she was billeted in the home of a counterrevolutionary who "made life impossible . . . by giving [her] very difficult, heavy work to do." But she was proud to have survived the experience. Some *brigadistas* faced physical threats from local counterrevolutionaries who left dolls with ropes around their necks with notes on the doors where they were staying that read, "The next one will be you!" These were far from being hollow threats, given the murders of several literacy volunteers during the campaign and the terrorism perpetrated by armed antigovernment gangs in the countryside.[210]

* * *

Sexual harassment was occasionally another problem young female *brigadistas* had to face. "Mercedes" recalled: "On my second night there, one of the uncles [neighbors] wanted me to sleep with him. I told him that if he bothered me, I'd get the militia in. That calmed him down!"[211] Monica was fifteen, and before she left, her aunt and uncle had warned her mother: "Beatriz, you know how it is: one goes and two come back." As it was, Monica found herself in a difficult situation and was physically beaten by one of the sons of the family she was staying with. Soon afterward she was sexually molested by an older, married neighbor. "I wasn't only embarrassed I was shocked that a married man could court me. I worried that I might have done something to encourage him," she recalled.[212] Considering her accommodation in a two-roomed house, Alba Margarita Cortina said: "Imagine what my mother would have thought when she realized that I was housed with a fifty-year-old widower and six young girls!"[213] In general, however,

Figure 2.6. The anti-Castro movement view of the literacy campaign. Movimiento Unidad Revolucionaria, "Can this happen in the Americas?" (1963). This pamphlet was first published in Spanish as "Conozca lo que le ocurrirá a usted y a su país." (c1962). Courtesy of the Cuban Heritage Collection, University of Miami Libraries, Coral Gables, Florida.

young female *brigadistas* were watched over most vigilantly and lovingly by their *campesino* host families.²¹⁴

Nevertheless, *brigadistas* like Rosalía Rouce Leal often encountered resistance from elderly learners who "didn't hide the fact that they believed [she] was incapable of teaching them a single letter of the alphabet." Sometimes, she confessed, she "almost begged them to pay attention and learn." Perceptively, she acknowledged: "If for me it was hard, for them it was worse, as their hands were clumsy and three of my students had problems with their eyesight. What joy we all felt when they were finally able to write their names! They showed a childlike enthusiasm." When all three of her pupils were able to read and write, Rosalía said, was "one of the greatest joys of my life."²¹⁵

Antonio Villaverde was worried about his two sons who were teaching in the Escambray, where counterrevolutionary bands were operating. On one occasion, his twelve-year-old son called home and sounded "rather strange." Thinking it "might be an SOS," Dr. Villaverde said, "we called him back and asked him if he wanted to come home, if he was afraid. Of course, he said no."²¹⁶

Backup and support for the *brigadistas* were readily available in the form of the *"enlace"* (local team leader or coordinator), usually a teacher (often not much older than themselves) who acted as both a personal and teaching adviser.²¹⁷ Lourdes Hernández Domenech was a young volunteer teacher in Villa Clara and one of the *brigadista* coordinators. She remembered an eleven-year-old boy whom she took to the house where he was to stay; he was quite happy until it was time for her to leave and she went to the door. "You're not staying with me?" he asked. "OK, I'll come with you," he said. It was the first time he had ever been away from home and would only agree to stay when Lourdes promised to visit every day—which she did.²¹⁸

Regular gatherings of *brigadistas* were encouraged every Sunday (a non-teaching day), which some found helpful.²¹⁹ But others, like "María," preferred to stay with the family with which she was billeted, sometimes putting on little plays or shows for the neighbors.²²⁰ *Brigadistas* frequently participated in local projects; for example, Alba Margarita Cortina helped deliver books collected by her mother's FMC group, which also arranged to bring a shipment of clothes and toys in a big truck. Her *brigadista* team also helped build a cultural center, a project initiated by a Baptist minister, and she proudly recounted how she had helped paint the center, the first time in her life she had done any manual work.²²¹ This experience of manual labor was an essential part of the learning exchange between *brigadistas* and their pupils, and a fundamental aspect of José Martí's approach to education. He had recommended incorporating manual work into the school curriculum, urging that "the pen should be used in schools during the afternoon; but during the morning the hoe."[222] The development of a new attitude to manual labor emphasized by Che Guevara was where Marxist theory and Martí's ideas intersected.[223] This "work-study principle" became an essential feature of Cuba's educational revolution.[224]

This was undoubtedly a big challenge for many of the middle-class city kids, who had probably done very little, if anything at all, around the house at home—but one generally approached with a different spirit from that of the Pedro Pans, who often resisted all attempts to get them to tidy their own rooms, let alone wash the dishes or participate in other household chores. "Since the majority of the [Pedro Pan] children's parents were of the property owning middle class and accustomed to having servants in their homes," Ruby Hart Phillips observed, "it has been somewhat hard for the youngsters to adjust themselves to servantless living. Both in foster homes and in the centers here the children felt at first they were being imposed upon when they were told to clean their rooms or do other household chores."[225]

In contrast, many of the *brigadistas'* letters reflect great pride in their successful integration into farm life and learning many new skills. One *brigadista* assured Fidel that he was of such great assistance to his family that "they didn't want me to return to my parents!"[226] Young Nestor Falcón adopted a more plaintive tone in his letter, writing: "the labor was intense... but I wasn't concerned by the exhaustion, or the rain, or the nights of hard work, or the privations—for me, a youth who had never been apart from his parents before."[227] Others, like Leopoldo Cabrera, proudly wrote he had harvested "100 *latas* of coffee," while experiencing very rough living conditions: "The last two months I spent eating yuca and boniato because food was scarce. The only way to get [to where I was staying] was by mule. Rain set in and the roads were destroyed, so no one could reach us at Esperanza. You had to walk twenty-four kilometers."[228]

Nancy was only thirteen when she taught in Oriente province. She wrote: "[T]his has been one of the most beautiful things of our Revolution.... To the world we are small, but even if we are small, we have made a gigantic decision—greater than any weapons. The imperialists have now been exposed, and they cannot overthrow what is every day stronger, to the point where even children have decided that they are ready to fight for this socialist revolution, and we promise Fidel to defend our country and our liberty."[229]

* * *

Forty years after the campaign, Armando Hart contended that the humanist spirit of the revolution was not an "intellectual abstraction . . . foreign to real life." This was most evident, he said, in the literacy campaign, "when a hundred thousand Cuban young people went to the valleys and mountains to the homes of peasants and became members of their families. There, they learned about the vicissitudes and material problems of the *campesinos'* lives. They made friends; established human relationships; and, as an essential component of life, gained a memorable experience, forged human ties, and felt emotions that they will treasure as long as they live."[230]

Participating in the literacy campaign was an accelerated coming-of-age experience for most *brigadistas*, as was the abrupt separation from their parents for the Pedro Pans. But for most of the young Cubans who flew off to Miami with Operation Pedro Pan, it was not something in which they had had a choice, nor was such a prolonged separation anticipated. A former *brigadista*, who later, as a Cuban diplomat, had contact with many émigrés in the United States, came to understand how some of the Pedro Pans whisked out of the country felt their parents had denied them the opportunity to participate in something historic. Jesús Arboleya suggested the trauma the Pedro Pans experienced was because they felt they had been removed from "the important things that were happening in Cuba at the time." He thought this explained why so many former Pedro Pan children "feel they have to show how successful they were in the United States. Maybe they were jealous of our experiences as young people in events that had a big impact in the world—the Cuban revolution. I felt I was part of something big, whereas they did nothing by themselves."[231]

This statement goes some way in explaining the apparently irreconcilable or dramatically dissonant arguments about the nature of the literacy campaign by proponents and critics of Operation Pedro Pan. The campaign has been criticized most often by observers convinced that such a massive mobilization of the population could only have been achieved through coercion. On the other hand, U.S. educationalist Jonathan Kozol argued that the reason for the mass participation of Cuban youth in the literacy effort was

Figure 2.7. Literacy *brigadistas* celebrating the end of the campaign, December 1961. Courtesy of Prensa Latina photo archive.

"self-evident" from the stories he heard in Cuba, stories that were still fresh in the memories of both learners and *brigadistas* more than ten years after what is commonly referred to in Cuba as "the Great Campaign."[232]

Through the campaign, young Cubans became more aware of the society and the world in which they lived, and they were inspired—not indoctrinated or compelled—to join the literacy effort. It was a life-changing experience for many. They might have written their letters to Fidel conscious of what they were expected to say, and in the hope of a reward in the form of a scholarship (which most received), but it is impossible to ignore the sincerity of the sentiments they expressed. Recognizing the natural optimism, altruism, and self-confidence of youth, as well as its energy and enthusiasm, the revolutionary government offered them an opportunity to experience firsthand the realities of life for the majority of Cubans, to reenvision their country and, in the process, remake themselves. And they grabbed that chance with both hands.

Antonio Gramsci contended that if the head is captured, the heart and hands will follow.[233] The Cuban literacy campaign seems to be a case where the heart was captured and the head and hands followed. Far from being "blank slates," the *brigadistas*' letters, memoirs, and interviews reveal all the contradictions and "imperfections" of Cuban youth at the time of the campaign—as children of their environment, as Che confessed he, too, had been. Yet by overcoming the individualism of the past and practicing solidarity, not charity, he said, each one of us becomes the "architect of that new human type . . . who will be the representative of the New Cuba."[234]

"As we change our world, we change our thinking about it," wrote educationalist John Holst, and that changes us.[235] For the *brigadistas*, like the Pedro Pans, the year 1961 brought about an accelerated maturity—but in a far more positive way because it was an experience they had chosen. For many young Cubans, the literacy campaign was almost like a religious conversion. "I never could have known that people lived in such conditions," recalled young Armando Valdéz:

> I was the child of an educated, comfortable family. Those months, for me, were like the stories I have heard about conversion to a new religion. It was, for me, the dying of an old life and the start of something absolutely new. I cried, although I had been taught men must not cry, when I first saw the desperation of those people—people who had so little. . . . *No, they did not have "so little," they had nothing!* . . . I did not need to read of this in Marx, in Lenin, in Martí. I did not need to read of what I saw before my eyes. I cried each night. I wrote my mother and my father. I was only twelve years old. I was excited to be part of something which had never happened in our land before.[236]

The literacy campaign left a lasting legacy, not only in creating what Armando Hart called an "immense legion of men and women occupying diverse positions of responsibility" in subsequent decades as scientists, technicians, teachers, economists, and a wide range of other professions. He was convinced that, as "one of the most emotional acts in the humanism of the revolution—our humanist revolution," the hundreds of thousands of Cubans who participated in that campaign retained "the enthusiasm and emotion that that victory inspired."[237]

On the other hand, when one looks at the images of the literacy *brigadistas* and listens to their stories, it is understandable why middle-class or conservative parents might have been horrified at the prospect of their children—most especially their daughters—turning into such self-confident, committed, and independent-minded young people. But far from losing their families, the *brigadistas* returned feeling part of a larger Cuban, human family, as "global citizens."[238] The literacy campaign "was only possible as part of the revolutionary process," Armando Hart explained, "but at the same time it gave a tremendous impulse to that revolutionary process."[239] The campaign certainly transformed Cuba's political culture, but, above all, the *brigadista* experience was fundamental to the transformation of a generation of young Cubans who were swept along by the revolutionary humanism of the literacy campaign, and who learned, in an intimate and enduring manner, the "why" of the revolution.

3

The *Patria Potestad* Hoax

When Cuban mothers were asked to complete government surveys concerning the care and schooling of their children in October 1960, the U.S. media raised the alarm, saying this was a sign the government was preparing to "nationalize" children along "communist" lines.[1] A few weeks later, another report said: "Castro's threat to make every child a virtual ward of the state [has] caused panic among Cuban parents, and they are sending their youngsters off to Miami, unaccompanied, at the rate of 1,000 a month."[2] The *Miami Herald* claimed that on 1 January 1961 the government would assume custody over every Cuban child and none of them would be allowed to leave the country; the same article mentioned that special visas were available for children whose parents might be having difficulty obtaining visas for themselves.[3] Many Cubans readily believed such rumors because, *Time* magazine reminded them, "As Lenin himself once said: 'Revolution is impossible as long as the family exists.'"[4]

The Catholic church hierarchy had already decided by May 1960 that the communist enemy was no longer "at the door" but now "within our home," and said to be undermining all human values, including matrimony and the family.[5] In November 1960, the church-sponsored National Confederation of Parents' Associations urged resistance to the government's alleged intention to eliminate *patria potestad* or (parental authority) and destroy young Cubans' souls, reminding parents of their "inalienable right" and "most sacred duty" to raise their children in the teachings of the church, "the spiritual mother of all Christians."[6]

Over the following months, there were frequent references in the U.S. and anti-Castro media to a supposed new government "law" to eliminate parents' authority over their children, along with plans for a mass indoctrination campaign and the prohibition of religious instruction to children.[7] The counterrevolutionary underground issued warnings that "Dictator Castro" had already prepared a decree that would make every child in Cuba "a ward of the state."[8] Wendell Rollason, director of the Inter-American Affairs Commission set up to assist the Miami community to deal with the influx of Cuban refugees, told the Senate subcommittee looking into the Cuban refugee problem in December 1961 that the "[Communist] party line ... as we know is first to grab on to the children." The new deadline for this to take place, he asserted, was now 1 January 1962.[9]

Some Cubans today recall with amusement how these "*bolas*" or rumors became something of an urban myth; apparently those Cuban children sent to the Soviet Union who were unable to be indoctrinated were returned to the island as the canned pink meat the Russians were sending to Cuba in those years. This absurdity was said to have been confirmed when a child's ring was found in one of these cans.[10] Although the government repeatedly denied and often ridiculed these stories, as Joan Didion observed, no "rumor spread goes unrewarded."[11] Cubans, who witnessed the sudden departures of many of their friends and family, recognized that "for a parent to send their child away—a child of any age—that parent must have had a great fear."[12]

A cartoon by an exiled Cuban artist, published in Miami, captured the climate of fear promoted by the anti-Castro movement. Most Pedro Pans have explained that their parents decided to send them to the United States with Operation Pedro Pan because they had been convinced by these ongoing rumors that they were about to lose custody of them and control over their education. "My mother was so frightened. She had such a fear—real or imagined by her, I don't know," recalled Rosa Irigoyen.[13]

At the moment when the first discussions about the child evacuation scheme were taking place in Miami, the barrage of U.S. media reports about the threat to parental rights and the gross exaggeration of the numbers of children being sent out of Cuba may well have contributed to, or even stoked, the exodus. The Cuban media countered these inflammatory reports by ridiculing the rumors and explaining that all new government measures were designed to "strengthen the Cuban family," not undermine it.[14] Furthermore, by urging parents to register their children, the government said it had no intention of denying parents' rights or *patria potestad* but instead sought to protect children's rights.[15] *El Mundo* suggested this "infamy" and other equally ludicrous "*bolas*" (rumors) had taken in some "simple and

Figure 3.1. "Here, Catalina, hide him. This pair isn't like the Batista soldiers. They came for the livestock; these come for the kid." Courtesy of the Lourdes Casal Library, Center for Cuban Studies, Brooklyn, New York.

ingenuous souls," even though, if such a law were implemented, "it would create insuperable material difficulties for the government."[16]

Desperate Cubans were reported to be taking to small craft to reach the sanctuary of the United States to prevent their children's dispatch to the Soviet Union, and instances of collective hysteria occurred.[17] In Guanabo, a beach suburb of Havana, women apparently gathered their children and hid them in their houses when a cry was raised that trucks were coming to collect them and load them onto Russian ships.[18] According to *Time* magazine, fifty mothers in Bayamo signed a pact to kill their children rather than hand them over to Fidel Castro.[19] Msgr. Bryan Walsh and others repeated these stories without questioning their veracity, asserting that children were "picked up off the streets and never seen again," and orphanages "emptied and all the children sent to Russia for indoctrination."[20]

A Pedro Pan said it felt like "Communist demons were closing in fast" on his family.[21] A Cuban exile described how parents searched frantically for visas, tickets, suitcases, and medicines for their children as the panic about *patria potestad* spread: "Would history repeat itself? Would our children be sent to Russia as had happened to thousands of Spanish children during the Civil War? Our children? No! We had to put them somewhere safe, to take them out of Cuba. It was necessary to act quickly and very discreetly."[22]

The specter of children being transported to socialist countries is often explained because of Cuban memories of the Spanish Civil War.[23] The Basque and other Spanish children were, in fact, sent to several countries, including Britain, France, and Mexico, not just the Soviet Union, and the reception the child refugees received was extremely varied.[24] Most of the children sent to the Soviet Union (overwhelmingly the progeny of Communist Party or leftist parents) were unable to be repatriated or reunited with their parents because of subsequent international events—the total rupture of all communications between Spain and Russia—and not because they were "held as hostages" by Stalin as some proponents of Operation Pedro Pan have inferred.[25]

Comparisons between the experiences of the Cuban and Spanish child refugees also overlook the fact that large areas of Spain were under full-scale aerial and military attack, and thousands of civilians were being killed and wounded. In Cuba, counterrevolutionary violence was extensive, but it never reached the level of a sustained civil war. Moreover, none of those justifying Operation Pedro Pan have noted the contradiction that while the United States welcomed the Pedro Pans and other Cuban refugees "with open arms," all efforts to bring the Basque children to the United States were blocked, even though President Roosevelt's wife, Eleanor, lobbied hard for their admittance.[26]

Anticommunism and the Family

As discussed in chapter 1, the political discourse of the Cold War clearly informed the response to the Cuban revolution in the United States and, to a large extent, on the island itself. In line with its "ideology of benevolent domination," the United States felt obliged to call Cubans' attention to the "anti-democratic, subversive activities of Communists in the service of foreign totalitarianism," not viewing this as an "intrusion into the domestic affairs of Cuba but an obligation to the Free World and to the security system of the Americas."[27]

As the U.S. media drew a "paper curtain" around revolutionary Cuba, pronouncements about a "Red embrace [of] Cuba" and the island's imminent economic collapse must have had an impact among the Cuban middle class, so attuned to the opinion of their closest neighbor.[28] With Cubans having long been subjected to U.S. anticommunist propaganda, two North American researchers commented: "[O]ne can understand why the switch in trade and official affection from the United States to the socialist bloc should come as a shock to substantial segments of the [Cuban] population. The wonder is not that so many have gone over to the opposition . . . but that so many have resisted the psychological pressures generated by the economic war and remained loyal to the revolution."[29]

If Cuba was an economic colony of the United States, Fidel observed at the founding congress of the Cuban Communist Party "we were also [colonized] ideologically."[30] Many Cubans who now consider themselves communists were petrified to encounter such a person who they were told devoured children.[31] The *patria potestad* hoax in Cuba reiterated the classic Cold War trope that communism meant, or even required, the destruction of the family unit.[32] Probing the psychology and politics behind the postwar retreat into "domestic containment," Elaine Tyler May explained how home and family promised "security in an insecure world."[33] Even though the new government's measures directly affecting the Cuban family were generally aimed at reinforcing the family, especially families of the urban and rural poor, in an atmosphere of rapid and radical social transformation, many changes were perceived as threatening the traditional family.[34]

Therefore, the response to the scare campaign cannot just be explained in terms of naivety or simple deception. The "diversionary campaign" about *patria potestad* was totally absurd, commented a Cuban journalist, but nevertheless, "for reasons of class," it suited some parents to believe the rumors, and for that reason they were more than ready to send their children "to the promised land of Walt Disney—the United States."[35]

Some government actions inevitably made some Cubans, who were well-primed on anticommunist propaganda, fearful of the course the revolution was taking and hence susceptible to the *patria potestad* scare. First, as discussed in chapter 1, the revolutionary government's efforts to create a desegregated, secular, free, universal system of education provoked an angry response from middle-class parents and church leaders committed to maintaining the elitism, racial purity, and profitability of private schools. Moreover, brainwashing or indoctrination was the way communists were supposed to maintain control over their captive populations, so everything the revolutionary government did regarding education was understood to be part of that process. Thus, leading Catholics interpreted the education reforms as an attempt to create a Soviet-style education system. The nationalization of the entire education system, including church-run schools, *Newsweek* said, converted all schools into "instruments of government propaganda," representing "a giant stride toward all-out Communism."[36]

In December 1960, on the same day the first Pedro Pans arrived in Miami, the Cuban government announced the introduction of a comprehensive file (*ficha escolar acumulativa*) for all school students—those attending both state and private schools—whereby a student's academic progress could be tracked.[37] This, according to the *Miami Herald*, "touched off widespread reports that the state planned to assume all responsibility for children of poor families up to the age of fifteen."[38] Education Minister Armando Hart explained that the concept was to give teachers a tool to assist the "integral formation" of each child and had "nothing to do with false versions about *patria potestad*, although," he commented, "it appears that some religious schools are distorting the facts."[39]

The establishment of *círculos infantiles* (child-care centers) in Cuba also fed the *patria potestad* scare campaign. The government's conscious push to integrate women into the workforce and political life inevitably provoked a hostile reaction from more socially conservative elements of Cuban society. Prior to the revolution, the concept of universally accessible child care was virtually unknown; charity-run crèches existed for children of very poor families, and only wealthy families could afford kindergarten and preschool fees.[40] Although the Federation of Cuban Women (FMC) campaign in support of this new project generated great enthusiasm, and hundreds of thousands of pesos were raised, the idea of the *círculos* touched a nerve in a country that tended to sentimentalize children and venerate motherhood to an excessive degree. Rumors circulating about the government's plans to assume custody of the nation's children suggested the child-care centers were where children removed from their families would be placed, allegedly in order to "poison their infantile souls with lies about communism."[41] Feverish statements were published in the exile media claiming that every child "who enters a [state-run child-care center] will return converted into a spy against his own family."[42]

Beyond facilitating the integration of women into economic and political activity, the day-care program was promoted by the government as part of the process of molding the new Cuban citizen, encouraging the development of a sense of community and solidarity rather than competitiveness and individualism. The centers were racially mixed, and children were encouraged to be independent and engage in productive labor, such as making gardens, so that they might enjoy "the fruits of their own labor."[43] This appalled some middle-class Cubans who had an ingrained cultural prejudice against manual work of any kind, although making gardens is an almost universal part of preschool and elementary school curriculums today in many countries. Moreover, there was another element of class prejudice underlying some of the opposition to the *círculos*. When the government announced its plan to bring young women from the countryside to work in the centers, Alfred Padula noted, "bourgeois mothers were horrified. Commit their children to the hands of ignorant peasants! As one *burguesa* had said of her children, 'I don't want them to be brought up common.'"[44]

Ironically, although the establishment of the *círculos* in Cuba was regarded by some as a step toward destroying the family, in his testimony to the Senate Subcommittee on the Cuban refugee problem in December 1961, Fr. Walsh recommended the expansion of the day-care program at the Catholic Hispanic Center in Miami for the children of working Cuban émigré mothers and an increased subsidy from the federal government.[45]

As the Cuban government prepared for a final push in the literacy campaign in August 1961, the government asked the FMC to work with parents to devise a special program (*Plan Asistencial*) of educational activities and television and radio broadcasts to occupy elementary school students when the official school year would have begun.[46] *El Mundo* promptly reassured parents that this program was absolutely voluntary and insisted it had nothing to do with the "failed lie about the suppression of *patria potestad*."[47] The Minister of Education insisted that "the participation of parents in scholastic activity is going to become more intense in Cuba . . . because under socialism parents not only educate [their children] in the home but also cooperate in [a wide range] of educational activities." He went on to explain that those who believed the "big lie and stupid calumny" promoted by the counterrevolution, "demonstrate a total ignorance of the concepts of Marxism-Leninism about the family and its application in socialist countries."[48]

Nevertheless, the rumors persisted, and U.S. media reports quoting "unnamed sources in Havana" continued to be published about the new "law," which was said to be causing widespread consternation, even among supporters of the government. Cubans were reported to be ready to resist this "new measure . . . [which] would go beyond anything that has been done even in the Soviet Union or China."[49] The U.S. Senate Subcommittee investigating the Cuban refugee problem in December 1961 was informed, as hard fact, that a law eliminating *patria potestad* was "sitting on [Fidel Castro's] desk."[50]

As the war of words intensified between the Cuban government and its opponents about who best defended children, the family, and parental rights, all government measures regarding children and education were seeds falling on soil already well cultivated by anticommunist diatribes emanating from Washington, the U.S. media, and the Vatican. And this hyped-up scare campaign soon took a material form with the printing and mass distribution of a fake government decree, revealing a more shadowy element behind the rumors and a deliberate attempt to manipulate parents' anxieties.

Caso Imprenta (Print Shop Case)

On 17 September 1961, the Cuban press reported mimeographed copies of a law proposing the removal of children from their families had been found, but said no family "should worry about their children, and no one should give credit to the unfounded rumors that have been circulated. . . . [So] credulous mothers should relax and understand they have been used for counterrevolutionary ends."[51] Similar disclaimers were made on Havana International Service, broadcast in English to North America, and Cuba's Radio Mambí, the latter ridiculing the idea that Premier Nikita Khrushchev had asked President Osvaldo Dorticós to send Cuban children to the Soviet Union because the socialist state did not have enough children of its own.[52]

As a result of a tip-off from a printing worker, the day before (16 September), Cuban state security had raided a print shop in Old Havana and discovered a printing mold of a supposed new revolutionary government decree proclaiming that, from January 1962, all children over the age of three would be taken into state care, and parental access would be severely restricted. Lázaro Garrido, the print shop proprietor, was arrested along with two of his employees. Garrido was well known for his affiliation to the

Catholic church and the anti-Castro Revolutionary Movement of the People (MRP).[53] Copies of a similar law on *patria potestad* were found in another print shop in Cienfuegos, a town about 150 km southeast of Havana. Other raids netted copies of the "law," chain letters to accompany the phony laws, and flyers with a brief message: "Martí told us—don't let them take your children away." These letters urged women to defend their children in the streets, like a "wild animal defends its cubs ... with sticks, with stones, with our fingernails, with whatever it takes."[54]

The government measures proposed in the various versions of this fake *patria potestad* law that were printed and apparently widely circulated throughout Cuba in 1961 were extreme, if not absurd: they applied to children from three to twenty years of age, with parental access being limited to two days per month; a census of all children would be conducted by the Integrated Revolutionary Organizations (ORI) to ensure compliance with the law; and any breaches of this "law" were to be considered "a counterrevolutionary crime and punishable by two to fifteen years' imprisonment." One of the "Transitory Dispositions," or clauses, stated that no Cuban minor would be permitted to leave the country.[55] The reference to the role of the ORI was, for some, especially inflammatory, as this was the new revolutionary organization that included members of the former communist party, the Popular Socialist Party, and therefore tended to reinforce the Cold War trope that communists were intent on poisoning children's minds.

Fidel Castro was outraged and waded into the debate on 19 September 1961, accusing "imperialism" and "falangist [fascist] priests" of having nothing to use against the revolution, so they had to "grab hold of God" and religion, despite the fact that "no church [could] say that its activities had been interfered with." Because the revolution had taken nothing from the people, he asserted, they had to "invent something." Fidel reminded his audience that the same scare tactic had been used to undermine the Russian revolution, although he insisted no socialist revolution had ever passed any such law about removing children from their families. He further lambasted the idea saying that the government simply did not even have enough resources to care for those children "truly in need," such as orphans and those abandoned by their parents. Fidel then went on to draw attention to the fact that the decree was allegedly signed by President Dorticós in Havana on a date when he was actually abroad. Defending the day-care program, he announced that three thousand former domestics were currently being retrained for "useful employment," and he condemned the appalling slave-like conditions for nannies previously working in private homes. Capitalism is "the enemy of motherhood and children," he said, proclaiming the revolution had been made "for the children."[56]

Fidel went on to say it was "sad" that some Cuban parents were sending their children away to be educated in the United States, but the government had placed no restrictions on anyone leaving, "much less children," he said. "We respect the sentiments and the rights of every family, above all. We have respected this, even [in the case] of our worst enemies."[57]

Not many copies of the phony decree were retrieved by Cuban state security forces, but anecdotal evidence suggests that various versions of the fake law were widely distributed across the island. Despite all evidence to the contrary, some Cuban Americans still insist that children were actually removed from their families and placed in "ideological indoctrination" camps.[58] Nicolás Ríos said everyone in his church congregation had copies of the fake law, although he never believed it was genuine. "The church was very hostile to the government at that time," he said, "opposed to the taking over of private property and the schools, the teaching of Marxism, the influence of communists in the government—everyone knew this."[59]

The sting in the tail of the fake law for many Cubans was its reference to the prohibition of the teaching of any form of religion to minors.[60] Religious themes were a constant feature of anti-Castro propaganda; the first issue of the exile paper *Rescate* published a cartoon portraying Fidel Castro as the anti-Christ, fleeing from the hand of the "people of Cuba" bearing a cross.[61] Returning to discuss the *patria potestad* hoax a week after the print shop raid, Fidel Castro felt obliged to reiterate that the "revolution never prohibited anyone's belief."[62]

The full story about the *patria potestad* "law" was published in *Revolución* on 23 September 1961, accusing "counterrevolutionary elements" of trying to take advantage of establishment of the *círculos infantiles* in order to spread rumors. Pornographic material was alleged to have been found in the same Havana print shop, "destined to poison the minds of our youth."[63] The initial Cuban state security report quickly identified the CIA and "falangist clergy" as the main culprits of the fraud, to which mothers especially were said to have fallen victim.[64]

The government now went on the offensive, and the Cuban media went into overdrive on the issue. *Bohemia* published a special supplement on children, outlining the benefits the revolution had bestowed on Cuba's smallest

Figure 3.2. "Copies of a false 'law' discovered in print shop." *Revolución*, 23 September 1961.

citizens, reiterating Martí's maxim that "no one is more important than a child."[65] *Verde Olivo* gave extensive coverage to the issue, publishing statements by Education Minister Armando Hart and Justice Minister Alfredo Yabur.[66] A few weeks later, *Bohemia* again ran several pages in which Cuban parents commented on the *patria potestad* hoax.[67] A spate of articles also appeared about the importance of the family unit in the Soviet Union in the Popular Socialist Party's paper *Hoy*.[68]

Cuban state security officials today claim to have evidence that the fraudulent "law," as printed and distributed in various versions throughout Cuba, was originally drafted in the United States.[69] The evidence for this appears to be the confession of a former Cuban CIA agent, a lawyer, who said he had assisted with checking the legal language of the fake law, an act he later deeply regretted. The same former agent also confirmed the CIA's role in Operation Pedro Pan as part of its broader anti-Castro project.[70]

Washington's Cuba Project

Cuba's fate was never going to be left in the hands of its people. In adopting the CIA's proposed "Program of Covert Action against the Castro Regime" in March 1960, the Eisenhower administration planned "to bring about the replacement of the Castro regime with one more devoted to the true interests of the Cuban people and more acceptable to the [United States]," while ensuring that Washington's hand was well hidden, in keeping with the CIA policy of "plausible denial."[71] The policy of "plausible denial" had been outlined in the National Security Council Directive 5412/1 of 12 March 1955, explaining: Covert actions were to be conducted so that "any U.S. Government responsibility for them is not evident to unauthorized persons and that if uncovered, the U.S. Government can plausibly disclaim any responsibility for them."[72] The 1975 U.S. Senate Commission headed by Senator Frank Church acknowledged the secret war against Cuba was a classic example of a covert action program.[73]

The Cuba Project included the development of a gigantic Miami operations base; the establishment and promotion of a Cuban government-in-exile; the training and arming of a paramilitary force that would carry out sabotage and terrorist actions in readiness for the invasion that took place in April 1961 at the Bay of Pigs; and an extensive propaganda effort.[74] The CIA's propaganda campaign focused on targets and themes that had proven successful in the past, such as appeals to the church to involve women in anticommunist actions, efforts to undermine the economy, and generally encouraging a wave of noncooperation with the government by all sectors of the population.[75]

Although President John F. Kennedy dismantled much of the National Security Council structure created by his predecessor, he made no changes to the leadership of the CIA, and he committed his administration to pursuing and even enhancing President Eisenhower's Cuba policy.[76] A week after Kennedy's 20 January 1961 inauguration, the Joint Chiefs of Staff sent a memorandum on Cuba to Defense Secretary Robert McNamara, warning that the Castro government was "steadily increasing [its] military strength" and that "Communists" were tightening their hold over the military, police, government finances, and propaganda. The memo concluded: "Unless the United States takes immediate and forceful action, there is a great and present danger that Cuba will become permanently established as a part of the Communist Bloc, with disastrous consequences to the security of the Western Hemisphere. [Therefore, the] primary objective of the United States in Cuba should be the speedy overthrow of the Castro Government, followed by the establishment of a pro-U.S. Government, which, with U.S. support, will accomplish the desired objectives for the Cuban people."[77] The assumption here, of course, was that the national interests of Cuba and the United States were identical.

At the top of the agenda for the newly minted president's consideration was whether to implement the CIA's plan to utilize Cuban émigrés in a planned invasion—what became the Bay of Pigs operation—that had been approved by Eisenhower on 6 December 1960, only weeks before his departure from office.[78] This date is significant, because it was precisely at this time that Fr. Bryan Walsh was in Miami to prepare the ground for Operation Pedro Pan as a way to protect the families of anti-Castro activists. Thus, the initiative for the children's airlift was incontrovertibly tied to the invasion plan scheduled to take place a few months later, as admitted by most of the main participants in the operation.[79] An essential element of the invasion plan was to be an internal uprising against the government.[80] An additional memorandum from the Joint Chiefs of Staff to Defense Secretary Robert McNamara on 27 January 1961 discussed the need to intensify the "information offensive" warning the Cuban people of the Castro government's increasing alignment with China and the Soviet Union and their growing isolation from the "Inter-American System"; greater employment of radio broadcasting was recommended to achieve this objective.[81]

The budget allocations of the Cuba Project illustrate the priorities of the anti-Castro effort, propaganda being the largest expense, and an intensive and extensive psychological warfare campaign was launched in the hope of undermining popular support for Fidel in Cuba and Latin America.[82] The prevailing belief among Cold Warriors was that the Soviets were effectively using brainwashing techniques to elicit confessions from political dissidents, and that communists maintained control over entire populations through manipulating people's minds through state propaganda as well as terror. The CIA therefore sought to add this to its own bag of tricks with the creation of a special program in 1953 to study methods of mind control, known as Project MKUltra.[83]

President Eisenhower was "the nation's prime enthusiast" for psychological warfare (or "psywar"), and this was part of his "New Look strategy" of covert operations, reflecting his desire to avoid the casualties and costs of conventional warfare.[84] The logic was that communist leaders could be easily overthrown if sufficient "encouragement" was given to the "oppressed populations."[85] As defined in a U.S. Joint Chiefs of Staff publication, psychological warfare consists of "[p]lanned operations to convey selected information and indicators to foreign audiences to influence their emotions, motives, objective reasoning, and ultimately the behavior of foreign governments, organizations, groups, or individuals."[86]

Although generally aimed at foreign countries, its target audience can often also be the U.S. domestic population. Different aspects of psychological warfare can include "gray" operations that involve "public propaganda secretly sponsored [that] do not require a secret agency to run them"; and "black" operations, designed to be attributed to the other side and carried out by a secret agency in order to hide the actual source of the propaganda.[87] The *patria potestad* hoax was a classic example of black propaganda.

As the easiest to implement and least dangerous of all covert actions, Cold War propaganda operations utilized the skills of thousands of "talented collaborators" as writers, journalists, publicists, radio technicians, and broadcasters.[88] One such "talented collaborator" in the Cuba Project was a former Office of Strategic Services (OSS) officer and "American actor-turned-agent," David Atlee Phillips, who was recruited by E. Howard Hunt for an operation in Guatemala when the democratically elected government of President Jacobo Árbenz was deemed by Washington (as Fidel Castro would be some years later) to be "endanger[ing] the hemisphere."[89] Phillips and Hunt got to work preparing a vast quantity of prerecorded "terror broadcasts," articles, pamphlets, and leaflets in Spanish for dissemination throughout Guatemala, and they also trained Guatemalan émigrés in the art of psychological warfare.[90]

Prior to the 1950 Guatemalan election, a warning was issued in the name of the Regional Planters Association stating that if Árbenz won, "women would be raised up to the same height as men and children would be taken away." This same propaganda tack was used again in 1954 against President Árbenz's agrarian reform, claiming the government intended to seize men's wives and children.[91] A few weeks before the U.S.-backed invasion, Phillips and his team launched a clandestine radio program that proved to be highly effective in the effort to oust Árbenz, which became known as "Operation Success."[92] The Catholic church also played a vital role in Guatemala, a deeply religious country. Shortly before the coup in April 1954, Archbishop Rossell y Arellano issued a pastoral letter, alerting Catholics that "anti-Christian communism—the atheist doctrine of all time—is stalking our country under the cloak of social justice." Guatemalans were called on to "rise as one against this enemy of God and country."[93]

In the lead up to the 1961 Bay of Pigs invasion, CIA director Allen Dulles told President Kennedy that he was more confident about success in Cuba than he had been about Guatemala in 1954.[94] But the Cubans, too, were looking to draw lessons from history. As a young itinerant revolutionary, Che Guevara was an eyewitness to the coup against President Árbenz in 1954, and he readily assured the *Havana Times* in July 1959, "what happened in Guatemala will not happen here."[95]

Through the first year or so of the revolutionary government, probably on assignment for the CIA, David Phillips ran a public relations business in Havana. He was summoned to Washington in early 1960 to become chief of propaganda for the CIA's Cuba Task Force.[96] Phillips's CIA personnel file described him as "an outstanding propagandist" who had "fluent Spanish with excellent area knowledge."[97] On arrival in Washington, he asked about the goals of the Cuba Project. "The Guatemala scenario" was the reply.[98] Establishing a clandestine radio station would be his first assignment, with the collaboration of his old friend Howard Hunt.[99] A key element of the CIA's Cuba Project was to be a "gray" radio station (Radio Swan) operating from Swan Island, off the coast of Honduras, that would be presented as "the major voice of the opposition."[100] Phillips and Hunt were given sixty days in which to get the station operational.[101] While Cuban exiles and the CIA were anxiously waiting for Kennedy's green light for the invasion at the Bay of Pigs, "psychological warfare activities were going full blast," Hunt recalled.[102]

Radio Swan

On air by 17 May 1960, Radio Swan proved to be one of the CIA's most ambitious, if not its most notorious, psywar operation. To maintain its appearance as a commercial radio station, Radio Swan ran advertisements for Coca-Cola, Goodyear, Pan American Airlines, and other businesses nationalized by the Cuban government after July and August 1960, payments for which might have eased the rapidly escalating financial burden the CIA was assuming in supporting leading exiles, their families, and numerous exile publishing ventures based in Miami.[103] Advertisements were placed in U.S. papers on behalf of the "Cuban Freedom Committee," soliciting donations for radio broadcasts to "help drive communism from Cuba"; checks were to be sent to "Christianform" at a Washington address, an organization later identified as a CIA front.[104] The *New York Times* also printed a similar fund appeal, headlined "What Can We Do about Cuba?" "International Communism" was said to be about to invade Cuba, thereby threatening "Western Christian civilization."[105]

Many of the anti-Castro groups played on the theme that the revolutionary government posed a threat to religious belief and practice, and they used the Christian symbol of the fish in their propaganda, especially around the time of the Bay of Pigs invasion.[106] Because of its impact in Guatemala, David Phillips urged the Cuban Revolutionary Council (the Miami-based "government-in-exile" headed by José Miró Cardona) to make greater use of the Christian fish symbol, offering the "large quantities of fish prop[aganda]" that the CIA had on hand.[107] That symbol became the logo of the leading anti-Castro group, Revolutionary Unity (UR), whose slogan was God, Homeland, and Liberty.[108]

The Cuban government immediately tried jamming Radio Swan's signal but only succeeded in the Havana area. Addressing the UN General Assembly in September 1960, Fidel Castro denounced the broadcasts as a "new [imperialist] aggression."[109] Cuba's Radio Mambí condemned the "hysterical parrots of Radio Swan," and President Osvaldo Dorticós warned Cubans to "be alert for lies and attempts to destroy the revolution through psychological warfare."[110] The Honduran government, which was engaged in a dispute with the United States over the sovereignty of Swan Island, also sent a protest note to Washington.[111]

Radio Swan's effectiveness, however, was somewhat limited because its independent façade was so transparent. Particularly damaging was its tendency to exaggerate, if not issue outright lies. "It was a shame," remarked *New York Times* correspondent Ruby Hart Phillips, "that the propaganda against Castro could not have been more facts and less adjectives."[112] Daniel Braddock, chargé d'affaires at the U.S. embassy in Havana, suggested "greater respect for facts would lend [Radio Swan] more weight."[113] In a memo of 10 February 1961, the Voice of America director expressed his opinion that Cubans listened to VOA "for confirmation," but tuned in to Radio Swan "for titillation."[114]

After the failed invasion, President Kennedy's special assistant Arthur Schlesinger proposed that Radio Swan be "liquidated as soon as possible in its present form."[115] In the CIA's own assessment, its drive for "scoops" had led to sensationalism and "statements that were obvious lies to listeners," undermining the station's "credibility and reputation."[116] Renamed Radio Americas in mid-1961, the clandestine station continued broadcasting from Swan Island, encouraging acts of sabotage.[117] "No doubt about it," wrote former CIA chief Richard Bissell, all kinds of "nutty schemes were born of the pressure" of those years, including a plan to convince Cubans of the imminent second coming of Jesus Christ, who would deal with Castro, the anti-Christ.[118]

A CIA report issued just prior to the Bay of Pigs attempted invasion noted: "Cuban women have become the leaders of opposition activity" and were therefore seen as an important target for propaganda campaigns.[119] The *patria potestad* scare campaign had a distinctive David Phillips scent about it, recycling the same themes concerning children and the family that had proven so effective in Guatemala.[120] In October 1960, Radio Swan's evening news bulletin announced: "Cuban mothers, don't let them take your children away!" After reminding listeners that Radio Swan had previously alerted Cubans to new laws such as the Urban Reform Law, the existence of a secret new "law" was announced that would remove children from their families when they turn five to be held by the state until they are eighteen, by which time, it was said, "they will be materialist monsters." Fidel Castro was said to be about to proclaim himself "Mother Superior of Cuba," and Cubans were admonished to go to church and "follow the instructions given you by the clergy." The next day, the Caribbean News bulletin announced that priests and nuns were to be made state employees and that Education Minister Armando Hart would become "Pope" to ensure all Cuban children were properly "indoctrinated" as communists. Addressing Cuban mothers, the broadcaster said: "They can take away your clothes, your food, and even kill you, but no one can remove your right to raise your [own] child." Women were told to be ready to sacrifice themselves rather than deliver their children to these "beasts."[121]

The Cuban media condemned such reports as "obviously too stupid for anyone with common sense [to believe]."[122] Nevertheless, the exile press, much of which according to Howard Hunt was funded by the CIA, persisted with these alerts: "Cuban Mother, defend your child" shrieked a full-page advertisement in *Bohemia Libre*: "Cuban mother . . . the classic dictatorships of Cuba . . . could only take away your child's life. The Castro dictatorship aspires to more: it aspires to take away his soul—that is, his religion, his sense of nationality, his dignity as a free person."[123]

But although the Cuban media ridiculed such suggestions, within a few months, Operation Pedro Pan was under way, convincing CIA propagandists that they had indeed hit on a vein that could be tapped.

Caravan of Sorrow

As part of his propaganda assignment for the CIA, Phillips engaged the services of a New York public relations firm run by Lem Jones to distribute the press statements of the supposed Cuban government-in-exile (the Cuban Revolutionary Council) in preparation for the Bay of Pigs invasion, a plan that the U.S. government continued to deny. One of this PR agency's first activities was to organize a busload of Cuban women traveling from Miami to New York in September 1960 to coincide with Fidel Castro's appearance at the UN General Assembly.[124] The goal was to dramatize the fears Cuban mothers had for their families in the face of the increasingly open "communist" character of the revolutionary government. But this "freedom ride"—as it was portrayed—was beset by problems from the beginning. Six of the women were pregnant and suffering badly from morning sickness. When the bus driver objected to the frequent rest stops, one woman threatened him, saying she had a gun in her handbag. It was left to Annette Aaron from the Lem Jones agency to defuse the situation. Aaron had had "easier assignments," but there were "compensations" because much of the tab of the "Cuban account" was picked up by Washington.[125]

The "Caravan of Sorrow," as it was called, achieved some publicity; the women, all dressed in black with dark glasses, were photographed outside St. Patrick's Cathedral in New York, declaring themselves to be refugees mourning "the death of freedom in Cuba."[126] A few months later a similar tour of women through several Latin American countries was organized and paid for by the CIA.[127] At a press conference in San José, Costa Rica, the women said their mission was "to awaken the conscience of mothers all over America to the threat that Castro-Communism is to them and their children"; they stated there was "irrefutable evidence that the Cuban regime will very soon put into effect a legal project which will transfer *patria potestad* to the state."[128] A few weeks later, a Costa Rican newspaper ran an advertisement with a sketch of Fidel Castro grabbing a child while a mother desperately tried to save her, saying: "This is happening in Cuba ... don't let it happen here!"[129]

Responding to these melodramatics, women in Cuba organized a petition to be sent to the United Nations, demanding an end to the U.S. "imperialist policy ... against the peoples of Latin America," and a women's rally was organized to highlight the sacrifice made by the mothers of those who had died during the revolutionary war to overthrow Batista.[130] By the time the fraud of the *patria potestad* law was exposed in September 1961, the government was fighting a counterrevolutionary terrorist offensive on many fronts, while remaining committed to the successful completion of the national literacy campaign.[131] Even so, the rumor-mongering continued, the exile media reporting in early 1962: "[Castro,] who had sent his own son behind the Iron Curtain, [was] ... persisting in his efforts to take Cuba's children from their parents. Although his Cuban-Communist dictatorship has not yet dared decree that Cuban children belong to the state, it is acting as if it—not the mothers and fathers—exercise parental authority."[132]

Msgr. Walsh was convinced that the supposed departure of Fidelito, Castro's own twelve-year-old son, for the Soviet Union helped confirm the rumors about the plans of the revolutionary government, even though Fidelito was simply a member of a delegation of young Cubans that made a short trip to Russia and other socialist bloc countries.[133] The departure of this youth delegation, however, unfortunately coincided with the discovery of the fake law in September 1961.[134]

The effectiveness of the hoax about *patria potestad* in spreading alarm and dissension in Cuba was duly noted in Washington. A memo from Roger Hilsman, assistant secretary for intelligence and research in the State Department, assessed the situation in Cuba following the April 1961 invasion debacle. "Castro remains in firm control in Cuba," he wrote, accepting that it would be "unlikely" that the government would be seriously threatened from within in the foreseeable future. But he continued: "The only remaining independent institution within Cuba, the Catholic church, has been greatly weakened during the past few months by the state seizure of the church schools and the deportation of most of the clergy including some native priests. Other non-governmental institutions . . . have been under state domination for over a year. These institutions, as well as the present state-organized literacy campaign, have facilitated the intensification of government propaganda and indoctrination."[135]

Hilsman then went on to mention that the "alleged recent government proposal to remove or reduce parental jurisdiction over children carries greater potential loss of popular support than any other measure suggested to date." Government leaders, he added, had gone "to [great] pains to deny that such measures would be implemented." Although in the short term, he concluded, the prospects for the opposition were poor, "extreme measures, such as the removal of children from parental to state tutelage, could upset this estimate."[136]

* * *

Some Cuban émigrés still insist that it was "common knowledge" that Fidel Castro planned to implement "draconian policies," among which was "the revocation of the *patria potestad*."[137] Msgr. Walsh quoted the "rumored" decree without comment in his 1971 article; he also insisted that he was told by unnamed people in the Cuban government that there had been "a definite plan to reduce parents' rights to take their children out of the country without the permission of the government."[138] Carlos Franqui, onetime July 26 Movement supporter and editor of *Revolución* newspaper, was similarly convinced that the plans for implementing the *patria potestad* law "really did exist."[139] Some Cuban Americans will still swear that it was only the public outcry that prevented the law from being instituted.[140] A former school principal, Josefa Gasset-Torrado, asserted: "Every Cuban mother I spoke to was willing to take to the streets if the measure went through. It was *vox populi* in Havana—mothers were just not going to let their children be taken from them. That is why the government backed down."[141]

The testimony of some of the key players in the Operation Pedro Pan drama sheds important light on the origin and purpose of the *patria potestad* hoax. Ramón ("Mongo") Grau and his sister Leopoldina ("Polita") Grau were arrested in 1965 for anti-Castro activities, including their participation in assassination plots against the Cuban leader himself. Both had close links to the CIA, and on arriving in Miami they were lauded for their role in assisting Operation Pedro Pan.[142] When asked about the *patria potestad* scare by *Miami Herald* journalist Sergio López, Ramón Grau admitted: "The entire thing was a propaganda test to hurt Fidel. . . . The idea was to create panic [among Cuban parents]. . . . It was hoped that this would foster unrest and rebellion against him."[143]

Earlier, on her release from prison in 1976, Polita Grau, a leader of Rescate's women's group, was interviewed by Cuban journalist Luis Báez, who queried her about the alleged threat to *patria potestad*.[144] She admitted to having "encouraged the rumor that the communist government was the absolute owner of the *muchachos* [kids] and that parents would lose their rights over their children. That they would be sent to Russia." She explained that a false revolutionary government law about this was drafted and printed.[145]

> Luis Báez: You sincerely believed in this?
> Polita Grau: In reality, no.
> Luis Báez: Then why did you do it?
> Polita Grau: It was a way to destabilize the government. So that the people would begin to lose faith in the revolution.
> Luis Báez: A very cynical attitude.
> Polita Grau: That's possible, but we were at war against the government. In a war, anything is permitted.[146]

Former Cuban CIA agent Tony Veciana recently published his memoir, in which he claimed responsibility for the fake *patria potestad* law as well as another fabricated law about the revolutionary government's monetary policy that led to a run on the banks. But it was not his intention, he said, to "divide families" and was "sorry for those who were hurt" by Operation Pedro Pan and never reunited. The goal, he explained, "had been only to deepen the discontent with the government, to sow more instability, and hopefully, to create the conditions for its downfall."[147]

Other Cuban anti-Castro activists have similarly expressed some regret for their part in the circulation of the fake law and the rumor campaign about *patria potestad*. "I believe that to use such an apocryphal law for a political objective in whatever circumstance must be condemned," said Arturo Villar, a Miami businessman and former leader of a counterrevolutionary group. He described the hoax as neither "clean nor intelligent" and an "unconscionable" tactic.[148] On his deathbed, Ángel Fernández Varela, a lawyer and former Cuban CIA operative, felt impelled to confess to his family his role in drafting the fake law that fueled the hysteria, and what his son Álvaro described as the CIA's "sinister immorality play" that was Operation Pedro Pan. His father was a "fervent Catholic" with a penchant for James Bond movies, said Álvaro, a man who "spent his whole life trying to help others in need—never seeking the limelight," but he died with a "heart heavy with guilt" over Operation Pedro Pan.[149]

Thus, it would appear the evidence supports the Cuban government's claim that the *patria potestad* law was a total fraud instigated by the CIA, and that the scare campaign was unfounded and cynically manipulated by the church and CIA-backed anti-Castro forces that sought to overturn the revolutionary project. What is also clear, however, is that the hoax regarding the new "law" was a potent factor contributing to a general atmosphere of uncertainty, if not hysteria, among some Cubans insofar as these rumors struck a chord with those already anxious about the pace of reform and social change they were witnessing. This led more conservative sectors of Cuban society to fear what might be coming next as the revolution rapidly evolved far beyond the initial goals of dismantling Batista's repressive apparatus and his crony-run economy.

When, on the eve of the Bay of Pigs invasion in April 1961, Castro pronounced that the revolution under way in Cuba was a "socialist" revolution, the worst fears of his political opponents were confirmed.[150] By the end of 1960, the ground had been well prepared by the repeated warnings about communism emanating from Catholic church pulpits, CIA radio broadcasts, and anti-Castro propaganda about the imminent threat to children and families. But why Operation Pedro Pan developed on such a massive scale, nevertheless, was due to other factors that came into play.

4

Operation Pedro Pan and the Children Who Could Fly

By December 1960, some supposedly terrified Cuban parents were reported to have responded to "Castro's threat to make every child a virtual ward of the state" by sending as many as one thousand children a month to Miami.[1] Was the *patria potestad* hoax intended to spur an exodus on this scale? Similar scare campaigns in other countries had not provoked the same response—but this was the result in Cuba, once the networks for collecting children's names and passports and distributing visa waivers and tickets were established. Moreover, the unprecedented foster care program for refugee minors funded by the U.S. government, under the auspices of Miami's Catholic Welfare Bureau, was a definite inducement.

Most of the Pedro Pan children remember the atmosphere before they left Cuba as one of "near-delirium," and every Pedro Pan can vividly recall the day they left Cuba: the glass wall of the *pecera* (fishbowl) in the airport departure lounge through which they could see their parents' anguished faces but not hear their voices; the crying of children on the plane; the rejoicing of adult passengers on landing in Miami; the disorientation and anxiety they experienced arriving in a foreign country to be met by strangers.[2]

Msgr. Walsh always maintained that the organizers of the child airlift simply responded to Cuban parents' wishes.[3] "All Pedro Pan did," he said, "was to create a window of opportunity for Cuban parents to exercise their rights." Their fears were "very real," he said, heightened by the experience of the literacy campaign and the government's education reforms.[4] In that situation, said a former Pedro Pan, in effect, Cubans chose "to sacrifice their children to a free society [rather] than to a totalitarian one."[5]

Here it is important to distinguish between the three components of what is commonly referred to as "Operation Pedro Pan": the *patria potestad* hoax, the organized airlift evacuating children to Miami, and the program set up to care for the unaccompanied minors in the United States. Initially, Operation Pedro Pan and the campaign about the threat to *patria potestad* were not directly linked. As already explained, Operation Pedro Pan was first conceived as a way to protect the children of opponents of the revolutionary government. What ensured the success and scale of the child evacuation scheme, however, was the simultaneous establishment of the program by (then) Fr. Walsh, as director of the very modest Catholic Welfare Bureau in Miami—the Cuban Children's Program, and the highly irregular visa waiver system that facilitated the entry into the United States of an unlimited number of Cuban children on the basis of a simple letter signed by Fr. Walsh.

This program was clearly in line with the U.S. immigration policy framed in the context of the Cold War to encourage flight from socialist bloc countries. Fr. Walsh had been involved with an earlier program under which almost fourteen hundred young Hungarians (most of them boys in their mid- to late teens) were admitted into the United States following the Soviet repression of the 1956 popular uprising.[6] The political bias of the U.S. immigration policy was bluntly spelled out by Republican Representative Walter H. Judd in May 1959: "Every refugee who comes out [of Cuba] is a vote for our society and a vote against their society." The welcome mat was therefore promptly laid out for any and every Cuban fleeing from the revolution. "Our people opened their homes and hearts to the Hungarian refugees four years ago. I am sure we will do no less for the distressed Cubans," said President Dwight D. Eisenhower two days before he was succeeded by Senator John F. Kennedy as president in January 1961.[7]

The U.S. covert war against the Cuban revolution relied on emigration from the island to fulfill several functions: to drain Cuba of the human capital needed for its development; to discredit the revolutionary social project; and to establish a support base and recruits for the counterrevolutionary movement.[8] Unquestionably the lack of an immigration quota or any restrictions on disaffected Cubans entering the United States spurred the exodus.[9] Msgr. Walsh recalled: "We also knew we could still expect many more children from Cuba, since a great many Cuban families [already] had passports, with multiple entry Tourist B1 Visas. As soon as their parents knew that care was available in Miami [more] children would come."[10]

A meeting in the White House in late October 1960 reviewed the Cuban refugee situation and took note of the presence of "unattached" minors in the Miami area, a problem that was "expected to become more serious as plans are now being developed by the Castro regime to make children wards of the state"; some of these children were reported to be "roaming the streets" seeking food and shelter.[11] Nevertheless, on the eve of the 1960 presidential election, Tracy Voorhees reported to a meeting at the State Department that the problem in Florida was "not actually very large or very serious," with only a few thousand Cuban refugees needing assistance. He drew attention to the fact that the problem had received considerable publicity, and therefore, the administration needed to be seen "doing something suitable ... not necessarily related to the *actual needs* of the situation." In response, Undersecretary Douglas Dillon identified "important reasons of foreign policy" as the reason the Cuban refugees should not be permitted "to fall into a situation where they could be *portrayed abroad* as in difficult straits in the United States." It was important, he argued, that U.S. policy toward the Cubans "reflect credit upon the United States response to the needs of these victims of Castro's oppression."[12]

Toward the end of 1960, President Eisenhower approved an initial amount of $1 million to assist the resettlement of Cuban refugees and establish the Cuban Refugee Emergency Center in Miami. Up to that time, the Catholic Diocese of Miami had borne the greatest burden of aid to the Cuban refugees through the Catholic Hispanic Center, created most "providentially" by Bishop Coleman Carroll in 1959.[13]

On 7 November 1960, General Edward Lansdale urged a review of the Cuba Project that President Eisenhower had approved the previous March, emphasizing the need to appeal to "the warm understanding and sympathetic approval of the people of the Free World," and urging "a series of political actions which can isolate the Communist leaders from the [Cuban] people ... and enlist the support of world opinion.... First, and easiest," he said, was the "need to call world attention to the significance of Cuban refugees in a strong enough manner to make the world choose the anti-Castro side." He recommended that publicity focus on the "helpless victims of terrorism": children and the aged.[14] Within a month of this memo, initial steps were taken to support Fr. Walsh's Catholic Welfare Bureau's efforts to find foster homes for the trickle of Cuban children turning up in Miami with no family friends or relatives to care for them, and federal funds were promised.[15] Despite Tracy Voorhees's estimate in his January 1961 report to the president that one thousand Cubans were arriving each week, U.S. media, such as the *New York Times*, tended to grossly inflate that figure up to five times that number.[16]

An examination of Washington's pre- and postwar refugee policy shows that it was applied very selectively and discriminatorily.[17] When the plight of German refugee children was discussed in joint hearings of the U.S. Senate and House of Representatives in April 1939—on the urging of those who were organizing a British program for child refugees from Europe—it was argued that to admit children to the United States without their parents was "against the will of God."[18] In fact, anti-Semitism, anticommunism, and anti-immigrant sentiment determined the rejection of the bill that would have allowed 20,000 Jewish and other "non-Aryan" German children to come to the United States. Ultimately, only 240 child refugees from German-controlled parts of Europe arrived.[19] And after the war, only 375 children were admitted under the Displaced Persons Act of 1948, in marked contrast to the policy adopted on the Cuban children, for whom direct presidential proclamations established no limit.[20]

The Cuban Children's Program was particularly unique in that, apart from placing no limit on the number admitted, the federal government financed foster care for refugee children for the first time, and this was through a religious agency.[21] In fact, the entire program established for Cuban refugees was totally unprecedented as a comprehensive program run by the U.S. government.[22] By January 1961, 6,500 Cuban children were already enrolled in public and parochial schools in the Miami area, for whom the fifty-dollar enrollment fee was waived along with other charges; and by August, the number of Cuban children in public schools alone had risen to 8,500.[23] Tracy Voorhees praised the work done by the Catholic Diocese, but the Kennedy administration resisted calls to extend federal aid to Catholic schools.[24] The fact that by early 1961 public schools in Miami-Dade were struggling to cope with the influx of Cuban students makes all the more extraordinary the government's decision to facilitate the arrival of even more refugee minors.

The Cuban Children's Program was nevertheless defended in highly emotional and political terms: "Each of us can swell with pride," said Wendell Rollason, a lawyer with the Miami-based Inter-American Affairs Commission, for being "a small but vital part in the drama of taking from the grasp of communism but one little child." In a rhapsodic vein, he continued, saying "thousands of little minds" would not now "be warped by Communist

Figure 4.1. "Last one in . . ." Msgr. Bryan Walsh had a framed copy of this cartoon hanging in his apartment when this researcher interviewed him there in March 2000.

indoctrination . . . [or] taught that there is no God . . . [or to] spy on their parents."[25] Within a short few years, the Cuban Children's Program became the major part of the federal government's refugee program, which totaled $138.6 million through June 1964.[26] When the issue of the high cost of this program was raised, Fr. Walsh pointed out that the burden would have been much greater on the public school system if a significant number of Pedro Pans had not been enrolled in Catholic private schools, a cost met by the local diocese.[27]

A Boy Called Pedro

Some families were already sending their children off to the United States during 1960. Noel Betancourt was seventeen when his parents dispatched him and his younger brother to Miami. "You had to have lived those years in Cuba to understand what it was like," he said. "America was seen as the big protector. Uncle Sam would fix everything, as had happened ever since 1902." Noel and his brother left in November 1960, entering the United States on student visas, indicating they had been admitted to the University of Miami. This was not in the least unusual, given the long tradition of upper- and middle-class Cuban youth studying in the United States. What was unusual in the case of the Betancourt brothers was that Noel's younger brother had not yet graduated from high school; he was only fifteen.[28]

Msgr. Walsh loved to recite the tale of "Pedro," a story that became almost mythologized and has been cited in virtually every account of the exodus of the Cuban children.[29] According to the monsignor, one day in November 1960, a fifteen-year-old boy called Pedro Menéndez was brought to his office, having arrived alone in Miami, where apparently he found himself passed from one household to another, with no one being in a position to care for him, even on a temporary basis.[30] During an interview with Msgr. Walsh, this researcher had the opportunity to inquire after young Pedro, knowing that he kept close tabs on hundreds of his former charges. But Msgr. Walsh could not say what had happened to the legendary Pedro, which might suggest that young Pedro was in fact just that—a myth.[31]

Toward the end of 1960, the U.S. media reported that every plane leaving Cuba for the United States carried a few unaccompanied children, and desperate parents at Havana airport were said to be begging adults with reservations to give up their seats to children.[32] Constant media references to support services available to unaccompanied Cuban "students" may well have further stimulated departures. As the director of the modest Catholic Welfare Bureau in Miami, Fr. Walsh had just returned from Puerto Rico, where he had been studying Spanish for three months.[33] The encounter with young Pedro, he said, drew his attention to the potential number of homeless Cuban children in Miami, but uppermost in his mind was how this foster care scheme could be funded.[34] Three Miami voluntary children's agencies (the Catholic Welfare Bureau, the Children's Services Bureau, and Jewish Family and Children's Services) agreed to cooperate in caring for Cuban children. This prompted the resolution of the Cuban Refugee Committee (part of Dade County Welfare Planning Council) on 22 November 1960 to include an appeal for federal funds for foster care in institutions or family homes for Cuban children arriving in the United States "to avoid coercive regimentation."[35]

With Washington already feeling pressure to be seen doing something for the latest "fugitives from communism," Tracy Voorhees recommended that the government access the $1 million emergency fund (if it should "prove necessary beyond what private charity can do") to assist the Cuban refugee children found to be "in extreme need."[36] So in mid-December 1960, when

Fr. Walsh first met with James Baker, the director of the elite Ruston Academy in Havana, the priest readily assured him that he would have federal funds for foster care of Cuban children—a better option than a boarding school, which Baker had initially proposed. As a result, they agreed to work together.[37]

James Baker had come to Miami with his own scheme. As U.S. and Cuban companies were seized by the revolutionary government after July 1960, many businesspeople and managers relocated to Miami in the expectation that Washington would soon step in and solve the Cuba problem in general and the Fidel Castro problem in particular. This was not an unrealistic expectation, given the number of previous occasions the United States had intervened in Cuban politics.[38] Meanwhile, the Cuban and U.S. business executives would sit it out in Miami.

The students at Ruston Academy were children of expatriate U.S. businesspeople, diplomats, and wealthy Cubans, and the talk in Havana about the imminent government takeover of all private schools was undoubtedly in Baker's mind.[39] Not surprisingly, therefore, among the most enthusiastic backers of the child evacuation scheme were members of the American Chamber of Commerce, including executives from Shell and Standard Oil, whose Cuban interests had been taken over by the state. Wanting to keep their support low profile, donations toward the twenty-five dollars needed for each Pedro Pan's plane ticket plus other expenses were directed to the Catholic Welfare Bureau's account.[40] Parents were then given money orders with which they could purchase tickets for their children.[41] Texaco, IBM, and Ford were among other private companies sponsoring the airlift of the children.[42]

There was, however, another dimension to James Baker's scheme, which he candidly explained to Fr. Walsh at their first meeting. Some of his friends, he said, were active in the counterrevolutionary movement. Fr. Walsh was convinced these parents were "afraid to get more involved in the underground because their children might be taken away," so the plan was that the children of anti-Castro fighters would be kept safe in Miami until the situation was "solved by the U.S. Marines."[43]

Another incident is often mentioned as providing the impetus for Operation Pedro Pan and the Cuban Children's Program. In November 1960, a Cuban mother brought her two children to the Key West Juvenile Court saying she had smuggled them out of Cuba because she was afraid they would be sent to Russia for indoctrination; she appealed for help in finding them suitable foster homes while she returned to Cuba to join her husband.[44] Interestingly, in citing this case, Msgr. Walsh added his own intriguing twist to the story, explaining that the parents were "actively opposed to the Castro regime," and that the mother returned to Cuba in order "to continue her work in the counterrevolutionary movement."[45] Significantly, the original 1962 article about this case made no mention of the mother's political activity.[46] It is unclear whether Walsh had additional information about the case, knew the woman concerned, or whether he just chose to add his own political embellishment to the story.

Thus, two distinct objectives behind the airlift of Cuban children become evident: on the one hand, the official site of the Operation Pedro Pan Group, Inc., presents it as a straightforward program established "at the request of parents in Cuba to provide an opportunity for them to send their children to Miami to avoid Marxist-Leninist indoctrination."[47] On the other, the operation emerges as intimately bound up with the effort to undermine and overthrow the revolutionary government, in the prelude to the planned U.S.-backed invasion. In his 1971 article, Msgr. Walsh was remarkably open about this aspect of Operation Pedro Pan; only later was this element downplayed as the child "rescue" scheme became mythologized by the Cuban-American community in the United States.

Children of the Counterrevolution

Until he met James Baker, Fr. Walsh said he was simply planning to assist Cuban children already in Miami needing care.[48] Now Baker's scheme captured the priest's imagination. In agreeing to take responsibility for the young refugees without his bishop's approval, Walsh said he decided that to "save 200 kids from communism" was "worth [his] career."[49] He evidently thrilled at the idea of "sharing the worries of families we did not even know, hundreds of miles away in a life and death struggle in the Cold War," but was convinced that if the Cuban authorities "got wind of a mass movement of unaccompanied children, they would clamp down right away."[50]

Addressing a national conference at the end of January 1961 to discuss the resettlement program for Cuban refugees, Fr. Walsh carefully distinguished Cubans from other "political exiles" from Latin America fleeing dictatorships, reminding his audience that the "situation in Cuba [was] just another step in what is part of a worldwide conspiracy to destroy religious and civil liberty." The arrival of the Cubans in the United States, he said, presented an "opportunity and indeed privilege of helping them and [thereby] playing an active role in the fight against Communism."[51]

Over the years, the flight of the Pedro Pans has inspired numerous fictional accounts for young readers, in which the children of underground activists heroically resisting "Castro's totalitarian regime" are spirited to the safety of the United States.[52] But the documentary record of the actual airlift of the Cuban children reveals another dimension to this story.

In October 1960, members of the Revolutionary Recovery Movement (MRR), a leading underground anti-Castro group, met with Miami-based exile Dr. Manuel (Tony) Varona, who offered them economic help for travel and accommodation for family members who wanted to leave Cuba.[53] By then, the U.S. government was actively assisting the rising counterrevolutionary movement, and not always very discreetly. Telegrams from the U.S. embassy in Havana often ask for similar special assistance for Castro's political opponents arriving in Miami.[54] When fifteen oppositionists escaped from a Cuban prison, U.S. ambassador Bonsal was again quick to alert the State Department that they might be heading for Key West by boat, mentioning that Fidel Castro had been on television accusing the U.S. embassy of "supporting and actively cooperating with counterrevolutionary groups."[55]

A month later, the same Tony Varona reported to the State Department that underground activists had concerns about their families left in Cuba. For this reason, he argued, it was of "great operational interest to expedite visas for family members," but he complained there had often been "bureaucratic delays."[56] The clear implication was that if their families were guaranteed protection, as Msgr. Walsh explained, the anti-Castro forces would be more eager to fight Castro.[57] Varona told the State Department meeting that the refugee crisis in Miami had now assumed "serious proportions" and merited official attention. Humanitarian work in Miami, he said, was "only just beginning" but was becoming a "drain on funds" that could otherwise be "used in more productive ways."[58] He failed, however, to specify what these "more productive" activities might be. CIA agent Howard Hunt later recalled that Varona was persistent in demanding financial assistance for the families of "destitute" anti-Castro Cubans, while also requesting a monthly budget of $745,000 for the political activities of the Revolutionary Democratic Front (FRD).[59]

At his first briefing on Cuba as president, John F. Kennedy was told that Cuba was "now for practical purposes a Communist-controlled state," and it was decided to step up "covert measures against Castro, including propaganda, sabotage, political action and direct assistance to the anti-Castro Cubans in military training."[60] The U.S. government, however, was still officially denying involvement in the training of an exile force for an invasion of Cuba, and the New York Times went so far as to suggest that the Cuban government might need to "produce [that is, fabricate] an invasion" in order to prove the truth of the rumors.[61] It turned out that during the Bay of Pigs invasion, Varona's son, brother, and nephew were all captured, along with former president Miró Cardona's son—so Varona's plea for the "protection" of family members clearly had a personal motive.[62]

Holding the children of anti-Castro fighters in the United States might have served multiple purposes. First, it meant parents could continue fighting in the underground without the pressure of having to worry about their children. It has also been suggested that the presence of those children in the United States gave the CIA a means of "ensuring compliance" on the part of Cuban counterrevolutionaries, who were viewed as notoriously unreliable.[63] In other words, the CIA might have had in mind doing exactly what Wendell Rollason accused the Cuban government of doing, when Pelleyá asserted it was seizing children of captured members of the underground as a means of "retaliation" or warning to others if they did not "knuckle under."[64]

This research found no evidence that this occurred in revolutionary Cuba. On the other hand, the Cuban investigation uncovered cases where U.S. visas and places on flights were offered for children of potential agents as inducements to participate in various underground activities. Popular singers Tony Álvarez and Olga Chorens had two daughters they wanted to get out of Cuba; when they sought the aid of Castro oppositionist Ramón Grau, he convinced them to assist Operation Pedro Pan by transporting children's passports and distributing visas on their concert tours around Cuba.[65] In another case, José Luis Pelleyá Jústiz was recruited to the CIA by Warren Pyne, the manager of Pan American Airlines in Cuba; when he was arrested in 1964, he declared that he had obtained a visa waiver for the younger son of Carmen González in return for her assistance in removing an official stamp from the Ministry of State, where she worked. This stamp was later used to falsify travel documents for Cubans leaving for the United States.[66] In yet another case, in return for a U.S. visa for his younger son, Bartolomé Pérez García was asked to do a "favor" by a key figure in the underground; this "favor" was the delivery of poison capsules to the organizer of a banquet at the Havana Hilton (today the Habana Libre) with which to assassinate leaders of the government. Pérez initially agreed but later refused.[67]

The U.S. government was nevertheless worried that too many opponents of the revolution were fleeing to Miami and the impetus of the anti-Castro movement was being dissipated. The chargé d'affaires at the U.S. embassy in Havana on 16 December 1960 suggested that the impending rupture of diplomatic relations between the United States and Cuba would have the benefit of closing the "escape valve" of easy access to U.S. visas so that the departure of Cuban dissidents would no longer be facilitated. It was too easy for Castro to rid himself of "elements of discontent," Daniel Braddock argued. On balance, he considered breaking relations with Cuba appeared "to be in the U.S. interest."[68] When diplomatic relations were severed on 3 January 1961, there were some fifty thousand visa requests pending at the U.S. embassy in Havana.[69]

Thus, in the months leading up to the Bay of Pigs invasion, when rumors were rife about the CIA training Cuban exiles in camps located in Florida and Guatemala, one "escape valve" was shut, while another (for the children of Castro's opponents) was opened. It can therefore be assumed that among the first batch of Pedro Pans sent by James Baker to Fr. Walsh's care in Miami were offspring of members of the anti-Castro underground. By guaranteeing their families' safety, Operation Pedro Pan served to encourage—if not impel—Castro's opponents to keep up pressure on the revolutionary government.

Sergio Díaz explained the circumstances in which he sent his six-year-old son to Miami in January 1961:

> I became a member of the underground soon after we learned that Castro was a communist. . . . [A]nd it was rumored that the communists were about to take control of all of the schools. We also learned that Castro was about to stop all children over five years old from leaving Cuba. I spoke to one of my friends [in the resistance] who had access to a waiver and asked to use it to get my son out of the country. I knew that we were about to have a large military action to overthrow Castro. . . . I was afraid that if I didn't act immediately, my son might not get out. . . . We had no family in the United States and I couldn't

send my son to live on the streets. That was when I learned that there was a program to place children in foster homes until my wife could get to the United States. I knew then what I had to do.[70]

By the time the Bay of Pigs invasion took place in April 1961, the scheme to bring the Cuban children to the United States was on what Msgr. Walsh described as a "firm foundation," with a "formal" relationship established with the U.S. government.[71] The plan was that James Baker would get the children out of Cuba, and Fr. Walsh would "provide shelter for those who had no one here [to care for them]."[72] Under the initial scheme worked out in December 1960, the children would enter the United States on student visas, assisted by staff at Coral Gables High School, who completed the required I-20 student visa forms indicating that the young Cubans were to be enrolled at their high school. Agnes Ewald of Coral Gables High School supplied the forms to Norma Lemberg, a former Havana resident, who, with the assistance of Dr. Sergio Giquel, delivered the documents to Cuba.[73]

At this time, the Catholic Welfare Bureau in Miami had only a handful of children in its care, but despite the fact that rumors were circulating in Havana that no children would be allowed to leave Cuba after 1 January, Fr. Walsh and James Baker were acting on the assumption that many more children would be on their way when their parents learned that care was available in Miami.[74] But once the U.S. embassy was closed in Havana, other means had to be found to facilitate the children's flight from Cuba and entry into the United States. This was the magical visa waiver system, which, along with the Cuban Children's Program, became one of the central pillars of Operation Pedro Pan.

The Visa Waiver System

After the 3 January 1961 closure of the U.S. embassy, a special visa waiver system for Cubans was instituted; it was described by Robert Hale (director of the U.S. State Department's visa office) as "a matter of sound and humanitarian national policy, and in keeping with the traditional role of the United States as a haven for those fleeing persecution."[75] By the end of 1961, the Immigration and Naturalization Service was receiving twelve hundred visa waiver applications from Cubans every working day, while the U.S. government picked up the tab for the children's flights as an additional incentive offered by Washington.[76]

James Baker now came up with the idea of the Jamaica route: with the cooperation of the British embassy in Havana, children could fly to Jamaica, where they would receive visas from the U.S. embassy in Kingston and travel on to Miami the next day. This, Fr. Walsh surmised, had the advantage of deceiving Cuban authorities that the children were going to school in Jamaica, not the United States. But this more complicated and more expensive route proved unnecessary when it became clear that the visa waivers signed by Fr. Walsh (or even photocopies) would be accepted by both the Cuban and U.S. immigration authorities.[77] Even so, young Cubans like Nelson Valdés were still being put on planes in April 1961 with British visas, believing they were going to London, only to find they were transferred to flights to Miami after arriving in Nassau in the Bahamas.[78]

It is noteworthy that all contemporary official accounts of the Cuban child refugees fail to mention the special entry arrangements and the clandestine network established for bringing the children out of Cuba; moreover, the Pedro Pans were usually referred to as "students," implying they were being admitted on student visas (not visa waivers). For Katherine Brownell Oettinger, head of the U.S. government's Children's Bureau in 1962, which oversaw the welfare program for the young Cuban refugees, it was all a bit mysterious—or perhaps, she chose not to probe this aspect of the airlift. She simply remarked on the "surprisingly large number" of unaccompanied Cuban children arriving in the United States, sent by parents who evidently viewed the separation as preferable to "the alternative—indoctrination with the malignant seeds of communist dogma."[79] Similarly, a 1963 article published in *Children* magazine made no mention of any special assistance children received in order to leave Cuba, avoiding mention of the Miami priest's unprecedented visa waiver authority and stating that the children arrived on "student visas." It described the children's situation as the "unfortunate" result of "hasty parental plans."[80] In general, however, the children's departures were hardly the result of an emergency situation or "hasty parental plans," as children often had to wait several months for their paperwork to be completed.

When the *Miami Herald* first announced the evacuation program for Cuban children in March 1962, the cloak-and-dagger side of the operation was dramatized: "The Communists are certain to call it child smuggling. No one is telling exactly how it is done. No one will. The risk of reprisal is too great."[81] It was the Children's Bureau of the Department of Health, Education, and Welfare (DHEW) report about the program in 1967 that made the first public mention of James Baker and Fr. Walsh's "direct discussions" with the State Department and the Immigration and Naturalization Service that resulted in the Miami priest being granted authority to bring in 225 children on "student" visas. By the time the federal government took over the program in February 1961, the report said, "visa waivers were being granted in blocks of 500."[82]

The Pedro Pans' visa waivers actually took the form of letters signed by Fr. Bryan O. Walsh on Catholic Welfare Bureau letterhead and addressed (in Spanish) "To whom it may concern." There was space for the name and birth date of the child and then the words: "has been granted a 'Visa Waiver' by the Department of State on the request of the Catholic Welfare Bureau, Inc." These letters explain that Pan American and KLM Royal Dutch Airlines had been advised to accept these documents in lieu of a U.S. visa.[83]

It remains an intriguing, and still unexplained, aspect of Operation Pedro Pan how a young Miami priest came to be authorized by the U.S. government to sign visa waivers for as many Cuban minors as he chose. This special entry arrangement was certainly a unique feature of the Cuban Children's Program, and how it was established sheds considerable light on the nature of Operation Pedro Pan and the political agenda at work.

James Baker and his family left Cuba, arriving in Miami on 5 January 1961, without abandoning his plans to evacuate children, despite the closure of the U.S. embassy in Havana. Before departing, Baker organized a group of "trustworthy friends" to keep the program going.[84] From this moment, however, things become rather curious. Fr. Walsh received a call from Frank Auerbach of the State Department's visa office (supposedly on Baker's prompting) summoning him to Washington. On 8 January, a Sunday afternoon, he met Auerbach at one of the side doors of the State Department building; they then met with Robert Hale (director of the visa office), a representative of the British embassy, and possibly a representative of the CIA. For the first time, the option of the "visa waiver" was discussed that would enable the children to board direct flights to Miami without a valid visa, which would normally incur a fine of one thousand dollars. "The question," Walsh said, was now "whether the Cuban authorities would cooperate in allowing such a child to leave. This we could only find out by trying."[85]

Msgr. Walsh never explained why all this had to take place after hours, but from his comments in interviews and articles, he clearly enjoyed the atmosphere of intrigue and conspiracy enshrouding this meeting, later comparing this encounter to a scene from the popular 1960s TV series, *The*

F.B.I.[86] Whether this cloak-and-dagger routine was necessary, however, can only be speculated. The former director of Cuba's Center for Historical Investigations on State Security (CIHSE) has claimed that Walsh had actually met David Phillips, the key propagandist in the CIA's Cuba Project, at that meeting.[87] Although this is possible, as Phillips was working in Washington at the time, there appears to be no evidence to support this statement.[88] Whatever the case, it took only twenty-four hours for the State Department to approve young Fr. Walsh's "blanket authority" (as a representative of the Catholic Welfare Bureau) to issue visa waivers to as many Cuban children between the ages of six and sixteen as he wished. Of course, he stressed, all this was "verbal ... we had nothing in writing."[89]

When questioned, Msgr. Walsh could not explain why parents were unable to leave with their children, except to say "[f]or one reason or another, the U.S. government did not see fit to give them visa waivers."[90] Some Cuban and other commentators have pointed out that if there had been a genuine concern for families, parents should have been allowed to leave with their children.[91]

Prior to the April 1961 invasion, Washington had decided that visas for adult refugees should be issued sparingly, in order to keep the anti-Castro forces active on the ground in Cuba. But after the Bay of Pigs disaster, the Kennedy administration reassessed its approach to Cuba, and while the strategy of another invasion was not abandoned, it was agreed there was an urgent, practical need to get oppositionists out of Cuba. Therefore, the National Security Council meeting of 5 May 1961 decided that all Cuban nationals entering the United States would be given refugee status.[92] Bishop Coleman Carroll of the Catholic Diocese of Miami put an even more radical proposal to the Senate Subcommittee on Cuban refugees, suggesting that "airlines should be permitted to board [all] passengers in Havana for the United States without visa waivers or visas."[93]

A concession was made by the State Department in September 1961, when it was agreed that any Cuban child could apply for visa waivers for their parents, and that is what many of them did.[94] This meant the visa waiver system became a means by which families wanting to leave Cuba could send their children out as "students" and subsequently come themselves on visa waivers initiated by their children.[95] Thus, although the visa waiver system for unaccompanied children was not originally intended to fulfill this purpose, it soon became a means of facilitating the emigration of Cuban families, which no doubt proved to be an added stimulus to

Operation Pedro Pan, especially for those Cubans who had no other relatives already in the United States.[96] This was confirmed by Robert Hale of the State Department's visa section in his testimony to the Senate Subcommittee hearings on Cuban refugees.[97]

Msgr. Walsh saw this as an "unforeseen outcome" of Operation Pedro Pan, insofar as it opened the door for tens of thousands of Cubans to come to the United States when the Freedom Flights began on 1 December 1965.[98] And he was proud of the part he claimed to have played in the Cuban Adjustment Act (1966) that fast-tracked Cubans' residency status in the United States.[99] The Cuban government, on the other hand, argued that this and other U.S. legislation served to encourage illegal and dangerous emigration from the island.[100] This preferential immigration policy for Cubans was only partially rescinded in the last days of the Obama administration.[101]

Msgr. Walsh also took some credit for the family reunifications that occurred in December 1962 as a result of the exchange negotiated between Washington and Havana for the release of members of Brigade 2506, who had been captured during the Bay of Pigs invasion.[102] A significant State Department memo, written after the 1962 Missile Crisis had cut off all commercial air traffic between the United States and Cuba, noted the humanitarian benefits of restoring flights, as the Cuban government had proposed, but concluded "it was more important to isolate Castro's regime" than to allow the flights to resume.[103] At that point, there were 4,100 children in care in the United States, and most of these had to wait at least another three years to be reunited with their parents.[104]

It can hardly have been considered an ideal emigration arrangement for children to be sent abroad in advance of their parents, given the trauma and uncertainty experienced by any child in such circumstances, especially when there was no guarantee when or if parents would be able to leave. Torres believed most parents who wanted to leave Cuba, if "given the opportunity to travel with their children, would have chosen to leave together; however, this was not an option."[105] But many parents were still convinced the separation would only be a matter of months, and they might not have been ready to emigrate as a family, which meant they would forfeit all their assets and property in Cuba if they did not return within three months, as one mother explained.[106] Because of this, some parents chose to stay in Cuba in the hope of "riding out the storm."[107]

In reality, the visa waiver system adopted for Cubans was "a legal fiction" created for those who wanted to escape "Cuban Communism."[108]

Immigration authorities at Miami airport were instructed to admit minors arriving with what must have appeared to be rather suspect paperwork, often simply copies of letters with Fr. Walsh's signature. Some commentators have suggested this might have represented a violation of U.S. immigration laws, pointing out: "At no other time in the history of the United States were so many people allowed to circumvent established U.S. immigration procedures. It was not only extraordinary that a private individual was given authority to fulfil sensitive governmental function, but that the constitutionally mandated and clearly demarcated separation between church and state was ignored."[109] The U.S. government apparently even went as far as actually paying for the transport costs to the United States of adult Cuban refugees, not just children, for those who had visas issued prior to July 1961; this free airlift cost the U.S. government $350,000.[110]

Pedro Pan as an Anti-Castro Activist

Some of the children entrusted to the care of the Catholic Welfare Bureau were themselves anti-Castro activists, including those who had been active in Catholic youth groups like Mario A. Martínez-Malo, who recalled: "I knew about the training camps [for the Bay of Pigs] because I had been educated at Belén [College]. Most *Belemitas* at the university were closely associated with the Catholic University Association [ACU], . . . [which] provided many of the original [invasion] Brigade members [including its leader Manuel Artime]."[111]

Msgr. Walsh readily admitted "a certain number" of parents were active opponents of Fidel Castro, but he also explained that some parents were concerned about their children's political involvement, which they feared might "get the whole family into trouble."[112] He said his agency found they had to deal with "two types" of political Pedro Pans: those who had joined revolutionary youth groups and who were showing what he described as "the first effects of [government] indoctrination"; and others, who had been actively involved in anti-Castro activities through organizations such as Young Catholic Workers and Young Catholic Students. Both types, said Msgr. Walsh, "presented with special problems due to their anger against their parents for having shipped them to Miami."[113] No doubt conflicts arose between the two groups as well, but Walsh was known to run a tight ship, with liberal use of the *paleta* (a wooden paddle) he kept on hand at all times.[114]

There can be no question, as already shown, that Cuban youth were highly politicized; some were already veterans of the fight against Batista, while others were drawn into political activism encouraged by the government. Other young Cubans were equally fervent in their opposition to Fidel. CIA operative Howard Hunt praised the extensive sabotage actions carried out by "student" members of the Revolutionary Student Directorate (DRE) prior to the Bay of Pigs.[115] This meant the CIA clearly had "operational interests" in spiriting those young activists out of Cuba if they were identified by the authorities.[116]

One émigré stated categorically that "kids [were sent] out of the country to prevent them from getting involved in things," and anecdotal evidence seems to support this view.[117] Berta Álvarez and her younger brother found themselves on opposite sides of the political divide in revolutionary Cuba. While she had organized student strikes against Batista at her convent school, her younger brother was influenced by the conservative political views of the priests at his Catholic college. After the revolution, Berta totally immersed herself in revolutionary political activity, while her brother, who was still at school, joined the anti-Castro movement. Berta's parents then decided to send her brother and younger sister to Miami with Operation Pedro Pan without telling her—a tragic blow for Berta.[118] Silvia Ríos's parents, too, sent her younger brother to Miami after he was encouraged by the Marist brothers at his college to participate in propaganda activities against the government.[119]

Nelson Valdés has offered another example of the high degree of political consciousness among many of the Pedro Pans. At the time of the Bay of Pigs invasion, Valdés had just arrived in Miami as a Pedro Pan and was living in Kendall, a camp for Cuban child refugees on the outskirts of the city. When the house parents (the Prunas) abandoned the camp, after learning that their son (part of the invading Brigade 2506) had been captured by the Cuban forces, the Pedro Pans took matters into their own hands and staged a riot to demand U.S. intervention in Cuba. Led by a sixteen-year-old dubbed "El Paranóico" by his fellow Pedro Pans, some of the boys stole horses from nearby ranches and galloped off into town. In response to Fr. Walsh's attempt to restore order, some of the teenagers went on a hunger strike. Furious, Walsh shouted at them in English that they were "not supposed to bite the hand that fed them" and threatened that any child who did not behave would be "sent back to the Communists."[120]

Despite the frequent depiction of Pedro Pans as young children or even babies, the vast majority of them were teenage boys. It seems to be the case that parents often sent their older children to Miami while keeping younger ones with them.[121] Here it is worth noting the gender imbalance between the Pedro Pans and the literacy campaign *brigadistas*, the majority of the latter being female. Is this because boys were viewed as more likely to be engaged in political activity (either for or against the revolutionary government) and therefore perceived as more at risk? There is, however, plenty of evidence of girls, like the Mendieta sisters, who were emulating their father's opposition to the revolution. Or did it reflect a more protective attitude toward daughters? On the other hand, the predominance of girls among the *brigadistas* might indicate that teaching was regarded as an acceptable female occupation. Considering the overprotection of daughters in more affluent Cuban families, it is somewhat ironic that Valentín Díaz made an instant decision to send his two daughters on their own to Miami as Pedro Pans when his eldest girl arrived home from school saying she was being sent to the countryside.[122]

Unfortunately, without more evidence in the form of interviews with the parents of Pedro Pans (most of whom would by now be extremely elderly or deceased), this can only be speculation. What is clear is that most (but not all) of the Pedro Pans came from more privileged Cuban families and had attended schools run by either the church or other private educational institutions, as Msgr. Walsh explained.[123] Certainly, some children from poorer families, and even some orphans, were sent to the United States with Operation Pedro Pan. But generally those involved with caring for the Cuban children in the United States observed that their charges were the "sons and daughters of once 'comfortably off' middle-class families." While commended for their good, although rowdy, behavior and their remarkably easy adjustment to their new situation, the Pedro Pans provoked some criticism for their determined resistance to helping with household chores, as one report noted: "The greatest source of trouble has come from the fact that many of the youngsters had been waited on by servants all their lives. Some children have been genuinely shocked when asked to take out the garbage or even to pick up their clothes."[124]

Sr. Miriam Strong, who had worked at the Catholic Hispanic Center in Miami, reported many Pedro Pans experienced a culture shock on arrival at their foster homes, because many had never seen a bed being made or "known anyone other than the hired cook to do the dishes, [and] had never imagined middle-class teenagers could think about carrying out the trash."

"Their mothers," she explained, "had not worked and [the children] had never considered that they might take jobs themselves, such as paper boys or delivery boys."[125]

How the young refugees adjusted to the experience of separation from their families and the hardships many of them had to endure might also be explained by the fact that it was usually their parents' decision, most often their fathers,' to send them to Miami. That is not to say teenage Pedro Pans had had no say in the matter or even that they were not excited at the prospect of a visit to the United States; but it was generally not their decision. In the case of the young literacy campaign volunteers, there may have been considerable pressure from peers or others, but no one went against their will. Anecdotal evidence shows that some defied their parents in signing up as *brigadistas*, while others retained a deep resentment against their parents for preventing their participation.

Pedro Pans like Nelson Valdés, who came from less prosperous families, apparently found themselves discriminated against in Miami; the rich kids, he said, went to the smaller foster homes, such as St. Raphael's, where Fr. Walsh lived with about eighty teenage boys, while the rest were sent to the camps before being transferred to foster homes or institutions all over the country.[126] One boy wrote to then Msgr. Walsh from the camp at Opa Locka, complaining about the terrible conditions there and feeling betrayed by promises made to him when he was transferred from St. Raphael's.[127] The wealthier children often attended Catholic colleges as scholarship students, while others were sent to local high schools.[128] Even so, some of the Pedro Pans from privileged backgrounds like Carlos Eire were shocked to find themselves targets of racial abuse and labeled "dumb shit spics" on arrival in the United States, and queried about the color of their skin, due to the general identification of Cubans with blackness.[129]

The Lure of the *"Beca"*

While the *patria potestad* hoax was a clear factor prompting parents to consider sending their children out of Cuba, some less prosperous parents were evidently lured by the perceived opportunity for their children to obtain what were referred to as *"becas"* (scholarships) to study in the United States. For Cuban children, study in the United States was highly advantageous but not something everyone could afford. As the wheels of Operation Pedro Pan were being set in motion in November 1960, *Bohemia* reported that

Havana's exclusive Catholic Villanueva University was offering Cubans the chance to study in the United States, apparently paid for by the State Department. Moreover, some young Cubans already studying in the United States, like the fifty girls who arrived in October 1960 to attend the Ursuline Sisters' school in New Orleans, eventually ended up in the care of the Catholic Welfare Bureau.[130] Thus, even before Operation Pedro Pan took flight, schemes were in place bringing young Cubans to the United States on student visas. This no doubt explains why the departures of the Pedro Pans failed to attract any special attention from the Cuban government.

One Pedro Pan suggested that parents readily "swallowed" what the priests and U.S. propaganda were saying because "it was an opportunity to go to the United States—heck—and with all expenses paid!" Besides, he added, parents were "happy to think their kids wouldn't be around if there was bloodshed. And maybe it wouldn't be for too long."[131] Ana Riewerts recalled urging both her divorced parents to send her to the United States, fully expecting she would be attending an exclusive private school after her Catholic college in Cuba was shut down. At thirteen, she was already politically active, distributing anti-Castro propaganda.[132]

The August 1961 currency exchange and tightening economic measures imposed by the Cuban government no doubt meant it was increasingly difficult for families to pay school fees for children already studying in the United States.[133] Early in the program, Fr. Walsh became aware that some Cuban students were returning home because no one could pay their tuition.[134] By sending their children back to the United States with Operation Pedro Pan, parents were relieved of the necessity to find dollars to pay for their schooling there. This is precisely what Román de la Campa's parents did in order to save money for the emigration of the entire family.[135]

One study of refugee children acknowledged the factor of "perceived opportunities" as a cause of family separations in situations such as Operation Pedro Pan that were "not directly related to threats of survival," finding that very few of the Cuban children experienced "impulsive" separations from their families and that children's departures were usually planned over some months. It was more the case that parents chose to spare their children "hardship" or remove them from "environments [they] believed to be morally harmful." The very existence of the special programs for unaccompanied Cuban children, the study concluded, "may have had a 'magnet effect' which actually cause[d] more separations" than would have otherwise occurred. The study also contrasted the special program for the Pedro Pans to the lack of such programs for the large number of Cuban teenage boys who arrived in the later Mariel exodus in 1980—children whom they argued were at far greater risk than the Pedro Pans.[136]

Thus, those who regard Operation Pedro Pan through the conspiracy lens alone, or alternatively as a desperate act by desperate parents, have overlooked this aspect of its irresistible attraction as a chance for parents to secure their children's future, especially to those Cuban families who were dismayed at the social turmoil of the revolution and who believed it was a temporary measure until the old order was restored. This was the promise of Pedro Pan—an operation that might well have been named for another children's story, *The Pied Piper of Hamelin*.

By the time President Kennedy issued a press statement about the Cuban Refugee Program on 3 February 1961, highlighting the special program for children, whom he described emotively as "the most defenseless and troubled group among the refugee population," Fr. Walsh had reported to U.S. DHEW secretary Abraham Ribicoff that in a little over one month, 174 unaccompanied minors had arrived, of whom 53 had been claimed by relatives or friends; the rest (121, along with 15 children who were already in Miami) were taken into the care of the Catholic Welfare Bureau or other agencies.[137] The situation was considered urgent, however, because it was said that the 200 children on James Baker's original list were ready to leave Cuba, and hundreds more would be on their way by the end of the month.[138]

Francisco (Pancho) Finlay (general manager for KLM airlines in Cuba) and his wife, Berta (a teacher at Ruston Academy), had already been dispatching children from Cuba during 1960, but the official start date of Operation Pedro Pan is usually acknowledged as 26 December 1960, when the first two children, the Aquino siblings, arrived in Miami and were taken into Fr. Walsh's care.[139] Vivian and Sixto Aquino had been taught by a British national, Penny Powers, at the elite Ruston Academy in Havana, and it was Powers who apparently suggested that they should be sent to Miami because they had been actively engaged in antigovernment activities.[140] The family had already come to the attention of Cuban authorities when the mother was briefly detained in Cuba on her return from a trip to the United States, accused of carrying a bomb in cartons of cigarettes.[141]

What distinguished Operation Pedro Pan from earlier arrivals of unaccompanied children was the simultaneous creation of the Cuban Children's Program. Although only about half of those children arriving in Miami as part of Operation Pedro Pan actually required foster care—the rest were claimed by family friends or relatives already in the United States—in reality, Operation Pedro Pan owed its existence to the Cuban Children's Program. Without the means to care for the young refugees, the idea of bringing so many children to the United States would have been totally impractical.

The real inducement offered to parents by the Cuban Children's Program is evident in a letter sent in February 1962 from two Cubans appealing to a former U.S. employer for assistance with their niece's airfare:

> A sister of ours has a daughter, twelve years old, whom the present regime forces to attend their schools of communist indoctrination, a system which is against her religious feelings. In order to spare their daughter this sacrifice, they want to take her out of the country. However, lacking the means and friends in the United States who could take charge of her, they wrote to the Spanish Catholic Center in Miami, about which they had been told that they helped Cuban children, giving them an education as well as the means to come to the United States, and, as a matter of fact, they immediately sent her parents the visa waiver for the girl, but not the passage money to Miami, and neither the parents nor we have any way of obtaining the dollars which the authorities insist on. It is for this reason that we come to you asking to send us a money order for $25—in the name of the girl, whose name is [DELETED].[142]

Msgr. Walsh usually insisted that the two programs—the evacuation of young Cubans from the island and the foster-care program in the United States—were different things, and he argued that he and other organizers had no way of influencing or encouraging parents to send their children out of the country. Nevertheless, he was always happy to take credit for both programs. Even before they took their first child into care, Fr. Walsh's project had already been transformed from being a welfare program into what became the Operation Pedro Pan airlift. Walsh even confessed they waited to see how many children would come from Cuba before taking responsibility for homeless kids already in Miami. "We knew only too well," he said "that as soon as word got out in Miami that we were taking children under care we would be inundated with requests." And that is precisely what happened. By the time funds did start flowing from Washington to Miami, Fr. Walsh's tiny agency had already assumed a debt of $100,000 for the Cuban Children's Program.[143] Walsh certainly must have been convinced not only of the righteousness of his cause, but also of its financial viability with support assured from the federal government.

It is also clear, however, that without Operation Pedro Pan, the Cuban Children's Program would never have grown to the size it did. It was a win/win situation for Fr. Walsh—the rescue mission would supply the numbers to justify the Cuban Children's Program funds and significantly expand and stabilize the services provided by the Catholic Welfare Bureau, as well as earn him credit in Washington (and Rome—he was promoted to monsignor in 1962) for saving innocent children from the clutches of "atheistic communism."

There is some evidence of Operation Pedro Pan and the Cuban Children's Program being used by parents simply to place children for safekeeping while they got on their feet in the new country. The mother of Carlos Muñiz and his older sister, Míriam, was on the same flight to Miami as her children but, as a single parent, she was not confident she would be able to care for her children immediately. So the children were instructed to pretend they had traveled from Cuba alone to ensure they would be taken into care—which is what happened.[144] Eloísa Echazábal's father arrived in Miami the day before she did; but it was decided that Eloísa and her younger sister should stay at Camp Kendall because their father had no job and was staying in a single, small room. Transferred to an orphanage in Buffalo, New York, and then to a Catholic-run orphanage, the sisters were reunited with their parents some nine months later.[145] How many similar cases might exist of Pedro Pans being placed in care while their parents established themselves in the new country can only be speculated.

The Role of the Catholic Church

There appears to be no question that a significant number of Catholic clergy participated in, or at least supported, the anti-Castro underground in activities ranging from propaganda to sabotage operations to armed actions. The cover of a contemporary pamphlet titled *Nuestra Postura*, published by the Democratic Christian Movement (MDC) of Cuba, shows an armed man bearing an automatic weapon above his head.[146] Some commentators have heaped praise on the "outstanding role" the churches and religious sects played in the anti-Castro struggle, explaining how in one instance the November 30 Movement used the cellar of a church to hide more than a ton of explosives. Some priests actually joined the underground movement as armed combatants; the Revolutionary Student Directorate (DRE), in particular, attracted hundreds of young Catholics to its ranks.[147]

The prominence in the Bay of Pigs invasion brigade of ACU leaders such as Manuel Artime, along with priests like Fr. Ismael de Lugo, who had fought for General Franco in Spain, certainly did nothing to alleviate the rising antagonism between the church and the revolutionary government.[148] When the Bay of Pigs invasion was proclaimed to be a "struggle . . . of those who believe in God against the atheists," Fidel Castro denounced the church as the "fifth column of the counterrevolution."[149] On May Day 1961, the Cuban leader did not mince his words, accusing the religious colleges of "poisoning the minds of Cuban youth" and announcing that the residency permits of all foreign priests would be revoked, eliciting a great cheer from the assembled masses.[150] The rector of Havana's San Carlos seminary, Fr. Carlos Manuel de Céspedes, later reflected: "Everything happened very fast. Fidel had admitted that our Revolution was a Marxist one . . . and those who solidly back[ed] the Revolution looked on Catholics as their sworn enemies. For their part, Catholics felt the same: it was a Communist Revolution, hence intrinsically bad. You had to fight it or flee."[151]

Was this counterrevolutionary activity of individual priests conducted without their superiors' knowledge or approval? When two European journalists interviewed Msgr. Agustín Román, who had been expelled from Cuba in 1961, and pressed him without success for a statement about the church's support for the anti-Castro underground, they were given a church document that described Operation Pedro Pan as "a notable example of the fruits obtained thanks to the willingness and organization of civil society on the island and to the human and ecclesiastical solidarity abroad." This same document also explained that the operation was "done through a network of people on the island, the Catholic church and the U.S. government." All the monsignor would say to the journalists, however, was: "It is enough for a priest to show the way to the Kingdom of God."[152]

It would appear that key sectors of the Catholic church did far more than to "show the way to the Kingdom of God" to the faithful: first, by promoting the scare campaign about parental authority, thereby helping to create the psychological and political conditions for the exodus; and then, by assisting the departures of the children that the propaganda campaign provoked. The Cuban report on Operation Pedro Pan accused the Catholic church in both Miami and Cuba of direct responsibility for Operation Pedro Pan, pointing out that it had provided "the necessary cadres connecting the networks of the CIA and the counterrevolutionary organizations."[153]

Considerable anecdotal evidence demonstrates the key role of Catholic clergy in the distribution of the Pedro Pans' visa waivers and churches as centers for the distribution and collection of passports.[154] Alex López, a Pedro Pan, remembered that parents like his gave their children's names for Operation Pedro Pan in the local parish church office in Matanzas.[155] Many other researchers provide substantial evidence of the involvement of the church in the exodus, but try to distinguish between the participation of individual members of the clergy and the church as a whole.[156] The official history of the exodus, according to the website of Operation Pedro Pan, Inc., states: "At no time was the Catholic Church as an institution in Cuba involved . . . [but] individual priests and religious did seek and receive visa waivers." But the same website also states that Pedro Pan was "a program created by the Catholic Welfare Bureau (Catholic Charities) of Miami in December 1960."[157]

Despite the official Pedro Pan group's categorical statement that the Catholic Welfare Bureau "had no means of influencing Cuban parents to send their children to the United States," and that this "was not its role or mission," the Cuban community in the United States has persistently made reference to "the church's heroic effort to rescue children in Operation Pedro Pan."[158] Furthermore, like Msgr. Román, the Catholic Diocese of Miami has continued to express pride in the scheme as one of its greatest achievements.[159] Msgr. Walsh specifically stated that the Catholic Welfare Bureau "administered *both programs*"—that is, the Cuban Children's Program and Operation Pedro Pan—with the blessing of the Miami diocese.[160] The monsignor was fond of recounting his conversation with Bishop Coleman Carroll after he had taken upon himself responsibility for the first two hundred Pedro Pans. Instead of chastising him as he feared, the bishop apparently asked why Fr. Walsh had agreed to accept only two hundred.[161]

It could be argued that these contradictory statements arise because over time the evacuation operation has become popularly identified or thoroughly confused with the Catholic Welfare Bureau's Cuban Children's Program. But the Catholic church also may not want to be identified with some of the murkier aspects of the anti-Castro struggle. Besides, the rift between the revolutionary government and the Cuban church healed remarkably quickly. The year following the 1961 expulsions from the island of over one hundred Catholic clergy, a "new era" opened for the Cuban church with the arrival of a couple of dozen new Cuban and foreign priests.[162]

When Bryan Walsh (by then a monsignor) visited Cuba to attend the funeral of Cardinal Arteaga Betancourt in March 1963, he was struck by the number of young seminarians present, as he had understood that the seminary had been shut down. He also met with the new papal nuncio and several bishops, including Archbishops Pérez Serantes and Alfredo Müller San Martín, who had both been outspoken opponents of the revolutionary government, but who had remained in Cuba.[163] Bishop Müller had exercised considerable political influence over the priests and Catholic youth of Cienfuegos and had actively encouraged families to send their children out of the country; his nephew Alberto was a leader of the counterrevolutionary group the DRE.[164]

In a private conversation, Archbishop Pérez Serantes told Msgr. Walsh the church was "better supported than ever before" because, with the departure of the rich, those religious Cubans who remained were "more generous." Msgr. Walsh also recorded that the archbishop said the church was "much to blame for the past, [and] that a renovation of spirit was needed among the clergy—more humility and more effort." Msgr. Walsh did note, however, that the papal nuncio, Msgr. Sacchi, mentioned that a Cuban and three Spanish priests remained in prison; but apparently they were about to be released.[165] This story suggests that the revolutionary government was far more tolerant of the church after the expulsion of the shipload of clergy in September 1961. The Vatican had condemned the expulsions, but it failed to excommunicate the leaders of the revolutionary government as the Cuban hierarchy had demanded.[166]

Subsequently, with only about two hundred clergy left on the island, Pope John XXIII urged the Cuban hierarchy "to abandon its impractical strategy of confrontation along with its short-sighted policy of counseling Catholics to leave Cuba."[167] In January 1962, the Cuban government appointed a new ambassador to the Papal Court, and within a decade, during his visit to Chile, and in the context of the rising tide of liberation theology, Fidel Castro was raising the idea of a strategic alliance between Christians and Marxists.[168]

In the years before his death in 2016, the Cuban leader hesitated to accuse the Catholic church as an institution of responsibility for Operation Pedro Pan, saying "one of the saddest things about it" was the involvement of some clergy, both in Cuba and Miami, but he said it was something the government did not want to "look into too closely." He insisted Cuba did not blame Rome or the Catholic church because many Catholics were good revolutionaries. Those who engaged in counterrevolutionary activities in Cuba, he said, were indeed sent to prison, but no priest was ever executed, contrasting the experiences in the Mexican and French revolutions and the Civil War in Spain.[169]

Some of those who had assisted the children's departures, such as Fr. Francisco ("Panchito") Ortiz, who became a respected figure in the diocese of Cienfuegos, later came to believe the operation "cast a tremendous shadow over the history of the church, due to the participation of religious people." Fr. Ortiz decided he and others should "ask the Cuban people for forgiveness for the pain and suffering" they helped cause through Operation Pedro Pan.[170] This, the Cuban report suggested, is one reason why the Catholic church as an institution has sometimes wanted to distance itself from the operation, especially in Cuba, where the exodus is viewed very negatively.[171]

It is also possible that the Catholic hierarchy adopted the CIA's protocol of "plausible denial." After all, as a former Pedro Pan remarked, "the church has had 2,000 years of conspiratorial experience."[172] Was Fr. Walsh, then just an ordinary priest, chosen to authorize the children's visa waivers rather than his bishop or other superiors in order to obscure the church's direct hand in the scheme? As with all such clandestine operations, it is highly unlikely that an official document or article will ever be found that states categorically that the Catholic church was urging parents to send their children out of Cuba, although church leaders were reportedly "counsel[ing] exile to their flocks" at the time.[173] The Cuban report included the testimony of a former double agent, "David," who was a twelve-year-old student at La Salle College in 1961 when one of the priests, Fr. Raúl Martínez González, tried to convince him of "the dangers of communism" and advised him to leave the country. Fr. Martínez was later identified as part of Ramón Grau's underground network in the parish of Sta. María del Rosario.[174] Two Marist brothers showed up at Sonia Almazán's home to convince her parents to send her younger brother to Miami, where they promised he would receive the same quality of private schooling he had been receiving in Cuba; but her parents told them that the family would leave together or not at all.[175]

With the 1961 nationalization of education, most of the religious who had taught at Catholic private schools left Cuba—voluntarily or otherwise.

Some of Cuba's most prestigious Catholic colleges, such as La Salle, relocated to Miami within months of the nationalization and were ready to commence the new school year in September 1961. It is quite probable that many Pedro Pans simply followed their teachers and their schools to Miami. Many priests and nuns, formerly living in Cuba, were immediately employed in the various homes and camps caring for Pedro Pans, as well as in Miami's parochial schools.

Thus, practicing what they preached, the vast majority of Catholic clergy and laity became émigrés themselves, assisted by a special program run by the Miami diocese.[176] This meant that the resistance began to lose one of its main points of support.[177] On the other hand, the arrival of thousands of Cuban Catholics brought tremendous benefits to the Catholic church in south Florida.[178] Addressing the Southeastern Regional Meeting of the National Conference of Catholic Charities in March 1962, Fr. Walsh announced with confidence: "The Church in the South is on the move . . . [and] is beginning to come out of the ghetto."[179]

From the start, the Catholic church was eager not only to have its part in establishing the Cuban Children's Program acknowledged but to make sure it was publicized as widely as possible, as donations began to flow into the church's coffers. In the last months of 1960, the Catholic Welfare Bureau was facing a 30 percent cut in its already extremely tight budget. Msgr. Walsh was astute enough to see the opportunities presented by the tide of refugees from Cuba. Within a few years, his tiny agency expanded from a small staff to a vast organization with an annual budget of millions of dollars offering services to tens of thousands.[180]

Msgr. Walsh later confessed that the Cuban refugees had "bestowed benefits on Miami that far outweigh[ed] any inconveniences or aggravations," attracting $195 million in federal aid. He also mentioned that 5,000 Cuban children were enrolled in local Catholic schools—an obvious boon for the church.[181] The benefits flowing to the Catholic church from Msgr. Walsh's work were highlighted at a dinner in his honor in Miami in May 1994.[182] By the time he retired in 1996, the Catholic Charities' budget had grown from $100,000 with a staff of eleven to $60 million with 421 staff. This was possible "thanks to Operation Pedro Pan," the Miami press reported.[183]

Fr. Walsh's prominence as director of the Cuban Children's Program was no doubt a factor in his promotion in late 1962 to monsignor—the youngest ever appointment to that office. Walsh himself acknowledged that the "payoff" for the Catholic Welfare Bureau was that it gave them "a very high

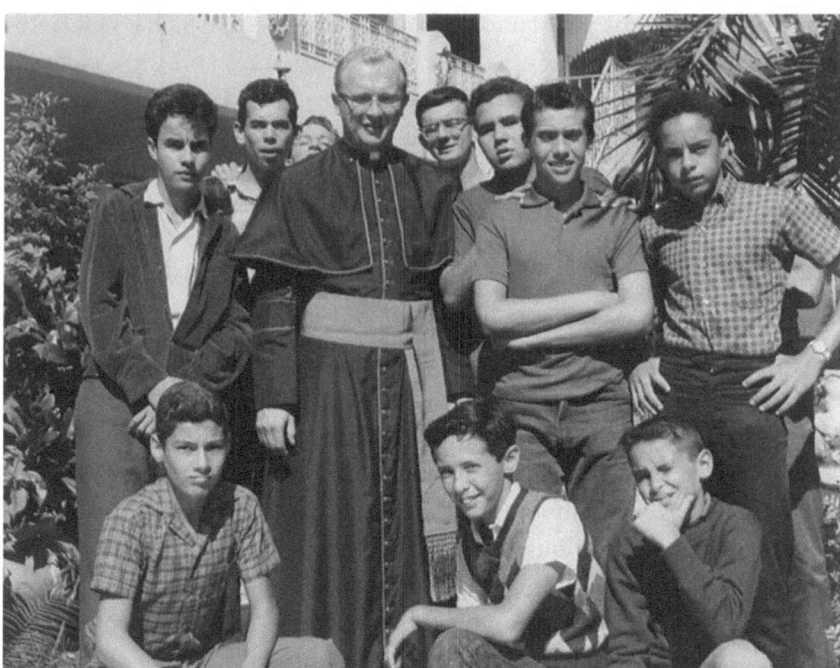

Figure 4.2. Fr. Bryan Walsh with Pedro Pans at St. Raphael's home. Courtesy of Barry University Archives and Special Collections, Miami Shores, Florida.

profile and . . . proved a valuable experience when [President Lyndon B.] Johnson's War on Poverty program was initiated." He also pointed out that his was the first agency under religious auspices to get a contract under that program.[184] Possibly President Kennedy's Catholic faith helped break down barriers to such federal aid to Catholic welfare agencies, establishing an unprecedented relationship between government and private and religious refugee organizations.

All the factors discussed above—parents' concerns about the supposed indoctrination of their children, the opportunity presented to Cuban families for *becas* in the United States, the demands of the anti-Castro underground movement, and Washington's political strategy—became concentrated and intensified after the debacle at the Bay of Pigs in April 1961. The momentum already building behind Operation Pedro Pan now became irresistible.

A Brigade 2506 Bay of Pigs veteran turned sociology professor observed that the failure of the "American-sponsored invasion" at the Bay of Pigs was "probably the most important factor in determining Castro's consolidation of power." By mid-1961, he recalled, "greater despair and frustration seized large numbers of Cubans who were disenchanted by the regime and whose only hope lay in escape from the island as quickly as possible."[185] In a private meeting with U.S. special envoy Richard Goodwin during an Organization of American States conference in Punta del Este in August 1961, Che Guevara made a point of thanking the U.S. government for the invasion because it had proved to be a "great political victory" for Cuba, uniting the Cuban people behind the revolution.[186]

Thus, the Bay of Pigs marked a watershed in the direction and tempo of the revolution. Within weeks Fidel Castro had pronounced the socialist character of the revolution; the education system was nationalized, and schools were closed for the literacy campaign; the first of the hundred thousand literacy *brigadistas* were mobilized; and the government announced the expulsion of all foreign priests from the island. By this time, a Pedro Pan remembered everyone saying: "'Communism is next. It [will be] the state control over the youth; taking away parental authority at home; state control over schools....' [Then] once the Bay of Pigs was over and Fidel Castro had declared the revolution Marxist-Leninist, there was no doubt. All the suspicions people had [held about the direction of the revolution] became a reality.... And panic spread."[187]

Parents' fears for their children were "very real," said a Cuban émigré in Miami. They "were more afraid about what was going to happen in Cuba at that moment than what might happen to them outside. They thought that they were saving their children. How else can you understand it? How could a parent send their children away alone?" he asked. "They thought the church would protect them and put them somewhere they would be safe," said his partner Silvia.[188]

Did Washington have a clear-cut strategy to frighten parents into sending their children out of Cuba, or was the intention just to create instability and undermine support for the revolutionary government, especially among the middle class? There certainly seems to be no basis for the argument that the Cuban children were in comparable danger to that faced by Jewish children in Nazi-occupied Europe or by children caught in the midst of other wars, civil strife, or ethnic conflicts. While admitting the Cuban government never passed a law eliminating *patria potestad*, James Baker insisted that Operation Pedro Pan was trying to save children from something far worse: "We were trying to help them escape from communist indoctrination," he said.[189]

"They were teaching us Marxism in school," remarked playwright Eduardo Machado, a Pedro Pan, "but my parents treated it like they were gassing us."[190] The founder of the Pedro Pan support group, Ely Chovel, also expressed some skepticism about whether the Pedro Pan children faced any serious threat in revolutionary Cuba, commenting: "That's Hollywood."[191] The exception to this, of course, were those young Cubans actually engaged in counterrevolutionary actions such as sabotage, armed resistance, or even terrorist acts against the Cuban government—as some clearly were.[192]

As discussed in earlier chapters, the social revolution under way in Cuba challenged the privileged lifestyle, value systems, and, to some extent, the religious beliefs of upper- and middle-class Cubans. But whether this justified the mass airlift of unaccompanied children to face the subsequent traumas of emigration and lonely exile in the United States is another matter. This is the "history of a crime," a Cuban diplomat insisted. "Who is the guilty side?" he asked. "Not the parents. The guilty ones were those who consciously played on parents' fears. Many parents later repented their decision, realizing they were wrong. Of course, everyone thought it would be only a temporary separation."[193]

"People always want to take care of their own," commented Noel Betancourt, an early Pedro Pan who eventually returned to live in Cuba. "The rich wanted to look after their children. The CIA wanted to take care of its own. The Catholic church had its own interests." On the other hand, he said, "this situation was taken advantage of by political forces who wanted to create a sense of chaos and disorder so as to weaken the support of those who really benefited from the revolution."[194]

Thus, Operation Pedro Pan can be understood as arising from the entanglement of many distinct threads. The *patria potestad* scare promoted by the CIA and the Catholic church reflected a Cold War mind-set and fed parental anxieties. But far from being overcome by panic, some families saw the Cuban Children's Program as an unprecedented opportunity for their offspring to study in the North. For Washington, Operation Pedro Pan served as an inducement to keep underground operatives active on the ground in Cuba and a quick, secure exit for young anti-Castro activists, while demonstrating U.S. concern for the plight of the latest refugees from communism. Consequently, once these elements converged, within a very short space of time, Operation Pedro Pan became practically and politically an effective cover, as well as an instrument, for those working against the Cuban revolution. What becomes apparent, however, is that the greatest value of Operation Pedro Pan was its function not just as a cover for the "other activities" of counterrevolutionaries on the island but as part of Washington's psychological warfare being conducted against the Cuban revolution—in Cuba, in the United States, and internationally.

5

The Dark Side of Neverland

Some scholars have argued that after the April 1961 Bay of Pigs debacle, the CIA "lost interest" in the children's exodus and disengaged itself from Operation Pedro Pan because it no longer served a purpose in the effort to overthrow Fidel Castro.[1] Others have proposed that the CIA only became involved at this time.[2] The evidence shows that the CIA interest in Operation Pedro Pan did not wane after the failed invasion, but, on the contrary, the evacuation scheme for Cuban minors was stepped up and became thoroughly entwined with the counterrevolutionary movement.[3]

At the time, the CIA noted with frank dismay that Castro had been "significantly strengthened" by the attempted invasion.[4] Letters written from Cuba to friends and relatives in this period reflect a disillusionment and desperation among those wanting to leave: "It is a cruel decision," wrote one man from Havana, "for it means leaving Mother and my brothers behind. But my daughter is a great responsibility and I have to get out of the country as soon as possible."[5]

From James Baker's initial estimate of 200 young Cubans requiring student visas in December 1960, the number quickly grew to 510.[6] By mid-April 1961, 657 Cuban children had already arrived in Miami under the program.[7] Within a year, another 7,000 reached the United States, about half of whom were taken into the care of the Catholic Welfare Bureau and other child welfare agencies.[8] When the Missile Crisis halted flights between Cuba and the United States in October 1962, there had been a further 6,270 arrivals, bringing the total number of Pedro Pans to 14,048.[9] In fact, the peak of over 200 arrivals a week was reached just a few months after the Bay of Pigs, in mid-1961.[10]

By September 1962, 19,000 Cuban children were enrolled in Miami-Dade public schools (representing about 10 percent of total enrollments in the area); and 4,300 were in the care of various agencies around the United States.[11] Some officials in the U.S. Department of Health, Education, and Welfare (DHEW), which was responsible for the Cuban Refugee Children's program, might well have breathed a sigh of relief when the seemingly endless flow of young Cubans from the island ceased the following month.

Thus, Operation Pedro Pan expanded dramatically at the precise moment when the revolutionary government seemed to be more secure, and therefore the expected period of separation of the young Cubans from their families was less finite. Why this might have been the case can be explained by several factors. First, despite repeated denials by the Cuban government, the *patria potestad* scare was revived and spread by Polita Grau's anti-Castro group Rescate.[12] Second, relations between the revolutionary government and the Catholic church hierarchy reached their lowest point, leading to the expulsion of over one hundred priests in September 1961. Third, when most private schools were nationalized on 1 June 1961 and all schools were closed for the second semester of 1961 to encourage teachers and students to join the literacy campaign, thousands of teenagers were out of school. Fourteen-year-old María regarded this as an "extended holiday," but middle-class parents no doubt became anxious about their children falling behind in their schooling.[13] Finally, as discussed above, the literacy campaign itself was interpreted by the counterrevolutionary movement as a mass indoctrination effort that was using young Cubans as its shock troops as well as its target.

Operation Mongoose

The day after the April invasion was decisively defeated, President Kennedy pledged to "intensify efforts" against Castro.[14] Fidel Castro was now Kennedy's personal enemy and no longer one "inherited from Eisenhower." Subsequently, getting rid of Castro became almost an obsession with the Kennedy brothers and some CIA officials in their "desire to get even."[15] The White House was now enveloped in "white heat" over the Castro issue, and a new version of the Cuba Project was proposed, which, according to former CIA director Richard Bissell, "bore a remarkable resemblance to the CIA's original plan for the Bay of Pigs," a plan he had overseen.[16]

Fidel Castro had good reason to feel "under siege," wrote Kennedy's special assistant Arthur Schlesinger: "Even if double agents had not told him the CIA was trying to kill him, the Mongoose campaign left little doubt that the American government was trying to overthrow him."[17] "We are at war with Cuba," said a CIA official.[18] The proximity of Cuba to the United States that had once involved intimacy and neighborliness now "implied peril"; Cuba had become a "malignancy" that no longer served U.S. interests, but rather threatened those interests.[19] Despite communication problems between the White House and the CIA during the attempted invasion, the fiasco never shook the common conviction that the United States had the right to remove the threat Castro supposedly represented. Rather than consider the option of dialogue, Kennedy committed his administration to intensifying the effort to overthrow the Cuban leader.[20]

The last shot had scarcely been fired at the Bay of Pigs when discussions began in Washington about a new scheme to remove Fidel Castro. Codenamed Operation Mongoose, this secret war remained undeclared by Congress and was to become the CIA's "most expensive failure," the cost of which ultimately included two presidencies.[21] Miami was converted into a hemispheric guerrilla training center, and the CIA's Miami station known as JM/Wave became the biggest of its kind anywhere in the world, outside its headquarters in Langley, Virginia; it was described by one operative as "a sprawling bureaucratic monster."[22] With a budget of well over $50 million a year, it employed hundreds of U.S. personnel, who ran thousands of Cuban agents and subagents, carrying out an extensive program of covert, economic, and psychological operations—including assassination attempts against Fidel Castro.[23] Cuban exiles not on the payroll often pretended they were because it gave them "cachet" and helped them raise funds.[24] Numerous fake businesses created as CIA fronts also employed hundreds of Cubans.[25]

This new comprehensive covert operation included various scenarios for U.S. military intervention in support of a projected internal revolt against the revolutionary government. General Edward Lansdale was brought in as operations chief, and Attorney General Robert Kennedy urged, "No time, money, effort—or manpower [should] be spared" in this "top priority" program.[26]

What distinguished Operation Mongoose from the previous Bay of Pigs invasion plan, however, was that it was run directly from the White House and also the scale on which it was conducted.[27] Officially set in motion on 30 November 1961, the operation was directed by the Special Group

(Augmented), with General Maxwell Taylor as chairman and Robert Kennedy as the president's representative.[28] The strategy of Operation Mongoose was contradictory because, although the main role was assigned to the domestic front in Cuba, in reality the CIA ran the show. For example, the key agents infiltrated onto the island with the task of reorganizing the clandestine movement were almost exclusively recruited and trained in the United States; and the Cuban Revolutionary Council, the government-in-exile headed by José Miró Cardona, had even less autonomy than it had at the time of the Bay of Pigs.[29] This dependence of the counterrevolutionary movement on Washington had obvious implications for those in Cuba running the evacuation scheme for children.

Therefore, while Operation Mongoose depended on the revitalization of the anti-Castro forces on the ground in Cuba, paradoxically, greater control was exercised from the United States.[30] President Kennedy's special assistant, Arthur Schlesinger, expressed his concern about this in July 1961, writing: "Despite the pretense of impartiality . . . [the CIA is favoring] those groups most willing to accept CIA identification and control."[31] Policy director of the CIA's Cuba Project Howard Hunt regarded the exiles as "not much more than puppets," who, he said, "had no choice but to do what we told them to."[32] The failed invasion had left the exiles "with feelings of astonishment and disillusionment, and in many cases despair." Their mistake, one exile leader lamented, "was that they thought too highly of the United States. They believed to the end it would not let them down. But it did."[33]

Even while President Kennedy was proposing the Alliance for Progress, an economic program for Latin America he envisaged as a new Marshall Plan, the National Security Council was assessing the possibilities for further military action against Cuba, having concluded that as "long as Castro thrives, his major threat—the example and stimulus of a working communist revolution—will persist."[34]

The question arose of what to do with the exile paramilitary force, which even prior to the invasion had been problematic.[35] "We tried the Cuban Legion and it didn't work," the National Security Council concluded early in May; instead, Cubans would be encouraged to join the U.S. armed forces, largely as a means of maintaining greater influence and control over them. But the option was left open that Cubans might still be consolidated into a separate unit, "should the need for such a unit ever develop."[36] The initial plan was to recruit four thousand Cubans into the U.S. armed forces as special forces, but the response was apparently disappointing.[37] When the Cubans realized they were not being trained specifically for a return to Cuba, there was said to be a "distinct loss of interest."[38]

This matter of a separate Cuban brigade remained a bone of contention between Washington and the exiles. Cuban exile leader José Miró Cardona energetically backed the idea of integrating Cubans into the U.S. armed forces when he testified to the Senate Subcommittee on Cuban refugees in December 1961.[39] But only a few months later, he and another prominent exile leader, Tony Varona, had lost patience and demanded that the exile Cuban Revolutionary Council (CRC) itself "be given the wherewithal to invade Cuba and overthrow the Castro regime."[40] Meanwhile, the Special Group (Augmented) set the month of October 1962 as the date for a new invasion plan in support of the Cuban effort to overthrow the "Communist regime" in Cuba.[41] By early 1962, the State Department was convinced that the success of Operation Mongoose would depend on "decisive U.S. military intervention."[42] Many Pedro Pan parents, like Gabriel Orozco's father, who was active in the counterrevolutionary underground, believed that the U.S. invasion planned for October 1962 would be successful and allow the children to return soon after.[43]

Miró Cardona, whose own son had been part of the exile invading force Brigade 2506, went as far as to request mandatory military service for all male Cuban émigrés under the age of fifty.[44] As the majority of Pedro Pans were teenage boys, they may well have been viewed as potential recruits in the medium- if not short-term for these military plans, and many, like Juan Pujol, did end up in the U.S. Army.[45] Federal government assistance for the Cuban refugees ceased at age nineteen, so those not engaged in tertiary study might have joined up for economic reasons. A number of Pedro Pans were drafted into the U.S. military, anyway, after they became naturalized U.S. citizens. Others, like Tony Daltabuit, enlisted voluntarily because, he said, "I wanted to show that I was a good American and would defend my new homeland. I joined the Army and served in Vietnam with the hope that we could crush the communists."[46]

That teenage Cuban refugee boys attracted special attention in this post–Bay of Pigs recruitment drive is evident in a November 1961 CIA paper: "#2. Agent training: There are currently some [DELETED] Cubans already trained or now in training as activists who can be infiltrated to organize the resistance and develop sabotage activities. In addition, there are some

[DELETED] Cuban students in training for infiltration to conduct Agit/Prop activities."⁴⁷

All the Pedro Pan boys in Albuquerque, where Nelson Valdés found himself, knew where the office was if you wanted to sign up. "It wasn't a regular army recruiting office but one run by Cubans on Central Avenue," he recalled. Nelson and a friend signed up in August 1962, but their military careers were thwarted when the Missile Crisis broke out a few months later.⁴⁸

Some young exiles lost patience with their elders and took their own initiative. In August 1962, a group of Revolutionary Student Directorate (DRE) members organized a raid on Havana, launching bombs from two boats off the shore. Hailed in Miami for their courage and audacity, the students' action was not regarded favorably in Washington, and the *New York Times* argued the act "played right into [Castro's] hands" because the Cuban government had been using the fear of another U.S. attack to maintain its popular support.⁴⁹

Nevertheless, the refugees were a vast and fertile recruiting ground for the foot soldiers required in this new phase of the covert war against Castro. The CIA never really considered Cubans temperamentally suitable as agents but had little choice; only a few Cubans apparently became "agents in the formal sense," although many were on the payroll for more than a decade.⁵⁰ The CIA seemed to have an "insatiable need" for more agents, recruited from the thousands of Cubans arriving in Florida every month, who were processed at the CIA-run Opa Locka detention center; they were then employed in a wide variety of jobs, including everything from pilots of small boats, to cooks and housekeepers at commando camps, to house parents, cooks, cleaners, teachers, and caretakers at the camps accommodating the Pedro Pans.⁵¹

U.S. Refugee Policy after the Bay of Pigs

After the Bay of Pigs, with 116,000 émigrés now resident in the United States, the U.S. government reviewed its refugee policy.⁵² It was agreed that Cuban nationals holding U.S. visitors' visas would be given "refugee status" and assisted under a new DHEW program. This switch in policy was not, however, predicated on humanitarian considerations, evident in the fact that Cuban émigrés would be "eligible to apply for travel privileges" as well as citizenship.⁵³ Roberto Suero, representing the Cuban Refugee Center, explained that the refugees needed to come and go and, in this regard, Wendell Rollason reported that the immigration and state departments had been tremendously cooperative. But he urged that the refugees needed even greater flexibility in order to be able to move in and out of the United States.[54] This cooperation extended to the Kennedy administration offering a free airlift for Cubans wanting to leave the island, at a cost of $350,000 and an additional $10 million set aside to meet "unexpected refugee migration problems."[55]

This proviso for travel privileges for Cuban refugees agreed to in May 1961 was regarded as important, not just for the infiltration and exfiltration of agents.[56] The State Department recognized the propaganda advantage of sending exiles on speaking tours of Latin America to expose the alleged horrors of Castro's Cuba, which required the right of reentry into the United States—not something usually granted to refugees or parolees.[57] Prior to the Bay of Pigs, Manuel Artime, a leading figure of the Cuban Revolutionary Council (CRC), made an extensive tour of Central and Latin America with the assistance of the CIA to rally support for action against Fidel Castro.[58] Other speaking tours had already been organized of groups, such as the Cuban Feminine Crusade, which visited Colombia in December 1960 representing Cuban women "who have suffered under Fidel Castro's dictatorship and who have organized to fight communism in Latin America."[59] In 1962, the CIA was specifically assigned responsibility to organize these trips throughout Latin America.[60] The mayor of Miami told the Senate Subcommittee that one of the "byproducts of the Cuban Refugee Program . . . had been the utilization of some of this outstanding talent in the Alliance for Progress program."[61]

The National Security Council now recommended that Cuban refugees in Miami should be encouraged to locate to other areas, implying that their U.S. sojourn was expected to be longer than originally anticipated, and acknowledging that their vast numbers were placing an impossible burden on south Florida. Now that Cubans were regarded as "an immigrant group," DHEW secretary Abraham Ribicoff was instructed to encourage them "to continue their trades"—in other words, to find work. At the same time, the State Department was instructed to do what it could to supply visas to those Cubans who wanted to get out of Cuba.[62] A child resident in the United States could immediately apply for visa waivers for their parents and other family members, and many of them did.[63]

A meeting of State Department officials with representatives of the CRC in May 1961 was told that extra planes were needed to transport people out of Cuba; Pan American Airlines was bringing about 100 Cubans to the United States each day, but hundreds of others were being turned away; flights were fully booked through October.[64] By January 1962, between 1,700 and 2,000 Cubans were arriving in the United States each month, and *Newsweek* reported 10,000 Cuban refugee children were enrolled in Dade County schools.[65] Although the visa waiver system had never been intended to facilitate the mass migration of Cubans to the United States, 70,000 visa waiver applications were granted in the first ten months of 1961, and 1,200 requests were received each working day, two-thirds of which were approved.[66] Miami lawyer Wendell Rollason described the visa waiver program as "the very lifeblood for the average Cuban in his hopes and plans to escape the ravages of communism," saying the impact of this upon the Cuban people had been "electric."[67]

Curiously, Rollason failed to inform the Senate Subcommittee of the extraordinary authority the State Department had vested in him, allowing him, like Fr. Walsh, to issue visa waivers to Cuban refugees, supposedly to encourage them to "vote with their feet." Rollason's authority was specifically intended to assist underground fighters who had no relatives already in the United States to claim them.[68] The high volume of visa applications had raised some security concerns; Immigration and Naturalization Service (INS) official James Hennessy remarked that U.S. officials were dependent on Cuban exile organizations to vet incoming refugees.[69] Due to the bitter factionalism between rival exile groups, Rollason, who had a background in immigrant rights' law, was apparently brought in as a more "neutral liaison." But whatever the motive, there was absolutely no historical precedent for this arrangement whereby private individuals—Fr. Walsh and Wendell Rollason—were given the authority to grant visa waivers. Rollason said he was on the CIA payroll at this time, which raises a question about Fr. Walsh's relationship with the agency—a relationship he always denied.[70]

In a January 1962 review of Operation Mongoose, General Lansdale pointed out that the Cuba Project still needed far more hard intelligence than was available.[71] To address this problem, an "Interrogation Center" was established at Opa Locka in February with thirty-seven personnel, although the quality of the information was found to be "not as good as in the past."[72] The Cuban Refugee Center also became essential in this regard as it registered about two-thirds of Cubans arriving in Miami, thoroughly probing the political views of each new arrival.[73]

The Pedro Pans were probably not exempt from this intelligence gathering process, especially those who had been active oppositionists in Cuba or children of anti-Castro activists. A CIA memo on the Cuba Project prepared in late January 1962 mentions an assessment was being made of more than one hundred people "to determine their suitability to be sent back to Cuba as agents in the guise of students."[74] It is not beyond the realm of possibility that some of these potential agents were teenagers who had arrived as part of Operation Pedro Pan, as Nelson Valdés's story about the Albuquerque recruiting office suggests.[75]

This comprehensive interview program for newly arrived Cubans was evidently important not only as intelligence gathering but also as a means of recruiting CIA operatives.[76] As their numbers swelled, however, it became evident it was just too easy for Cubans to tell U.S. officials what they wanted to hear.[77] General Lansdale candidly admitted to the National Security Council that a lot of the Cubans then in the United States were "Castro agents."[78] The deputy chief of the CIA's Miami station, Ted Shackley, believed there were hundreds of Cuban agents operating in Miami. Indeed, by the end of 1961, the Cuban government was quite confident about the level of penetration by its counterintelligence agents of exile groups in the United States.[79]

Operations Pedro Pan and Mongoose

From April 1961, Ramón ("Mongo") Grau and his sister Leopoldina ("Polita") stepped in to carry on with the child evacuation scheme after other organizers were arrested or fled into exile. Polita had been involved from the beginning with James Baker's group, but Ramón always liked to present himself as the instigator of Operation Pedro Pan. As the nephew and niece of a former Cuban president (Ramón Grau San Martín), they were well connected to the highest diplomatic, political, and social circles, but Mongo believed that Cuban state security never took him seriously because of his reputation as a "playboy."[80] Far from concealing his links to the CIA, after spending twenty-two years in prison, and once safely ensconced in Miami, Ramón Grau proudly boasted about having been a CIA "operative."[81]

In his memoir, Grau also claimed to have been authorized as the Catholic Welfare Bureau representative in Cuba, but this was denied by Msgr.

Walsh.[82] Walsh readily acknowledged Ramón Grau as "a man of great courage who took tremendous risks to help the children of Cuba," but he was also quick to point out that the child rescue mission was never his initiative. Msgr. Walsh further explained it was Polita who had the connections with the Catholic church and was "Number One" within the group that James Baker had originally put together. "Poor old Mongo," Walsh laughed, implying that Ramón Grau's memory was not what it should have been.[83] Nevertheless, Msgr. Walsh was the first person Grau asked to see on arriving in Miami from Cuba in 1986, as the Miami priest was apparently instrumental in securing his release and assisting in bringing the rest of his family to the United States.[84]

The Grau siblings were assisted in Operation Pedro Pan by employees at a travel agency in Old Havana and airline executives Pancho Finlay and Tony Comellas of KLM and Pan American, respectively, whose cooperation ensured that passenger lists with false names were maintained so that children's names with visa waivers could be substituted at the last minute.[85] Most of the underground activists, however, who assisted Operation Pedro Pan at this time were involved in other, more significant counterrevolutionary activities, as were Polita and Ramón Grau.[86]

In this new phase of Operation Pedro Pan following the invasion debacle, the evacuation of children may well have been a "sideline" of the counterrevolution, but it became a convenient cover for these "other activities," especially the movement of operatives out of and around the island. In fact, it was precisely at this moment after the Bay of Pigs that the U.S. government saw the usefulness of the operation. The possibility of using the same evacuation mechanisms for "non-combatants" (civilians) as those used for agents and their families was raised in a memo sent in late April 1961 to Defense Secretary Robert McNamara.[87]

As a leader of the counterrevolutionary group Rescate, Polita Grau was regarded by Cuban intelligence as a more serious adversary than her brother.[88] Polita was well connected with the Catholic hierarchy and was also the link with an intriguing character, Penny Powers (Phyllis H. Powers), a British national who had taught at James Baker's school, the Ruston Academy.[89] Polita later identified Penny Powers as the central figure in the Cuban side of the operation; Msgr. Walsh also said she was the "key liaison in the Havana group."[90] Ramón Grau described Penny Powers as the most "anticommunist" woman he ever knew, and he confirmed she was the main link between himself and Fr. Walsh, via the British embassy.[91] When questioned about whether Penny Powers might have been a British agent, James Baker commented she was a "very intelligent, dedicated woman and the kind of person British intelligence would use, or find helpful."[92] After interviewing Penny Powers in Havana in 1993, María de los Angeles Torres confirmed that she was a British intelligence officer and "the central coordinator for the underground effort during Operation Pedro Pan."[93]

Msgr. Walsh told this researcher he kept in touch with Penny Powers through the British ambassador in Havana.[94] A letter written to Msgr. Walsh in early 1963 by Mike McCann at the British embassy in Tokyo suggests that Walsh had lost contact with Penny Powers at this time. Obviously aware of the child "rescue" program, McCann expressed his "great regret" that the most "successful" immigration program from Havana was no longer possible. He informed Msgr. Walsh that the British consul-general in Miami (a Mr. Smitherman) would let him know when Penny Powers's "whereabouts" became known.[95]

The Cuban researchers discovered that Penny Powers had traveled to Miami in November 1960, a trip preceding that made by James Baker, leading them to speculate whether the whole child evacuation scheme might have been her idea; on the other hand, it is possible James Baker sent her on that trip.[96] Apparently not implicated in any counterrevolutionary activities other than Operation Pedro Pan, Penny Powers remained in Cuba, running an international school she established in October 1965; she died peacefully in Havana in 1996.[97]

Ramón Grau and his sister Polita were arrested in early 1965 for their part in assassination attempts against Fidel Castro and other counterrevolutionary activities, and they served twenty-two and fourteen years, respectively, in prison.[98] Despite frequent claims to the contrary, not one of the central figures in Operation Pedro Pan working in Cuba was ever charged for participating in the child evacuation scheme, other than those involved with printing the fake *patria potestad* law and other counterrevolutionary activities such as sabotage, subversion, or armed attacks.[99] The involvement of key personnel in Operation Pedro Pan in the broader covert war against Castro does not, however, prove that the child rescue scheme was an essential part of Washington's Cuba Project.[100]

But apart from its origin as a means of protecting the children of anti-Castro activists in the lead-up to the Bay of Pigs, the operation can also be shown to be closely linked to the actual "infiltration and exfiltration" of underground operatives and CIA agents to and from the island helping "endangered adults escape the island."[101] In February 1961, the director of the Ruston Academy, James Baker, wrote to the former U.S. ambassador to Cuba, Philip Bonsal, pleading special consideration for Pedro Pans aged sixteen to eighteen, because delays in their obtaining the required security clearance from the State Department might cost them their lives. Baker urged that the names of such young anticommunist fighters should be able to be substituted on passenger lists at the last moment.[102] This is apparently what happened. In his memoir, Ramón Grau explained the special code word "King Size" was used to alert contacts in Miami about adult counterrevolutionaries departing on children's visa waivers. Apart from the 14,000 Cuban children Ramón Grau claimed to have "saved," and for which he said he had the "blessing and cooperation of the church"—and also "of God"—Grau asserted he had rescued another 28,000 people "from Castro's clutches."[103]

The Cuban report supported Ramón Grau's claim that many adults fraudulently used the children's visa waivers and the false passports he prepared with his little team of forgers.[104] Operation Pedro Pan, therefore, was a convenient vehicle as well as a cover for the CIA and the counterrevolutionary movement. It is possible that a letter dated 16 August 1962 from Fr. Walsh in the Museum of South Florida (now the History/Miami Museum) archives on Cuban refugee children also relates to the transport of agents out of Cuba.[105] This letter might have been the result of a failure to follow the procedure required for children over the age of sixteen, who needed a security clearance from both the U.S. immigration and state departments.[106] There is another possibility, that the individuals referred to in the letter might have been some of Ramón Grau's "King Size" Pedro Pans (adults using children's visa waivers), as only three given names are listed for one female passenger: Marta Inocencia Pilar.

The CIA reported in November 1961 that there were a number of Cubans in Florida, including students, "already trained or now in training as activists who can be infiltrated to organize the resistance and to develop sabotage activities." This CIA paper discussed the use of a small fleet to accomplish "Infiltration/Exfiltration" of agents to ensure the creation of "a secure underground organization." Larger scale infiltrations of men and materiel for sabotage, and perhaps ultimately guerrilla activities, were envisaged. The CIA stressed "every effort [should] be made not only to possibly forestall identification of U.S. Government support but also to avoid any appearance of U.S. Government control or ultimate responsibility."[107]

This is where Operation Pedro Pan directly intersects with the covert war against Cuba. An example of this is the case of Sara del Toro, who was arrested in 1961 but later lauded in Miami as a heroine of Operation Pedro Pan.[108] In one interview, she described her role as a courier between Havana and Miami for Manuel Ray, the U.S.-based leader of the Revolutionary Movement of the People (MRP), not mentioning her part in the child exodus.[109] On other occasions, however, she preferred to talk about assisting Fr. Walsh by bringing a "suitcase filled with visa waivers" back into Cuba.[110] Sara del Toro's life story was dramatized in a "historical novel" that portrays her "heroism" in carrying out anti-Castro terrorist activities and assassination plots as well as her involvement in Operation Pedro Pan.[111] In reality, Sara and her husband, Amador Odio, were imprisoned for participating in assassination plans and various acts of sabotage, including arson that destroyed the famous El Encanto and La Epoca department stores. No mention was made in their trial of their role in evacuating children from Cuba.[112]

Similarly, Margarita Oteiza, a former Ruston Academy student and later English teacher at her old school, has been presented as another heroine of Operation Pedro Pan, but she also proudly identified herself as an "underground operative" in the anti-Castro struggle.[113] Such examples provide clear evidence of how Operation Pedro Pan was so interlocked with the counterrevolution as to be inseparable from it, at a time when the Cuban counterrevolution was increasingly run from the White House. Certainly, the main players in the Operation Pedro Pan drama never distinguished between their actions in extracting children from Cuba and their other (sometimes terrorist) activities—except when it served to portray the program as a humanitarian effort unrelated to the U.S. government's more shadowy regime-change project.[114]

The CIA and Pedro Pan

Suspecting that "security, not humanitarian concerns" lay behind the expansion of a program that originally served as a means for parents in the anti-Castro underground to protect their children, Chicago professor and former Pedro Pan María de los Angeles Torres brought a Freedom of Information Act (FOIA) case against the CIA in 1994, demanding the declassification of government records on the evacuation scheme for Cuban children. "Nobody involved with the operation hides the fact that the CIA was involved," she told the *Miami Herald*. Therefore, she asked, "Why is it that the CIA will not put forth the information?"[115]

The *Miami Herald* editors responded: "Was the CIA involved in Operation Pedro Pan . . . ? No, the CIA says. Yes, says a Chicago political scientist. . . . Plausible deniability is of course part of the CIA's *modus operandi*. Yet it's also plausible that the agency, trying to discredit Fidel Castro, would have tried to turn Cuba's middle class against him by circulating rumors that he was going to take children away from their parents to be raised by communist cadres. Such rumors *did* circulate in Cuba." The *Miami Herald* editorial, however, concluded "no harm except embarrassment could come from revealing the CIA's role, if any." Nothing could "detract from what's important—that is, Msgr. Walsh and Miami's [Catholic] archdiocese conducted a splendid example of charity and humanity for which thousands of parents and children remain grateful today."[116]

This response—that it was of no concern that Operation Pedro Pan might have been part of a U.S. covert action program—reveals how central the exodus of the Cuban children became to the creation myth of the émigré community. When a Miami journalist challenged the conventional wisdom that the operation was "one of the most moving stories of Cubans fleeing Communist repression in their homeland"—one of "heroism and compassion"—and suggested, instead, that there was a "dark side of Peter Pan"—"Washington's sinister manipulation of Cuban parents' fears"—there was a flurry of letters from other Pedro Pans expressing gratitude to those who had rescued them. The trauma of separation, said one, was "nothing compared to the trauma under which those who stayed in Cuba have been living for the last 30 years."[117]

It is clear, however, that something more than "charity and humanity" or "heroism and compassion" was behind Operation Pedro Pan. In an interview with *Diario las Américas* in Miami in January 1998, Msgr. Walsh himself admitted it "might have been the case that the CIA was involved [in Operation Pedro Pan] as it was in everything to do with Cuba in those days. If there was a plan or a plot, we didn't know about that"; he and others, he said, just carried on to ensure parents could exercise their "human right to educate their children according to their own values, not Marxist values."[118] In another interview, he chuckled, "if the CIA didn't know what we were doing, they were negligent. It was their job to know everything that was going on with Cuba in Miami." He was adamant, however, that he had "no evidence whatsoever, and never have had, of direct CIA involvement, and I knew many people in the CIA." The interviewer asked him if he had contact with the CIA, to which he answered: "No . . . yes. They visited me about other things because I was involved in a lot of things [related] to Cuba."[119] Msgr. Walsh consistently denied any personal knowledge of CIA involvement in Operation Pedro Pan, but he told the Washington Post: "Not to have had the CIA at least watching [the airlift scheme] would be ridiculous." Moreover, he admitted some of the parents were cooperating with the CIA in Cuba. Nevertheless, the CIA continues to insist the agency "[has] no relevant documents on the subject."[120]

In March 1999, the U.S. District Court in Illinois brought down a final judgment on Torres's case against the Central Intelligence Agency, stating that it might have been a "reasonable guess" that the CIA was the "likely mother lode on the subject [of Operation Pedro Pan] . . . but the facts have turned out to the contrary—because the evacuation of Cuban children turned out not to be a CIA operation at all." The Pedro Pan group evidently felt this decision represented the definitive rebuff to all speculation about the CIA's role in the child exodus and posted it on their website. To reach its decision, the court had reviewed 723 pages of documents the CIA provided, but these remained classified as "Sensitive Compartmented Information."[121] Despite this legal setback, Torres persisted with her argument that the only reason for the CIA to withhold documents related to Operation Pedro Pan was because of a fear that it "could lead to unraveling the entire anti-Castro tapestry." She was also told by one archivist that because the program involved "friendly governments," such as Britain, this made declassification of documents more sensitive.[122] This is highly likely because of the central role played by the British teacher Penny Powers and officials at several embassies. Although one British chargé d'affaires admitted his embassy had "pushed the limits of diplomatic immunity" and was declared a *persona non grata* and withdrawn from Cuba, in general, all staff at foreign embassies were left alone.[123]

Addressing a conference on Pedro Pan at Florida International University in 2001, Msgr. Walsh told the story of how he had been contacted recently by "Don Holding" (actually, Don *Bohning*), a longtime Miami journalist, who asked him if he remembered [NAME DELETED]. The journalist was convinced Walsh must have known this person because "he was active in the CIA in Miami in the early 1960s." This unnamed person had asked Bohning about Operation Pedro Pan. "I began to laugh," said

Msgr. Walsh. "I told Don that I had been expecting this call since a professor at DePaul University, Dr. de Torres, had requested from the CIA the release of all documents relating to Operation Pedro Pan under the U.S. Freedom of Information Act." But, he said, the name "had never been used, except in conversation by the Catholic Welfare Bureau."[124]

That same year, 2001, the Catholic magazine *Oye* published an article quoting a CIA spokesperson, Anya Guilsher, who said several documents had been identified that mentioned the departures of unaccompanied children "but it was clear that there was no CIA activity or involvement in that exodus." On the other hand, Guilsher was reported to have explained it was no secret that the CIA did seek to generate opposition to the Castro regime in the 1960s, but she stated: "[W]e have uncovered no information to suggest that any unintended or intended purpose of these efforts was to induce parents to send their children unaccompanied to Florida."[125]

To date, it has not been proven that "Operation Pedro Pan" was the actual name the CIA or organizers gave the child evacuation scheme, and it does not appear to be a "classic CIA operation."[126] Torres's investigation apparently confirmed that Pedro Pan was not a CIA cryptogram, even though the list of the agency's cryptograms remains confidential. Nevertheless, Torres remained convinced Operation Pedro Pan was a "classified operation, at least in its origins until 1962."[127] The program to "rescue" the children was clearly organized and promoted by anti-Castro Cubans and others with the support of, and largely funded by, the CIA and the U.S. government. Moreover, there can be no doubt there is a substantial amount of CIA and State Department documentation that is still classified, particularly that relates to propaganda campaigns and psychological operations conducted in those years.[128]

Propaganda Wars

In Operation Mongoose, the battle on the propaganda front was to be just as intense as the military fight against Fidel Castro. Propaganda was a top priority for the CIA's new chief of operations, General Edward Lansdale, who was a dedicated advocate and practitioner of psychological warfare.[129] "It was really kind of surreal working with Lansdale," recalled former United States Information Agency (USIA) deputy director Donald Wilson. "[He] really thought if you said something on the radio, people would believe it.... He thought one statement or blast could move people's minds, [but] it doesn't work that way."[130] One of the general's more crackpot schemes was to spread the word that "the Second Coming of Christ was imminent" and that Christ was returning in order to deal with Castro, "the anti-Christ."[131] The *patria potestad* hoax was just one example of these often absurd but deadly serious psywar campaigns launched against Cuba, and the plight of the Cuban child refugees featured prominently in the propaganda effort to undermine the moral standing of the revolution.[132]

After the invasion debacle of April 1961, President Kennedy's special assistant Arthur Schlesinger outlined the U.S. "mission," as he saw it, which was "to redefine the conflict in Cuba in a way which will transform current opinion not only within this hemisphere but in Europe, Africa and Asia." The problem he identified was the "current widespread view . . . that the conflict is between the Castro regime, which, for all its excesses, is at least dedicated to the welfare of the Cuban people, and a crowd of émigrés, whose aim is to bring back the old order to Cuba." The conflict, he suggested, should be portrayed not as a bilateral one but rather as between "the totalitarian (or communist) and the libertarian (or social democratic) wings of the Cuban Revolution."[133]

The State Department acknowledged the example of the Cuban revolution was having an impact in Latin America because, while "others have talked of social reform . . . , Fidel Castro has actually accomplished a radical social revolution in Cuba, and has done so in defiance of the Yankees with the support of an apparently more powerful patron." This was said to present "a danger that the Cuban example will set the pattern of the impending social revolution in Latin America."[134]

After the August 1961 Organization of American States conference in Punta del Este, Uruguay, President Kennedy's special adviser Richard Goodwin wrote to the president proposing the intensification of the covert action program against Cuba and the immediate establishment of a "psychological warfare group" in the State Department to highlight "the Sovietization of Cuba, repression of human rights, failure of the Cuban economy, etc." But he advised this should not appear as "official U.S. propaganda."[135] Goodwin and Schlesinger were clearly alert to the fact that there was a sensitivity in Latin America to overt U.S. intervention in the continent, especially after the Bay of Pigs.[136]

The challenge the Kennedy administration faced on the Cuba issue was not only international public opinion. "A job remains to be done here [in the United States]," Schlesinger advised the president, referring to a poll that showed 65 percent of the U.S. population was against armed intervention in Cuba and only 44 percent supported indirect help to the anti-Castro forces. "Again official government hand-outs are not going to be effective," he wrote, and he suggested countering the solidarity work of the Fair Play for Cuba Committees in the United States with "*Fair Play for Cubans Committee*s under liberal sponsorship," which could circulate stories about Castro's authoritarianism and offer Manuel Ray as a spokesperson, especially to labor and student audiences, as his counterrevolutionary group, the MRP, had not been so identified with the Bay of Pigs.[137]

Although most mainstream U.S. media kept up the diatribes against Fidel Castro and the revolution, among the most consistently strident was the *U.S. News and World Report*, which regularly called for another U.S. invasion and highlighted, among the many alleged crimes of the revolution, the "regimentation of children." It also constantly repeated the *patria potestad* rumor, asserting: "The big fear now is that on January 1 [1962], the Government will take children over three years of age away from their parents as in the commune system in Red China."[138]

An unusual collection of letters from Cuba in the years 1961–1963 somehow ended up in the Tamiment archive of U.S. labor and progressive movements located at New York University. A description of the collection explains these letters had been "solicited by Norman Jacobs of the *New Leader* for a special supplement on Cuba under Castro that NL planned but never published. . . . Contains original letters as well as English translations, copies of which were apparently sent to the CIA."[139]

It is possible these were collected for use in Washington's propaganda offensive against the Cuban revolution; a common theme in these letters is the urgent desire to get out of Cuba; shortages of food, clothing, and medicines were pointed out; and conditions in the prisons and instances of political repression were also mentioned. Correspondents give detailed descriptions of bombings and sabotage taking place, often reported quite favorably if not enthusiastically. Some of the letters seem to have been written with a foreign audience in mind; one letter, for example, complained: "[O]ur friends are still following a blind policy that may have the direst consequences: allowing this cancer that is threatening America to consolidate gradually up to the point when it will spread to other countries, some of which may be in danger of being lost to democracy. There can be no peace in the hemisphere while the regime of the Communists and Fidel Castro persists in Cuba."[140]

Another Cuban correspondent, verging on hysteria, wrote: "An invasion is an absolute must. The Cuban people have done and continue to do what they can; they are rebelling and demonstrating against the regime; the [anti-Castro] guerrillas prove it and so do the recent street demonstrations (in El Cano and Cárdenas). Russia takes everything out of the country, the mass of workers and peasants do not want to work.... Please get to work on this very soon as very soon we will have nothing more to eat, and they keep on executing people and killing them in the streets and now, on top of that, we have foreign mercenaries in our country."[141]

In March 1962, General Lansdale discussed the refugee question with President Kennedy, who asked: "Wouldn't it be better to shut the doors to the people trying to get out, so that they would be forced to stay and take action against the regime?" To this Lansdale responded: "Once we are committed to helping [the Cubans] stage a revolt, provide arms, and are willing to go all the way in being sure that they will win, then we might consider closing our doors.... [But for the moment], with 2,000 people fleeing every week, we would be foolish to remove this symbol of our sympathy and cut off the source of intelligence information and recruits."[142]

The depiction of desperate refugees fleeing Castro's Cuba was "good optics" in the U.S. and international media, justifying Washington's efforts to isolate and undermine the revolutionary government. By the time Operation Pedro Pan was revealed to the U.S. public in March 1962, this propaganda effort against Cuba was in full swing. That same month, the *Miami Herald* ran a front-page article headlined: "Plight of Cuba Today: Agony, Hunger, Fear."[143]

This propaganda value of the Cuban refugees had been identified early in the Cuba Project: "Our propaganda line should be in favor of the 'poor Cubans,'" wrote Gerard C. Smith, assistant secretary of state for Policy Planning, in July 1960: "Our case would be improved if Castro took military steps to block the flow of refugees. A few pictures of Castro's men shooting refugees attempting to escape would do more to hurt Castro than a host of economic sanctions."[144]

Sadly for that idea, few such photo opportunities presented themselves as the Cuban government's policy was generally to allow those who wanted to leave to do so. But if Fidel Castro would not oblige, others were more than willing. A Joint Chiefs of Staff paper of 12 March 1962 discussed "Justification for U.S. Military Intervention in Cuba"; among many suggestions in this paper was Point 4: "We could develop a Communist Cuban terror campaign in the Miami area, in other Florida cities and even in Washington.

The terror campaign could be pointed at Cuban refugees seeking haven in the United States. We could sink a boatload of Cubans en route to Florida (real or simulated). We could foster attempts on lives of Cuban refugees in the United States even to the extent of wounding in instances to be widely publicized."[145]

Wendell Rollason, as director of Miami's Inter-American Affairs Commission, drew attention to the inestimable role of the Cuban "students," whom he described as "[o]ne of the greatest and finest groups fighting communism." They were, he said, "a tremendous bunch of clean kids. They have gotten onto TV in debates in Latin America with the pro-Castro people and the results have been electrifying. You can do more sending these kids [on speaking tours] than you can the gray-haired politician, whom everybody tends to suspect of ulterior motives. But with the Latin American tolerance and appreciation of the youngster in politics, the position the students hold in politics in Latin America is high."[146]

It should be explained here that the Pedro Pans were often referred to as "students," including by Msgr. Walsh. Speaking tours by students as well as by teachers, jurists, and student, labor, and women's groups were recommended by the CIA as part of this propaganda offensive.[147] In February 1962, in a review of the Cuba Project's "Political Support Plan," General Lansdale recommended tours by the exiles in Latin America to "give personal witness against the communist regime and ask support for the people recapturing their freedom."[148] Youth could be particularly effective in this campaign, as shown by a *Miami Herald* article in April 1962 that reported the story of sixteen-year-old Gary Anderson: "The Cuban Communist government shot his father," the article began. Gary, the son of an American businessman who owned a chain of gas stations in Cuba, was now a guide for "Operation Amigo," a tour agency that conducted tours of the Cuban Refugee Center in Miami for Latin American youth, which Gary believed "counters Communist propaganda by letting young Latin Americans see for themselves what U.S. democracy is like."[149] The Pedro Pans were also brought along to meetings of the American Legion and Catholic church groups as "miniature icons of anticommunism" to bear witness to the horrors of Castro's Cuba.[150]

In 1961, Miami's Channel 4 (WTVJ) aired a documentary, *The Plight of Pepito: Cuba's Lost Generation,* depicting a six-year-old child refugee looking lost and bewildered on arriving in the United States with his two parents, who never appear in the film. Pepito is a "symbol," says narrator Ralph

Renick, and if U.S. citizens devote themselves to these young exiles, they will be adding "new soldiers to the ranks of democracy. For when they grow up, they will champion the cause of liberty."[151]

Thus, the young refugees could evidently help to win over U.S. public opinion to support Washington's ongoing regime change project in Cuba after the embarrassment of the Bay of Pigs defeat. But they had yet another role to play. The de facto open-door policy to refugees from Cuba had provoked resentment among the local population, particularly in the Miami area. Signs on apartment buildings for rent sometimes read "No Cubans, no pets, and no children."[152] As part of the "Psychological Support Plan" of Operation Mongoose, it was felt necessary to "create [an] atmosphere of a 'crusade' for human liberty" in order to ensure domestic support for President Kennedy's policy with regard not just to overthrowing Castro, but also for the assistance program for the ever-larger numbers of Cuban émigrés arriving on U.S. soil. In this regard, General Lansdale recommended "visits of prominent U.S. and Latin American personalities to Cuban refugee camps in Florida."[153]

Growing Resentment against Cuban Refugees

Not all U.S. citizens were ready to open their arms to welcome their Cuban neighbors; the refugees placed a significant burden on Miami, which was experiencing a mild recession and relatively high unemployment. Although locals might have sympathized with their predicament, the Cuban refugees were seen as taking jobs and housing from local residents. Resettlement outside Dade County was seen as the only viable—and urgent—solution.

The Senate Subcommittee hearings into the Cuban refugee problem in December 1961 discussed at length this rising tide of resentment—if not outright hostility—toward the Cubans.[154] A recently screened television program, *Crisis Amigo*, was shown to the senators; introduced by WTVJ news director Ralph Renick, excerpts of the script were included in the minutes of their proceedings. This documentary stressed that the government's response to the Cuban refugee crisis was "in the best tradition of the United States as a political sanctuary. But Washington has heard little—or preferred not to—of the plight of the Americano. He's the Miamian who lost his job to a Cuban, suffered educational setbacks, and surrendered meekly to invasion of his customs."[155]

Antagonism was said to be growing, "not because the refugees are Cuban ... but because there are lots of them." Moreover, the documentary continued, many of the Cubans arriving "would not have been permitted to enter the United States except as political exiles—we have imported everything from petty thieves to narcotics pushers." Nor were the Cuban child refugees exempt from criticism in this documentary; they were reportedly responsible for a "disciplinary problem" in Dade County schools because "the Cuban teenager prefers to talk rather than listen," and there was said to be an "undercurrent of trouble between Cuban and American students." The situation had apparently improved since the "ill-fated Cuban invasion," and now "Cuban teenagers are less cocky and arrogant." The documentary concluded with the comment that the subcommittee would "find the Cuban problem a tough nut to crack. The shell is emotionalism, but the kernel is economic." Furthermore, the narrator added, "unless we move to relieve the economic and cultural pressures, the imminent explosion may be heard around the world. ... If Fidel Castro turned in his fatigues today and just faded away, more than 50 percent of the Cuban refugees would not return home. ... The answer is compulsory resettlement [and] Washington confesses it has been negligent in this direction."[156]

The U.S. government, therefore, had to walk a tightrope between being seen to be doing something for the "refugees from communism" while not inflaming local community sentiments about special jobs, housing, and other programs for Cuban émigrés. The solution was a relocation program to spread the burden (and impact) beyond Miami and Florida, which also meant relocating thousands of Pedro Pans all over the country.[157] This became important because, when Cuban parents eventually made it to the United States, families were only permitted to reunite where the children were—not Miami. The Cuban children were said to have shown a greater willingness than their parents to be located outside of Miami and placed with American families, but, in fact, they were given no say in the matter.[158]

Thus, the Cuban refugee exodus was becoming a serious national problem. But while the Cuban Children's Program was a publicly announced federally funded program, the special government assistance the unaccompanied minors received to reach U.S. shores was kept under wraps.[159] Addressing the Senate Subcommittee on Cuban refugees in December 1961, Fr. Walsh was quite circumspect about this aspect of the program, stressing that any publicity it received "would be interpreted perhaps as propaganda by the Cuban regime ... and might lead to a shutoff of exit permits for these children."[160]

Could it be that one of the reasons Walsh wanted to keep it quiet was that the Catholic church did not want to draw attention to the highly unusual situation of an ordinary parish priest having the State Department's authority to sign visa waivers, and also the fact that the Cuban Children's Program was funding private school fees for some of the Pedro Pans attending Catholic colleges? The Children's Bureau received bundles of letters complaining about the assistance given to the Cuban children, some suggesting it was a way the Catholic church could "assure its political power" and "enrich itself at the expense of the U.S. taxpayer."[161]

Katherine Oettinger of the Children's Bureau, which was responsible for the Cuban Children's Program, referred to the "delicate aspects" of this service.[162] Msgr. Walsh explained they "never knew when the Cuban government was going to crack down and we didn't want to place the parents still in Cuba in danger if their children were being used for propaganda" in the United States. But he gave no explanation of how the children might have been "used for propaganda," only stating they "never allowed the children to be photographed and were very careful in this regard."[163]

This perceived need for secrecy did present a dilemma for the organizers of the scheme from the beginning because, while not revealing how the children made it to the United States, they urgently needed to solicit support for those in their care. This first arose at the National Resettlement Conference in Miami in late January 1961, which planned to convince the rest of the country that "the refugees posed a national problem and that Miami needed the help of the nation." At this time, Operation Pedro Pan was just getting under way, and Walsh was aware that some media were "beginning to get wind of what was going on." Msgr. Walsh recalled that they decided to admit to the "presence of unaccompanied Cuban children, but would say nothing about helping them get here. We did indicate that the less said the better, since we were convinced that any publicity would have quick repercussions in Cuba."[164]

It is possible that Fr. Walsh and others involved in the care of the Cuban children sincerely believed that if a spotlight was put on the "rescue" operation, it would be harder to get children out of the country, or that parents back in Cuba might be identified as oppositionists. But there is no evidence of Cuba stopping the departures of the children, even after the Cuban government's exposé of the fake *patria potestad* law in September 1961. Msgr.

Walsh suggested the reason why the Cuban government might have turned a blind eye to the departures of children was because leading members of the Cuban government "had a personal interest in the continuation of the exodus," that is, because they wanted to send their own children out of the country before defecting. He mentioned one case, that of a Cuban diplomat stationed in Europe who got his children out of Cuba before defecting.[165] There can be no doubt that Operation Pedro Pan hit very close to home among some of the Cuban government leaders; addressing the first group of young Cuban Americans who returned to the island in 1978, Armando Hart (then minister for culture) spoke with great bitterness about the removal of his brother Enrique's children as part of Operation Pedro Pan by their mother. Enrique had been a prominent leader of the July 26 Movement and had died in the revolutionary war.[166]

There could be another explanation, however, for the need for secrecy enshrouding Operation Pedro Pan: The fact that the same networks were used by the anti-Castro underground to spirit adults engaged in counter-revolutionary activities out of (and into) the country. Exposing those networks would have jeopardized the entire counterrevolutionary movement on the island. Besides, maintaining an aura of secrecy was "central to the escape narrative," suggesting that Cuban children were in imminent danger.[167] Discussing the origins of the program at a 2001 conference at Florida International University, Msgr. Walsh again avoided giving a direct answer about Operation Pedro Pan's links to Washington's more sinister schemes, saying, "some revisionist historians and commentators both in the U.S., the U.K. and Cuba have engaged in an on-going campaign to portray Operation Pedro Pan . . . as a dirty tricks campaign conceived by the CIA to mislead Cuban families and panic them into sending their children abroad. If there was such a plan, it would seem strange that it should be wrapped in complete secrecy for some sixteen months and then largely escape the scrutiny of the media in the U.S. and the Castro regime until some thirty years later."[168]

In fact, the exodus of the Cuban children was never an absolute secret, and it could be argued that the articles in the U.S. media describing the arrival in Miami of "thousands" of unaccompanied minors from Cuba helped to fuel the panic and encourage the exodus.[169] In general, however, the flight of the children out of Cuba was not widely reported until March 1962. Msgr. Walsh always explained the decision to announce the child rescue operation at that time was in order to seek support for the program; and certainly the numbers of children arriving presented a significant challenge to find placements for them all and made it harder to keep the operation secret. But Msgr. Walsh insisted, despite the evidence to the contrary, they were not feeling more confident that the departures would not be stopped by the Cuban government; the problem, he said, was that the understanding with the media on Operation Pedro Pan had collapsed and that Cleveland's *Plain Dealer* was about to run with the story.[170]

"We decided to put a positive twist on it and appealed for foster homes," as a "preemptive strike," Msgr. Walsh recalled.[171] He and DHEW secretary Ribicoff held a press conference in Miami on 7 March 1962 where they announced that 7,778 unaccompanied Cuban refugee children had come to the United States for whom foster families were desperately needed.[172] A few days earlier, the National Catholic Welfare Council (NCWC) News Service reported on the program that had brought almost 8,000 unaccompanied minors to the United States, and followed up this report with an appeal for foster homes for the Cuban children.[173]

The Cuban report accepted this "preemptive strike" argument about why Operation Pedro Pan was announced at that time. The Cleveland *Plain Dealer* had reported on 22 February 1962 that ten to fifteen refugee children from "Communist-controlled Castro Cuba" had been placed in the local Palmdale Catholic home, having arrived on "official waivers or exit visas"; the young Cubans were reported to be "among the first of the estimated 3,000 unaccompanied child refugees" to be settled in the Midwest. The children had been sent out of Cuba by their parents, the article said, because of "increasing communization of the Cuban schools" and "rumors that the Communist state would take children away from their families."[174]

Cleveland had been one of the pilot cities to receive relocated Cuban refugees.[175] Nevertheless, despite the Cleveland paper's best efforts to win local sympathy for the refugees, that city became the scene of a public demonstration of growing animosity toward the Cubans because of the special treatment they received.[176] Kathryn Close, editor of *Children* magazine, pointed out: "As with all programs involving aliens, the Cuban program has met with resistance in some communities . . . [and] resentment has been expressed over 'doing more for the Cuban children than we are doing for our own.'"[177]

At the Miami press conference, Secretary Ribicoff directly addressed the urgency of the resettlement issue, calling on the mayors of all cities to accept the Cuban refugees because Miami had "done a great job in helping the victims of Castro's tyranny," but it was "unfair to expect Miami to carry the whole load." He referred to the incident in Cleveland where the local mayor snubbed arriving refugees as "unfortunate" and a "misunderstanding." He was, however, quick with the reassurance that "when the opportunity comes for [the refugees] to return to Cuba, the Federal Government will do everything to speed their return—in only a matter of hours."[178] The *New York Times* report of the press conference similarly argued that the Cubans were expected to return home soon.[179]

Some researchers have offered some useful insights into the backlash against the Cubans pouring into Miami and how the pathetic situation of the refugee children was used to counter this community hostility.[180] But in an interview, Msgr. Walsh firmly denied the decision to publicize Operation Pedro Pan was based on an attempt to deflect or soften resistance to the Cuban Refugee Program by highlighting the vulnerability of the children. His denial does not sit well with the evidence.

A Remarkable Coincidence

The *New York Times* suggested that Operation Pedro Pan had been "a carefully guarded secret . . . [until] its size gave it away."[181] But here a remarkable coincidence occurred. On 20 February, only a week or so before Fr. Walsh and Secretary Ribicoff's 7 March 1962 press conference, the CIA's General Lansdale prepared a comprehensive review of the Cuba Project. In "Activity #3: D. Psychological Support Plan," he proposed a propaganda offensive focusing on the Cuban refugees to commence in the month of March. He suggested "prominent U.S. and Latin American personalities" should be encouraged to visit the Cuban refugee camps in Florida "to demonstrate concern for plight of refugees, *particularly parentless children*." First Lady Jacqueline Kennedy, the memo stressed, "would be *especially effective in visiting children refugees.*" There were reported to be one thousand children in one camp near Miami, and Mrs. Kennedy was said to have had a big "impact on Latin Americans" during a recent visit to Venezuela and Colombia. The USIA was assigned responsibility for this task as part of the propaganda effort to "[c]reate atmosphere of a 'crusade' for human liberty."[182]

Although Msgr. Walsh always argued that the *Plain Dealer* had so inopportunely exposed the child rescue operation, the journalist John P.

Leacacos reported that he had challenged State Department officials about the secrecy surrounding the program and had been told, on the contrary, "they would be happy to have the American loving care of the Cuban children publicized because of its propaganda value," even though there was an "official State Department ban or censorship or requested voluntary censorship on discussing the matter."[183] It should also be pointed out that Leacacos filed his article from Washington on 22 February, citing "authoritative sources," only two days after General Lansdale's 20 February memo on the Cuba Project mentioned above.

Therefore, it seems impossible to believe that there is no connection between General Lansdale's proposal about a propaganda offensive focused on the Cuban children and the public announcement of Operation Pedro Pan. Moreover, the appeal for foster parents for the homeless Cuban children was framed in highly political terms: "We can think of few better ways to 'fight communism' than to care for the children who flee from it. Interested?"[184] Such appeals stirred a deluge of inquiries from patriotic Americans, but many of them wanted assurance that the young Cubans needing foster homes were "white."[185]

When the Missile Crisis of October 1962 stranded thousands of Pedro Pans, the DHEW Children's Bureau made a similarly politically charged appeal for foster parents: "Many American families, feeling concern for children separated temporarily from their parents and desiring to do something to help young refugees from Communism, have volunteered to take a Cuban child or children into their homes. Many of these families see this as an opportunity to demonstrate to the young Cubans in their care what democracy and our American way of life mean."[186]

Despite Fr. Walsh's stated concern that the Pedro Pans might be used as the "innocent victims of power politics and clashing ideologies," such appeals portray the children as political trophies in a way that foreshadowed the attitude adopted by much of Miami's Cuban-American community to Elián González decades later.[187] In the interview with this researcher, Msgr. Walsh boasted, "we *got* the nephew of [Cuban] President Dorticós," and he mentioned that children or relatives of several other prominent figures or supporters of the revolutionary government came to the United States as part of Operation Pedro Pan.[188]

"The Lost Apple"

As an integral part of Operation Mongoose, the USIA was kept fully appraised and was involved in top-level planning for the anti-Castro operations that developed overt propaganda to complement the CIA's psychological warfare projects. Following the March 1962 public announcement of Operation Pedro Pan, General Lansdale suggested more could be done to "exploit the emotional possibilities of the 8,000 children that were under the protection of the United States."[189] Reporting a few months later, Donald Wilson of the USIA outlined the projects his organization was working on, "within the general framework . . . of exploiting Castro defectors and children refugees." One film, *La Tierra Prometida* (The Promised Land), about the economic failures of the revolution, had already been produced, and two others (unnamed) were said to be in production, focusing on Castro's "mistreatment" of children and organized labor.[190] WTVJ's short documentary focusing on a refugee child, *The Plight of Pepito: Cuba's Lost Generation*, broadcast in 1961, no doubt had already had a positive impact.

The USIA subsequently released a rather poignant short documentary titled *The Lost Apple* (the title taken from a traditional Spanish children's song) evidently designed to win sympathy for the predicament of the little refugees and encourage U.S. families to foster them, but the political message was very thinly veiled.[191] Featuring a sad and lonely little boy called Roberto (with an uncanny likeness to Elián González), the narrator asks: "Why would Papa and Mama do this? How could they send you to a far and lonesome place where you have no friends? CASTRO!" is the answer, uttered by the narrator (Carlos Montalban) in a melodramatic tone.[192]

CIA documents from mid-1962 make explicit reference to a USIA film on the Cuban child refugees in the Miami camps, but there was apparently some dispute over whether or not the children's faces should be shown. The USIA was asked to investigate reports that voluntary agencies and DHEW were opposing any publicity or pictures of children in the Miami area "for fear Castro would not permit others to leave." This same memo mentions that "social service people are preparing articles for broad distribution on child welfare of Cubans in Florida, Venezuela, and Uruguay."[193] As part of the propaganda offensive in Latin America, Robert Hurwitch, the project officer for Operation Mongoose, planned for Katherine Oettinger's article about the Cuban refugee children in the United States to be translated into Spanish for circulation in Latin America.[194]

Another memo to General Lansdale, on 24 July 1962, mentioned the "Film on Children in Miami Orphanages," stating:

> Last week USIA was asked to clarify statements on inability to get into orphanages [sic] in Miami area to take pictures. USIA reported money appropriated, superb director appointed and highly professional staff organized to do the job, but were not given permission by voluntary agencies to take "close ups" and therefore project dropped. CIA sided with voluntary agencies' point of view—that there might be repercussions on parents remaining in Cuba. I took a stand that they could show backs of heads and point out that their faces not filmed in order to protect those remaining from Communist tyranny. USIA will look again with view to handling as part of "youth" film starting off with tiny tots and moving through Cuban students.[195]

Somehow the issue of whether or not to show the children's faces was resolved, because *The Lost Apple* features the faces of several individual children in the camp, so obviously those pushing the propaganda value argument won. Released in English and Spanish versions, this documentary raises other questions because it was shown in the United States, as well as in Latin America, in contravention of the 1948 Smith-Mundt Act, which forbids the circulation of USIA propaganda domestically without open acknowledgement.[196] In responding to the idea that Operation Pedro Pan had any links to the CIA or the propaganda campaign against the Cuban revolution, Msgr. Walsh conceded that this USIA documentary was "the only effort by the U.S. Government to use the [operation] for propaganda purposes." But he said, "[b]y the time it was released in 1963, the program had come to an end with the October Missile Crisis."[197]

That may be the case, but several copies of the draft script for *The Lost Apple* are in Msgr. Walsh's archive held at Barry University, suggesting that he was heavily involved in the project. Moreover, one of the producers of the documentary wrote to the Catholic Welfare Bureau in March 1963, expressing his gratitude for the favorable response the bureau had had to the film, because, he said, he had expected them to be "our severest critic." He went on to explain that the film had been made for the USIA, and that "extensive distribution through all possible channels in Latin America" was projected, and seventy channels of the National Educational Television network would broadcast it in the United States, making it available to schools and other organizations. Correspondence in Msgr. Walsh's archive indicates

Figure 5.1. Pedro Pans in Portland, Oregon, learn to salute the U.S. flag. "Tidal wave of Cuban children flows silently out of country," *Oregonian*, 8 March 1961. Courtesy of Barcroft Media, London, U.K.

that the Catholic Welfare Bureau was also actively promoting the documentary.[198] Nowhere in the credits of this film, however, is any mention made of the USIA.

Thus, the story of the rescue of the children served as a powerful indictment of Cuba's revolutionary project, and the young Pedro Pans themselves were constantly praised for how well they adjusted to their situation and how grateful they were for a chance to grow up in a "free country."[199]

The Pedro Pans as a U.S. "Investment"

There is yet another aspect to *The Lost Apple* that suggests the Pedro Pans might have been regarded by their hosts not just as eloquent accusers of Castro's communism, sources of intelligence, or potential recruits for future military adventures. Their sojourn in the United States was also seen as an opportunity for them to be trained as ambassadors and future leaders of a U.S.-style democratic political system—in other words, as an investment to ensure the historical, political, and economic bonds between the two nations were retained.

In the film *The Lost Apple*, a Spanish priest reminds the children assembled at the camp for a talent night that their presence "here under the sheltering skies of the United States, far from the land where you were born, torn from the warmth of your parents—is a constant reminder that there is something very wrong in the world." He urges them to be "boys and girls with a great sense of responsibility. There is a new society, a new world waiting ahead of you, a new homeland you have to build. And that new homeland can only be built with new men. That is what Cuba is waiting for from all of you."[200]

Now the Pedro Pans are no longer seen as simply innocent victims in a Cold War conflagration but are urged to become junior freedom fighters against the evil that had supposedly overcome their homeland. In other words, the Pedro Pans were to be the shock troops of Washington's longstanding "civilizing mission" in a future, post-Castro Cuba. Thus far, Cuban exiles had seemed incapable of winning the fight against Castro, and their frustrated handlers in Washington were becoming convinced of "the urgent necessity . . . to locate, train and support such Cuban nationals as will be capable of establishing a new non-Communist government once Castro is overthrown."[201] The Pedro Pan children were obvious targets for this "re-education" program. The anti-Castro DRE took very seriously its particular role in "eradicating the seeds of Marxism-Leninism" that had been planted in the minds of the youth who had stayed in Cuba.[202]

Among the most ardent advocates for taking advantage of the sojourn of young Cubans in the United States was James Baker, former director of the Ruston Academy in Havana. He presented the December 1961 Senate Subcommittee hearings on the Cuban refugee problem with a several-page "Memorandum on Preparing Refugees to Contribute to Education for Democracy in Cuba." The problem he identified was that of counteracting

"Communist indoctrination" and "reorienting" schoolchildren once "Castro and his communistic government are overthrown," something he acknowledged would be a "colossal" task: "If we are to rewin young Cubans to the side of freedom, we must return as well prepared to convince people of the value of democracy as were the Communists to sell their program when they took over the country in 1959."[203]

The special targets for this reeducation campaign were to be the one thousand Cuban teachers in Miami and the thousands of Cuban secondary and college students now studying in the United States: "It is of paramount importance that both students and adults return to Cuba firm believers in democracy, prepared to defend their country from the unceasing attacks of the Communists that will remain behind after Castro and his followers have fled."[204]

A research group was proposed to study indoctrination methods supposedly used in Cuba and then to work out how to counter them; special courses would be offered for refugees, including an after-school program for Cubans attending junior and senior high school in Miami. The stated objective was "To prepare a program and educational materials to be used in the post-Castro period: (a) to combat positively the effects of Communist brainwashing on Cuban children and youth of the primary and secondary levels; and (b) to develop in these students a comprehensive understanding of and belief in democracy."[205]

Although this program was based on the understanding that Castro's demise was imminent, the memo noted that if the training of teachers was completed before it was possible for them to return to Cuba, they could be deployed to "other Latin American countries faced with a shortage of teachers and a threat from Communism."[206]

Tracy Voorhees's January 1961 report on the Cuban refugee situation had already recognized the opportunity presented by the presence of a large number of Cuban children in U.S. schools, commenting that they were "generally a very high type of student from ambitious, education-minded families." He quoted a Miami school principal as saying: "There are a lot of very fine people coming into our schools. They can be fine ambassadors for us, if they return sometime to Cuba; or fine potential citizens of the United States, if we handle things right here."[207] Sr. Miriam Strong, an employee at the Catholic Hispanic Center in Miami, also stressed the importance of bringing young Cubans to the United States because, she said, "[t]o free these minds of Castroism will be the most difficult task of the period of reconstruction. Getting children out of Cuba and caring for them in their exile is the immediate, most urgent, problem of the adults today."[208]

Katherine Oettinger of the DHEW Children's Bureau saw the same advantage to Operation Pedro Pan: "When the program will end, no one can predict at present.... [But its] impact will be felt long after its termination. In the long run, the peace of the world and the preservation of free societies depend on the development of the individual capacities of children and of a vast 'common market' of ideas, knowledge, cultural interchange, and good will. The program for the displaced children from Cuba represents a long-term investment on this side of the ledger."[209]

As it was, the CIA had been actively recruiting students from many Latin American countries since 1960 in order to prepare them to be leaders on their return to their respective countries.[210] At the exact moment Operation Pedro Pan was taking off, FBI director J. Edgar Hoover wrote, "there is a group of young Cubans who want to go to college here in this country and that is a wonderful opportunity. The communists always went after the youth first and we ought in this country to see if we can't place these young people into schools and indoctrinate them with democracy."[211] Msgr. Walsh himself was involved in a leadership program for young Latin Americans, with a weighty element of Christian proselytizing, but this, of course, was not considered "indoctrination."[212] As Karen Dubinsky remarked somewhat wryly: "Where we 'educated,' communists 'brainwashed.'"[213]

The Cuban report suggested it was the Ruston Academy teacher Penny Powers who proposed to Ramón Grau a "parallel plan" to Operation Pedro Pan in October 1961 called the Organización Nacional de Asistencia Social (National Organization of Social Assistance, or ONAS). This was the creation of a scholarship scheme to reeducate young Cubans once the revolution was overthrown. Students would be held in "concentration camps" in order to "reeducate them and 'de-intoxicate' them from the preachings of [José] Martí and the revolution and at the same time catechize them with the annexationist and traitorous ideas of those who want to sell out the country and convert them into faithful servants of the U.S. Empire."[214]

While this might be considered something of an exaggeration, Operation Pedro Pan clearly did involve an element of reeducation or counter-indoctrination. A memo to Secretary of Defense McNamara in April 1962 expressed concern about a serious problem expected to arise in a post-Castro scenario because "the continuing indoctrination of the Cuban youth is creating a growing nucleus for a communist underground after the elimination of the present government . . . a problem for the future which is steadily increasing in magnitude." The memo urges that U.S. intervention in Cuba should take place as soon as possible.[215]

Penny Powers, like James Baker, saw the reeducation of young Cubans who had been influenced by the social revolution under way in Cuba as an essential aspect of Operation Pedro Pan. "This should be an opportunity," wrote Penny Powers to former U.S. ambassador Bonsal, "for the children to see American life at its best form, so that they would realize that Communism has nothing to offer them in comparison with democracy."[216] She became concerned that the inappropriate placement of the children in orphanages and negative impact of the separation of siblings undermined the possibility of the "intensive preparation" she hoped they would receive during their U.S. sojourn. Furthermore, she said, this added to the anxieties for their parents back in Cuba.[217]

This sheds a rather different light on Operation Pedro Pan beyond its stated goal as a "rescue" mission and exposes it as part of a long-term U.S. political strategy based on the general view in Washington that Cubans were temperamentally incapable of governing themselves and needed a firm guiding hand.

* * *

In conclusion, despite the court ruling rejecting the FOIA case María de los Angeles Torres brought against the CIA, the evacuation scheme was intimately bound up with Washington's Cuba Project, the covert war to undermine and overthrow the Cuban government, in various ways. First, the CIA instigated and promoted the *patria potestad* hoax, which played on Cold War anticommunist fears and anxieties arising from the profound social changes taking place in revolutionary Cuba. Although a mass exodus may not have been the original intention of the scare, it became one of the main factors driving the departures. This was achieved through the CIA's subversive broadcasts on Radio Swan and a broad range of propaganda materials, including the fake law, that were widely distributed through clandestine and Catholic networks.

Initiated in the lead-up to the 1961 U.S.-backed Bay of Pigs invasion as a means of guaranteeing the safety of the children of anti-Castro fighters while their parents were encouraged to stay on the island and participate in the attempted violent overthrow of the Cuban government, Operation

Pedro Pan also proved to be a way to expedite the departure of young antigovernment activists whose cover had been blown. Furthermore, the networks spiriting children out of the country were also engaged in what have been described euphemistically as "other pro-democratic activities," including sabotage, assassination plots, and terrorist actions against the Cuban government, which, after the Bay of Pigs debacle, were even more run directly from Washington.

Furthermore, U.S. visas and places on flights were offered to the children of potential agents as inducements to participate in various underground activities.[218] The massive scale of the child exodus proved to be a convenient cover for the "exfiltration" of agents (dubbed "king-size" Pedro Pans) in the intensified covert operations conducted in preparation for a second invasion attempt, planned for October 1962, a plan derailed by the Missile Crisis that same month.

Once on U.S. soil, the Pedro Pans were seen by Washington policymakers as potential—and often very willing—recruits in military, intelligence, and propaganda programs against the Cuban government as junior spies, soldiers, or ambassadors representing an alternative "democratic" Cuba. Therefore, it is impossible to argue that the U.S. government and its agencies, including the CIA, had no knowledge of or involvement in Operation Pedro Pan.

Cuban children continued to trickle into Miami after October 1962, but the Missile Crisis is generally accepted as bringing about the end of Operation Pedro Pan. The failed Bay of Pigs invasion had been a significant setback, but for the anti-Castro exiles, the Kennedy-Khrushchev accord of October 1962 was even more devastating because of the noninvasion agreement reached between Washington and Moscow.[219] Furthermore, the 1961 literacy campaign and the revolutionary government's second effort to defeat small armed bands of counterrevolutionaries operating in the Escambray mountains in June 1962, along with the second agrarian reform law of October 1962, all combined to deal a fatal blow to the counterrevolution.[220] After the Missile Crisis, Operation Mongoose was "quietly mothballed," and Chief of Operations General Lansdale, still a close ally of Robert Kennedy, was "tactfully relieved of his responsibilities."[221]

Nevertheless, exile groups continued to launch raids against Cuba, which the U.S. government tolerated while appearing to take a greater distance from these counterrevolutionary activities.[222] By the end of 1962, the anti-Castro forces were generally in disarray, many of their leaders having been captured or in exile, so the child evacuation scheme was becoming far more difficult.[223] But the cancellation of direct commercial flights between Cuba and the United States sealed the fate of the thousands of now-stranded children.

Havana and Washington signed an agreement regarding the repatriation of the captured Bay of Pigs invaders in December 1962, but when Cuba proposed the resumption of flights toward the end of 1962, Washington refused, wanting to avoid the appearance of responding to Castro's demand.[224] The refugee problem was reported to be having a continued "depressing impact" on the Miami area; even though 56,000 Cubans had been relocated to other states by March 1963, over 100,000 remained (of whom 60,000 were receiving aid), and they were proving hard to dislodge.[225] Speaking at the Cuban Refugee Center in Miami in early 1963, director of the Cuban Refugee Program John Thomas reminded his audience that the program had been "the most liberal, generous, and realistic program ever put into effect, anywhere in the world," and he urged Cubans to consider resettlement outside the Miami area, explaining this did "not in any way diminish the importance which the United States gives to the future building of a free and democratic Cuba."[226]

Thus, while the Pedro Pans were encouraged to claim their parents, the U.S. government sought ways to staunch the seemingly never-ending flow of Cuban refugees into Florida and to move those already there to other states. The Pedro Pans, having been shipped all over the United States, then came to perform yet another function—that of "anchors"—due to the U.S. policy that children and parents could only be reunited wherever the young refugees had been placed, not in south Florida.[227]

The lack of direct flights from Cuba not only helped to isolate the island politically and economically but also made it more difficult and expensive for Cubans to leave. By early 1963, the only "Free World" air services to Cuba were from Mexico and Spain, leaving several thousand Pedro Pans stranded in the United States and possibly thousands of others in Cuba still holding Fr. Walsh's visa waivers.[228] The matter of family reunification was not properly settled until December 1965, but even in April 1967 the Children's Bureau reported it still had 375 young Cubans in its care.[229]

For obvious reasons, it has suited the main proponents of Operation Pedro Pan to overlook the U.S. government's resistance to appeals for family reunification, and to obscure the entire program behind a humanitarian façade, carefully separating it from some of the less savory activities of the anti-Castro counterrevolutionary movement.[230] Thus, what emerges is not a picture of a compassionate response to a situation of social and political turmoil but rather a dark tale of "intrigue and deception," of the cynical manipulation of parents' deepest fears, and a callous disregard for Cuban families.[231] As one of the key players in this drama remarked: "In a war, anything is permitted."[232]

6

The Pedro Pan Paradox

If secrecy was so crucial to Operation Pedro Pan in order to smuggle the children out from under Fidel Castro's nose, it should have been far more difficult to spirit the children out of Cuba after Fr. Bryan Walsh and U.S. Department of Health, Education, and Welfare (DHEW) secretary Abraham Ribicoff went public about the program in March 1962. But several thousand more unaccompanied children were able to leave the island until the Missile Crisis in October of that year stopped all flights to the United States. Why this was the case, Msgr. Walsh explained, was always the biggest "single mystery of the whole thing. . . . We expected every day to be the last day. We just could not understand that the [Cuban] government was allowing this to happen."[1]

So, how much did the Cuban government know about Operation Pedro Pan at the time? A former Pedro Pan was told by a Cuban Ministry of the Interior official, Colonel Tony de la Guardia, that they knew about the "monsignor's children." Apparently de la Guardia "admitted that the Cuban government always followed the children closely and had spies among the workers of the temporary shelters in Miami."[2] This is possible because the staff at the camps were mostly Cuban émigrés themselves, and Cuban state security was highly successful in penetrating exile groups in the United States, to the point where the effectiveness of screening procedures was queried at the Senate Subcommittee hearings on Cuban refugees.[3] Two Cuban defectors in the 1980s asserted that nearly all Cuban CIA agents recruited in the 1960s were double agents, although this is probably something of an exaggeration.[4]

After the U.S. embassy in Havana was closed in January 1961, Fr. Walsh flew to Kingston to investigate the possibility of sending the children via

Jamaica, where they could collect U.S. visas and then proceed to Miami. At the airport, he was surprised when a Cuban came up to him and asked if he was there to meet the Cuban children, recalling, "Pedro Pan was supposed to be a secret and we were trying to avoid giving the Cuban authorities the impression that there was a wide-scale organized effort to help children leave the island. We were sure that this would bring about reprisals against parents and others in Cuba who were cooperating."[5]

Clearly delighted with what he imagined as a cloak-and-dagger escapade, he continued, "I tried to look innocent and told him that we were simply curious to see the flight. But by now we were beginning to feel that we were really involved in an international intrigue."[6] Were the Cuban authorities watching out for children or just monitoring adult émigrés? The Jamaica route, however, soon proved to be an unnecessary, more complicated, and more expensive option than simply putting the children on direct Havana-Miami flights with Walsh's visa waivers in their hands.

Recently appointed as monsignor, Walsh also made a brief visit to Havana in March 1963 to attend the funeral of Cardinal Arteaga Betancourt, a trip that was quite remarkable on several counts, not least of all for the fact that he and Miami's Bishop Coleman Carroll were able to travel to Cuba (admitted for one day without visas as "passengers in transit") and meet with several leading figures in the church hierarchy, such as archbishops Enrique Pérez Serantes and Alfredo Müller San Martín, who remained on the island despite their open hostility to the revolutionary government. It is clear in the fourteen-page report Msgr. Walsh wrote about this trip that he was well known in Havana, because at one point he found himself surrounded by Cubans who wanted to discuss the situation of children and relatives in Miami.[7] Whom his report was written for was never explained, although it is possible that Msgr. Walsh prepared it with the intention of sending it to the State Department as a firsthand account of the situation on the island, relishing as he did his bit part in what he perceived as a great Cold War spy drama.[8]

Whether Msgr. Walsh's trip proved that the Cuban government was unaware of Operation Pedro Pan and the participation in the scheme of leading religious figures is not clear. It is possible the Cuban government was simply monitoring the situation and not particularly concerned about the departures of the children at this time. After a thorough review of the trial records of those involved in Operation Pedro Pan, the Cuban report concluded that the existence of the organized scheme was exposed primarily by some of the main protagonists themselves, such as Msgr. Walsh and others, despite their attempt to "obscure their real goals by portraying their actions as humanitarian and legal."[9] A former head of Cuban state security asserted that the full extent of Operation Pedro Pan only became known when Polita Grau revealed everything to an informer placed in her prison cell after she was arrested in 1965, that is, after the operation had apparently ended.[10]

On another occasion, Msgr. Walsh related what Ramón Grau had told him about an encounter with an intelligence officer just before his release from prison in Cuba. The officer supposedly told him, "We should have shot you years ago." Grau asked: "Why? For trying to kill Fidel Castro?" "No, for stealing our children," the officer responded.[11] This could, however, just be an example of bravado on Grau's part, or maybe also on Walsh's. The obituary published in the *New York Times* on Ramón Grau's death chose to highlight his and his sister's role in child smuggling rather than their criminal conviction for their part in a plot to assassinate Fidel Castro.[12]

Teté Cuervo, who worked at the Havana travel agency that was issuing tickets for the Pedro Pans, was arrested at the time of the Bay of Pigs invasion. She repeated the "cover story" to the Cuban state security officers who questioned her: that the children were traveling to the United States on *"becas"* (scholarships). María de los Angeles Torres became convinced that Cuban security knew about the child airlift program because so many of the parents were underground activists, like Cuervo's husband, who had participated in the invasion.[13] This suggests that Cuban authorities were far more interested in the activities of adults rather than the departures of the children.

It is significant that Penny Powers (the former Ruston Academy teacher) and prominent members of the Catholic clergy, along with an unknown number of staff at various foreign embassies who had actively promoted or participated in the program, remained at liberty in Cuba.[14] Although she had no formal diplomatic accreditation, Penny Powers was somehow authorized by the British government to stamp visa waivers into Cubans' passports for travel to Jamaica.[15] Certainly, relations between the U.S. and British embassies were reported to be extremely close at this time, to the point where they read one another's cables, and the British assumed a significant role in U.S. affairs when the U.S. embassy in Havana was closed in January 1961.[16]

Penny Powers might have been in a position to denounce Ramón Grau to the Cuban authorities but apparently chose not to. Instead she brought him food during his first two years in prison and looked after his aging uncle, the former president of Cuba. Although Cuban authorities claim to have learned of Penny Powers's role in Operation Pedro Pan after the scheme ended, in a footnote, the Cuban report mentioned that because Powers was a close associate of the Grau siblings she was being watched by Cuban state security in late 1964.[17] Msgr. Walsh recalled Penny Powers was "violently anti-Fidel" and had declared she "would not leave Cuba until Fidel left first." Powers ran a small school for children of European diplomats after the Ruston Academy closed, and Msgr. Walsh believed she had the protection of the British embassy. "We never mentioned her," he said, "because we didn't want to make her life more difficult."[18]

In an interview a few years before her death, Penny Powers said that from prison Ramón Grau asked her to act as a double agent for him against the Cuban government when she was still working for British intelligence. Penny Powers and Ramón Grau apparently fell out at some point when Powers refused a gift he sent from prison.[19] It is important to note that Ramón and Polita Grau were arrested in February 1965, while Penny Powers opened the Hillside International School in October of that year—presumably with the approval of the Cuban government—and lived in Havana until her death in 1996.[20] Powers was made a Member of the British Empire (MBE) in 1981 by Queen Elizabeth II for her "services to education in Cuba," not, as has been suggested, for "her struggle against oppressive regimes."[21] Could Penny Powers have already been a double agent? Or, as former U.S. diplomat Wayne Smith pointed out, maybe Powers never actually violated any Cuban law.[22] This seems to be a mystery that might never be solved.

What conclusion can be drawn from the fact that no one was ever arrested or charged in Cuba for assisting the exodus of the children?[23] There can be no doubt that the Cuban government was acutely aware of the campaign about *patria potestad*, especially after the September 1961 raid on the print shop where copies of the fake law were found, and those responsible for printing and distributing it were arrested and jailed. Moreover, the thousands of children departing as unaccompanied minors can hardly have escaped notice; an official in the passport office of Cuba's Department of Foreign Relations, recalled parents coming to her office in late 1960 begging for passports for their children to be expedited. "They were not interested in leaving [themselves], but only wanted passports for their children," she said.[24] When the Marist Brothers' College was expropriated following the June 1961 nationalization of education, government officials discovered a group of priests at Villa Marista processing children's passports and visa waivers, together with counterrevolutionary propaganda and a significant amount of U.S. dollars.[25]

The fact that unusually large numbers of children were boarding flights without their parents, along with frequent U.S. media reports about how Miami-Dade County schools were bursting at the seams with Cuban students, meant that while the Cuban government may not have been aware of the mechanics of the operation, it cannot have failed to realize what was happening. *New York Times* journalist Ruby Hart Phillips described how her sister was subjected to close scrutiny by immigration officials when she left Cuba in December 1960 with a six-year-old Cuban child, for whom she had assumed guardianship. "Hundreds of children were being sent out of Cuba," Phillips explained, "and the authorities were not pleased to see an American taking one." She said she knew of one North American who helped "several hundred children leave Cuba," but she mentioned no name.[26]

Nevertheless, there is no evidence of any attempt to stop the children leaving, apart from an incident in September 1961 when the *New York Times* reported shots fired at Havana airport when authorities "refused to allow a group of children to fly to the United States without their parents."[27] The Cuban report explained this incident arose because of the Ministry of the Interior's new, tighter restrictions on exit permits related to changes in the urban reform law, and the insistence that the tickets used by departing passengers matched the name on their passports.[28] As already discussed, KLM and Pan American airlines kept passenger lists with false names, for which the names of Pedro Pans were substituted at the last minute—a highly irregular protocol.[29] It might also be significant that this incident occurred the day after copies of the fake *patria potestad* law were discovered by Cuban security forces.

In August 1961, the world had witnessed the overnight erection of the Berlin wall and, because Fidel Castro had declared the Cuban revolution as socialist a few months earlier, inevitably those aware of the tight controls many socialist bloc countries placed on citizens wanting to leave began to fear that the revolutionary government would impose similar restrictions.[30] As it was, generally no such restrictions were established on Cuban would-be emigrants—except for doctors, some other professionals, and later, boys approaching the age of military service.[31] But a central feature of the *patria potestad* scare campaign was regular mention that the revolutionary government intended to block the departure of all children from the island, the date for which kept changing as the supposed date of implementation was passed.

When he first denounced the *patria potestad* hoax in September 1961, Fidel Castro explained rather bluntly why the Cuban government imposed no restrictions on citizens leaving the country: "Let the parasites go!" he said. "No one loses anything." The 500-peso departure charge, he added, would give five families an income of 100 pesos each, and departing émigrés might leave a house large enough for ten people. "It is sad to see those children taken to be educated over there," said Fidel, "but we respect the feelings and the rights of each family, above all else."[32]

The Cuban government's policy of "letting them go" meant that Operation Pedro Pan became "a vehicle that allowed the kids to leave and then the parents to follow."[33] The government might have allowed the émigrés and their children to leave because they were considered "poor material for conversion to communism" or because it could use the money obtained from the fares and from the property goods they were forced to relinquish.[34] Although in the short term, the exodus and the brain drain it represented had a significant impact on the economy, ultimately it proved to be a natural "cleansing" process that actually strengthened the revolution.[35] This might have been somewhat of a miscalculation on the part of the U.S. government because, whether the Cuban government was motivated by pragmatism or a conscious political strategy, the outcome of the flight of so many disaffected citizens or outright opponents was to weaken dissent significantly within Cuba, enabling the consolidation of support for the revolution and an acceleration in the pace of reform.

The argument that the Cuban government did not know much about (or had accepted) the departures of the children is therefore credible to a certain extent. The Ministry of the Interior was only established in June 1961 and faced a tense situation of increasing hostilities emanating from within and outside the country as Operation Mongoose was ramped up.[36] As explained in the previous chapter, invasion plans were not abandoned—another attempt being scheduled for October 1962—and armed gangs were active in the Escambray mountains, while terrorist attacks and sabotage continued in the cities and countryside.

Referring to the rather irregular appearance of the children's visa waiver letters, which were sometimes just copies, Msgr. Walsh suggested that the Cubans had such a bureaucratic mentality that they would accept any official-looking paperwork they were presented with.[37] But this hardly explains why, if the Cuban government objected to the departures, they let the children go. The Cuban researchers insisted that although the government was aware of the consequences of the *patria potestad* scare, it was "very far from imagining" the scope of the operation and the extent of the involvement in the scheme of different U.S. government agencies, including the CIA, and foreign diplomats, as well as sectors of the Catholic church in Cuba and the United States. The Cuban report, nevertheless, affirmed that the government always "respected the right of parents to freely decide the destiny of their children." Even so, paradoxically, the report argued that the entire operation—not just the *patria potestad* hoax—was a "criminal action" that was said to have "rescued" children from a revolution made precisely "to liberate them from exploitation"—despite the fact that no one in Cuba was ever charged with the crime of organizing or assisting the children's departures.[38]

A decade after Operation Pedro Pan, Fidel Castro was still angry about the *patria potestad* hoax and, during a visit to Chile, he recalled how psychological warfare had been employed against the Cuban revolution: "With what lack of scruples, with what cynicism did they launch and propagate one of the most shameless, the lowest and most infamous of lies . . . [that the revolution] was going to deprive mothers of their rights over their children. . . . [This led to] possibly several thousand women sending their children to the United States because of that base rumor."[39]

When a bust of the late Msgr. Walsh was unveiled in Miami in June 2009, the Cuban leader was prompted to return to the subject in his regular newspaper column, "Reflections," referring to the episode as "one of the most repugnant acts of moral aggression carried out against our country" and a "cynical publicity maneuver that would have been the "envy of Goebbels." The revolution, Fidel said, was made "voluntarily . . . by a free people," and he pointed out that over the years around a million Cubans had been able to leave. He scathingly described the priest as "the mastermind behind the operation . . . under the orders of the bishop of Miami." "There was no reason why [those children] had to be dragged into that tragedy. . . . None of them," he asserted, "required to be saved."[40]

Over the years, the Cuban government moderated its language regarding the fate of the Pedro Pans, expressing sympathy for the trauma most experienced by being separated from their families. When, in 1978, Fidel Castro met with the first group of young Cubans to return to the island—those who had left with Operation Pedro Pan or as children with their families in the 1960s—he expressed concern that they might blame his government for their exile: "You might ask," he said, "'Why did you let us go?' But, what else could we do? I want you to understand well that one of the things that produced a mass exodus from the country was something totally fabricated, which was the story about *patria potestad* that they produced as an apocryphal law, totally false, and they made it appear like a stolen document.... [T]hat was one of the things that led to a mass exodus from the country, and many families sent their children away, before leaving themselves."[41]

The "real fear" about the *patria potestad* law, Fidel admitted, was understandable because it "coincided with a particular psychological moment, because there were so many revolutionary laws of one kind or the other."[42] Many Pedro Pans, nevertheless, still struggled to understand their parents' decision to send them away, harboring feelings of resentment and rejection.[43] These sentiments were explored in Eduardo Machado's play, *Havana Is Waiting*, in which the character Federico (a Pedro Pan like Machado) returns to Cuba and attends a rally in Havana for Elián González's return, and remarks: "I wish someone would have fought to get me back."[44]

This researcher interviewed two former senior figures in Cuban state security, both of whom acknowledged that the Cuban government might have had a vague idea of what was happening, but each offered a different answer to the question of why so many children were permitted to leave as unaccompanied minors.

Retired General Fabián Escalante, a former head of Cuban state security, explained it was a simple matter of priorities. "The priority in those days was to stop the bombs going off," he said, referring to the widespread terrorist attacks and sabotage campaigns conducted by antigovernment groups. Besides, he pointed out, the resources and personnel of the newly created Ministry of the Interior in those years were limited and extremely inexperienced: "In Havana, there were only 200 [Cuban agents] trying to follow thousands, maybe 2,000 or 3,000 counterrevolutionaries."[45]

Would the government have stopped the departures if it was fully apprised of what was happening? The second interviewee was retired Colonel José Buajasán, a kindly looking man who, in different circumstances, said he might have become a Catholic priest. In the early 1960s, he led a tiny team assigned to counteract the propaganda the anti-Castro groups were spreading. He answered this question with a question: "How could we have

Figure 6.1. Poster for the 2017 documentary, *Elián*, directed by U.S. journalist Tim Golden and Irish filmmaker Ross McDonnell. With kind permission of Fine Point Films, Belfast, Ireland.

stopped them? [The children] were being sent out of the country with their parents' consent. If we had prohibited this, wouldn't this confirm that the government had indeed assumed *patria potestad* over Cuba's children?"[46]

Operation Pedro Pan, María de los Angeles Torres concluded, effectively "turned parents' worst fears—that their children would be taken from them—into grim reality."[47] The Cuban report went as far as suggesting parents who chose to send their children out of Cuba were actually relinquishing their rights to the organizers of the program.[48] Some of the Pedro Pans agree: "My mother sent me away so that she would not lose *patria potestad*," said Francisco, "but the irony is that she did not lose it in Cuba, she lost it here, when I came to the United States through her own decision that had nothing to do with events in Cuba."[49] With some bitterness, Román de la Campa pointed out: "We ended up in camps after all—not in Eastern Europe, but in distant sites [in the United States] that our parents had never seen or perhaps even heard of, and without their direct knowledge. We were saved from Prague but were sent instead to naval bases in Opa Locka, orphanages in Toledo, camps in Jacksonville."[50]

A former U.S. diplomat in Havana, Wayne Smith, reflected, "I've never understood the argument that the separation of the children from their families and sending them to the United States protected the human rights of the families, in that, as we now know, the rumors were false, the children [who stayed in Cuba] were not separated from their families, and so the painful experience was really not necessary."[51]

The Case of Little Elián González

But the paradox of the Pedro Pan story does not end there. On Thanksgiving 1999, a five-year-old child was found floating on an inner tube in the Florida Straits after his mother and several other Cubans had drowned in an effort to reach Florida. Ironically, when young Elián González was held captive by his relatives in Miami for several months, in the fury unleashed in the Cuban-American community to any idea of the child's return to his surviving parent—his father in Cuba—somehow the principle of *patria potestad* was trumped by the toxic exile politics of Miami. It was not a "custody matter," said Republican Senator Orrin Hatch, but a case where the child might be returned "to one of the last prison nations in the world."[52] The Cuban American National Foundation produced posters portraying Elián as "Another child victim of Fidel Castro" to protest the Cuban president's expected attendance at the World Trade Organization forum in Seattle in December 1999.[53]

The little boy was wrapped in an American flag and showered with toys in an obscene effort to answer the question posed by a *Washington Post* editorial: "[Is it] better to grow up with one's father in a tyranny or with extended family in a democracy?"[54] Former Pedro Pans (mainly those still living in Florida) fell over each other to express their gratitude for having had the chance to come to the United States in an endless recital of the narrative of their "escape" and subsequent success in the land of freedom and opportunity.[55]

Infuriated, Fidel Castro issued a call to arms and pronounced the child was "a symbol of the billions of children [in this world who] should be educated, fed and given the opportunity of a healthy and dignified life." Therefore, he expressed confidence that "the enemy" would "not be able to withstand our morale, our truth and our irrepressible forces, and . . . will have no alternative but to return Elián as soon as possible."[56] When the conflict dragged on, Fidel recalled the experience of Operation Pedro Pan, which he described as a "mass kidnapping."[57] This statement has been erroneously interpreted as reflecting the Cuban government's view that the island's children were "the property of the state," thereby confirming that parents' fears in the early 1960s were justified.[58] This ignores the fact that both the Cuban and U.S. governments repeatedly insisted on the application of the principle of *patria potestad* in Elián's case.

In reality, the Pedro Pans had left the island with their parents' consent, and in accordance with Cuban law at the time. The key difference in the case of Elián González was that he had left Cuba with his mother illegally and without his father's agreement as required by Cuban law.[59] In fact, most countries' child custody laws require the consent of both parents or guardians for a child to leave the country.

The international political wrangle over Elián González, nevertheless, exposed the extent to which Operation Pedro Pan had marked the psyche of a fractured nation.[60] At stake was the exile image of Cuba as the ultimate, absolute hell, an image that would be invalidated if the child was returned to his father. The debate was framed in such Manichean terms that returning Elián to Cuba was regarded by Cubans in Miami as the same as sending him back to a concentration camp or a slave plantation. Elián's great uncle Lázaro even suggested that it would have been better for the child to have been eaten by sharks than returned to Cuba. After all, commented Miami priest Fr. Francisco Santana, "Elián is so important, because the exile community... began precisely by the concept of 'Save the Children.'"[61]

Nevertheless, some Cuban Americans could see the contradictions in the argument that the child should remain in Miami, arguing that Elián's father's custody claim "was based on the same notion of *patria potestad* on which the parents of the 14,000 [Pedro Pans] ... had relied."[62] The head of the U.S. Interests Section in Havana, Vicki Huddleston, remarked that the intransigence of Miami's Cuban-American community to return the child to his father enraged every Cuban citizen on the island. "It was terrible propaganda against us," she said, "more effective than forty plus years of Fidel's propaganda."[63]

Despite the furious resistance in Miami to any idea that the child might be repatriated to Cuba, Msgr. Walsh, too, privately supported returning Elián to his father, explaining, "The whole foundation of Pedro Pan was the inalienable rights of parents to decide the education of their children. [Elián's father] has the same right. . . . It is an inalienable right, unless the parents are unfit parents. That's fundamental to the whole question."[64]

On this point, Fidel Castro repeatedly insisted the government respected "the rights of parents who want to take their children with them [to the United States]. We respect this right as steadfastly as we are defending the rights of this father . . . in his fight to get his son back."[65] Ironically, here the U.S. and Cuban governments—and Fidel Castro and Bryan Walsh—found themselves on the same side, although Msgr. Walsh did not make his views public at the time, no doubt because of the extraordinary political pressure exerted by the Cuban-American community. Although the overwhelming majority of Miami's Cubans apparently supported Elián remaining in the United States, many expressed a different opinion privately.[66] Ely Chovel, founder of the Pedro Pan Group, was publicly vilified for advocating the child's return to his father's custody in Cuba.[67] Another former Pedro Pan, Eloísa Echazábal, said she, too, felt under great pressure not to speak what she "felt in her heart"—that Elián belonged with his father.[68]

Significantly, the U.S. Court of Appeals eventually ruled in June 2000 that "Communist re-education and indoctrination are not necessarily 'persecution' as defined in U.S. asylum law," thus rejecting the application for asylum made on the child's behalf.[69] This removed the final obstacle to Elián's return to Cuba on 28 June.

The Fate of Pedro Pan Carlos Muñiz

But perhaps the greatest paradox of all, in this tale replete with many ironies, is that of the case of Carlos Muñiz, a Pedro Pan, whose fate was to be assassinated at the age of twenty-six by the very same counterrevolutionary exile forces that had "rescued" him as a child from Cuba.[70] Carlos, at the age of eight, and his older sister Míriam came to Miami on the same flight as their mother, who had told them to pretend they had traveled alone so that they would be taken into care while their widowed mother found her feet. The family eventually settled in Puerto Rico, where, as a student, Carlos became influenced by that island's struggle for independence. Muñiz was part of a group of fifty-five young Cuban Americans who returned to Cuba in December 1977, a visit that opened the way for the first dialogue between Cubans on the island and those living "in the exterior" (abroad) at a time when intransigent exiles were pronouncing: "Dynamite is the only language in which we will engage in dialogue."[71]

Just as some Pedro Pans internalized the message that they were the future leaders of their nation and felt obligated to show their gratitude to "the American People who embraced [them]," others, like Carlos Muñiz, came to feel responsible for seeking a dialogue and reconciliation with the land of their birth.[72] But the visits of these young émigrés back to Cuba provoked a violent reaction among some terrorist exile groups, like Omega 7. The travel agency Muñiz ran that organized trips to Cuba was firebombed, and he and others in his group began to receive death threats in anonymous telephone calls. Carlos Muñiz was assassinated in his car on Saturday 28 April 1979, shot at from a passing vehicle a few blocks from his mother's house in a residential street of San Juan. No one was ever charged for this crime, although Omega 7 claimed responsibility. At his funeral, Carlos's mother was handed a wreath with the message: "To that son of a bitch."[73]

"My mother took the decision to send me [out of the country]," commented a former Pedro Pan, "[b]ut the decision to return was mine." She had felt a need to return "in order to close the circle and to make peace with ourselves, our history and our country."[74] But the participation in what became known as the Antonio Maceo Brigade that organized trips of young Cuban Americans to Cuba sometimes caused intractable divisions within families. "Going back meant you were breaking someone's heart," said Guillermo Grenier, whose mother regarded him as going to visit "assassins," even though, as seems evident from Carlos Muñiz's case, the assassins did not reside in Cuba.[75] It is far from uncommon for immigrant families to experience a pronounced rift between generations, as children usually adapt to the new country more easily than their parents; the main difficulties for Cuban émigré families integrating into U.S. society often arose because of "parental insistence on preservation of Cuban cultural patterns and the Cuban youngster's faster [adaptation]."[76] But in the case of Cuban-American families, the political gap between different generations often became quite extreme.[77]

Young Cuban Americans living in New York and Boston in the early 1970s started to publish a magazine, *Joven Cuba*, at about the same time another group coalesced around a similar magazine, *Areíto*, in Miami.[78] They saw themselves as having been "born in the midst of a society in change," and then growing up "in another society in crisis." At this time, the United States, their adopted homeland, was being shaken by the Civil Rights movement, the war in Vietnam, and student protests. Confused about their identity, the young Cuban émigrés asked: "Are we part of a historical continuity or do we live in the past?"[79] Their parents had fled Cuba to protect middle-class and Catholic understandings of childhood and family life, only to be horrified by the countercultural lifestyle their children were exposed to in the land that was supposed to be their refuge from "the Revolution's godlessness and amorality."[80] One Cuban émigré parent remarked: "Fidel Castro took my property and left me with no country, but the United States took my children."[81]

Finding themselves alone in a strange land without their parents, the Pedro Pans quickly had to learn self-reliance and independence and often had to assume responsibility for younger siblings. This experience left many of them with feelings of abandonment by their parents and a sense of a lost or stolen childhood. "When I arrived in Miami," recalled María Emilia Castagliola, who left Cuba as a fourteen-year-old with Operation Pedro Pan, "my eyes were swollen by tears. Once I stepped off the plane, I never cried again."[82]

Some Pedro Pans who were unhappy, including some who were abused in foster homes or institutions, chose not to tell their parents about their situation so as not to worry them. When others, like Ana Mendieta, did write home describing her placement in an orphanage and then in a foster home, where she and her sister were treated like maids, she was told she was "exaggerating" and that her mother was suffering badly herself.[83] Ed Canler's mother responded to his description of Camp Matecumbe for Pedro Pans

Figure 6.2. This statue of José Martí was erected facing the U.S. Interests Section in Havana in 2000 during the international conflict over the Cuban child Elián González. (Photo by the author.)

as a "green hell" saying, "Well remember, you were in a red hell. So get over it!"[84]

By the time Candi Sosa's parents arrived in the United States, she no longer considered herself a child; she felt she had lost her innocence, having been repeatedly sexually abused by her foster father. She was not the child she had been, and nor were her parents the same, she said, so that those who reencountered one another "had familiar faces, but the people behind those faces were strangers."[85] Candi's mother, Ana, had known nothing about what had happened to her daughter but said she had suffered terribly from "nerves" during the two-and-a-half-years separation. Her young son was also a Pedro Pan but was separated from his sisters; he later developed severe anxiety and depression from which he never recovered. Nevertheless, Ana had no regrets about the decision she had made.[86]

Thus, although "Pedro Pan" proved to be a totally inappropriate metaphor for the exodus in that, as many of the young Cubans quickly discovered, their childhood ended the moment they boarded their flight to Miami, they began to feel that they really had arrived in "Neverland, the Land of the Lost Children" depicted in J. M. Barrie's original children's tale. When Ely Chovel paid young Elián a visit in his great uncle's Miami home on 28 December 1999, she told him the story of how she came to the United States as a young girl with Operation Pedro Pan. "He kept asking me to teach him how to fly like Peter Pan," she recalled. "I want to fly, I want to be Peter Pan," he repeated. When she asked him why, he whispered, "So I can go wherever I want to."[87]

Conclusion

Ambassadors, Soldiers, or Spies?

> La mitad de una vida, vacia por dentro...
> Y porqué?... por ignorancia y por mentiras.
> Cuarenta anos, la mitad de una vida,
> gastados, perdidos, sin nada por dentro.
> "La Mitad de Una Vida"[1]

As the dramatic year of 1962 drew to a close, with Moscow and Washington reaching an accord that resolved the October Missile Crisis, Operation Pedro Pan had largely served its purpose in the covert and propaganda war against the Cuban revolution. The counterrevolutionary networks in Cuba on which the operation had relied were significantly weakened by this time, even the CIA admitting that the anti-Castro movement was losing its "effectiveness."[2] Most importantly, however, the evacuation scheme was no longer as viable with the cancellation of direct flights between the United States and Cuba.

At this point, policymakers in Washington were more concerned with isolating Cuba than reuniting stranded children with their families, and "saving" more Cuban children was somehow no longer a priority.[3] Certainly, the number of children requiring placements was overwhelming U.S. foster-care agencies, and young Cubans arriving in Miami during 1962 were often more likely to find themselves sent to orphanages and other inappropriate placements. Fourteen thousand children had left, but if the operation had continued, maybe it would have been 50,000 children, commented a former Pedro Pan. "Where do you put 50,000 children?" she asked.[4] But why stop the evacuation effort, even if it was more difficult at this time? Were the minds of those children remaining in Cuba no longer in peril?

Whether or not the Cuban government knew the extent of Operation Pedro Pan, it accepted the children's departures as a decision made by their parents and made no attempt to stop them leaving; whether this was due to pragmatism or a political strategy, no one was ever charged with assisting the exodus. But the whole scheme had been built on both lies and a lure that targeted the middle and upper classes of Cuba.

The lies responsible for the panic were that the revolutionary government was intent on eliminating parental authority, destroying the Cuban family, outlawing religious worship, and shutting off the exit of those citizens uncomfortable or angry about the social, political, and economic changes taking place on the island. The *patria potestad* hoax, however, was likely to be of less concern to the urban or rural poor, whose families were strengthened and benefited significantly from the measures introduced by the revolutionary government with schools and health care for their children. Furthermore, poorer Cubans' ties to the Catholic church were far more tenuous than those of their wealthier compatriots, making them less susceptible to scaremongering about threats to religious freedom.

The lure was the coveted opportunity of an all-expenses paid U.S. "scholarship" in the form of the Cuban Children's Program. Therefore, far from being a desperate and impulsive act to "save" their children, some Cuban parents just took advantage of the apparent opportunity Operation Pedro Pan presented for their children's advancement. It was also a decision based on the false expectation that the separation would be brief, due to what turned out to be unfounded confidence that the United States would successfully step in to "correct" the revolutionary course of New Cuba.

The airlift was facilitated by a politically motivated and unprecedented U.S. immigration policy in which a lowly Miami priest was given authority to allow the entry into the United States of an unlimited number of Cuban minors, while the immigration of family groups was deliberately made more difficult in order to create or aggravate tensions on the island. In celebrating the scheme as "an example of personal sacrifice" among all the "heroic actions" of the anti-Castro counterrevolutionary struggle, the main proponents of Operation Pedro Pan have largely chosen to overlook or downplay most of these facts.[5]

Operation Pedro Pan might have been only part of a U.S. strategy of political subversion and psychological warfare—or a "sideline" of that covert war—but it was certainly an effective part of that strategy. If the *patria potestad* hoax and the departure of so many children did not actually influence most Cubans to turn against the revolutionary government, both factors served at least to confuse or disorient those disturbed by or opposed to the rapid and radical social and political transformation of their country.

Revolutions act like "a social cyclone," observed a former Catholic youth activist. "It was a moment when the old society was being totally broken up," he said, "a moment of confusion and confrontation."[6] "In 1961, I was crazy, I think," a Cuban woman recalled in 1967. "We were all a little crazy then," she said. "There was so much happening—the Revolution changed so many things so fast . . ."[7]

Operation Pedro Pan undoubtedly tapped fears, prejudices, and insecurities among largely white and previously privileged Cubans in a highly volatile political situation. Therefore, parents of some social classes were inevitably tempted to take up an offer to put their children out of harm's way, especially those parents (or parents of offspring) who were actively engaged in antigovernment activity.

But the evacuation scheme was rooted in a Cold War mind-set and agenda. A former Pedro Pan recalled with anger, "I began to feel part of a great hoax of an enormous manipulative machine. . . . What had happened is that the Americans were using the Cubans: the mass emigration [and] the children who arrived alone. . . . [T]he departure of the children had been a propaganda tool. And what came out of the [Miami] camps was a wounded generation."[8]

Ambassadors, soldiers, or spies—the Pedro Pan children were envisioned in Washington as all of these—and the plight of the young Cuban refugees was destined to play a vital role in the U.S. propaganda war against Cuba: first, in the effort to undermine the moral standing and influence of the Cuban revolutionary project, especially in Latin America; second, to firm up domestic support for Washington's covert Cuba Project; and third, to soften resistance in U.S. communities to the influx of large numbers of Cuban émigrés.

The Pedro Pans were also regarded by those who had purportedly saved them as a source of intelligence, informers, and also potential anti-Castro fighters in Washington's covert war against the Cuban revolution—as some already were before they left Cuba and others became in the United States. The revolt of the Pedro Pans at Camp Kendall in Miami during the Bay of Pigs invasion in an effort to convince the U.S. government to back the exile force more decisively clearly demonstrated the young refugees' heightened political consciousness and fervent dedication to the anti-Castro cause.

Furthermore, the Pedro Pans were seen by their "saviors" (and came to see themselves) as a U.S. "investment" in Cuba's political future as ambassadors for or leaders of a post-Castro, "democratic" Cuba. One fifteen-year-old girl postmarked letters written to her mother from Miami "*Territorio libre de América,*" mocking how revolutionary Cuba was presenting itself after the literacy campaign as the first nation in the Americas free of illiteracy.[9] Thus, the Pedro Pans grew up boosted or burdened by the idea that they were "the sweet hope of [their] homeland," as one of them said, feeling obliged to express their gratitude for the opportunities given to them and pressured not to question the circumstances of, or reasons for, their departure from Cuba or what happened to them in the country that welcomed them.[10]

Not every Pedro Pan became successful in their adopted homeland as is often suggested, and some, like the young Cuban Americans who created the Antonio Maceo Brigade, bravely faced condemnation and even violence from their peers and fellow émigrés for advocating reconciliation with the land of their birth.[11] Nevertheless, the story of their "rescue" ultimately became central to the creation myth of the Cuban community in the United States in order to justify Cubans' uniquely privileged status as political exiles, as distinct from other Latin Americans fleeing war, repression, and economic disaster.[12] The welcome extended to the Pedro Pans certainly stands in stark contrast to the recent U.S. government policy of deporting or even interning the tens of thousands of unaccompanied children who have arrived from Central America since 2014, with one Miami journalist going as far as suggesting the border children should be sent to the U.S.-run camp for "enemy combatants" at the occupied territory of Guantanamo Bay, Cuba.[13]

"Miami or the mountains—that's the story of my family!" remarked Sonia Almazán somewhat ruefully. Having grown up in an upper-class family in Cienfuegos, she joined the literacy campaign with great enthusiasm, but watched with dismay as all her friends, neighbors, and ultimately her entire family departed for the United States.[14] Thus, although exile is usually understood as something suffered only by "those who voluntarily or involuntarily give up their native soil," Teresa de Jesús Fernández said she experienced a form of "internal exile" in the absence of her childhood friends who left her behind in Cuba.[15]

Cubans who remained on the island came to see Operation Pedro Pan as exacerbating the schisms that developed within many middle-class

Cuban families in the wake of the revolutionary hurricane that swept the island. Berta Álvarez found it difficult to talk about how her parents sent her younger brother and sister to the United States while she was away in the countryside teaching literacy, so that she never even had the chance to say goodbye to her siblings. "I was a revolutionary," she said. "It was a time of great enthusiasm, more than anything inspired by a great sense of justice, to make Cuba what we always wanted it to be—to eliminate injustice against the poorest sectors of the population."[16]

Families like Berta's, however, need not have been split if Cubans had been allowed to determine the fate of their nation and their families without interference from their powerful neighbor. But Washington's Cuba Project involved a cruel and calculated immigration policy that resulted in the unnecessary and unexpectedly prolonged separation of Cuban families.

Why is there such resistance in Washington to releasing documents related to this episode of U.S.-Cuban history? Even the editors of the *Miami Herald* commented in 1998 that "the hoarding [by the U.S. government and its agencies] of information on Cold War activities, including longtime U.S. involvement in Central America and Cuba . . . [has been] particularly egregious."[17] María de los Angeles Torres's FOIA case against the CIA revealed there is undoubtedly a significant amount of documentation about the exodus of the children that has yet to be declassified. The U.S. District Court that heard her case reviewed 723 pages of the documents the CIA provided, but these were not released to the public and remained classified as "Sensitive Compartmented Information."[18]

An earlier effort by Felix Masud-Piloto to obtain U.S. government documents on Cuban migration to the United States was similarly frustrated.[19] A subsequent FOIA request made by journalist Yvonne Conde for documents from the State Department, the Immigration and Naturalization Service, and the CIA specifically related to the exodus of the Cuban children was denied on the basis of "state security."[20]

There can be no doubt there are many other CIA, State Department, United States Information Agency (USIA) and other U.S. government agency documents relating to the exodus of the Cuban children that could well shed further light on the political origin, nature, and purpose of Operation Pedro Pan, especially regarding the propaganda and psychological warfare aspects of the exodus—whether or not it is ever confirmed to have been an actual CIA operation.[21] The State Department clearly bears considerable responsibility for using the Cuban refugees, and not just the children, for its political goals.²² Is it the case, as has been suggested, that those documents regarding the operation are still considered as "sensitive" because of the involvement of other nations' embassies and diplomatic staff?²³ Even so, it is hard to imagine why they should remain classified at this point in time.

In recent decades, the abuse of children in the care of state or church-run institutions in many countries has been exposed, and the damage done to countless young lives has finally begun to be acknowledged. Reluctance on the part of the organizers of Operation Pedro Pan to accept responsibility for the abuse of young Cubans in their care appears to be further proof of the political agendas at work then and now.²⁴ Alex López and Candi Sosa are just two former Pedro Pans who have spoken out about the sexual abuse they suffered while in the care of the Catholic Welfare Bureau. The question of how widespread or serious the abuse suffered by Pedro Pans was has become quite controversial in the highly polarized debate about the scheme. Both Torres and Yvonne Conde have been lambasted by defenders of the "orthodox" version of the Pedro Pan story for raising this issue and resisting pressure to remain silent about the negative side of their experience. When this researcher asked Msgr. Bryan Walsh his opinion of Conde's book, he simply chuckled, saying the way to hit the best-seller list was to write about "a miserable childhood" like Frank McCourt (a fellow Irishman) had done with his then recently published book *Angela's Ashes*.²⁵

When Torres was interviewed by María Hinojosa on U.S. National Public Radio in the series "Who Tells the Story?" the Future Media Group that produces the LatinoUSA weekly radio program felt obliged to publish a "Statement from Operation Pedro Pan [Group], Inc.," which explained that, out of the thousands of testimonials they had reviewed, "only a very small fraction was abused, less than 1 percent of the 14,148 [sic] total," concluding, "All in all, it is our contention, based on the evidence available, that Pedro Pan children in the Cuban Children's Program fared significantly much better than American-born children in both institutional and foster home care during the 1960s."²⁶

This may well be the case, but it fails to acknowledge the real anxiety and trauma experienced by many Pedro Pan children resulting from their sudden, extended exile and separation from their families. A Miami journalist went as far as describing the entire operation as "totally immoral" and "nothing less than child abuse on a national scale."²⁷

The sense of rootlessness, pain, and anger experienced by many Pedro

Pan children was captured in a poem titled "Disconnected," posted on a website created for former Pedro Pans in the late 1990s:

> They were lifted up,
> abruptly,
> from the only ground their little feet had ever known,
> they were disconnected,
> from the earth.
>
> Catapulted to a different land,
> where the ground lay covered with a frigid white substance
> and harshness descended upon them
>
> Like they had never known before
> split off geographically;
> and then spiritually to cope,
> their tender Souls were emptied out,
> depleted.
>
> Where once there was innocence
> now it was lost
> and they are still flying, soaring, depleted,
> confused
> disconnected from their Truth,
> hoping to land, someday . . .
> somewhere.[28]

More than a few Cubans on the island boast they still have unused visa waivers signed by Fr. Walsh in their possession. The program is generally regarded as having ended in October 1962 when air traffic from the island to the United States ceased as part of Washington's effort to isolate Cuba. But small numbers of children continued to reach the United States by boat and also by air through countries such as Spain and Mexico, apparently with the collaboration of the Catholic church in Cuba and Spain.[29] The last Miami camp for Cuban children was only closed in 1981. Who was organizing these departures from Cuba? Who were these children? Was this still a convenient exit route for counterrevolutionary activists? Was this a way for Cuban security agents to penetrate exile organizations as some State Department officials suspected?[30] Cuban counterintelligence agents did, in fact, successfully infiltrate many Miami-based exile organizations.[31]

Some Cubans, in fact, made the reverse journey to the Pedro Pans—that is, they had been attending high schools in the United States but returned to Cuba after the revolution, either as instructed by their parents—possibly because with the currency reform it was harder to find the U.S. dollars to pay for tuition—or because the students themselves chose to return. Their stories would be fascinating to pursue as a parallel experience to the very many memoirs written and published by former Pedro Pans.

Looking beyond the passion, hyperbole, and persistent Cold War rhetoric that still envelopes issues touching on U.S.-Cuba relations, even after President Barack Obama's December 2014 initiative of restoring diplomatic ties, the episode of Operation Pedro Pan remains an open wound for many individual Cubans and their families. One Cuban, who left the island as a child and knew many Pedro Pans as friends and classmates in Miami in the 1960s, reflected on the undeniable human cost of the program, saying, "it was one of the most sinister maneuvers hatched by the CIA and the U.S. government against [Cuba]. They took advantage of the political ignorance of the people, the mirage of the 'American way of life,' the anticommunism carefully manipulated over the years, and they didn't hesitate to destroy and tear apart those families that were supposedly their allies against Castro, by using those children for their political objectives."[32]

The exodus of the children from revolutionary Cuba has generally been portrayed by defenders and detractors of the operation as an episode in the Cold War—either as a desperate humanitarian rescue or as a sinister CIA conspiracy. Although Operation Pedro Pan did not necessarily begin as a coherent and comprehensive U.S. program, four distinct elements soon came together to drive the scheme: the scare campaign about *patria potestad*, the evacuation scheme, the extraordinary visa waiver system, and the Cuban Children's Program—all of which determined the massive scale of the exodus. Thus, like all migration processes, Operation Pedro Pan was driven by push *and* pull factors. The apparent opportunity of a highly prized U.S. "scholarship" was irresistible to some Cuban families: as one Pedro Pan remarked, it was like "offering the whole store to someone just asking for candy."[33]

By recognizing the fact that most Pedro Pans were teenagers and not small children as they have frequently been portrayed, they no longer appear simply as innocent weapons in an international political conflict. Instead, it is clear that many of that generation of young Cubans displayed an active political agency. With this perspective, discourse on Operation Pedro Pan can move beyond the kidnap-or-rescue dichotomy in which it has largely been mired.

* * *

In conclusion, neither the Cuban revolution nor Operation Pedro Pan can be understood solely within the context of the Cold War. The hubris of the revolution was that it showed that a small Latin American nation could choose to chart its own course. Tensions between the neighboring countries had simmered since the nineteenth century, when the newly formed United States of America began to cast avaricious eyes southward and saw Cuba as a ripe fruit destined to fall by natural and divine law into its grasp, codified as the Monroe Doctrine. Fidel Castro's proclamation that the revolution would "Cubanize" Cuba was understood in Washington as an affront to the United States' long self-imagined benevolence and protection of the island, but it thrilled and inspired many Cubans, especially the youth.

The revolutionary project Cubans embarked on in 1959 initiated a process of social transformation that profoundly affected how Cubans saw themselves, their nation, and its place in the world. How individuals and families reacted to this was largely determined by class, race, and age. What is remarkable is how quickly the revolutionary transformation of Cuba was accomplished, given the proximity of the United States and the hegemony of its culture over the island.

Defense of Cuba's revolutionary project was never going to depend solely or even primarily on force of arms. On the fiftieth anniversary of the Cuban revolution, Lisandro Pérez argued that its power had been successfully consolidated in the early 1960s, largely because it had been able to "[capitalize] on political values and ideals" that had long been part of Cuba's national identity. He concluded that despite the significant costs entailed, many Cubans were still "not ready to throw the revolution out with Fidel. . . . Too many have a stake in the continuation of a system that once changed their lives for the better."[34]

Cubans' stake in their revolution was far more than a matter of the material benefits it brought the majority—benefits that can be and have been eroded at different times. What cannot be reversed so easily is the change in consciousness among Cuban citizens—a sense of sovereignty and independence, a sense of community, solidarity, and social justice. This new consciousness or *conciencia* was achieved not through indoctrination or coercion but by establishing participation as the essential element of Cuba's revolutionary political culture, demonstrated most powerfully and effectively by the 1961 national literacy campaign that meant a generation of Cubans came to feel the revolution was *their* revolution. The organizers of Operation Pedro Pan admitted as much at the time in acknowledging that it would be a "colossal" task to reverse this among young Cubans in particular.[35]

Of course, this *conciencia* among Cubans today remains uneven, imperfect, and still very much in flux. But how else can the survival of the revolutionary project for six decades be explained? Examining the first years of the revolution and, in particular, the impact of their experiences on the generation that reached maturity in those years, might help explain how that revolutionary project somehow survived the economic catastrophe Cubans suffered in the 1990s following the collapse of the Soviet Union. Miami or the mountains might then be a metaphor for the choice the Cuban people faced in the early years of the revolution, a choice between the Old Cuba that was eventually transplanted across the sea, ninety miles to the north, and the New Cuba that was struggling—and continues to struggle—to be born on the island.

NOTES

Introduction

1. Erwin Potts, "8,000 Cuba Children Saved from Castro Brainwashing in 'Operation Exodus,'" *Miami Herald*, 8 March 1962, 1.
2. "8,000 Fidel Won't Get," *Miami News*, 8 March 1962, 2A.
3. Grupo Areíto, *Contra Viento y Marea* (Havana: Casa de las Américas, 1978), 17; Yvonne M. Conde, *Operation Pedro Pan: The Untold Exodus of 14,048 Cuban Children* (New York: Routledge, 1999), xii. See also Maya Bell, "Operation Pedro Pan," *Orlando Sentinel*, 10 December 195.
4. Alex López, interview by author, Washington, D.C., 10 September 2001. All interviews, unless otherwise identified, were conducted by the author. See bibliography for complete list.
5. Victoria Viejo, interview in Estela Bravo and Olga Rosa Gómez, eds., *Operación Peter Pan: Cerrando el círculo en Cuba* (Havana: Casa de las Américas, 2013), 76 (my translation).
6. Rosa Otero, interview in Marina Ochoa and Guillermo Centeno, dirs., *Del Otro Lado del Cristal* (Havana: ICAIC, 1995) (my translation).
7. Silvia Ríos, interview by author, Miami, 11 May 1999.
8. Raquel Mendieta Costa, "Only Fragments of Memoir," in María de los Angeles Torres, ed., *By Heart/De Memoria: Cuban Women's Journeys in and out of Exile* (Philadelphia: Temple University Press, 2003), 134.
9. Cuban Mission to the United Nations, "Illegal Migration from Cuba to the U.S.," press release, 2 August 1999.
10. Dan Merica, "Trump Unveils New Restrictions on Travel, Business with Cuba," CNN, http://edition.cnn.com/2017/06/16/politics/trump-cuba-policy/index.html, 17 June 2017.
11. Msgr. Bryan O. Walsh, "Cuban Refugee Children," *Journal of Inter-American Studies and World Affairs* 13 (July–October 1971): 380–83.
12. Anita Casavantes Bradford, *The Revolution Is for the Children: The Politics of Childhood in Havana and Miami, 1959–1962* (Chapel Hill: University of North Carolina Press, 2014), 4.
13. María Cristina García, *Havana USA: Cuban Exiles and Cuban Americans in South Florida, 1959–1994* (Berkeley: University of California Press, 1996), 83–84.

14. María de los Angeles Torres, *The Lost Apple: Operation Pedro Pan, Cuban Children in the United States, and the Promise of a Better Future* (Boston: Beacon Press, 2003), 216.

15. Dirk Johnson, "The Elián González Case: The Refugees; Children of 'Operation Pedro Pan' Recall Painful Separations from Parents," *New York Times*, 22 April 2000.

16. María de los Angeles Torres, "Elián and the Tale of Pedro Pan," *Nation*, 27 March 2000, 21.

17. Flora González, "I Was an 'Elián' of the Early 1960s," *Boston Globe*, 3 February 2000.

18. Gabriel Orozco Sr., interview in Bravo and Gómez, *Operación Peter Pan*, 129 (my translation).

19. Richard R. Fagen, Richard A. Brody, and Thomas J. O'Leary, *Cubans in Exile: Disaffection and the Revolution* (Stanford, CA: Stanford University Press, 1968), 3–5.

20. Everett M. Ressler, Neil Boothby, and Daniel J. Steinbock, *Unaccompanied Children: Care and Protection in Wars, Natural Disasters, and Refugee Movements* (New York: Oxford University Press, 1988), 118–19.

21. Walsh, "Cuban Refugee Children," 379, 412. Of the 14,048 Pedro Pans who arrived, 6,486 received foster care as part of the Cuban Children's Program. Later in his article, Walsh gives the figure 7,464 as the number of children taken into care. There is no explanation of this quite significant discrepancy.

22. For example, see Román de la Campa, *Cuba on My Mind: Journeys to a Severed Nation* (London: Verso, 2000).

23. Grupo Areíto, *Contra Viento y Marea*, 22–23 (my translation).

24. Lillian Guerra, *Visions of Power in Cuba: Revolution, Redemption, and Resistance, 1959–1971* (Chapel Hill: University of North Carolina Press, 2012), 23.

25. This was codified in the 1966 Cuban Adjustment Act.

26. John F. Thomas, "U.S.A. as a Country of First Asylum," *International Migration Review* 3, nos. 1 and 2 (1965): 10.

27. For a thorough examination of the longstanding, fraught relationship between the two nations, see Louis A. Pérez Jr., *Cuba in the American Imagination: Metaphor and the Imperial Ethos* (Chapel Hill: University of North Carolina Press, 2008) and *Cuba and the United States: Ties of Singular Intimacy* (Athens: University of Georgia Press, 1980).

28. Louis A. Pérez Jr., *On Becoming Cuban: Identity, Nationality, and Culture* (Chapel Hill: University of North Carolina Press, 1999), 490.

29. Lars Schoultz, *That Infernal Little Cuban Republic: The United States and the Cuban Revolution* (Chapel Hill: University of North Carolina Press, 2009), 92.

30. William M. LeoGrande and Peter Kornbluh, *Back Channel to Cuba: The Hidden History of Negotiations between Washington and Havana* (Chapel Hill: University of North Carolina Press, 2014), 18.

31. Schoultz, *That Infernal Little Cuban Republic*, 137–39.

32. #481 A Program of Covert Action against the Castro Regime, 16 March 1960, in *Foreign Relations of the United States* (hereinafter *FRUS*), *1958–1960, VI: Cuba* (Washington: U.S. Government Printing Office, 1991), 850–51.

33. #603 Memorandum of a Conversation, Department of State, 1 November 1960: "Cuban Refugees in Florida," *FRUS, 1958–1960, VI*, 1111 (my emphasis).

34. "President Orders Cuba Refugee Aid, *New York Times*, 4 February 1961, 1–2.

35. Stephen Rabe, *The Most Dangerous Area in the World: John F. Kennedy Confronts the Communist Revolution in Latin America* (Chapel Hill: University of North Carolina Press, 1999), 19, 15.

36. #607 Memorandum from the Secretary of Defense's Deputy Assistant for Special Operations (Lansdale) to the Deputy Secretary of Defense (Douglas): "Cuba," 7 November 1960, *FRUS, 1958–1960, VI*, 1116.

37. Flora González, interview in Ochoa and Centeno, *Del Otro Lado del Cristal*.

38. Quoted by Pérez, *On Becoming Cuban*, 482–83.

39. Marcia del Mar, *A Cuban Story* (Winston-Salem, NC: John F. Blair, Publisher, 1979), 23–24.

40. Roger Hilsman, Memorandum: "Estimates and Evaluations on Cuba," 3 November 1961, Declassified document #65D438, 480. National Security Archive, Washington, D.C.

41. Hugo Chaviano, "Cuban Parents' Fears Were Real," *Chicago Tribune*, 21 January 1998, 12. See also "Even 7-Year-Olds Spy for Castro Now," *U.S. News and World Report*, 17 April 1961, 16.

42. Dr. Carlos Cortina, testimony of 4 December 1962 to U.S. Senate Subcommittee hearings, Cuban Refugee Problem, Washington, D.C.: Government Printing Office, 1963, 383.

43. Walsh, "Cuban Refugee Children," 383.

44. Walsh, interview by author, Miami, 20 March 2000. Interestingly, he went on to say that Elián González's father had "the same right."

45. Walsh, "Cuban Refugee Children," 395.

46. Contemporary U.S. media reports about the literacy campaign include "Cuba's Children's Crusade," *Newsweek*, 3 April 1961; "Cuba: Redder Schoolhouse," *Newsweek*, 19 June 1961; "F is for Fidel," *Time*, 6 October 1961.

47. Michelle Chase, *Revolution within the Revolution: Women and Gender Politics in Cuba, 1952–1962* (Chapel Hill: University of North Carolina Press, 2015), 3.

48. See "The History of Operation Pedro Pan," PedroPan.org, n.d., www.pedropan.org/category/history.

49. Victor Andres Triay, *Fleeing Castro: Operation Pedro Pan and the Cuban Children's Program* (Gainesville: University Press of Florida, 1998), 103.

50. Antoni Kapcia, *Cuba: Island of Dreams* (Oxford: Berg, 2000), 99.

51. The Antonio Maceo Brigade was formed by young Cuban Americans, some of them former Pedro Pans, who advocated closer ties between the Cuban community in the United States and the island.

52. Ramón Torreira Crespo and José Buajasán Marrawi, *Operación Peter Pan: Un caso de guerra psicológica contra Cuba* (Havana: Editora Política, 2000).

53. The report of the Cuban investigation into Operation Pedro Pan was only partially completed in 2000, but it was nevertheless published as a book as a salvo in the custody battle over Elián González. This is the reason I refer to the book throughout this text as "the Cuban report."

54. Torreira and Buajasán, *Operación Peter Pan*, 389.

55. See "Men of Conscience," *Miami Herald*, 17 September 1986; Herbert Buchsbaum, "Cuban 'Peter Pan' Honored," *Miami Herald*, 2 October 1986.

56. María de los Angeles Torres and Estela Bravo were among the few researchers who conducted interviews with some parents. See Torres, *Lost Apple*, and Bravo and Gómez, *Operación Peter Pan*.

57. Torres, *Lost Apple*, 11; Fabiola Santiago, "Author Awaits Unwritten End to Unfolding Saga of Pedro Pan," *Miami Herald*, 2 June 1999.

58. "For Juan Pujol, Suffering of Separation during Pedro Pan Was for the Best," *Miami Herald*, 16 May 2009.

59. Conde, *Operation Pedro Pan*, 225, 215–16.

60. Torres, *Lost Apple*, 250–51, 267.

61. Casavantes, *Revolution Is for the Children*; Karen Dubinsky, *Babies without Borders: Adoption and Migration across the Americas* (New York: New York University Press, 2010).

62. For example, the 1963 United States Information Agency (USIA) film on the refugee children, *The Lost Apple*, the Pedro Pan Group website, and the covers of Conde's and Casavantes's books all use images of Pedro Pans as very young children, images that inevitably evoke a powerful emotional response and contribute to the desperate rescue narrative about Operation Pedro Pan.

63. See Philippe Ariès, *Centuries of Childhood: A Social History of Family Life* (New York: Vintage Books, 1962). Casavantes uses a broad definition of a child as one aged between five and sixteen; see *Revolution Is for the Children*, 8, 11.

64. Torreira and Buajasán, *Operación Peter Pan*, 72 (my translation).

65. See Helen Brocklehurst, *Who's Afraid of Children: Children, Conflict, and International Relations* (Burlington, VT: Ashgate Publishing, 2006), 6–11.

66. Francisco Méndes, interview in Bravo and Gómez, *Operación Peter Pan*, 180 (my translation).

67. Walsh, "Cuban Refugee Children," 383–84.

68. Dubinsky, *Babies without Borders*, 25.

69. Gene Miller, "'Peter Pan' Means Real Life to Some Kids," *Miami Herald*, 9 March 1962, 11A; Erwin Potts, "8,000 Cuba Children Saved from Castro Brainwashing," *Miami Herald*, 8 March 1962, 1.

70. Bryan O. Walsh, "The Origins of Operation Pedro Pan," paper for presentation at Pedro Pan Conference, Florida International University, Miami, 20–21 April 2001, box 44, Monsignor Bryan O. Walsh Papers, Barry University, Miami Shores, Florida (hereinafter Walsh Papers). Renick presented a "Tribute to Monsignor Bryan Walsh" at the testimonial dinner in his honor, held in Miami 24 February 1978; see box 53, Walsh Papers.

71. See http://razonesdecuba.cubadebate.cu/series/fidel-habla-sobre-operacion-peter-pan-video/.

72. The term *patria potestad* originated in the Spanish Civil Code, which "regarded the husband as the protector of his wife, whom she was obliged to obey" under Article 58. Furthermore, Article 154 established children as "entirely subject to the disposition of the parents, with little or no protection guaranteed by the state." Lowry Nelson, *Rural Cuba*, (New York: Octagon Books, 1970), 176–78.

73. For example, see Ileana Fuentes, "Portrait of Wendy, at Fifty, with Bra," in Andrea

O'Reilly Herrera, ed., *ReMembering Cuba: Legacy of a Diaspora* (Austin: University of Texas Press, 2001).

74. There has also been bitter wrangling among the Pedro Pans themselves regarding the use of the name or brand "Pedro Pan." See Pedro Pan Foundation documents 1978–1993, box 12, Walsh Papers.

75. See http://pubsys.miamiherald.com/cgi-bin/pedropan/index. Also Juan Carlos Chávez, "Flights' Logs Record Cuba's Child Exodus," 4 January 2009, https://www.orlandosentinel.com/news/os-xpm-2009-01-04-pedropan04-story.

76. Sonia Otieza, "Los 'niños de Pedro Pan' no pueden olivar," *El Nuevo Herald*, 9 June 1992.

77. Anders Gyllenhaal, "Recovered Notes Give Birth to Herald's Pedro Pan Database Project," *Miami Herald*, 16 May 2009. See also Luisa Yañez, "Base de datos sobre el histórico éxodo de la Operación Pedro Pan," *El Nuevo Herald*, 12 May 2009; and Luisa Yañez, "Cubans Reconnect with Past through Pedro Pan Database," *Miami Herald*, 17 May 2009.

78. Conversation with Gladys Gómez-Rossié, Miami, 2 May 2016. Gladys is the community relations coordinator at the Cuban Heritage Collection, University of Miami.

79. Eduardo Galeano, quoted by María López Vigil, *Cuba: Neither Heaven nor Hell* (Washington, D.C.: EPICA, 1999), v.

Chapter 1. A Revolutionary Hurricane Sweeps Cuba

1. Fidel Castro, *Fidel Castro Reader* (Melbourne: Ocean Press, 2007), 108.

2. Damián J. Fernández, *Cuba and the Politics of Passion* (Austin: University of Texas Press, 2000), 62.

3. Lisandro Otero, "Utopia Revisited," in Ambrosio Fornet, ed., *Bridging Enigma: Cubans on Cuba* (Durham, N.C.: Duke University Press/*South Atlantic Quarterly*, 96, 1997), 21.

4. Andrés Suárez, *Cuba: Castro and Communism* (Cambridge, MA: MIT Press, 1967), among other scholars, argued the enactment of the agrarian reform as the moment the revolution became transformed into a social revolution, 54. Others argue the "definitive turn" in the direction of the revolution occurred in mid-1960 with the extensive nationalizations of U.S. and Cuban businesses. See Silvia Pedraza, *Political Disaffection in Cuba's Revolution and Exodus* (New York: Cambridge University Press, 2007), 68.

5. Pérez, *Cuba in the American Imagination*, 239.

6. See Pérez, *On Becoming Cuban*.

7. I have chosen here to use the more gender-neutral term "New Cuban" rather than New Man, acknowledging that the concept, as it was understood in revolutionary Cuba, implied a new, *global* citizen with an internationalist consciousness—not simply a Cuban nationalist.

8. Elizabeth Sutherland, *The Youngest Revolution: A Personal Report on Cuba* (London: Pittman Publishing, 1970), 97.

9. Ernesto Che Guevara, "Socialism and Man in Cuba," in David Deutschmann, ed., *Che Guevara Reader: Writings on Politics and Revolution* (Melbourne: Ocean Press, 2004), 212–28.

10. Ernesto Che Guevara, *Reminiscences of the Cuban Revolutionary War* (Melbourne: Ocean Press, 2006), 83.

11. Universidad Popular, *Educación y revolución* (Havana: Imprenta Nacional de Cuba, 1961), 271.

12. "Una revolución es una lucha a muerte entre el future y el pasado," in *El Pensamiento de Fidel Castro: Selección Temática. Tomo 1, Volumen 2. Enero 1959–abril 1961* (Havana: Editoria Política, 1983), 443–45.

13. Fidel Castro, *Fidel in Chile: Major Fidel Castro's Speeches during His Visit to Chile* (New York: International Publishers, 1972), 207–8.

14. Tzvi Medin, *Cuba: The Shaping of Revolutionary Consciousness* (Boulder, CO: Lynne Rienner Publishers, 1990), 7.

15. Fernández, *Cuba and the Politics of Passion*, 88. Richard R. Fagen also argued that all political systems since Plato "develop procedures for creating the types of citizens thought necessary for their survival and growth." Richard R. Fagen, *The Transformation of Political Culture in Cuba* (Stanford, CA: Stanford University Press, 1969), 2–3.

16. Guevara, "Socialism and Man in Cuba," in *Che Guevara Reader*, 217.

17. The Spanish word *"conciencia"* can be translated as both conscience and consciousness and implies both the thinking process and a moral sense of conscientiousness and commitment. See Joseph Kahl, "The Moral Economy of a Revolutionary Society," in *Trans-Action*, April 1969, 32. Marifeli Pérez-Stable defines *conciencia* as "proletarian class-for-itself consciousness." See Marifeli Pérez-Stable, "Politics and Conciencia in Revolutionary Cuba" (Ph.D. diss., State University of New York, Stony Brook, 1985), 19.

18. Rafael Hernández, Haraldo Dilla, Jennifer Dugan Abbassi, and Jean Díaz, "Political Culture and Popular Participation in Cuba," *Latin American Perspectives*, 18, no. 2 (1991), 43–44. See also Guerra, *Visions of Power*, for a detailed examination of how a new relationship between the individual and the revolutionary state emerged in the early 1960s.

19. Torres, "Elián," 21.

20. Elizabeth Sutherland described revolutionary Cuba as "a land of youth." Sutherland, *Youngest Revolution*, 95.

21. Jaime Suchlicki, *University Students and Revolution in Cuba, 1920–1968* (Coral Gables, FL: University of Miami Press, 1969), 21.

22. See "Program Manifesto of the 26th of July Movement" (November 1956), in Rolando E. Bonachea and Nelson P. Valdés, eds., *Cuba in Revolution* (New York: Anchor Books, 1972), 113–40. See also Gladys Marel García Pérez, *Insurrection and Revolution: Armed Struggle in Cuba, 1952–1958* (Boulder, CO: Lynne Rienner Publishers, 1998).

23. Suchlicki, *University Students*, 75.

24. Herbert Matthews, "Populace Revolt in Santiago de Cuba," *New York Times*, 10 June 1957.

25. Julia Sweig, *Inside the Cuban Revolution: Fidel Castro and the Urban Underground* (Cambridge: Harvard University Press, 2002), 96–112.

26. Hart Phillips, *Cuba: Island of Paradox* (New York: An Oblonsky Book, Astor-Honor, 1959), 294–95.

27. Jean-Paul Sartre, *Sartre on Cuba* (New York: Ballantine Books, 1961), 88–89.

28. Sweig, *Inside the Cuban Revolution*, 136.

29. Phillips, *Cuba: Island of Paradox*, 341–42.
30. Sweig, *Inside the Cuban Revolution*, 159. Ricardo Alarcón later became Cuba's foreign minister and then president of the National Assembly.
31. Fidel Castro, *La Revolución Cubana, 1953/1962* (Mexico, D.F.: Ediciones Era, 1972), 142.
32. *Bohemia*, 18–25 January 1959, 1. Ironically, the young rebel (Antonio Chao Flores) featured on this cover was later tried and executed on 11 August 1962 for counterrevolutionary activities; he was then twenty-two. See Enrique Encinosa, *Cuba en Guerra: Historia de la oposición anti-Castrista 1959–1993* (Miami: Cuban American National Foundation, 1994), 119–21.
33. Fagen, *Transformation of Political Culture*, 147.
34. This was a phrase noted by Fidel Castro from José Martí's *Collected Works*, which he studied intensively while imprisoned on the Isle of Pines. Mario Mencía, *Time Was on Our Side* (Havana: Editora Política, 1982), 260.
35. Pablo Medina, *Exiled Memories: A Cuban Childhood* (New York: Persea Books, 2002), 109.
36. De la Campa, *Cuba on My Mind*, 58.
37. Sartre, *Sartre on Cuba*, 88–89.
38. When John F. Kennedy was elected at the age of forty-three in 1960, he was regarded as extraordinarily youthful for a U.S. president. The U.S. constitution requires candidates for the presidency to be at least thirty-five years old.
39. Quoted by Nelson Valdés, "Cuban Political Culture: Between Betrayal and Death," in Sandor Halebsky and John M. Kirk, eds., *Cuba in Transition: Crisis and Transformation* (Boulder, CO: Westview Press, 1992), 209.
40. Oscar Lewis, Ruth M. Lewis, and Susan M. Rigdon, *Neighbors: Living the Revolution: An Oral History of Contemporary Cuba* (Urbana: University of Illinois Press, 1978), 479.
41. Quoted by Karol Roccena Ortiz, "Accounts of Desperate Times: Six Refugee Life Histories" (Ph.D. diss., University of California, Irvine, 1983), 295.
42. Alfred L. Padula Jr., "The Fall of the Bourgeoisie: Cuba, 1959–1961" (Ph.D. diss., University of New Mexico, 1974), 477.
43. Raúl Castro's speech of 19 July 1960, quoted by Anne Luke, "Youth Culture and the Politics of Youth in 1960s Cuba" (Ph.D. diss., University of Wolverhampton, U.K., 2007), 63.
44. R. Hart Phillips, "Youth of Cuba Collecting Funds for Arms against 'Aggressor,'" *New York Times*, 27 March 1960.
45. "Vigoroso llamamiento a Toda La Juventud Para Estrechar Filas. Hay que Defender A Cuba," *El Mundo*, 28 October 1960, 1. See also "Acuerdos del Primer Pleno de la Asociación de Jóvenes Rebeldes," in José Bell, Delia Luisa López, and Tania Caram, eds., *Documentos de la revolución cubana 1960* (La Habana: Editorial de Ciencias Sociales, 2008), 298–303.
46. #271 Memorandum from the Chairman of the Board of National Estimates (Kent) to Director of Central Intelligence (Dulles), 3 November 1961, in *FRUS, 1961–1962, X*, 670.
47. Luke, "Youth Culture," 106, 195.

48. Fidel Castro, "La Nación entera, de pie, no teme a nada" in *Manual de Capacitación Cívica* (Havana: MINFAR, 1960), 279–97.

49. R. Hart Phillips, "Castro Movement of Children Rises," *New York Times*, 7 August 1959.

50. "Ellos querián vestirse así el Día de Reyes!" *El Mundo*, 5 January 1961. Three Kings' Day, or Epiphany (January 6), is the traditional day for giving Christmas gifts in Spain.

51. R. Hart Phillips, "Castro Movement of Children Rises," *New York Times*, 7 August 1959, 6. See also Casavantes, *Revolution Is for the Children*, 58–60.

52. "Responde Cuba a los E.U. Nacionalizadas 167 Empresas Yanquis. Producción, Educación y Organización Son las Tareas de la Juventud Cubana," *El Mundo*, 25 October 1960, 1.

53. "Even 7-Year-Olds Spy for Castro Now," *U.S. News and World Report*, 17 April 1961, 16.

54. Kapcia, *Cuba: Island of Dreams*, 99.

55. Leo Huberman and Paul M. Sweezy, *Cuba: Anatomy of a Revolution*, 2nd ed. (New York: Monthly Review Press, 1961), 93.

56. Ileana Fuentes, "Portrait of Wendy, at Fifty, with Bra," in O'Reilly, *ReMembering Cuba*, 60.

57. Of Conde's 428 Pedro Pan respondents, 67 percent were aged between twelve and seventeen. Conde, *Operation Pedro Pan*, 222.

58. Walsh, "Cuban Refugee Children," 383–84; Katherine Close, "Cuban Children away from Home," in *Children*, 10, no. 1 (January–February 1963), 8.

59. Directorio Revolucionario Estudiantil, *Ideario* (DRE pamphlet, n.d.). Directorio Revolucionario Estudiantil en exilio, Cuban Heritage Collection, University of Miami Libraries, Coral Gables, Florida.

60. See Guillermo Ricardo Paz Vásquez, "My Story," PedroPan.org, 26 July 2014, www.pedropan.org/content/my-story.

61. Suchlicki, *University Students*, 95. See also Joseph Holbrook, "Catholic Student Movements in Latin America, Cuba, and Brazil, 1920s to 1960s" (Ph.D. diss., Florida International University, 2013).

62. This protest was reported in *Revolución*, 12 April 1961.

63. Torreira and Buajasán, *Operación Peter Pan*, 44–45.

64. Nicolás and Silvia Ríos, interview by author, Miami, 11 May 1999. Silvia and her partner were both practicing Catholics and left Cuba in 1973.

65. Torres, *Lost Apple*, 98.

66. *Quincena* 5 (March 1960): 7, 50–52.

67. Carrie Hamilton, *Sexual Revolutions in Cuba: Passion, Politics, and Memory* (Chapel Hill: University of North Carolina Press, 2014), 143.

68. Lois M. Smith and Alfred Padula, "The Cuban Family in the 1980s," in Sandor Halebsky and John M. Kirk, eds., *Transformation and Struggle: Cuba Faces the 1990s* (New York: Praeger, 1990), 178; Lewis et al., *Neighbors*, 530.

69. Chase, *Revolution*, 173–74. See also "Serán unidas en matrimonio cuatrocientas mil parejas," *Revolución*, 22 November 1960, 13. The responsibilities of parenthood were further reinforced in Cuba with the adoption of the Family Code in 1975.

70. Rachel M. Hynson, "Sex and State Making in Revolutionary Cuba, 1959–1968" (Ph.D. diss., University of North Carolina, 2014).
71. Torreira and Buajasán, *Operación Peter Pan*, 101–2.
72. Huberman and Sweezy, *Cuba*, 101; see also Smith and Padula, "Cuban Family," 177.
73. Oscar Lewis, Ruth M. Lewis, and Susan M. Rigdon, *Four Women: Living the Revolution: An Oral History of Contemporary Cuba* (Urbana: University of Illinois Press, 1977), xxii.
74. Nelson, *Rural Cuba*, 178; Phillips, *Cuba: Island of Paradox*, 358.
75. Tony Mendoza, "Going Back," in O'Reilly, *ReMembering Cuba*, 79.
76. Nelson, *Rural Cuba*, 186–87. Oscar Lewis et al. offered many examples of these prerevolutionary dysfunctional Cuban families in *Four Women*, *Four Men*, and *Neighbors*.
77. Guevara, *Reminiscences*, 82.
78. Max Azicri, *Cuba: Politics, Economics, and Society* (London: Pinter Publishers, 1988), 55. See also Helen Safa, "Hierarchies and Household Change in Postrevolutionary Cuba," *Latin American Perspectives*, 36, no. 1 (January 2009): 42–52.
79. Lewis et al., *Four Women*, xv.
80. Lewis et al., *Neighbors*, 530.
81. "Waifs Aided by Cuba," *New York Times*, 16 October 1959. See also Sheryl L. Lutjens, "Restructuring Childhood in Cuba: The State as Family," in Roslyn Arlin Mickelson, ed., *Children on the Streets of the Americas: Homelessness, Education, and Globalization in the United States, Brazil, and Cuba* (London: Routledge, 2000), 150.
82. See articles about homeless children in *Revolución*, 17 September 1959, 14 October 1959, and 15 October 1959. See also Casavantes, *Revolution Is for the Children*, 50.
83. See Fidel Castro's speech, 19 September 1961, exposing the fake *patria potestad* law in *Obra Revolucionaria* 33 (27 September 1961): 13–31.
84. Nancy Stout, *One Day in December: Celia Sánchez and the Cuban Revolution* (New York: Monthly Review Press, 2013).
85. Mirta Muñiz, interview by author, Havana, April–May 1999. See also the picture of very young child planting a tree with the caption: "Only men and women? That was before. Now even small children like this one want to add their grain of sand in the service of the revolution, that is to say, in defense of Cuba." *Bohemia* 23 (July 1961): 68 (my translation).
86. Fernández, *Cuba and the Politics of Passion*, 68.
87. The term Afro-Cuban is used here to refer to any Cuban of African descent.
88. See announcements of the forthcoming "Gran Concentración" in *Revolución* 22 July 1959, asking Habaneros to welcome into their homes *campesinos* from the provinces.
89. Guerra, *Visions of Power*, 37–38, 67–74.
90. Margaret Randall, *Cuban Women Now: Interviews with Cuban Women* (Toronto: Women's Press, 1974).
91. Rachel Hynson, "'Count, Capture, and Reeducate': The Campaign to Rehabilitate Cuba's Female Sex Workers, 1959–1962," in *Journal of the History of Sexuality* 24, no. 1 (January 2015): 125–53.
92. Randall, *Cuban Women Now*, 209. By late 1961, 103 former domestics were reported to be working in banks; see *La Calle*, 9 November 1961, 6.

93. Chase, *Revolution*, 197. See also José A. Moreno, "From Traditional to Modern Values," in Carmelo Mesa-Lago, ed., *Revolutionary Change in Cuba* (Pittsburgh: University of Pittsburgh Press, 1971), 46.

94. "Creación de la Federación de Mujeres Cubanas," in Bell et al., *Documentos de la revolución cubana 1960*, 265–85.

95. Chase, *Revolution*, 131.

96. Stout, *One Day*, 342.

97. *Bohemia, Edición de la libertad*, 1 February 1959, 98.

98. Aleida March, *Remembering Che: My Life with Che Guevara* (Melbourne: Ocean Press, 2011).

99. Marvin Leiner, *Children Are the Revolution: Day Care in Cuba* (Harmondsworth: Penguin Books, 1978), 3, 6–7.

100. John M. Kirk, *José Martí: Mentor of the Cuban Nation* (Tampa: University of South Florida, 1983), 127.

101. Chase, *Revolution*, 4–5.

102. Quoted by Elizabeth Stone, ed., *Women and the Cuban Revolution* (New York: Pathfinder Press, 1981), 41.

103. Vilma Espín, "La Batalla de la igualdad no es solo de las mujeres, es de toda la sociedad" (Havana: Editorial de la Mujer, 1988), 6 (my translation).

104. Lois M. Smith and Alfred Padula, *Sex and Revolution: Women in Socialist Cuba* (New York: Oxford University Press, 1996), 122, 176.

105. "Graduadas 357 Muchachas Campesinas en la Escuela 'Ana Betancourt,'" *Bohemia*, 20 August 1961, 40.

106. See Randall, *Cuban Women Now*, 56–57.

107. See Comisión Nacional de Alfabetización de Ministerio de Educación, *Cumpliremos! Temas sobre la Revolución para los Alfabetizadores* (Havana: Imprenta Nacional de Cuba, 1961); and MINFAR, *Manual de Capacitación Cívica* (Havana: Ministerio de las Fuerzas Armadas Revolucionarias, 1960).

108. Lois M. Smith, "Sexuality and Socialism in Cuba," in Halebsky and Kirk, *Cuba in Transition*, 178.

109. *Bohemia*, 18 June 1961, 131 (my translation).

110. Carollee Bengelsdorf and Alice Hageman, "Emerging from Underdevelopment: Women and Work in Cuba," *Race and Class* 19, no. 4 (1978): 367–68.

111. Lewis et al., *Four Women*, xiii.

112. Geoffrey E. Fox, "Honor, Shame, and Women's Liberation in Cuba: Views of Working-Class Émigré Men," in Ann Pescatello, ed., *Female and Male in Latin America* (Pittsburgh: University of Pittsburgh Press, 1973), 274–89.

113. Ann E. Halbert-Brooks, "Revolutionary Teachers: Women and Gender in the Cuban Literacy Campaign of 1961" (master's thesis University of North Carolina, Chapel Hill, 2013).

114. Candace Johnson, "Framing for Change: Social Policy, the State, and the Federación de Mujeres," *Cuban Studies* 42 (2011): 35–51.

115. The different reactions of Cuban children and their parents to the revolution and the literacy campaign were dramatized in Melinda López's play *Sonia Flew* (New York:

Dramatists Play Service, 2009). Randall, *Cuban Women Now*, 102–3, described the sometimes heated atmosphere at meetings held to convince parents to let their children participate in the literacy campaign.

116. Smith and Padula, *Sex and Revolution*, 84; Chase, *Revolution*, 189–92.

117. *Denunciamos Imperdonable Crimen Comunista en Cuba*, 3. Pamphlets Collection 2: History and Politics in Cuba, Cuban Heritage Collection, University of Miami Libraries, Coral Gables, Florida. See also "En Cuba roja," *Bohemia Libre*, 27 August 1961, quoted by Chase, *Revolution*, 187.

118. Central Intelligence Agency, Information Report: "Signs of Discontent among the Cuban Populace; Activities of the Government to Strengthen the Regime," 6 April 1961, 2. http://nsarchive.gwu.edu/bayofpigs/19610406.pdf.

119. Dubinsky, *Babies without Borders*, 35.

120. James Baker, interview by Miguel González-Pando, Cuban Living History Project of Florida International University, https://libtube,fiu.edu/Play/344. (Part 1).

121. Chase, *Revolution*, 187.

122. Langston Hughes, "Cuban Color Lines, 1930," in John Jenkins, ed., *Travelers' Tales of Old Cuba* (Melbourne: Ocean Press, 2010), 144.

123. Alejandro de la Fuente, *A Nation for All: Race, Inequality, and Politics in Twentieth-Century Cuba* (Chapel Hill: University of North Carolina Press, 2001), 260.

124. De la Fuente, *Nation for All*, 264.

125. Fidel Castro, "Quizás el más difícil de todos los problemas: la discriminación racial. Comparencia en el Canal 12 televisión, 25 [March] 1959," in Fidel Castro, *El pensamiento de Fidel Castro. Selección temática. Tomo 1/2. Enero 1959–abril 1961* (Havana: Editora Política, 1983), 398.

126. Devyn Spence Benson, "Not Blacks, but Citizens! Racial Politics in Revolutionary Cuba, 1959–1961" (Ph.D. diss., University of North Carolina at Chapel Hill, 2009), 2.

127. Hugh Thomas, *Cuba or the Pursuit of Freedom* (New York: Da Capo Press, 1998), 208–9.

128. Rafael Duharte Jiménez, "The 19th Century Black Fear," in Pedro Pérez Sarduy and Jean Stubbs, eds., *AfroCuba: An Anthology of Cuban Writing on Race, Politics, and Culture* (Melbourne: Ocean Press, 1993), 37–46.

129. Lewis et al., *Four Women*, 332–36.

130. See, for example, Alfredo's story in Oscar Lewis, Ruth M. Lewis, and Susan M. Rigdon, *Four Men: Living the Revolution: An Oral History of Contemporary Cuba* (Urbana: University of Illinois Press, 1977).

131. De la Fuente, *Nation for All*, 286.

132. As recalled by Antonio Villaverde, interview by author, Havana, 28 April 1999.

133. Devyn Spence Benson, *Antiracism in Cuba: The Unfinished Revolution* (Chapel Hill: University of North Carolina Press, 2016), 126.

134. De la Fuente, *Nation for All*, 275, 269–71.

135. Ibid., 269–71; see also José Martí, "My Race," in Philip S. Foner, ed., *Our America: Writings on Latin America and the Struggle for Cuban Independence by José Martí* (New York: Monthly Review Press, 1977), 313.

136. Maurice Zeitlin, *Revolutionary Politics and the Cuban Working Class* (Princeton,

NJ: Princeton University Press, 1967), 280–85. For a discussion of the contradictory nature of the revolutionary government's efforts to eliminate racism, see Benson, *Antiracism in Cuba*.

137. De la Fuente, *Nation for All*, 264.

138. Carlos Eire, *Waiting for Snow in Havana: Confessions of a Cuban Boy* (New York: Free Press, 2003), 3–4.

139. "Ley de Reforma Urbana," 14 October 1960, in Bell et al., eds., *Documentos de la revolución cubana 1960*, 111–29.

140. Lewis et al., *Neighbors*, xv.

141. Alina Fernández, *Castro's Daughter: An Exile's Memoir of Cuba* (New York: St. Martin's Press, 1998), 44.

142. Tomás Gutiérrez Alea, dir., *Memorias del subdesarrollo* (ICAIC, 1968).

143. Nicolás Ríos, interview by author, Miami, 11 May 1999; Fidel Castro, "Democracia es esta," in Bell et al., eds., *Documentos de la revolución cubana 1960*, 260–64.

144. Ana Riewerts, phone interview from New York by author, 16 May 2002. After initially reducing rents in 1959, in October 1960 the revolutionary government nationalized all urban housing, ensuring that all tenants achieved ownership of their rented homes over a period of time and landlords received a compensation payment of up to $600 per month. See Padula, "Fall of the Bourgeoisie," 321–22.

145. Antonio Villaverde, interview by author, Havana, 28 April 1999.

146. Padula, "Fall of the Bourgeoisie," 26, 537.

147. Frantz Fanon, *The Wretched of the Earth* (London: Penguin Books, 1990), 27–28.

148. Pérez, *On Becoming Cuban*, 498.

149. Ibid., 13.

150. "Terry's Guide to Cuba, 1929," in Jenkins, *Travelers' Tales*, 134–35.

151. Sutherland, *Youngest Revolution*, 97–102.

152. Fanon, *Wretched of the Earth*, 169.

153. "¿Que lee el pueblo?" in *Bohemia*, 7 May 1961, 122–23. This article reported what books the Cuban people were reading (or encouraged to read), the best sellers being various editions of the works of José Martí (600,000 copies) and the Spanish classic *El ingenioso hidalgo Don Quijote de La Mancha* by Cervantes (340,000), the latter being the first book to roll off the presses at the new national printing house in 1959.

154. Inocencia, interview by Lewis et al., *Four Women*, 431.

155. David Forgacs, ed., *The Gramsci Reader: Selected Writings, 1916–1935* (New York: New York University Press, 2000), 234.

156. Guevara, "Socialism and Man in Cuba," in *Che Guevara Reader*, 216–17.

157. Fagen et al., *Cubans in Exile*, 87.

158. Pérez, *On Becoming Cuban*, 500; Susan Eckstein, *The Immigrant Divide: How Cuban Americans Changed the U.S. and Their Homeland* (New York: Routledge, 2009), 15–17.

159. "Don Feliciano, a Native, Replaces Santa in Cuba," *New York Times*, 21 December 1959; R. Hart Phillips, "Cuba Celebrates Christmas Gaily," *New York Times*, 25 December 1959.

160. Archbishop Enrique Pérez Serantes, "Vida Nueva," in Conferencia de Obispos Católicos de Cuba, *La Voz de la Iglesia en Cuba* (Mexico: Obra Nacional de la Buena

Prensa, 1995), 53–59. In this same pastoral letter he asked the government to consider abolishing the right to divorce (guaranteed in the 1940 Constitution) as a "cancer" that undermined the family.

161. Margaret E. Crahan, "Catholicism in Cuba," *Cuban Studies* 19 (1989): 5. Article 55 of the 1940 Constitution (reinstated in February 1959) officially established that all education would be *"laica"* (nonreligious) but religious instruction could be conducted in private educational centers. José Bell, Delia Luisa López, and Tania Caram, eds., *Documentos de la revolución cubana 1959* (La Habana: Editorial de Ciencias Sociales, 2008), 57.

162. John M. Kirk, *Between God and the Party: Religion and Politics in Revolutionary Cuba* (Tampa: University of South Florida Press, 1989), 175–76.

163. Sergio Arce, *The Church and Socialism: Reflections from a Cuban Context* (New York: Circus Publications, 1985), 189–93.

164. Nelson Valdés, "Cuban Political Culture: Between Betrayal and Death," in Halebsky and Kirk, *Cuba in Transition*, 215.

165. Melchor W. Gastón, Oscar A. Echeverría, and René F. de la Huerta, "Por qué reforma agraria?" unpublished study [1958] on behalf of the Catholic University Association (Agrupación Católica Universitaria), Havana, quoted by Schoultz, *That Infernal Little Cuban Republic*, 53.

166. Moreno, "From Traditional to Modern Values," 477.

167. Crahan, "Catholicism in Cuba," 7.

168. Padula, "Fall of the Bourgeoisie," 455n118; Torreira and Buajasán, *Operación Peter Pan*, 10–11.

169. See Denise Urcelay-Maragnes, *La Leyenda Roja. Los voluntarios cubanos en la guerra civil española* (León: Editorial Lobo Sapiens, 2011).

170. Eusebio Leal, interview in Marina Ochoa, dir., *Never Ever Neverland* (ICAIC, 2015).

171. Padula, "Fall of the Bourgeoisie," 418–19.

172. Kirk, *Between God and the Party*, 106.

173. Leslie Dewart, *Cuba, Church, and Crisis* (London: Sheed and Ward, 1964), 154–56; see also Lillian Guerra, "To Condemn the Revolution Is to Condemn Christ," *Hispanic American Historical Review* 89 (2009): 104–5.

174. Dewart, *Cuba, Church, and Crisis*, 15–16.

175. Bishop Alberto Martín Villaverde, "La Reforma Agraria y la Iglesia Católica," 5 July 1959, in *La Voz de la Iglesia*, 80–83 (my translation).

176. "La Reforma Agraria y El Arzobispado de Santiago de Cuba," 21 July 1959, in *La Voz de la Iglesia*, 85 (my translation).

177. Crahan, "Catholicism in Cuba," 7.

178. Padula, "Fall of the Bourgeoisie," 496, 143, 453–54.

179. Crahan, "Catholicism in Cuba," 5–8.

180. Casavantes, *Revolution Is for the Children*, 88.

181. Pedraza, *Political Disaffection*, 58.

182. Sr. Miriam Strong, "Refugees from Castro's Cuba: 'Of Fish and Freedom': A Historical Account of the Cuban Refugees Received and Relieved by His Excellency Bishop

Coleman F. Carroll in the Catholic Diocese of Miami, Florida, 1959–1964" (master's thesis, Fordham University, 1964), 133.

183. Grupo Areíto, *Contra el viento y marea,* 27 (my translation).

184. José Buajasán, interview in Ochoa, *Never Ever Neverland.*

185. Dewart, *Cuba, Church, and Crisis,* 149–50.

186. R. Hart Phillips, "Castro Censures Catholic Parley," *New York Times,* 29 November 1959, 19.

187. See "Castro v. the Virgin," *Time,* 22 September 1961, 48.

188. "As Anti-Communists Speak up in Cuba," *U.S. News and World Report,* 1 August 1960, 8.

189. Quoted by Alice L. Hageman and Philip E. Wheaton, eds., *Religion in Cuba Today: A New Church in a New Society* (New York: Association Press, 1971), 67.

190. Trial testimony of Reynold González of 18 October 1961, Cuban Ministry of the Interior Archives, quoted by Jesús Arboleya, *The Cuban Counterrevolution* (Athens, OH: Center for International Studies, Ohio University, 2000), 61.

191. "Por Díos y por Cuba," 16 May 1960, *La Voz de la Iglesia,* 107–14.

192. "Circular colectiva del episcopado Cubano," 7 August 1960, *La Voz de la Iglesia,* 115–18 (my translation).

193. Kirk, *Between God and the Party,* 84.

194. R. Hart Phillips, "Cubans See Test for Church Near," *New York Times,* 22 August 1960.

195. "Roma o Moscú?" pastoral letter of 13 November 1960, in *La Voz de la Iglesia,* 135–41.

196. "Provocación contrarrevolucionaria en la Iglesia de la Milagrosa," *Revolución,* 12 December 1960, 1.

197. See "A Program of Covert Action against the Castro Regime," March 1960, in Peter Kornbluh, ed., *The Bay of Pigs Declassified: The Secret CIA Report on the Invasion of Cuba* (New York: New Press, 1998), 103–9.

198. #607 Memorandum from the Secretary of Defense's Deputy Assistant for Special Operations (Lansdale) to the Deputy Secretary of Defense (Douglas): "Cuba," 7 November 1960, *FRUS, 1958–1960,* VI, 1116.

199. Fidel Castro speech of 4 March 1961, quoted in Hageman and Wheaton, *Religion in Cuba,* 130–32.

200. Quoted by Gerald E. Poyo, *Cuban Catholics in the United States, 1960–1980: Exile and Integration* (Notre Dame, IN: University of Notre Dame Press, 2007), 76.

201. Padula, "Fall of the Bourgeoisie," 468.

202. "Cuba: 'To the Palace,'" *Newsweek,* 25 September 1961, 54.

203. Hageman and Wheaton, *Religion in Cuba,* 28; see also Poyo, *Cuban Catholics,* 78.

204. Nicolás Rios, interview by author, Miami, 11 May 1999.

205. Lewis et al., *Four Women,* 177.

206. Hernández et al., "Political Culture," 41.

207. López Vigil, *Cuba,* vii.

208. Arce, *Church and Socialism,* 189.

209. Poyo, *Cuban Catholics,* 78, 11.

210. Torreira and Buajasán, *Operación Peter Pan*, 68.
211. Eusebio Leal in Bravo and Gómez, *Operación Peter Pan*, 289 (my translation).
212. Quoted by Hageman and Wheaton, *Religion in Cuba*, 30.
213. Padula, "Fall of the Bourgeoisie," 490.
214. Huberman and Sweezy, *Cuba*, 6.
215. Nelson, *Rural Cuba*, 236; and World Bank survey, quoted by Richard Jolly, "Education," in Dudley Seers, ed., *Cuba: Economic and Social Revolution* (Chapel Hill: University of North Carolina Press, 1964), 171.
216. Rolland G. Paulston, "Education," in Mesa-Lago, *Revolutionary Change*, 385.
217. Theodore MacDonald, *Making a New People: Education in Revolutionary Cuba* (Vancouver: New Star Books, 1985), 17.
218. Quoted in Jolly, "Education," 346.
219. Casavantes, *Revolution Is for the Children*, 24–26, 30.
220. Pérez, *On Becoming Cuban*, 159–60.
221. See Bell et al., eds., *Documentos de la revolución cubana 1959*, 57–58, for articles 55 and 56 on education in the Ley Fundamental de la República, the 1940 Constitution that, with some minor adjustments, was reinstated 7 February 1959.
222. Jacob Canter, U.S. public affairs officer, 1952–1953, quoted in Pérez, *On Becoming Cuban*, 404.
223. James Baker, "The Beginning of the Pedro Pan Program in Cuba," sent to Msgr. Walsh, 25 May 1998, box 26, Walsh Papers.
224. Pérez, *On Becoming Cuban*, 408.
225. Samuel Bowles, "Cuban Education and the Revolutionary Ideology," *Harvard Educational Review* 41, no. 4 (1971): 477–81.
226. R. Hart Phillips, "Urrutia Will Let 300 Foes Depart," *New York Times*, 8 January 1959, 3.
227. Armando Hart, "Dos Capítulos del Mensaje Educacional a la Nación. Educación, Socieday y Estado," in *Nueva Revista Cubana* 2, no. 1 (January–March 1960): 162–71 (my translation). See also *Cuba y la Conferencia de Educación y Desarrollo Económico y Social* (Havana: Editorial Nacional de Cuba, March 1962) sect. d, "Principales problemas en relación con el contenido y orientación de la enseñanza, 24–28, quoted in Jolly, "Education," 348–51.
228. Jolly, "Education," 347. See also Armando Hart, "Sobre el Año de la Educación" (29 January 1961), in Fidel Castro, *Educación y Revolución* (Mexico, D.F.: Editorial Nuestro Tiempo, 1983), 17.
229. Anna Lorenzetto and Karel Neys, *Methods and Means Utilized in Cuba to Eliminate Illiteracy: UNESCO Report* (Havana: Editora Pedagogica, 1965), 16.
230. Eugene F. Provenzo Jr. and Concepción García, "Exiled Teachers and the Cuban Revolution," *Cuban Studies* 13, no. 1 (winter 1983): 2; "Two Cuban Teachers Say They Fled Castro's Communist Restraints," *New York Times*, 5 December 1962. See also Dr. Carlos Cortina, testimony of 4 December 1962 to U.S. Senate Subcommittee hearings, *Cuban Refugee Problem*, 363–69.
231. Torreira and Buajasán, *Operación Peter Pan*, 162.

232. See #278 Despatch from the Embassy in Cuba to the Department of State: "Growth of Communism in Cuba," 14 April 1959, *FRUS, 1958–1960, VI*, 462.

233. Pérez, *Cuba in the American Imagination*, 244–45.

234. R. Hart Phillips, "Cuba Gives Pupils Poem Scoring U.S.," *New York Times*, 27 November 1960, 34. Phillips describes a pamphlet titled "So-Called Democracy," distributed at Cuban schools after the clash at the Organization of American States (OAS) meeting in Costa Rica in August 1961. The story describes the exploits of little Pancho, depicting the United States as a shark that gobbles up little sardines (Latin American countries), and Uncle Sam is identified as the Ku Klux Klan. See also R. Hart Phillips, "Anti-U.S. Songs a Cuban Weapon," *New York Times*, 15 January 1961, 2.

235. "Text of Appeal to Cubans to Revolt against Castro Regime," *New York Times*, 9 April 1961.

236. Bell et al., eds., *Documentos de la revolución cubana 1959*, 336.

237. Ley 680, "Bases y normas reguladoras de la Reforma Integral de la Enseñanza," in Bell et al., eds., *Documentos de la revolución cubana 1959*, 227–72.

238. Poyo, *Cuban Catholics*, 71, 71n70. See also articles 46–48 of Law 680 on education reform in Bell et al., eds., *Documentos de la revolución cubana 1959*, 258.

239. R. Hart Phillips, "Cuba Revamping School System," *New York Times*, 26 July 1959, 26.

240. Torreira and Buajasán, *Operación Peter Pan*, 42.

241. "Coeducación en todas las escuelas públicas," *Diario de la Marina*, 8 September 1959.

242. Quoted by Torres, *Lost Apple*, 112.

243. Fidel Castro, *Fidel and Religion: Conversations with Frei Betto on Marxism and Liberation Theology* (Melbourne: Ocean Press, 2006), 159.

244. Oscar Rego, "Saludan los Dueños y Directores de Escuelas Privadas la Nacionalización de la Enseñanza," *Bohemia*, 4 June 1961, 17.

245. See "La Salle High marks 50th: Rededicated Building Honors Msgr. Bryan O. Walsh, Schools Link to Pedro Pan," Archdiocese of Miami, 14 December 2011, www.miamiarch.org/CatholicDiocese.php?op=Article_111213234218763.

246. Thomas, *Cuba*, 1131–33.

247. Quoted by Pérez, *On Becoming Cuban*, 400.

248. Ibid., 401.

249. Casavantes, *Revolution Is for the Children*, 42.

250. See Margarita Oteiza (former Ruston student and later English teacher at that school), interview by Eloísa Echazábal and Carmen Romañach, Miami, 31 March 2010, https://www.youtube.com/watch?v=R2HxEExZdOA.

251. Padula, "Fall of the Bourgeoisie," 488–91.

252. Kirk, *Between God and the Party*, 97.

253. Fidel Castro's speech of 1 May 1961, in Hageman and Wheaton, *Religion in Cuba*, 135–36.

254. Abel Prieto, "Cuba's National Literacy Campaign," *Journal of Reading* 25, no. 3 (December 1981): 216.

255. "Ley de nacionalización de la enseñanza. Junio de 1961," in Teresa Fernández So-

neira, *Cuba: Historia de la Educación Católica 1582–1961, Tomo II* (Miami, FL: Ediciones Universal, 1997), 397–98.

256. José Miller, director of Havana *patronato* (synagogue), interview by author, Havana, 26 April 1999. See also Abraham Dubelman, "Cuba," in *American Jewish Year Book*, vol. 63 (Philadelphia: American Jewish Committee and Jewish Publication Society of America, 1962).

257. Tom Miller, *Trading with the Enemy: A Yankee Travels through Castro's Cuba* (New York: Atheneum, 1992).

258. Dana Evan Kaplan, "Fleeing the Revolution: The Exodus of Cuban Jewry in the Early 1960s," *Cuban Studies* 36 (2005): 129–54.

259. Department of Health, Education, and Welfare [DHEW], Children's Bureau, *Cuba's Children in Exile: The Story of the Unaccompanied Cuban Refugee Children's Program* (Washington, D.C.: U.S. Government Printing Office, 1967), 3.

260. "1000 Muchachas a la Universidad Patricio Lumumba," *Verde Olivo*, 19 November 1961, 28.

261. "In Cuba, Another Communistic Move," *U.S. News* and *World Report*, 6 February 1961, 8.

262. "Communism in Cuba: Noose Gets Tighter," *U.S. News* and *World Report*, 18 September 1961, 16. Fidel Castro's twelve-year-old son (Fidelito) did not leave Cuba to study in the Soviet Union at this time, but he did participate in a youth delegation to various socialist countries in September 1961. See Juan Arcocha, "La más joven delegación que ha salido de Cuba," *Revolución*, 18 September 1961, 2.

263. Candi Sosa, interview in *Escape from Havana: An American Story* (CNBC Documentary, 2010).

264. Conde, *Operation Pedro Pan*, 26. The government did establish a scholarship program for gifted children. Regarding the "Promising Student Campaign" that sent Cuban students overseas, primarily to the Soviet Union, see del Mar, *Cuban Story*, 58.

265. "Cuban Students in New York," *New York Times*, 26 March 1961.

266. "Red Target: Youths," *U.S. News and World Report*, 19 February 1962, 55.

267. Eire, *Waiting for Snow*, 87.

268. Conde, *Operation Pedro Pan*, 215.

269. "African Savages Take Over Her School: A Cuban Girl Flees in Terror," *Miami Herald*, 27 August 1962, quoted by Dubinsky, *Babies without Borders*, 36.

270. Walsh, "Cuban Refugee Children," 382–83.

271. Jesús Díaz, dir., *Lejanía* (ICAIC, 1985), quoted by Dubinsky, *Babies without Borders*, 30.

272. *Plan Asistencial* (Attendance Plan) was an activity program for elementary schoolchildren run by the Ministry of Education with the involvement of parents, the FMC, and other mass organizations from the commencement of the 1961 school year while teachers were mobilized for the final effort of the literacy campaign. See advertisement for television and radio programs in *Revolución*, 6 November 1961, 8.

273. Chase, *Revolution*, 199.

274. George Southworth, "80 Cuban Boys in Miami—a Day in Their New Life," *Miami Herald*, 8 March 1962, 10A.

275. Agustín Tamargo, quoted by Smith and Padula, *Sex and Revolution*, 156.
276. Interview in Roccena Ortiz, "Accounts of Desperate Times," 293–304.
277. Ibid.
278. Del Mar, *Cuban Story*, 59.
279. Padula, "Fall of the Bourgeoisie," 555.
280. Francisco Méndez, interview in Bravo and Gómez, *Operación Peter Pan*, 179–91 (my translation).
281. Some Cuban interviewees recall the child on the second billboard as being an Afro-Cuban, and Casavantes, *Revolution Is for the Children*, 165, reproduced a different image from an anti-Castro pamphlet produced by the Junta Catequista Diocesana. A *New York Times* article also referred to these "propaganda posters." See Tad Szulc, "Castro Speeding Effort to Set Up Communist State," *New York Times*, 18 June 1961, 1, 3.

Chapter 2. *Alfabeticemos!* Let's Teach Literacy! Learning the "Why" of the Revolution

1. Msgr. Walsh, interview by author, Miami, 20 March 2000.
2. James Baker, "The Beginning of the Pedro Pan Program in Cuba," sent to Msgr. Walsh, 25 May 1998, box 26, Walsh Papers.
3. Antonio Villaverde, interview by author, Havana, 28 April 1999.
4. Armando Hart (former Minister for Education), interview by author, Havana, 17 January 2001.
5. Paulston, "Education," 379.
6. Huberman and Sweezy, *Cuba*, 97.
7. Guillermina Ares, *Alfabetización en Cuba: Historia y testimonios* (Havana: Editora Politica, 2000), 35–37; Ana Angélica Rey Díaz, *Conrado Benítez: Primer maestro mártir* (Havana: Editora Política, 1987), 8.
8. Fidel Castro's speech of 29 August 1960, Versión taquigráfica, CCP Library Archives, Havana, 17 (my translation).
9. Prieto, "Cuba's National Literacy Campaign," 215; Huberman and Sweezy, *Cuba*, 97.
10. See Fidel Castro's speech of 14 September 1959 at Camp Columbia in *La Fortaleza Conquistada* (Havana: Editorial Abril, 1987).
11. Fidel Castro's speech at the United Nations, 26 September 1960, in David Deutschmann and Deborah Shnookal, eds., *Fidel Castro Reader* (Melbourne: Ocean Press), 160.
12. Manuel Moro, interview by author, Havana, 3 May 1999. Moro was the assistant to Carlos Luis Herrera, the director of the National Literacy Commission's publicity department. For most of the campaign, Moro (then twenty-two) was the de facto director of publicity due to Herrera's other responsibilities.
13. Ares, *Alfabetización*, 46–47. See also Hart's opening address to the National Literacy Congress of 2–5 September 1961, in *Congreso Nacional de Alfabetización: Documentos* (Havana: Ministerio de Educación, 1961).
14. Fidel Castro's speech of 31 December 1960, quoted by Ares, *Alfabetización*, 51 (my translation). Each *brigadista* was set the goal of teaching six to ten people. See Fagen, *Transformation of Political Culture*, 182.
15. MacDonald, *Making a New People*, 62. By the end of August 1961, 985,329 illiterates

had been identified. Virgilio Gomez Fuentes, "Los principios socials aplicados a la organización y desarrollo de la gran campaña nacional de alfabetización," in *Alfabetización, Nationalización de la Ensañanza* (Havana: Ministerio de la Educación, 1961), 8–11.

16. Fidel Castro's speech in Santa Clara, 28 January 1961, quoted by Ares, *Alfabetización*, 52–53 (my translation).

17. Jolly, "Education," 201; Lorenzetto and Neys, *Methods and Means*, 40; Fagen, *Transformation of Political Culture*, 55n.

18. "Avanza la alfabetización en los llanos de Bayamo," *Bohemia*, 11 June 1961, 31 (my translation).

19. Herbert L. Matthews, *Revolution in Cuba* (New York: Charles Scribner's Sons, 1975), 182.

20. Guevara, *Reminiscences*, 83.

21. Mier Fables, interview in Jonathan Kozol, *Children of the Revolution: A Yankee Teacher in the Cuban Schools* (New York: Dell Publishing, 1978), 22.

22. Lorenzetto and Neys, *Methods and Means*, 15.

23. Abel Prieto, interview by Marvin Leiner, "The 1961 National Cuban Literacy Campaign," in Robert F. Arnove and Harvey T. Graff, eds., *National Literacy Campaigns* (New York: Plenum Press, 1987), 190.

24. Manuel Moro, interview by author, Havana, 13 January 2001.

25. Quoted by Leiner, "1961 National Cuban Literacy Campaign," 189.

26. See Fidel Castro, "Report to the First Congress of the Cuban Communist Party," in *First Congress of the Communist Party of Cuba, Havana 17–22 December 1975* (Moscow: Progress Publishers, 1976), 15–260.

27. Literacy campaign poster, Museo de la Alfabetización (National Literacy Campaign Museum), Havana.

28. José Martí, "Wandering Teachers," in Mirta Muñiz and Deborah Shnookal, eds., *José Martí Reader: Writings on the Americas* (Melbourne: Ocean Press, 1999), 47.

29. Armando Hart, opening address to the National Literacy Congress of 2–5 September 1961, *Congreso Nacional de Alfabetización: Documentos* (Havana: Ministerio de Educación, 1961), 27 (my translation).

30. Hart, "Sobre el Año de la Educación," in Castro, *Educación y Revolución*, 15–16 (my translation).

31. Manuel Moro, interview by author, Havana, 13 January 2001.

32. Jonathan Kozol, "A New Look at the Literacy Campaign in Cuba," in *Harvard Educational Review* 18, no. 3 (1978): 352.

33. José Martí, "Wandering Teachers," *José Martí Reader*, 48–50.

34. Educationalist Theodore MacDonald argued the primary reason for the Cuban literacy campaign's success, in contrast to Freire's work in Brazil, was "the fact that it took place in the context of total social revolution." MacDonald, *Making a New People*, 86.

35. Hart, "Sobre el Año de la Educación," in Castro *Educación y Revolución*, 21.

36. Jolly, "Education," 162, 201–2.

37. Fernando García, interview by Leiner, "1961 National Cuban Literacy Campaign," 191, 187.

38. Felix Roberto Masud-Piloto, *From Welcomed Exiles to Illegal Immigrants: Cuban Migration to the U.S., 1959–1995* (Lanham, MD: Rowman and Littlefield, 1996), 33–34.

39. Raúl Ferrer quoted by Leiner, "1961 National Cuban Literacy Campaign," 189.

40. See Armando Hart's speech at the 22 December 1961 closing rally of the literacy campaign, published in *Bohemia*, 31 December 1961, 37.

41. Fagen, *Transformation of Political Culture*, 55.

42. Jolly, "Education," 201–2.

43. Max Figueroa quoted by Fagen, *Transformation of Political Culture*, 59.

44. Lorenzetto and Keys, *Methods and Means*, 40; "Los Alfabetizadores Populares Infantiles," *Bohemia*, 26 November 1961, 99.

45. Raúl Ferrer quoted in Kozol, *Children of the Revolution*, 50.

46. Juan Martínez, letter to Fidel, n.d., Museo de la Alfabetización. Writing a letter to the prime minister was part of the literacy accomplishment test. The Museum collection includes thousands of these in bound volumes. Fagen commented that this gave "a special importance and individuality to the end of the process of becoming literate," and that this "must have been richer and more satisfying than passing a standardized test." Fagen, *Transformation of Political Culture*, 58. Jonathan Kozol also remarked on the "spontaneity and authenticity" of these letters. See Kozol, *Children of the Revolution*, 51.

47. Kozol, "New Look," 348.

48. Kapcia, *Cuba: Island of Dreams*, 111.

49. Jolly, "Education," 201–2.

50. Hart, "Sobre el Año de la Educación," in Castro, *Educación y Revolución*, 19–20 (my translation).

51. "National Coordinator Tells His Story," *Granma International*, 11 January 1987, 10.

52. Aldo Alvarez, "La Juventud Cubana en las Grandes Tareas de la Educación" (26 February 1961), in Castro, *Educación y Revolución*, 111.

53. "National Coordinator Tells His Story," *Granma International*, 11 January 1987, 10.

54. Gilberto Ante, "El brigadista enseña y aprende," in *Bohemia*, 3 December 1961, 20–21 (my translation).

55. Fidel Castro speech to *brigadistas*, 14 May 1961, in Fagen, *Transformation of Political Culture*, 183.

56. Rey Díaz, *Conrado Benítez*, 26.

57. "La alfabeticización ... Lo que dijo Fidel Castro," *Casa de las Américas* 1, no. 9 (November–December, 1961): 10.

58. "Children's Crusade," *Newsweek*, 3 April 1961, 51.

59. R. Hart Phillips, *The Cuban Dilemma* (New York: An Oblonsky Book, Astor-Honor, 1962), 305.

60. Conde, *Operation Pedro Pan*, 37.

61. Triay, *Fleeing Castro*, 7–8.

62. Fagen, *Transformation of Political Culture*, 181–82.

63. C. Fred Judson, *Cuba and the Revolutionary Myth: The Political Education of the Cuban Rebel Army, 1953–1963* (Boulder, CO: Westview Press, 1984), 16.

64. Prieto, "Cuba's National Literacy Campaign," 220.

65. *Revolución*, 26 April 1961, 8 (my translation).

66. MacDonald, *Making a New People*, 63.
67. Leiner, "1961 National Cuban Literacy Campaign," 177.
68. Johnson, "Elián González Case."
69. Kozol, "New Look," 344–45.
70. Che Guevara, "Socialism and Man in Cuba," in Deutschmann, *Che Guevara Reader*, 226–27.
71. Kozol, "New Look," 348.
72. Lorenzetto and Keys, *Methods and Means*, 72.
73. Kozol, "New Look," 364.
74. Pérez, *Cuba in the American Imagination*, 220, 244.
75. Mark Abendroth, *Rebel Literacy: Cuba's National Literacy Campaign and Critical Global Citizenship* (Duluth, MN: Litwin Books, 2009), 75, 78.
76. Raúl Ferrer quoted in Kozol, *Children of the Revolution*, 82–83.
77. Pérez, *Cuba in the American Imagination*, 223.
78. See Lillian Guerra, "The End of Fidelismo: Why Everything Is Possible Now," Cuba Counter Points, December 6, 2016, http://cubacounterpoints.com/archives/4749.
79. Paolo Freire and Raúl Ferrer quoted in Kozol, "New Look," 364, 367 (emphasis in the original).
80. Lorenzetto and Keys, *Methods and Means*, 72. For a discussion about the attempted suppression of the UNESCO Report on the Cuban literacy campaign at the Tehran literacy conference in 1965, see Kozol, *Children of the Revolution*, 77–81.
81. Anna Lorenzetto quoted in Kozol, "New Look," 361.
82. "María," interview in Kozol, "New Look," 373.
83. Lorenzetto and Keys, *Methods and Means*, 43.
84. Mirta Muñiz, interview by author, Havana, April–May 1999.
85. *Revolución*, 28 April 1961, 12.
86. *Revolución*, 31 May 1961, 1.
87. Lorenzetto and Keys, *Methods and Means*, 43.
88. "National Coordinator Tells His Story," *Granma International*, 11 January 1987, 10. See also Armando Hart's address to the 2–5 September 1961 congress on the literacy campaign, in *Congreso de Alfabetización* (Havana: Imprenta Nacional de Cuba, 1961), 9–28.
89. Armando Hart, interview by author, Havana, 17 January 2001.
90. Mirta Muñiz, interview by author, April–May 1999. Mirta Muñiz was a member of the propaganda department of the National Literacy Commission during the literacy campaign.
91. Ibid.
92. Mercedes Liriano Stuart, in Ares, *Alfabetización*, 63.
93. Inocencia Rodríguez Rodríguez, *Asociación de Jóvenes Rebeldes: Documentos para una historia de futuro* (Havana: Editorial Abril, 1989), 227–31.
94. Asteria Perdomo, in Randall, *Cuban Women Now*, 103.
95. Casavantes, *Revolution Is for the Children*, 113–14.
96. See Yamile Regalado Someillan's chapter 5 on the literacy campaign in "The Cartooned Revolution: Images and the Revolutionary Citizen in Cuba, 1959–1963" (Ph.D. diss., University of Maryland, College Park, 2009).

97. See *Bohemia*, 23 April 1961 (my translation).
98. See ad for the National Literacy Congress, *Bohemia*, 27 August 1961, 43; see also Lorenzetto and Keys, *Methods and Means*, 43.
99. Jolly, "Education," 199–200.
100. MacDonald, *Making a New People*, 55.
101. Fagen, *Transformation of Political Culture*, 57.
102. Kozol, *Children of the Revolution*, 9.
103. Mirta Muñiz, interview by author, Havana, April–May 1999.
104. Jolly, "Education," Table 5, 202.
105. Julie Marie Bunck, *Fidel Castro and the Quest for a Revolutionary Culture in Cuba* (University Park: Pennsylvania State University Press, 1994), 26, 86.
106. Kozol, "New Look," 354–55 (emphasis in the original).
107. Author's conversation with Juan Alfonso, Havana, 16 November 2000.
108. Liudmilla Chávez Verana in Ares, *Alfabetización*, 69; see also testimony of Gerardo Massaret Matamoros, interview in *Granma* 3 March 1982, 2.
109. Armando Hart, interview by author, 17 January 2001.
110. Patria Silva, interview by author, Havana, January 2001.
111. See the report of this atrocity in *Bohemia*, 3 December 1961, 66–72.
112. "Nosotros sabemos que las madres van a tener valor," *Revolución*, 30 November 1961 (my translation).
113. Oscar F. Rego, "Bombardeo y desembarco en Playa Girón," *Bohemia*, 18 June 1961, 66; and "Playa Girón: territorio libre de analfabetismo el 26 de julio," *Revolución*, 12 June 1961, 1.
114. See the Cuban Ministry of Education statistics in Jolly, "Education," Table 4, 200. See also Lorenzetto and Keys, *Methods and Means*, 45.
115. See the story about a "pretty young white woman" teaching a black family who lived under a bridge, *Bohemia*, 25 June 1961, 35–36.
116. Smith and Padula, *Sex and Revolution*, 37.
117. *Venceremos!* (Literacy Campaign primer), (Havana: Comisión Nacional de Alfabetización del Ministerio de Educación, 1961), 95.
118. Fidel Castro speech, 28 January 1961, Santa Clara, quoted by Ares, *Alfabetización*, 52–53 (my translation).
119. *Brigadista* identity card, Museo de la Alfabetización (my translation).
120. Fidel Castro to the AJR, 27 March 1961, quoted by Ares, *Alfabetización*, 72 (my translation).
121. René J. Mujica, "Some Recollections of My Experiences in the Cuban Literacy Campaign," *Journal of Reading* 25, no. 3 (December 1981): 222.
122. Fagen, *Transformation of Political Culture*, 183–84, 190–91. See also Fidel Castro's speech of 28 January, 1961, quoted by Ares, *Alfabetización* , 53 (my translation).
123. "Monica," in Lewis et al., *Four Women*, 67. Various interviewees made similar statements to this researcher.
124. Jorge Calderón's file, Museo de la Alfabetización (my translation).
125. Sergio Carles, Ciego de Avila, letter to Fidel, 4 January 1962, Museo de la Alfabetización (my translation).

126. Oscar, interview by MacDonald, *Making a New People*, 50.
127. Barbara ("Barbarita") Valenzuela, interview by author, Havana, 10 January 2001.
128. File of Yolanda Domínguez Vizcay, Museo de la Alfabetización (my translation).
129. Patria Silva, interview by author, Havana, 10 January 2001.
130. *Bohemia*, 2 April 1961, 15.
131. See cartoon in *Bohemia*, 3 December 1961, reproduced as Figure 2.1.
132. Manuel Moro, interview by author, Havana, 3 May 1999. In fact, 62 percent of the Conrado Benítez *brigadistas* were assigned to Oriente province, where the greatest number of illiterates lived. See also Jolly, "Education"; and Fagen, *Transformation of Political Culture*, 45.
133. Monica, interview in Lewis et al., *Four Women*, 68.
134. Vivian Vélez, personal conversation with author, Havana, 29 April 1999.
135. Angela Valdés, Ciego de Avila, letter to Fidel Castro, 16 January 1962, Museo de la Alfabetización (my translation).
136. Recruitment poster, Museo de la Alfabetización.
137. "National Coordinator Tells His Story," *Granma International*, 11 January 1987, 10.
138. Monica, interview by Lewis et al., *Four Women*, 67–68.
139. María Masud, interview by author, Dallas, 29 March 2003.
140. Ares, *Alfabetización*, 100. See also Lorenzetto and Keys, *Methods and Means*, 46. Of the 100,000 *brigadistas*, 70,000 received scholarships for 1962.
141. *Revolución*, 23 March 1961, 6.
142. *Revolución*, 26 December 1961, 13.
143. Nancy Urbino Pérez, Havana, to Fidel, January 8, 1962, Museo de la Alfabetización (my translation).
144. María Luisa Morena Díaz, Guanimar, Alguizar, letter to Fidel, 2 January 1962, Museo de la Alfabetización.
145. Marusa Vadel M, Havana, letter to Fidel, 14 January 1962, Museo de la Alfabetización (my translation).
146. Fidel Castro speech at the final campaign rally, 22 December 1961, *Bohemia*, 31 December 1961, 36–47.
147. See Matilde Serra Robledo et al., eds., *El pueblo dice . . . Vivencias de la Campaña de Alfabetización en Cuba* (Havana: n.p., 1999), 51–53 (my translation).
148. Leonela Relys Díaz, interview by Leiner, "1961 National Cuban Literacy Campaign," 178. See also Halbert-Brooks, "Revolutionary Teachers," for examples of young women defying their parents and joining the literacy brigades.
149. Randall, *Cuban Women Now*, 36.
150. María Masud, interview by author, Dallas, 29 March 2003.
151. Javier Salado, interview by author, Havana, 25 April 1999.
152. Manuel Moro, interview by author, Havana, 3 May 1999.
153. "A Oriente, tres mil brigadistas," *Revolución*, 28 April 1961, 12.
154. "Las Brigadas Conrado Benítez los esperan en Varadero," *La Calle*, 7 May 1961 (my translation).
155. "Enseñando el camino: Canción del padre del brigadista," *Bohemia*, 21 May 1961.

156. "10 respuestas a 10 preguntas sobre las brigadas de alfabetización," *Bohemia*, 16 April 1961 (my translation).

157. "Reporte de las Brigadas Conrado Benítez," *Bohemia*, 2 July 1961 (my translation).

158. Josefina Carpio Lage, Camaguey, letter to Fidel, 28 December 1961, Museo de la Alfabetización (my translation).

159. Dulce María Piñeiro in "Mensajes de los brigadistas," *Bohemia*, 12 November 1961 (my translation).

160. María, interview in Kozol, "New Look," 375.

161. Kozol, "New Look," 376.

162. On 5 May 1961, *Revolución* ran an article about children teaching literacy alongside their parents.

163. "National Coordinator Tells His Story," *Granma International*, 11 January 1987, 10.

164. Jesús Arboleya, interview by author, Havana, 23 April 1999.

165. A copy of this letter was published in "Ejército de Alfabetizadores Brigadas 'Conrado Benítez.' A los padres de los brigadistas," *Bohemia* 31 December 1961.

166. "Participarán en la Educación los Padres," *El Mundo*, 17 September 1961, 1; Ana Nuñez Machín, *La Epopeya: Historia de la Campaña de Alfabetización* (Havana: Editorial de Ciencias Sociales, 1983), 67n19. See also *Revolución* articles explaining the program, 15 and 18 September, 6 and 7 November 1961.

167. "Las muchachas campesinos se preparan para enseñar curso de corte y costura," *Bohemia*, 4 June 1961, 4–7. See also Vilma Espín et al., *Women in Cuba: The Making of a Revolution within the Revolution* (New York, Pathfinder Press, 2012), 30–31.

168. "Cuando lo cuente la historia," *Bohemia*, 30 June 1961, 36–37.

169. María del Carmen Ramón, "Escuelas Ana Betancourt: Cuando las campesinas llegaron al Hotel Nacional," CubaDebate, 31 July 2016, http://www.cubadebate.cu/noticias/2016/07/31/escuelas-ana-betancourt-cuando-las-campesinas-llegaron-al-hotel-nacional-fotos/.

170. Espín et al., *Women in Cuba*, 31.

171. The lanterns came to symbolize the campaign; 130,000 of them were imported from the People's Republic of China.

172. Oscar, interview by MacDonald, *Making a New People*, 50.

173. Jaime Saruski, "Los maestros en la Sierra," *INRA*, supplement, August 1960, 11.

174. Kozol, "New Look," 349

175. *Bohemia*, 30 July 1961, included a four-page spread covering the "Ten basic points for health" for "the teacher and the literacy teacher," who was urged to make every effort to achieve these goals in basic health concerning water ("friend or enemy?"), washing one's hands, maintaining a clean body and clean clothes, keeping animals outside the house, using a sanitary latrine, wearing shoes, paying attention to dental care, protecting food from flies, boiling milk, and washing fruit and vegetables well (my translation).

176. The public health questionnaire to be completed by the *brigadista* about the community in which they taught is in the Museo de la Alfabetización (my translation).

177. Manuel Moro, interview by author, 17 January 2001.

178. Mario Díaz, interview in *Cimientos* (Mundo Latino, 1995).

179. Raúl Ferrer, interview in Kozol, *Children of the Revolution*, 14.

180. El Indio Naborí, *Cartilla y farol: Poemas militantes* (Havana, 1982).
181. The back cover of the learner's primer (*Venceremos*) included a quote from Fidel: "Hay que convertir la educación en una virtud y la ignorancia en un vicio." See also "Lo que dice Fidel Castro," in *Casa de las Américas* 1, no. 9 (November–December 1961): 6.
182. *Brigadista* identity card, Museo de la Alfabetización NLCM (my translation).
183. Ferrer, interview in Kozol, *Children of the Revolution*, 14.
184. *Alfabeticemos*, 2 (my translation).
185. MacDonald, *Making a New People*, 62.
186. Lorenzetto and Keys, *Methods and Means*, 73.
187. Fagen, *Transformation of Political Culture*, 61.
188. Jesús Arboleya, interview by author, Havana, 23 April 1999.
189. Miguel, interview in Kozol, *Children of the Revolution*, 38.
190. Nilka Georgina Cuevas Durán, in Serra Robledo et al., *El pueblo dice*, 25 (my translation).
191. Nereyda Matos Martínez, Horgueta, letter to Fidel, 18 January 1962, Museo de la Alfabetización (my translation).
192. Julio Urrutia Vásquez, letter to Fidel, 1 January 1962, Museo de la Alfabetización (my translation).
193. Ana Mirta Trijillo Reyes, Las Doncellas, letter to National Literacy Commission, 21 September 1961, Museo de la Alfabetización (my translation).
194. Juana Kindelán in "Cartas de brigadistas," published in *Bohemia*, 20 August 1961, 10.
195. Cándida Rosa Orizondo Crespo in Serra Robledo et al., *El pueblo dice*, 25 (my translation).
196. Lidia Catalina Totman in Serra Robledo et al., *El pueblo dice*, 34 (my translation).
197. Maricela Leon Cotay, Madruga, letter to Fidel, 7 January 1962, Museo de la Alfabetización (my translation).
198. Mujica, "Some Recollections," 223.
199. María Luisa Morena Díaz, Guanimar, letter to Fidel, 2 January 1962, Museo de la Alfabetización (my translation).
200. Patria Silva, interview by author, 10 January 2001.
201. Raúl Fernández Alech, interview by Leiner, "1961 National Cuban Literacy Campaign," 181.
202. Oscar, interview by MacDonald, *Making a New People*, 49–51.
203. Ibid.
204. María de la Cruz Sentmanat, interview in *Bohemia*, 25 June 1961 66–67 (my translation).
205. *Bohemia*, 16 July 1961, 108–9.
206. Nilka Georgina Cuevas Durán, in Serra Robledo et al., *El pueblo dice*, 39–40 (my translation).
207. Examples of these eyeglass cases are displayed at the Museo de la Alfabetización.
208. Migdalia Martínez Pino, in Serra Robledo et al., *El pueblo dice*, 33.
209. Unidentified *brigadista*, in Serra Robledo et al., *El pueblo dice*, 27 (my translation).
210. Rogelina Ramírez Cossio in Serra Robledo et al., *El pueblo dice*, 43 (my transla-

tion); Raúl Fernández Alech, interview by Leiner, "1961 National Cuban Literacy Campaign," 181.

211. Mercedes, interview by MacDonald, *Making a New People*, 52.
212. Monica, interview by Lewis et al., *Four Women*, 66, 74, 76.
213. Alba Margarita Cortina, interview by author, Havana, 10 January 2001.
214. Sonia Almazán, interview by author, Havana, 12 May 2016. As a nineteen-year-old trainee teacher, Sonia was the coordinator or team leader for a group of *brigadistas*.
215. Rosalía Rouce Leal, in Serra Robledo et al., *El pueblo dice*, 29–30 (my translation).
216. Antonio Villaverde, interview by author, Havana, 28 April 1999.
217. Mirta Muñiz, interview by author, April–May 1999.
218. Lourdes Hernández Domenech, personal conversation with author, Havana, 25 January 2001. Her sixteen-year-old cousin, Manuel Asunce Domenech, became one of the most honored martyrs of the literacy campaign when on 26 November 1961 he was beaten and murdered and then strung up in a tree, beside the body of his pupil, an older peasant named Pedro Lantigua. These murders were reported in *Bohemia*, 3 December 1961, 66–72.
219. Alba Margarita Cortina, interview by author, Havana, January 2001.
220. María, interview in Kozol, *Children of the Revolution*, 32.
221. Alba Margarita Cortina, interview by author, Havana, 10 January 2001.
222. Philip S. Foner, ed., *On Education by José Martí: Articles on Educational Theory and Pedagogy, and Writings for Children from the Age of Gold* (New York: Monthly Review Press, 1979), 24, 128.
223. Che Guevara, "A New Attitude to Work," in David Deutschmann, ed., *Che Guevara and the Cuban Revolution*, (Sydney: Pathfinder/Pacific and Asia, 1987), 159–68.
224. Armando Hart, "La Revolución y los problemas de la educación," in *Cuba Socialista* 1, no. 4 (December 1961): 33–58. See also Denise Blum, "Cuban Youth and Revolutionary Values" (Ph.D. diss., University of Texas, Austin, 2002), 9.
225. R. Hart Phillips, "14,092 Children Sent Out of Cuba," *New York Times*, 9 March 1963, 2.
226. Sergio Camacho Santiago, Santa Clara, letter to Fidel, 31 December 1961, Museo de la Alfabetización (my translation).
227. Nestor Falcón, letter to Fidel, n.d., Museo de la Alfabetización (my translation).
228. Leopoldo Cabrera, Aguacate, letter to Fidel, 29 December 1961, Museo de la Alfabetización (my translation).
229. Nancy Urbino Pérez, Havana, letter to Fidel, 8 January 1962, Museo de la Alfabetización (my translation).
230. Armando Hart, "Qué aprendimos de la campaña de alfabetizacion?" in Felipe de J. Pérez Cruz, *La Alfabetización en Cuba: Lectura histórica para pensar el presente* (Havana: Editorial de Ciencias Sociales, 2001), xiii–xiv (my translation).
231. Jesús Arboleya, interview by author, Havana, 23 April 1999.
232. Critics of the campaign also point to the fact that only a minimal level of literacy was attained by most learners, and Kozol explained this would indeed have been a failure, except that the Cuban government immediately followed up with the "Battle for the Sixth Grade" among the population, and every newly literate Cuban who wrote to Fidel

received a book to encourage him or her to continue studying. Kozol, *Children of the Revolution*, 55–56.

233. Quintin Hoare and Geoffrey Nowell Smith, eds., *Antonio Gramsci: Selections from the Prison Notebooks of Antonio Gramsci* (New York: International Publishers, 1971), 366–67.

234. Che Guevara, "Speech to Medical Students and Health Workers" (20 August 1960), in Deutschmann, *Che Guevara Reader*, 112–17.

235. John D. Holst, *Social Movements, Civil Society, and Radical Adult Education* (Westport, CT: Bergin and Garvey, 2002), 15.

236. Armando Valdéz, interview in Kozol, *Children of the Revolution*, 22.

237. Armando Hart, interview in *Cimientos* (Mundo Latino, 1995).

238. See Abendroth, *Rebel Literacy*.

239. Armando Hart, interview by author, Havana, 17 January 2001.

Chapter 3. The *Patria Potestad* Hoax

1. "A Close Look at Cuba," *U.S. News and World Report*, 30 October 1961, 58; and "Cuba: Crises Phoney and Real," *Time*, 14 November 1960, 36.

2. "Miami: Refugee City," *U.S. News and World Report*, 5 December 1960, 62.

3. "When a Cuban Child Gets Here," *Miami Herald*, 30 December 1960, 1.

4. "Cuba: And Now the Children," *Time*, 6 October 1961, 41.

5. Arzobispo de Santiago de Cuba, "Por Díos y por Cuba," 16 May 1969, *La Voz de la Iglesia*, 107–14 (my translation).

6. Torreira and Buajasán, *Operación Peter Pan*, 93; Casavantes, *Revolution Is for the Children*, 111.

7. "Cuba: Sovietizing," *Newsweek*, 6 March 1961, 59; "Children's Crusade," *Newsweek*, 3 April 1961, 51; "Even 7-Year-Olds Spy for Castro Now," *U.S. News and World Report*, 17 April 1961, 16; "Cuba: Redder Schoolhouse," *Newsweek*, 19 June 1961; Richard Eder, "100 Priests Are Seized in Cuba: 6 More Castro Foes Executed," *New York Times*, 17 September 1961; "Cuba: And Now the Children," *Time*, 6 October 1961.

8. "A Close Look at Cuba," *U.S. News and World Report*, 30 October 1961, 58.

9. Wendell Rollason (director of the Miami-based Inter-American Affairs Commission) testimony of 7 December 1961 to U.S. Senate subcommittee hearings, *Cuban Refugee Problem*, Washington, D.C.: Government Printing Office, 1962, 159.

10. Sonia Almazán, interview by author, Havana, 12 May 2016.

11. Joan Didion, *Miami* (New York: Vintage Books, 1987), 123.

12. Jorge Cabañas, Ministry of External Relations (MINREX), interview by author, Havana, 4 May 1999. Cabañas later became the first Cuban ambassador to the United States appointed after diplomatic relations were restored in 2015.

13. Rosa Irigoyen, interview in Ochoa and Centeno, *Del Otro Lado del Cristal* (my translation).

14. "Serán unidas en matrimonio cuatrocientas mil parejas," *Revolución*, 22 October 1960, 13.

15. "Patria Potestad y enseñanza privada," *Revolución*, 28 October 1960, 1, 14. See also *Revolución*, 22 November 1960.

16. *El Mundo*, 1 December 1960, cited by Warren Miller, *90 Miles from Home: The Face of Cuba Today* (New York: Crest Books, 1961), 17. The article also reported a pronouncement, broadcast on the CIA's clandestine Radio Swan, that the government was adding a "mysterious substance" to bottled drinks that would act on the brains of Cubans and "convert them to communism."

17. "The New Exodus," *Time*, 18 August 1961, 33.

18. Torreira and Buajasán, *Operación Peter Pan*, 94–95.

19. "Cuba: And Now the Children," *Time*, 6 October 1961, 41.

20. Rev. Domenick Joseph Adessa, "Refugee Cuban Children: The Role of the Catholic Welfare bureau of the Diocese of Miami, Florida . . ." (master's thesis, Fordham University, 1964), 35; Walsh, "Cuban Refugee Children," 382.

21. Alfred Lanier, "Operation Pedro Pan's Code of Silence," *Chicago Tribune*, 15 January 1998, 23.

22. Mignon Medrano, *Todo lo dieron por Cuba* (Miami: Cuban American National Foundation, 1995), 25 (my translation).

23. Walsh, "Cuban Refugee Children," 382.

24. Dorothy Legarreta, *The Guernica Generation: Basque Refugee Children of the Spanish Civil War* (Reno: University of Nevada Press, 1984).

25. José Buajasán, interview in Ochoa, *Never Ever Neverland* (my translation).

26. See Legarreta, *Guernica Generation*, 170–80.

27. Lars Schoultz, "Benevolent Domination: The Ideology of U.S. Policy toward Cuba," *Cuban Studies*, 41 (2010): 1–19.

28. Robert Scheer and Maurice Zeitlin, *Cuba: An American Tragedy* (Harmondsworth, Middlesex, U.K: Penguin Books, 1964), 316; "Red Embrace in Cuba," *New York Times*, 12 May 1959; R. Hart Phillips, "Castro Actions Suit the Communists' Aims," *New York Times*, 29 November 1959; David Reed, "Castro Makes Trouble—And Has Troubles, Too," *U.S. News and World Report*, 12 December 1960, 49–51.

29. Huberman and Sweezy, *Cuba*, 189.

30. Fidel Castro, "Report to the First Congress of the Cuban Communist Party," in *First Congress of the Communist Party of Cuba, Havana 17–22 December 1975* (Moscow: Progress Publishers, 1976), 45.

31. Sonia Almazán, interview by author, Havana, 12 May 2016.

32. See pamphlet published by Cruzada Feminina Cuba, *Comunismo destruye la familia* (1963), quoted by Chase, *Revolution*, 184. See also *Conozca lo que le ocurrirá a usted y a su país* (Miami: Movimiento Unidad Revolucionaria, 1962), 17, collection 26, box 1, Grupos Políticos Cubanos en el exilio, Cuban Heritage Collection, University of Miami Libraries, Coral Gables, Florida.

33. Elaine Tyler May, *Homeward Bound: American Families in the Cold War Era* (New York: Basic Books, 1988), 3; see also Ellen Schrecker, *Many Are the Crimes: McCarthyism in America* (Princeton: Princeton University Press, 1998), 146.

34. Chase, *Revolution*, 13–14.

35. Jesús Díaz, *De la Patria y el Exilio* (Havana: Ediciones Unión, 1979), 28 (my translation).

36. "Profile," *Newsweek*, 15 May 1961, 56; see also "Catholics Fight Castro on Soviet-

Type Schools," *U.S. News and World Report*, 7 November 1960, 14; and "Cuba: Redder Schoolhouse," *Newsweek*, 19 June 1961, 50.

37. "Aplícase en las escuelas la 'Ficha Escolar Acumulativa,' *Revolución*, 26 December 1960, 1, 16 (my translation). See also "Revolución educacional en Cuba," EcuRed, http://www.ecured.cu/Revoluci%C3%B3n_Educacional_en_Cuba.

38. "Cuba Orders Complete Tab on Every Student," *Miami Herald*, 27 December 1960, 2A.

39. "Aplícase en las escuelas la 'Ficha Escolar Acumulativa,' *Revolución*, 26 December 1960, 1, 16 (my translation).

40. Leiner, *Children Are the Revolution*, 53.

41. Quoted by Chase, *Revolution*, 184.

42. Enrique Huertas, "Un siniestro plan para arrebatara los padres cubanas la custodia y educación de sus hijos," *Bohemia Libre*, 5 February 1961, quoted by Chase, *Revolution*, 184.

43. Randall, *Cuban Women Now*, 29, 132–34. See also Karen Wald, *Children of Che: Childcare and Education in Cuba* (Palo Alto, CA: Ramparts Press, 1978).

44. Padula, "Fall of the Bourgeoisie," 539.

45. Fr. Walsh testimony of 13 December 1961 to U.S. Senate Subcommittee hearings, *Cuban Refugee Problem*, 228.

46. See advertisement for Plan Asistencial television and radio programs in *Revolución*, 6 November 1961, 8; see also *Revolución*, 7 November 1961.

47. "Más acerca del Plan Asistencial," *El Mundo*, 20 September 1961, A4 (my translation).

48. Armando Hart, "La Revolución y los Problems de la Educación," *Cuba Socialista* 1, no. 4 (December 1961): 33–58 (my translation). See also "Niños: Realidad de la Nueva Generación," *Bohemia*, 10 September 1961, 78–79.

49. Richard Eder, "100 Priests Are Seized in Cuba; 6 More Castro Foes Executed," *New York Times*, 17 September 1961, 1, 41.

50. Wendell Rollason testimony of 7 December 1961 to U.S. Senate Subcommittee hearings, *Cuban Refugee Problem*, 159.

51. "Campañas Estúpidas," *El Mundo*, 17 September 1961 (my translation).

52. Foreign Broadcast Information Service (FBIS), Cuba #181, 19 September 1961.

53. José Buajasán, interview by author, Havana, 19 April 1999.

54. A copy of the chain letter and examples of other anti-Castro propaganda were made available to this researcher from the Center for Historical Investigations on State Security (CIHSE) archives (my translations).

55. Copies of various versions of this *patria potestad* law were made available to this researcher from the CIHSE archives. There is a slight variation between them, but their essential points are the same. One version of the law appears to have been "decreed" 31 August 1961 by Prime Minister Fidel Castro Ruz and President Osvaldo Dorticós Torrado, which is printed on Ministry of Education letterhead. Other "decrees" printed and circulated had different dates.

56. Fidel Castro's speech of 19 September 1961, in *Obra Revolucionaria* 33 (1961): 13–31.

This speech condemning the "counterrevolutionary hoax of *patria potestad*" was published in full over two days in *Revolución*, 20 and 21 September 1961 (my translations).

57. Ibid., 31.

58. Margarita Lora, "Peter Pan Wasn't Political," *Washington Post*, 21 February 1998, A17.

59. Nicolás Ríos, interview by author, Miami, 11 May 1999.

60. "The Church in Cuba," *Newsweek*, 9 October 1961, 94.

61. Examples of anti-Castro propaganda from the period were made available to this researcher from the CIHSE archives. See also the front page of the exile paper *Rescate*, 20 July 1960, reproduced in Elliston, ed., *Psywar*, 202.

62. Fidel Castro' speech of 22 September, *Obra Revolucionaria* 36 (11 October 1961): 15–16 (my translation).

63. "Descubren a impresores de copias de una falsa 'ley,'" *Revolución*, 23 September 1961, 8 (my translation).

64. *Caso Imprenta* [Print Shop Case], Cuban state security report, 18 September 1961. CIHSE Archives (my translation of copy in my possession).

65. "Niños—Primera Razón Revolucionaria" and "La vida en círculos infantiles," *Bohemia*, 1 October 1961, 52–61. See also *Revolución*, 20 and 28 September 1961. See also *El Mundo*, 20 September 1961, 4, 1; *Verde Olivo*, 1 October 1961, 25–27; *Revolución*, 6 October 1961; and *Bohemia*, 15 October 1961, 16–18.

66. "La patria potestad," *Verde Olivo*, 1 October 1961, 25–27; "Todos los derechos son para los niños," *Verde Olivo*, 8 November 1961. See also *El Mundo*, 17 and 20 September 1961, 4, 1; and *Verde Olivo*, 1 October 1961, 25–27.

67. "¡Hablan los Padres!" *Bohemia*, 15 October 1961, 16–18.

68. "El Socialismo en la URSS hace todos para que padres e hijos sean felices," *Noticias de Hoy*, 20 September 1961.

69. José Buajasán, interview by author, Havana, 19 April 1999.

70. See interviews with Angel Fernández Varela and Álvaro Fernández Pagliery, in Bravo and Gómez, *Operación Peter Pan*, 261–71 (my translation). Another former Cuban CIA operative also claimed responsibility for coming up with the idea of the fake law. See Antonio Veciana with Carlos Harrison, *Trained to Kill: The Inside Story of CIA Plots against Castro, Kennedy, and Che* (New York: Skyhorse Publishing, 2017), 89–91.

71. #481 A Program of Covert Action against the Castro Regime, 16 March 1960, in *FRUS, 1958–1960, VI*, 850–51.

72. Quoted by Rhodri Jeffreys-Jones, *The CIA and American Democracy* (New Haven: Yale University Press, 1989), 83.

73. U.S. Senate, *Alleged Assassination Plots Involving Foreign Leaders: An Interim Report of the Select Committee to Study Governmental Operations with Respect to Intelligence Activities* (Washington: U.S. Government Printing Office, 1975), 9.

74. A Program of Covert Action against the Castro Regime, 16 March 1960, which allocated $1.2 million and $1.3 million for propaganda and paramilitary expenses respectively for the 1961 financial year. See Peter Kornbluh, ed., *Bay of Pigs Declassified: The Secret CIA Report on the Invasion of Cuba* (New York: New Press, 1998), 103–9.

75. #281, "Memorandum from the Chief of Operations, Operation Mongoose (Lansdale)," *FRUS, 1961–1962, X*, 693.

76. John Prados, *Presidents' Secret Wars: CIA and Pentagon Covert Operations from World War II* (Chicago: Ivan R. Dee, 1996), 194. Kennedy did replace CIA director Allen Dulles with John McCone following the Bay of Pigs disaster.

77. #28 Memorandum from the Joint Chiefs of Staff to Secretary of Defense McNamara, 27 January 1961 in *FRUS, 1961–1962, X*, 57.

78. Mark J. White, ed., *The Kennedys and Cuba: The Declassified Documentary History* (Chicago: Ivan R. Dee, 1999), 4; Prados, *Presidents' Secret Wars*, 193.

79. James Baker, interview by Miguel González-Pando, Cuban Living History Project of Florida International University, https://libtube,fiu.edu/Play/344 (Part 1).

80. The CIA was also convinced the success of the invasion would depend on U.S. military intervention, but this was apparently not made clear to President Kennedy. See "Top Secret CIA 'Official History' of the Bay of Pigs: Revelations," National Security Archive, 15 August 2011,http://nsarchive.gwu.edu/NSAEBB/NSAEBB355/.

81. #29 Memorandum from the Joint Chiefs of Staff to Secretary of Defense McNamara, 27 January 1961, in *FRUS, 1961–1962, X*, 60.

82. Following the attempted invasion at the Bay of Pigs, the CIA inspector general prepared an initial report on the failed operation, in which he outlined the budget for the new Cuba Project of which $170,000,000 was allocated to propaganda; political action, $950,000; paramilitary, $150,000,000; intelligence, $250,000. See Kornbluh (ed.), *Bay of Pigs Declassified*, 24.

83. John D. Marks, *The Search for the Manchurian Candidate: The CIA and Mind Control* (New York: Times Books, 1979).

84. Jeffreys-Jones, *CIA and American Democracy*, 83–85.

85. Lawrence Soley, *Radio Warfare: OSS and CIA Subversive Propaganda* (New York: Praeger, 1989), 218.

86. Quoted by Elliston, ed., *Psywar*, 3.

87. Harry Rositzke, *The CIA's Secret Operations: Espionage, Counterespionage, and Covert Action* (Boulder, CO: Westview Encore, 1988), 163.

88. Ibid., 156.

89. Piero Gleijeses, *Shattered Hope: The Guatemalan Revolution and the United States* (Princeton, NJ: Princeton University Press, 1991), 299, 249. Howard Hunt later attained notoriety in the 1970s Watergate scandal under the Nixon administration.

90. Stephen Schlesinger and Stephen Kinzer, *Bitter Fruit: The Untold Story of the American Coup in Guatemala* (Garden City, NY: Anchor Books, 1983), 114.

91. Greg Grandin, *The Last Colonial Massacre: Latin America in the Cold War* (Chicago: University of Chicago Press, 2004), 44, 59.

92. Schlesinger and Kinzer, *Bitter Fruit*, 167.

93. Gleijeses, *Shattered Hope*, 287.

94. Christopher Andrew, *For the President's Eyes Only* (New York: HarperCollins, 1995), 261.

95. Quoted by Padula, "Fall of the Bourgeoisie," 548.

96. David Atlee Phillips, *The Night Watch* (New York: Ballantine, 1977).

97. Richard Bissell, CIA Deputy Director for Plans, "Biographic Summary of Certain Senior Officials," from "An Analysis of the Cuban Operation," 18 January 1962, reproduced in Elliston, ed., *Psywar*, 21.

98. Peter Wyden, *The Bay of Pigs: The Untold Story* (New York: Touchstone/Simon and Schuster, 1979), 22.

99. Soley, *Radio Warfare*, 223.

100. #481 A Program of Covert Action against the Castro Regime (Tab B: Propaganda), 16 March 1960, in *FRUS, 1958–1960, VI*, 850–51.

101. "Brief History of Radio Swan," Annex 2 (marked SECRET–EYES ONLY) to Memorandum No. 1 from Cuba Study Group to President Kennedy, Washington, 13 June 1961, reproduced in Elliston, ed., *Psywar*, 59–63.

102. Howard Hunt, *Give Us This Day* (New Rochelle, NY: Arlington House, 1973), 82–85.

103. Ibid., 44–47.

104. An example was an advertisement published in the *Wall Street Journal*, 29 November 1960, headlined "How You Can Help Drive Communism from Cuba." Donations were solicited on behalf of the Cuban Freedom Committee for radio broadcasts directed to "Cuban multitudes starving for news and facts of the democratic world from which they were so cruelly wrenched by the Castro dictatorship." Reproduced in Elliston, ed., *Psywar*, 203.

105. *New York Times*, 11 November 1960. The Cuban paper *Revolución* reproduced this ad as evidence of U.S. violation of Cuban sovereignty, 14 November 1960, 12.

106. For example, the group Revolutionary Unity (UR) issued small flyers with the symbol and a simple slogan, "Russians out of Cuba! Let not one remain." Copies of these and other examples of anti-Castro propaganda from the period were made available to this researcher from the CIHSE archives (Havana).

107. David Phillips, Cable to CIA Station, Miami, 25 March 1961, reproduced in Elliston, ed., *Psywar*, 48.

108. See UR propaganda in the CIHSE archives, Havana.

109. "Cuba Sees 'Aggression,' Charges Swan Island Broadcasts 'Piracy' by U.S.," *New York Times*, 15 September 1960, 12.

110. "Brief History of Radio Swan," in Elliston, ed., *Psywar*, 59–63.

111. "American Radio in the Caribbean Counters Red Campaign in Cuba," in *New York Times*, 9 September 1960, 1–2.

112. Phillips, *Cuban Dilemma*, 250.

113. #625 Notes on a Meeting of the Working Group on Cuba, Department of State, 22 December 1960, *FRUS, 1958–1960, VI*, 1186.

114. Memorandum from Henry Loomis to Morrow, "Broadcasting to Cuba," 10 February 1961, in Elliston, *Psywar*, 34. This memo is carbon copied to "Dave Phillips."

115. #208 Memorandum from the President's Special Assistant (Schlesinger) to the Political Warfare Subcommittee of the Cuban Task Force, 8 May 1961, *FRUS, 1961–1962, X*, 492.

116. "Brief History of Radio Swan," in Elliston, ed., *Psywar*, 60.

117. David Wise and Thomas B. Ross, *The Invisible Government* (New York: Random House, 1964), 336.

118. See Memorandum of 5 October 1961 from Thomas Parrott, secretary to the Special Group, quoted in a footnote in U.S. Senate, *Alleged Assassination Plots*, 142. For details of some psychological warfare operations proposed as part of Operation Mongoose, see also Memorandum from Department of Defense Project Officer for Operation Mongoose William H. Craig to Chief of Operations Lansdale, 2 February 1962, in White, *Kennedys and Cuba*, 100–105.

119. Central Intelligence Agency, Information Report, "Signs of Discontent among the Cuban Populace; Activities of the Government to Strengthen the Regime," 6 April 1961, National Security Archive, http://nsarchive.gwu.edu/bayofpigs/19610406.pdf.

120. David Phillips turned up working for the CIA a decade later in Chile when a successful effort was made to mobilize housewives to protest against the government of Salvador Allende in the March of the Empty Pots.

121. Transcripts of some of these Radio Swan broadcasts are retained in the CIHSE archives. See Torreira and Buajasán, *Operación Peter Pan*, 91–92 (my translation). See also Juan Carlos Rodríguez, *The Bay of Pigs and the CIA* (Melbourne: Ocean Press, 1999), 55–56. See also *Cuba–Girón: La gran conjura. Cuadernos de Estudios* (Havana: Centro de Investigaciones Operativas del MININT, April 1994) 34–36.

122. *El Mundo*, 1 December 1960, quoted by Miller, *90 Miles from Home*, 17.

123. "Madre Cubana: defiende a tu hijo," *Bohemia Libre*, 23 October 1960, reproduced and translated by Chase, *Revolution*, 199–201. See Hunt, *Give Us This Day*, 46.

124. Schoultz, *That Infernal Little Cuban Republic*, 135.

125. Wise and Ross, *Invisible Government*, 30; and Wyden, *Bay of Pigs*, 116–17.

126. "Cuban Women in Black in 'Mourning Journey,'" *New York Times*, 21 September 1960, 17. See also "Cubans Protest Castro Visit," *Washington Post*, 20 September 1960, A9.

127. Torres, *Lost Apple*, 92.

128. This press conference was reported in a letter from H. Franklin Irwin Jr., second secretary at the U.S. Embassy in San José, dated 19 December 1960, quoted by Conde, *Operation Pedro Pan*, 26.

129. Reproduced in Torres, *Lost Apple*, 94.

130. "Madres cubanas se dirigen a las NN.UU," *El Mundo*, 1 January 1961; "Concentración de madres de mártires," *El Mundo*, 11 January 1961.

131. Arboleya, *Cuban Counterrevolution*, 97.

132. "Mothers Becoming Frantic: Fidel No Family Man," *Times of Havana*, 16–18 March 1962, 1.

133. Walsh, "Cuban Refugee Children," 383.

134. Juan Arrocha, "La más joven delegación que ha salido de Cuba," *Revolución*, 18 September 1961, 2.

135. Roger Hilsman, memorandum, "Estimates and Evaluations on Cuba: Cuban Internal Political Situation," 3 November 1961. INR/RAR/P: AHHaynes:ff [Declassified document #65D438,480.], 1–2. Cuba Collection, National Security Archive, Washington, D.C.

136. Ibid., 3–7.

137. José Lucas Badue, letter to the editor, *New York Times*, 4 November 2001 (Cuba-L Direct news service).

138. Walsh, "Cuban Refugee Children," 382; also Walsh, interview by author, Miami, 20 March 2000.

139. Carlos Franqui quoted by Conde, *Operation Pedro Pan*, 40–41.

140. Gabriel Orozco Sr., interview in Bravo and Gómez, *Operación Peter Pan*, 135.

141. Conde, *Operation Pedro Pan*, 40–41.

142. Jennifer Mathieu and María A. Morales, "Exiles He Aided Bid Grau Farewell," in *Miami Herald*, 5 November 1998, 4B. See also Mirta Ojito, "Ramón Grau Alsina, 75, Cuban Who Aided Children's Escape," *New York Times*, 6 November 1998; and Luisa Yañez, "Ramón Grau Alsina, Anti-Castro Activist,"*Sun Sentinel, South Florida*, 4 November 1998.

143. Sergio López-Miró, "The Dark Side of Pedro Pan," *Miami Herald*, 29 November 1990, 31A.

144. Rescate was one of the leading counterrevolutionary groups that was well funded and with good political contacts due to some members' close association with the former Authentic Party government of Polita's uncle, Dr. Ramón Grau San Martín. Arboleya, *Cuban Counterrevolution*, 68–69.

145. Luis Báez, "Al líder de ustedes lo protege alguién más que el G-2," *Juventud Rebelde*, Havana, 28 November 1993, 6 (my translation). Why this interview conducted in 1976 was not published in Cuba until 1993 has never been explained.

146. Ibid.

147. See Veciana, *Trained to Kill*, 89–91.

148. Arturo Villar, interview in Ochoa, *Never Ever Neverland* (my translation).

149. Álvaro F. Fernández, "Operation Pedro Pan: A Horribly Black Mark on (U.S.) History," *Progreso Weekly*, 21–27 May, 2009. See also interviews with Ángel and Álvaro Fernández in Bravo and Gómez, *Operación Peter Pan*, 267 (my translation).

150. See Fidel Castro's speech of 16 April 1961 published in *Revolución*, 17 April 1961, 1.

Chapter 4. Operation Pedro Pan and the Children Who Could Fly

1. "Miami: Refugee City," in *U.S. News and World Report*, 5 December 1960, 62. See also Marcie Ersoff, "When a Cuban Child Gets Here," in *Miami Herald*, 30 December 1960, 1.

2. María Masud, interview by author, Dallas, 29 March 2003; see also Grupo Areíto, *Contra Viento*, 20–21, 40–43.

3. "The History of Operation Pedro Pan," PedroPan.org, n.d., www.pedropan.org/category/history.

4. Msgr. Walsh, interview by author, Miami, 20 March 2000.

5. José Lucas Badue, letter to the editor, *New York Times*, 4 November 2001 (Cuba-L Direct news service).

6. Laura Briggs, *Somebody's Children: The Politics of Transracial and Transnational Adoption* (Durham: N.C.: Duke University Press, 2012), 150–51; on the Hungarian program, see also Ressler et al., *Unaccompanied Children*, 44–50.

7. Both quoted by Masud-Piloto, *From Welcomed Exiles*, 33, 32.

8. Arboleya, *Cuban Counterrevolution*, 184–85.

9. Fagen et al., *Cubans in Exile*, 101.

10. Walsh, "Cuban Refugee Children," 399.

11. Quoted by Torres, *Lost Apple*, 61.

12. #603 Memorandum of a Conversation, 1 November 1960, *FRUS, 1958–1960*, VI, 1111 (my emphasis).

13. Adessa, "Refugee Cuban Children," 21–23.

14. #607 Memorandum from Lansdale on Cuba, 7 November 1960, *FRUS, 1958–1960*, VI, 1116.

15. Walsh, "Cuban Refugee Children," 386–87.

16. Tracy S. Voorhees, *Report to the President of the United States on the Cuban Refugee Problem* (Washington: U.S. Government Printing Office, 18 January 1961), 1; Marcie Ersoff, "When a Cuban Child Gets Here," *Miami Herald*, 30 December 1960, 1; "The Cuban Refugees," *New York Times*, 26 December 1960, 22.

17. See Arthur D. Morse, *While Six Million Died: A Chronicle of American Apathy* (New York: Random House, 1968), 61–62. Morse explains that over four hundred thousand quota slots for immigrants from Nazi-ruled countries went unfilled in the years 1933–1943.

18. Mark Jonathan Harris and Deborah Oppenheimer, *Into the Arms of Strangers: Stories of the Kindertransport* (New York: Bloomsbury Publishing, 2000), 149–51.

19. Briggs, *Somebody's Children*, 146–49.

20. Adessa, "Refugee Cuban Children," 11. See also the appendix to the DHEW Children's Bureau, *Cuba's Children in Exile*, 11–13.

21. DHEW Children's Bureau, *Cuba's Children in Exile* (appendix), 14.

22. Rafael J. Prohias and Lourdes Casal, *The Cuban Minority in the U.S.*, vol. 1 (New York: Arno Press, 1980), 7.

23. Tracey S. Voorhees, "Interim Report on the Cuban Refugee Problem," 19 December 1960, in *U.S. Department of State Bulletin* (Washington D.C., Government Printing Office, 9 January 1961), 46. See also Everett C. Parker, "Miami's Real Life Drama," *Christian Century*, 78/41, 11 October 1961.

24. Voorhees, *Report to the President* (18 January 1961), 5; "Keating Scores Kennedy Refusal of Catholic School Aid at Miami," *New York Times*, 12 February 1961.

25. Wendell Rollason testimony of 7 December 1961 to U.S. Senate Subcommittee hearings, *Cuban Refugee Problem*, 159.

26. More detailed figures are included in Thomas, "U.S.A. as a Country of First Asylum," 8; and DHEW Children's Bureau, *Cuba's Children in Exile*, 6. See also Appendix B, Tables 5 and 6, in the University of Miami 1967 study, which show the explosion of costs related to the unaccompanied children's program and education expenses for the Cuban children in public schools (not including expenses incurred by parochial schools). *The Cuban Immigration 1959–1966 and Its Impact on Miami-Dade County, Florida* (Coral Gables, Miami: University of Miami Research Institute for Cuba and the Caribbean, 1967).

27. See "Educational Program of the Dade Country Schools for Cuban Refugee Children and Adults," 1 December 1961, box 29, Walsh Papers.

28. Noel Betancourt, interview by author, Havana, 19 April 1999. As explained in the introduction, Pedro Pans are usually identified as those children who arrived between December 1960 and October 1962.

29. See Tina Montalvo, "Operation Pedro Pan Flew Kids to Freedom," *Miami Herald*, 15 June 1986, 4G.

30. Walsh, "Cuban Refugee Children," 387.

31. There is a Pedro Pablo Menéndez listed on the alumni list of Ruston Academy on the website that records he attended the school 1949–1956. Could this be the phantom Pedro? See http://www.rustonacademy.net/getstud-a.html. See also "Operation Pedro Pan Flew Kids to Freedom," *Miami Herald*, 15 June 1986, one of the many references to the legendary Pedro Menéndez.

32. "When a Cuban Child Gets Here," *Miami Herald*, 30 December 1960, 1.

33. Walsh, "Cuban Refugee Children," 387–88. See also Msgr. Bryan O. Walsh, 1997 interview by Miguel González-Pando, Cuban Living History Project of Florida International University, http://libtube.fiu.edu/Play/53 (Part One).

34. Msgr. Walsh, interview by author, Miami, 20 March 2000.

35. The minutes of this meeting are included as Appendix 1, in Adessa, "Refugee Cuban Children," 170–73. See also Walsh, "Cuban Refugee Children," 386–89.

36. Voorhees, "Interim Report" (19 December 1960), 47. Walsh had had contact with Voorhees in the earlier program for young Hungarian refugees.

37. Walsh, "Cuban Refugee Children," 390.

38. Morris H. Morley, *Imperial State and Revolution: The United States and Cuba, 1952–1986* (Cambridge: Cambridge University Press, 1987), 31.

39. See "Catholics Fight Castro on Soviet-Type Schools" in *U.S. News and World Report*, 7 November 1960, 14.

40. Walsh, "Cuban Refugee Children," 390–91; see also Johnson, "Elián González Case."

41. Torres, *Lost Apple*, 132.

42. Adessa, "Refugee Cuban Children," 26.

43. Walsh, "Cuban Refugee Children," 390; Msgr. Walsh, interview by author, Miami, 20 March 2000.

44. Katherine Brownell Oettinger, "Services to Unaccompanied Cuban Refugee Children in the United States," *Social Service Review* 36, no. 4 (1962): 378.

45. Walsh, "Cuban Refugee Children," 389. It is possible that the Cuban woman in this case was Sara del Toro, mother of ten children, who was one of Fr. Walsh's key contacts in Cuba. See Medrano, *Todo lo dieron*.

46. DHEW Children's Bureau, *Cuba's Children in Exile*, 1.

47. "The History of Operation Pedro Pan," PedroPan.org, n.d., www.pedropan.org/category/history. In 2001 Msgr. Walsh was identified as the author of this history of Operation Pedro Pan, but as of 2017 that is no longer the case. There is no explanation of this change.

48. Triay, *Fleeing Castro*, 17.

49. Walsh, interview in Lynn Geldof, *Cubans: Voices of Change* (New York: St. Martin's Press, 1991), 232.

50. Walsh, "Cuban Refugee Children," 393–98.

51. Fr. Bryan O. Walsh, "The Community Looks at the Problem: The Church," paper

presented at the National Resettlement Conference for Cuban Refugees, Miami, Florida, 30 January 1961, box 18, Walsh Papers.

52. See Kathlyn Gay, *Leaving Cuba: From Operation Pedro Pan to Elián* (Brookfield, CT: Twenty-First Century Books, 1999); and Ana Veciana-Suárez, *Vuelo a la libertad* (New York: Scholastic, 2004); María Armengol Acierno, *Children of Flight Pedro Pan* (New York: Silver Moon Press, 1994); and Cristina Díaz González, *The Red Umbrella* (New York: Alfred A. Knopf, 2010).

53. James G. Blight and Peter Kornbluh, eds., *Politics of Illusion: The Bay of Pigs Invasion Reexamined* (Boulder, CO: Lynne Reinner Publishers, 1998), 189.

54. See Telegram #1726 from Ambassador Bonsal, 13 October 1960. From Confidential U.S. State Department central files. Internal affairs decimal numbers 737, 837, and 937. Cuba, 1960–January 1963. #737.00/10–1360 CAA. Microfiche of Record Group 59, General Records of the Department of State and Telegram #1711 from Ambassador Bonsal, 10 October 1960, advising of arrival of ex-Minister of Foreign Relations Robert Agramonte Pichardo and wife. #737.00/10–1060 HBS. Microfiche of Record Group 59, General Records of the Department of State.

55. Telegrams to Secretary of State #1754 and #1771 from Ambassador Bonsal, 15 October 1960. From Confidential U.S. State Department central files. Internal affairs decimal numbers 737, 837, and 937. Cuba, 1960–January 1963. #737.00/10–1560 HBS. Microfiche of Record Group 59, General Records of the Department of State.

56. #614 Memorandum of a Conversation, Department of State, Washington, 29 November 1960, *FRUS, 1958–1960, VI*, 1133.

57. Walsh, interview in Geldof, *Cubans*, 232.

58. #614 Memorandum of a Conversation, Department of State, 29 November 1960, *FRUS, 1958–1960, VI*, 1132–1137.

59. Hunt, *Give Us This Day*, 44–45, 79–80. The Revolutionary Democratic Front (FRD), the so-called government-in-exile, was replaced by the Cuban Revolutionary Council (CRC) just before the Bay of Pigs invasion in April 1961.

60. #30 Memorandum of Discussion on Cuba, 28 January 1961, in *FRUS, 1961–1962*, X, 61–62.

61. Max Frankel, "Cuban Tensions Rise," *New York Times*, 6 November 1960.

62. Encinosa, *Cuba en Guerra*, 93; see also Victor Andres Triay, *Bay of Pigs: An Oral History of Brigade 2506* (Gainesville: University Press of Florida, 2001) 14.

63. Wixson, "Portrait of a Cuban Refugee," *Studies in Intelligence* (1964), quoted by Torres, *Lost Apple*, 61.

64. Rollason testimony of 7 December 1961 to U.S. Senate Subcommittee hearings, *Cuban Refugee Problem*, 159–60.

65. Testimony of Ramón Grau, quoted by Torreira and Buajasán, *Operación Peter Pan*, 223–24. The experience of the two girls, Lisette and Olguita, as Pedro Pans is also recounted in Conde, *Operation Pedro Pan*, 121–22.

66. Declaration by José Luis Pelleyá Jústiz at his trial, 31 October 1964, quoted by Torreira and Buajasán, *Operación Peter Pan*, 241–42.

67. Bartolomé Pérez García's trial testimony, quoted by Torreira and Buajasán, *Operación Peter Pan*, 184–85.

68. #623 Despatch from the Embassy in Cuba to the Department of State [Daniel Braddock, Chargé d'Affaires]: "Rupture Would Close Visa Escape Valve," 16 December 1960, *FRUS, 1958–1960, VI*, 1182–83.

69. Adessa, "Refugee Cuban Children," 3.

70. Sergio Díaz Sr., interview by Richard H. Wall Jr., "Operation Pedro Pan: An Examination of the Factors That Resulted in 14,048 Cuban Children Being Sent to the United States" (master's thesis, California State University, Long Beach, 2011), 49. Díaz was captured and imprisoned during the Bay of Pigs on 19 April 1961, but his wife and younger son were able to leave in June 1961.

71. Walsh, "Cuban Refugee Children," 412.

72. "The History of Operation Pedro Pan," PedroPan.org, n.d., www.pedropan.org/category/history.

73. Walsh, "Cuban Refugee Children," 391.

74. Ibid., 396–97, 399.

75. See Robert F. Hale's testimony, 13 December 1961, to U.S. Senate Subcommittee hearings, *Cuban Refugee Problem*, 205–8. James Hennessy, the executive assistant to the Immigration and Naturalization Service Commissioner, clarified that although about 80,000 visa waivers had been authorized by December 1961, only about 20,000 had actually arrived in the United States. James Hennessy testimony, 13 December 1961, to U.S. Senate Subcommittee hearings, *Cuban Refugee Problem*, 210.

76. García, *Havana USA*, 16–17.

77. Walsh, "Cuban Refugee Children," 399.

78. Nelson Valdés, interview by author, Dallas, 29 March 2003.

79. Oettinger, "Services to Unaccompanied Cuban Refugee Children," 378.

80. Kathryn Close, "Cuban Children away from Home," *Children* 10, no. 1 (January–February 1963): 5–6. *Children* was published by the Children's Bureau of the U.S. Department of Health, Education, and Welfare (Washington, D.C.). The documentary film made in 1962 on the child refugees in Florida camps also explained the young Cubans "escaped" from the island on "student visas." See Cliff Solway, dir., *The Lost Apple* (Talent Associates–Paramount, 1963).

81. Gene Miller, "'Peter Pan' Means Real Life to Some Kids," *Miami Herald*, 9 March 1962, 11A.

82. DHEW Children's Bureau, *Cuba's Children in Exile*, 1–2.

83. Adessa, "Refugee Cuban Children," reproduced a sample visa waiver as Appendix C, 176. Various versions of this visa waiver letter were distributed, and often just a copy of the letter, with the child's name and birthdate added, was sufficient for U.S. immigration authorities.

84. James Baker, "The Beginning of the Pedro Pan Program in Cuba," sent to Msgr. Walsh, 25 May 1998, box 26, Walsh Papers.

85. Walsh, "Cuban Refugee Children," 397, 400–401.

86. See Joe Cardona and Mario de Varona, dirs., *The Flight of Pedro Pan: An Untold American Story* (WPBT Channel 2, 1999).

87. Rodríguez, *Bay of Pigs*, 56.

88. David Phillips's children were students at Ruston Academy, Havana, so he would have known the director of that school, James Baker. See Torres, *Lost Apple*, 47, 88.

89. Walsh, "Cuban Refugee Children," 402.

90. Walsh, interview in Estela Bravo, dir., *Operación Peter Pan: Cerrando el círculo en Cuba* (BravoFilms, 2011).

91. Eusebio Leal, interview in Bravo and Gómez, *Operación Peter Pan*, 299 (my translation); María de los Angeles Torres, "Immigration Policies Aimed Exclusively at Youth Undermine Their Families," *La Prensa* (San Diego), 14 December 2012. She made the same point on the Smithsonian panel, "The Legacy of Operation Pedro Pan," 3 May 2011; see https://www.youtube.com/watch?v=UKWKSJ0Jr2Y.

92. "Notes on National Security Council Meeting," 5 May 1961, in White, *Kennedys and Cuba*, 52.

93. Bishop Coleman Carroll testimony of 6 December 1961 to U.S. Senate Subcommittee hearings, *Cuban Refugee Problem*, 19.

94. Adessa, "Refugee Cuban Children," 60.

95. Close, "Cuban Children away from Home," 5–6.

96. Michael McNally, *Catholicism in South Florida* (Gainesville: University Presses of Florida, 1982), 147.

97. Robert Hale testimony of 13 December 1961 to U.S. Senate Subcommittee hearings, *Cuban Refugee Problem*, 206.

98. Msgr. Bryan O. Walsh, "Operation Pedro Pan," Barry University Convocation, 40th Anniversary Convocation, 9 November 2001, box 18, Walsh Papers.

99. Msgr. Walsh, interview by author, Miami, 20 March 2000.

100. José Cabañas, interview by author, Havana, 4 May 1999. Cabañas was the first Cuban ambassador appointed after diplomatic ties were reestablished between Washington and Havana in 2015.

101. Julie Hirschfield Davis, "White House to End Exemption for Cubans Who Arrive without Visas," *New York Times*, 12 January 2017, www.nytimes/2017/01/12/world/americas/cuba-obama.

102. Msgr. Walsh, interview by author, Miami, 20 March 2000.

103. Quoted by María de los Angeles Torres, "Cuban Diaspora: Children Lost in Political Conflict," *Chicago Tribune*, 20 October 2002.

104. DHEW Children's Bureau, *Cuba's Children in Exile*, 4. Lourdes Rodríguez's study found the mean period of separation of the Pedro Pans from their parents was 4.9 years; see Lourdes Rodríguez-Nogués, "Psychological Effects of Premature Separation from Parents in Cuban Refugee Girls: A Retrospective Study" (Ph.D. diss., Boston University School of Education, 1983), 169. Of Conde's 442 respondents, almost half were separated for more than two years, and over 25 percent for four years or more; Conde, *Operation Pedro Pan*, 224.

105. Torres, *Lost Apple*, 267.

106. Raquel Canler, interview in Bravo and Gómez, *Operación Peter Pan*, 55 (my translation). See also "Exodus," *Time*, 22 August 1960, 30; and "Castro Cracks Down on Fleeing Cubans," *U.S. News and World Report*, 25 September 1961, 14.

107. Close, "Cuba's Children away from Home," 6.

108. Adessa, "Refugee Cuban Children," 54–55.

109. María de los Angeles Torres, "Open the Books on Operation Pedro Pan," *Miami Herald*, 18 December 1994, 5M. See also Gail Reed, "Flight of Fear," *Cuba Update*, February 1994 (New York: Center for Cuban Studies), 8.

110. Triay, *Fleeing Castro*, 36; Masud-Piloto, *From Welcomed Exiles*, 52.

111. Quoted by Triay, *Bay of Pigs*, 19.

112. Walsh, "Cuban Refugee Children," 383. Lourdes Rodríguez made the same observation about teenage activists in the anti-Castro underground; see Rodríguez-Nogues, "Psychological Effects," 58.

113. Walsh, "Cuban Refugee Children," 383–84.

114. Willy Chirino, interview in Cardona and de Varona, *Flight of Pedro Pan*.

115. Hunt, *Give Us This Day*, 85.

116. Torres, *Lost Apple*, 127.

117. Silvia Ríos, interview by author, Miami, 11 May 1999.

118. Berta Álvarez, interview by author, Havana, 5 May 1999.

119. Silvia and Nicolás Ríos, interview by author, Miami, 11 May 1999.

120. Nelson Valdés, interview by author, Dallas, 29 March 2003; Nelson Valdés, "Monsignor Bryan O. Walsh: A Personal Note," Cuba_L e-mail list, posted 22 December 2001.

121. For example, Raquel Canler sent her thirteen- and ten-year-old sons with Operation Pedro Pan but not her youngest six-year-old boy. Interviewed in Bravo and Gómez, *Operación Peter Pan*, 55.

122. Interview by Torres, *Lost Apple*, 119.

123. Walsh, "Cuban Refugee Children," 383.

124. Close, "Cuban Children away from Home," 3, 7.

125. Strong, "Refugees from Castro's Cuba," 84.

126. Nelson Valdés, interview by author, Dallas, 29 March 2003.

127. Angel Wong Alcazar to Walsh, 8 August 1964, box 26, Walsh Papers.

128. See Ed Canler's story in Bravo and Gómez, *Operación Peter Pan*, 45–49.

129. Eire, *Waiting for Snow*, 121. The anomaly of the acceptance of "colored" Cuban children in Miami-Dade schools that barred African American students was noted at the Senate Subcommittee hearings on the Cuban refugee problem, 6 December 1961, 274–81.

130. Torres, *Lost Apple*, 67.

131. Nelson Valdés, interview by author, Dallas, 29 March 2003.

132. Ana Riewerts, phone interview from New York by author, 16 May 2002.

133. "Keeping Them Poor," *Time*, 18 August 1961. See also radio interview with Fidel Castro on Currency Reform, 9 August 1961, FBIS (Cuba 1961). http://lanic.utexas.edu/project/castro/db/1961/19610809.html.

134. Fr. Bryan O. Walsh, "The Community Looks at the Problem: The Church," paper presented at the National Resettlement Conference for Cuban Refugees, Miami, Florida, 30 January 1961, box 18, Walsh Papers.

135. De la Campa, *Cuba on My Mind*, 37–38.

136. Ressler et al., *Unaccompanied Children*, 52, 118–19, 56, 167.

137. "President Orders Cuba Refugee Aid," *New York Times*, 4 February 1961, 1–2; Walsh, "Cuban Refugee Children," 411.

138. DHEW Children's Bureau, *Cuba's Children in Exile,* 1.
139. Walsh, "Cuban Refugee Children," 395–96; Torreira and Buhasán, *Operación Peter Pan,* 249.
140. Conde, *Operation Pedro Pan,* 51.
141. "Los primeros niños que dieron inicio a un programa histórico," *El Nuevo Herald,* 16 May 2009, http://www.el nuevoherald.com/noticias/especiales/operación-pedropan/article1995565.html.
142. Anonymous letter from Cuba, 13 February 1962, collection 39, Letters from Cuba, 1961–1962 Collection, Tamiment Archive, New York University Library, New York.
143. Walsh, "Cuban Refugee Children," 380, 392–95, 408, 397; DHEW Children's Bureau, *Cuba's Children in Exile,* 2–3.
144. Luis Adrián Betancourt, *¿Por qué Carlos?* (Havana: Editorial Letras Cubanas, 1981), 36.
145. "Eloisa's Story," Pedro Pan Exodus, http://pedropanexodus.com/eloisas-story.
146. Movimiento Democrata Cristiano de Cuba, "Nuestra Postura" (c1962). Collection 26: Grupos Políticos Cubanos en el exilio, Cuban Heritage Collection, University of Miami Libraries, Coral Gables, Florida.
147. Encinosa, *Cuba en Guerra,* 66.
148. Torreira and Buajasán, *Operación Peter Pan,* 60–61.
149. Kirk, *Between God and the Party,* 93–96.
150. Footage of Fidel's May Day speech (1 May 1961) in Ochoa, *Never Ever Neverland.* See also Martin Kenner and James Petras, eds. *Fidel Castro Speaks* (Harmondsworth, Middlesex: Penguin Books, 1972), 117–34.
151. Hageman and Wheaton, *Religion in Cuba,* 67–68.
152. *CRECED: Documento final* (Miami, Ediciones Creced, 1993), quoted by Hernando Calvo and Katlijn Declercq, *Cuban Exile Movement: Dissidents or Mercenaries?* (Melbourne: Ocean Press, 1999), 16, 19.
153. Torreira and Buajasán, *Operación Peter Pan,* 384, 79 (my translation).
154. Conde says that the Jesuit Sacred Heart of Jesus church became an important collection and distribution center for visas for Pedro Pans. Conde, *Operation Pedro Pan,* 66–67.
155. Alex López, interview by author, Washington, D.C., 10 September 2001.
156. Conde stated that members of the Catholic church "played a very important role" in the children's exodus, but argued this was spontaneous and not auspiced by the church as an institution. She also explained: "As most of the children attended Catholic schools, nuns and priests were trusted persons sought out by frantic parents." Conde, *Operation Pedro Pan,* 66–67.
157. "The History of Operation Pedro Pan," PedroPan.org, n.d., www.pedropan.org/category/history.
158. See Sandra González-Levy, "Church, Cuban Exiles Must Reaffirm Their Mutual Respect," *Miami Herald,* 11 December 1997, 33A.
159. Majorie L. Donahue, "Operation Pedro Pan: How Thousands of Children Shuffled under Castro's Nose," *Voice,* 3 March 1978. See also Bishop Thomas G. Wenski, "Ties

between the Cuban Catholic Church and the Archdiocese of Miami," paper delivered at LASA, Miami, 16–18 March 2000, box 17, Walsh Papers.

160. Walsh, "Cuban Refugee Children," 380 (my emphasis).

161. Msgr. Bryan O. Walsh, interview by Miguel González-Pando, Cuban Living History Project of Florida International University, http://libtube.fiu.edu/Play/53 (part 1). See also Donald P. Baker, "A Journey out of the Past for 'Pedro Pan' Project," *Washington Post*, 26 January 1998, A19.

162. Hageman and Wheaton, *Religion in Cuba*, 71. Dewart explained that the restriction of religious instruction to churches did not apply to seminaries, which continued to function normally, albeit with reduced numbers. See Dewart, *Cuba, Church, and Crisis*, 167.

163. Msgr. Bryan O. Walsh, "Recollection of Havana Trip," 25 March 1963, box 44, Walsh Papers.

164. Torreira and Buajasán, *Operación Peter Pan*, 274.

165. Msgr. Bryan O. Walsh, "Recollection of Havana Trip," 25 March 1963, 9–10, box 44, Walsh Papers.

166. Hageman and Wheaton, *Religion in Cuba*, 68.

167. Kirk, *Between God and the Party*, 110.

168. Dewart, *Cuba, Church, and Crisis*, 176–77; Crahan, "Catholicism in Cuba," 17.

169. Fidel Castro, *My Life: A Spoken Autobiography with Ignacio Ramonet* (London: Penguin Books, 2007), 238–39.

170. Interviewed in Torreira and Buajasán, *Operación Peter Pan*, 283, 384 (my translation).

171. José Buajasán, interview by author, Havana, 19 April 1999.

172. Ileana Fuentes, interview in Ochoa, *Never Ever Neverland*.

173. Kirk, *Between God and the Party*, 99. This researcher reviewed various contemporary publications of the Catholic church in Cuba, such as *La Quincena* (closed by the government in 1961), and while there were frequent warnings about the threat that communism posed to education of children and the family, there were no overt suggestions to parents that they should send their children to the United States.

174. Torreira and Buahasan, *Operación Peter Pan*, 269–70.

175. Sonia Almazán, interview by author, Havana, 12 May 2016.

176. Torreira and Buajasán, *Operación Peter Pan*, 68; McNally, *Catholicism*, 149.

177. Encinosa, *Cuba en Guerra*, 66.

178. See Bishop Coleman Carroll testimony of 6 December 1961 to U.S. Senate Subcommittee hearings, *Cuban Refugee Problem*, 14–15; see also McNally, *Catholicism*; and Poyo, *Cuban Catholics*.

179. Fr. Bryan O. Walsh, "Speech delivered at the Southeastern Regional Meeting of the National Conference of Catholic Charities," Richmond, Virginia, 26 March 1962, box 18, Walsh Papers.

180. Adessa, "Refugee Cuban Children," 43, 22–23. See also Casavantes, *Revolution Is for the Children*.

181. Msgr. Bryan O. Walsh, "Cubans in Miami," in *America*, 114, no. 9 (26 February 1966): 288.

182. Peggy Landers, "Priest honored for 40 years of church, civic service," *Miami Herald*, 24 May 1994, 1B.
183. Bea L. Hines, "Se retira héroe de refugiados Pedro Pan," *El Nuevo Herald*, 10 January 1996, 6A, quoted by Torreira and Buajasán, *Operación Peter Pan*, 381.
184. Msgr. Walsh, interview by author, Miami, 20 March 2000.
185. Juan M. Clark, "The Exodus from Revolutionary Cuba, 1959–1974: A Sociological Analysis" (Ph.D. diss., University of Florida, 1975), 58–59.
186. "Memorandum from Assistant Special Counsel Richard N. Goodwin to President Kennedy," 22 August 1961, in White, *Kennedys and Cuba*, 65.
187. Ileana Fuentes, interview in Ochoa and Centeno, *Del Otro Lado del Cristal*.
188. Nicolás and Silvia Ríos, interview by author, Miami, 11 May 1999.
189. James Baker, interview in Bravo, *Operación Peter Pan* (film).
190. Mireya Navarro, "A Return to Cuba: A Search for Himself," *New York Times*, 21 October 2001.
191. Ely Chovel, quoted by Dubinsky, *Babies without Borders*, 35.
192. Torres, *Lost Apple*, 238.
193. José Cabañas, interview by author, Havana, 4 May 1999.
194. Noel Betancourt, interview by author, Havana, 19 April 1999.

Chapter 5. The Dark Side of Neverland

1. Triay, *Fleeing Castro*, 27–29.
2. Reed, "Flight of Fear," 7.
3. Torres, *Lost Apple*, 136–37.
4. #223, CIA, "Program of Covert Action Aimed at Weakening the Castro Regime," 19 May 1961, in *FRUS, 1961–1962*, X, 555.
5. Letter from "Enzo," Havana, 15 July 1961, in collection 39, Letters from Cuba, 1961–1963. Tamiment Archive, New York University Library, New York.
6. Walsh, "Cuban Refugee Children," 390, 397; and DHEW Children's Bureau, *Cuba's Children in Exile*, 1.
7. Memorandum from Mildred Arnold, 24 April 1961, quoted by Torres, *Lost Apple*, 126.
8. By March 1962, a total of 7,778 young Cubans had arrived, of whom 3,486 were in care. See "Children Fly High in Secret Escape Routes from Cuba," *Miami Herald* (street edition), 8 March 1962, 3A; "8,000 Cuba Children Saved from Castro Brainwashing," *Miami Herald* (city edition), 8 March 1962, 1A.
9. Walsh, "Cuban Refugee Children," 379. This is usually the number of Pedro Pans mentioned by most researchers, although sometimes the figure of 15,000 is given.
10. Close, "Cuban Children away from Home," 4–5.
11. John F. Thomas, *The Cuban Refugee Program: Aiding Children and Youth* (report prepared for the DHE), 10 March 1964, box 29, Walsh Papers. Miami mayor Robert K. High estimated 21,500 Cuban students were enrolled in Miami-Dade schools, representing a significant "drain on the school facilities." See Robert High, testimony to U.S. Senate Subcommittee, 3 December 1962, in *Cuban Refugee Problem*, 336.
12. Pedraza, *Political Disaffection*, 84.
13. María Masud, interview by author, Dallas, 29 March 2003.

14. Kennedy's address to the Society of Newspaper Editors on 20 April 1961, quoted by White, *Kennedys and Cuba*, 40–43.

15. Thomas Powers, *The Man Who Kept Secrets: Richard Helms and the CIA* (New York: Alfred Knopf, 1979), 133; Jeffreys-Jones, *CIA and American Democracy*, 130–31.

16. Andrew, *President's Eyes Only*, 275; Richard Bissell, *Reflections of a Cold Warrior: From Yalta to the Bay of Pigs* (New Haven: Yale University Press, 1996), 199–200.

17. Arthur Schlesinger Jr., *Robert Kennedy and His Times* (Boston: Houghton Mifflin, 1978), 524.

18. Quoted by Morley, *Imperial State*, 149.

19. Pérez, *Cuba in the American Imagination*, 253–55.

20. Piero Gleijeses, "Ships in the Night: The CIA, the White House, and the Bay of Pigs," *Journal of Latin American Studies* 27 (1995) 42.

21. Warren Hinckle and William Turner, *Deadly Secrets: The CIA–Mafia War against Castro and the Assassination of JFK* (New York: Thunders Mouth Press, 1992), 6.

22. Morley, *Imperial State*, 150; Hinckle and Turner, *Deadly Secrets*, 126–27.

23. Lawrence Chang and Peter Kornbluh, eds., *The Cuban Missile Crisis, 1962: A National Security Archive Documents Reader* (New York: New Press, 1992), 5; see also David Corn, *Blond Ghost: Ted Shackley and the CIA's Crusades* (New York: Simon and Schuster, 1994), 67–94.

24. Don Bohning, *The Castro Obsession: U.S. Covert Operations against Cuba, 1959–1965* (Dulles, VA: Potomac Books, 2005), 1.

25. Wise and Ross, *Invisible Government*, 330.

26. U.S. Senate, *Alleged Assassination Plots*, 139–46. See also #280 Draft Memorandum for the Record, 1 December 1961, in *FRUS, 1961–1962, X*, 690.

27. Chang and Kornbluh, eds., *The Cuban Missile Crisis*, 5.

28. Andrew, *President's Eyes Only*, 275. A memo from Richard Goodwin to President Kennedy proposed that Robert Kennedy head the "command operation" against Castro as "the only effective way to handle an all-out attack on the Cuban problem." See #269 Memorandum from the President's Assistant Special Council (Goodwin) to President Kennedy, 1 November 1961, in *FRUS, 1961–1962, X*, 664–65.

29. Arboleya, *Cuban Counterrevolution*, 119. For other documents related to the establishment of Operation Mongoose, see *FRUS, 1961–1962, X*, 459–83, 666–84.

30. #272 Memorandum from Richard Bissell, 4 November 1961, in *FRUS, 1961–1962, X*, 673–74; #273 CIA Paper, "Types of Covert Action against the Castro Regime," 8 November 1961, in *FRUS, 1961–1962, X*, 675–76.

31. #244 Memorandum from Schlesinger to Goodwin on Cuban Covert Plan, 8 July 1961, in *FRUS, 1961–1962, X*, 620.

32. Hunt, *Give Us This Day*, 175.

33. Mario Lazo, *Dagger in the Heart: American Policy Failures in Cuba* (New York: Funk and Wagnells, 1968), 299–300. See also interviewees in Triay, *Bay of Pigs*.

34. #202 Cuba and Communism in the Hemisphere, 4 May 1961, *FRUS, 1961–1962, X*, 459–63. See also "The Americas: Launching the Alliance," *Time*, 18 August 1961, 30.

35. Prior to the April 1961 invasion, Arthur Schlesinger and Allen Dulles had warned about the "disposal problem" of the Cuban exile force. See #63 Memorandum from the

President's Special Assistant (Schlesinger) to President Kennedy, 15 March 1961, FRUS, 1961–1962, X, 157.

36. #206 Memorandum for the Record, NSC Meeting, 5 May 1961, FRUS, 1961–1962, X, 486; and #207 Memorandum from Secretary of Defense McNamara to His Special Assistant (Yarmolinsky), 5 May 1961, FRUS, 1961–1962, X, 489.

37. #228 Memorandum from Secretary of Defense McNamara to President Kennedy, 8 June 1961, in FRUS, 1961–1962, X, 571.

38. #342 Memorandum from Acting Chairman of the JCS (Anderson) to Secretary of Defense McNamara, 5 June 1962, FRUS, 1961–1962, X, 825; see also #313 Memorandum from the Deputy Secretary of Defense (Gilpatric) to Chairman of JCS (Lemintzer), 13 March 1962, in FRUS, 1961–1962, X, 770.

39. José Miró Cardona testimony of 6 December 1961 to U.S. Senate Subcommittee hearings, Cuban Refugee Problem, 6.

40. #317 Memorandum of Conversation, 29 March 1962, FRUS, 1961–1962, X, 777–78.

41. #291 Program Review by the Chief of Operations, Operation Mongoose (Lansdale), 18 January 1962, FRUS, 1961–1962, X, 710; #304 Program Review by Chief of Operations, Operation Mongoose (Lansdale), 20 February 1962, in FRUS, 1961–1962, X, 746.

42. #314 State Department, Guidelines for Operation Mongoose, 14 March 1962, in FRUS, 1961–1962, X, 771.

43. Gabriel Orozco Sr., interview in Bravo and Gómez, Operación Peter Pan, 137.

44. José Miró Cardona testimony of 6 December 1961 to U.S. Senate Subcommittee hearings, Cuban Refugee Problem, 6; Triay, Bay of Pigs, 75.

45. "For Juan Pujol, Suffering of Separation during Pedro Pan Was for the Best," Miami Herald, 16 May 2009.

46. Tony Daltabuit, interview by Wall in "Operation Pedro Pan," 83.

47. #273 Paper Prepared in the Central Intelligence Agency: Types of Covert Action against the Castro Regime, 8 November 1961, in FRUS, 1961–1962, X, 675.

48. Nelson Valdés, interview by author, Dallas, 29 March 2003.

49. "Reflections on Cuba," New York Times, 28 August 1962; see also "Young Cubans Relate Details of Attack Near Havana," New York Times, 27 August 1962.

50. Lourdes Arguelles, "The U.S. National Security State: The CIA and Cuban Émigré Terrorism," in Race and Class 23, no. 4 (1982): 292–93.

51. Hinckle and Turner, Deadly Secrets, 126.

52. See #202 Paper prepared for the National Security Council by Inter-Agency Task Force on Cuba. Cuba and Communism in the Hemisphere, 4 May 1961 in FRUS, 1961–1962, X, 467.

53. #205 Record of Actions at the 484d Meeting of the National Security Council, 5 May 1961, FRUS, 1961–1962, X, 482–83.

54. Roberto Suero testimony of 6 December 1961 to U.S. Senate Subcommittee hearings, Cuban Refugee Problem, 175; see also Wendell Rollason testimony of 6 December 1961 to U.S. Senate Subcommittee hearings, Cuban Refugee Problem, 161–62.

55. Robert W. Jones, "Free Transportation to USA Offered to Cubans with Visa Waivers," U.S. Department of State Bulletin, 45, 7 August 1961, 257–59. See also Masud-Piloto,

From Welcomed Exiles, 52; "Cuba: Operation Airlift," *Newsweek*, 31 July 1961, 39; and "U.S. Provides Airlift for Fleeing Cubans," *U.S. News and World Report*, 31 July 1961, 10.

56. #205 Record of Actions at the 483rd Meeting of the National Security Council, 5 May 1961 in *FRUS, 1961–1962, X*, 482–83.

57. #222 Memorandum of Conversation, Meeting with Representatives of the Cuban Revolutionary Council, 19 May 1961, in *FRUS, 1961–1962, X*, 549.

58. Haynes Johnson, *The Bay of Pigs: The Leaders' Story of Brigade 2506* (New York: W.W. Norton, 1964), 29.

59. Foreign Service Despatch to Department of State, from Viron Vaky, Second Secretary, American Embassy, Bogotá, Colombia, re "Cuba Series: Visits of Cuban Exiles," 7 December 1960, Confidential U.S. State Department central files. Cuba, 1960–January 1963. #737.00/12–760. This memo complained that the women did not get much press coverage in Colombia. Microfiche of Record Group 59, General Records of the Department of State.

60. Memorandum for General Lansdale from Lt. Col. Patchell, Subject: "Psychological Operations Group," 17 July 1962, states: "Trips Through Latin America: Agreed that need to have trips on a regular basis of notables throughout Latin America—not only politicians, but students, culture experts, musicians, performers, etc. CIA to present their projected program to group," in Elliston, ed., *Psywar*, 102–3.

61. Robert K. High testimony of 3 December 1962 to U.S. Senate Subcommittee hearings, *Cuban Refugee Problem*, 336.

62. #206 Memorandum for the Record, Debrief of NSC meeting 5 May 1961, *FRUS, 1961–1962, X*, 485–86.

63. Robert Hale (State Department visa officer) told the Senate Subcommittee that in 1961 the main beneficiaries had been parents, spouses, and children and "a limited number of persons" who did not meet other criteria. Robert Hale testimony of 13 December 1961 to U.S. Senate Subcommittee hearings, *Cuban Refugee Problem*, 205–6.

64. #222 Memorandum of Conversation, 19 May 1961, in *FRUS, 1961–1962, X*, 548–51.

65. #291 Program Review by the Chief of Operations, Operation Mongoose (Lansdale), 18 January 1962, *FRUS, 1961–1962, X*, 712; see also "They're OK," *Newsweek*, 4 December 1961. The article "Cuban Children Helped in Florida," *New York Times*, 27 May 1962, reported ten thousand "school-age youngsters" had already come, and five hundred more were arriving each week.

66. Robert Hale testimony of 13 December 1961 to U.S. Senate Subcommittee hearings, *Cuban Refugee Problem*, 205–6.

67. Wendell Rollason testimony of 6 December 1961 to U.S. Senate Subcommittee hearings, *Cuban Refugee Problem*, 158–59.

68. Torres, *Lost Apple*, 84–86.

69. James Hennessy testimony of 7 December 1961 to U.S. Senate Subcommittee hearings, *Cuban Refugee Problem*, 210–11.

70. María de los Angeles Torres, *In the Land of Mirrors: Cuban Exile Politics in the United States* (Ann Arbor: University of Michigan Press, 2001), 66–67. Rollason was arrested in Mexico in September 1964 on charges of bribery of government officials and fraud in getting Castro's opponents out of Cuba. Mexico was the only Latin American

country maintaining relations with Cuba at the time. See also Torres, *Lost Apple*, 84–86, 195.

71. #291 Program Review by the Chief of Operations, Operation Mongoose (Lansdale), 18 January 1962, *FRUS, 1961–1962*, X, 710–18. This review outlined thirty-two tasks ranging from intelligence collection to "psychological" programs through to the "use of U.S. military force to support the Cuban popular movement." An additional, thirty-third, task—the use of chemical weapons—to disrupt the sugar harvest was also considered. See U.S. Senate, *Alleged Assassination Plots*, 142–44.

72. #358 Memorandum from the Department of Defense Operations Officer for Operation Mongoose (Harris) to the Chief of Operations, Operation Mongoose (Lansdale), 23 July 1962, 865–67.

73. García, *Havana USA*, 18, 23, 216n29. See also Judith Edgette, "Domestic Collection on Cuba," in *Studies in Intelligence*, CIA, fall 1963, NND #947003, 41–42. National Security Archive, Washington, D.C.

74. #295 Memorandum Prepared in the Central Intelligence Agency for the Special Group, 24 January 1962. Tab A, Tasks Assigned to CIA in General Lansdale's Program Review, in *FRUS, 1961–1962*, X, 726.

75. Nelson Valdés, interview by author, Dallas, 29 March 2003.

76. Testimony of Vicente Munero Rojas to Cuban state security, 1964, quoted by Fabián Escalante, *The Cuba Project: CIA Covert Operations Against Cuba 1959–1962* (Melbourne: Ocean Press, 2004), 136.

77. Ronald Kessler, *Inside the CIA* (New York: Pocket Books, 1994), 44. Kessler puts this down to the U.S. CIA's officers' ignorance of Cuban culture. He quoted a Cuban CIA agent as saying: "They didn't understand the Cubans. Only a crazy would have thought in 1961 that the people would have gone against Fidel." Kessler, *Inside the CIA*, 45.

78. #206 Memorandum for the Record, a Debrief of NSC meeting, 5 May 1961, in *FRUS, 1961–1962*, X, 486. See also #228 Memorandum from Secretary of Defense McNamara to President Kennedy, 8 June 1961, in *FRUS, 1961–1962*, X, 571.

79. Corn, *Blond Ghost*, 85; Arboleya, *Cuban Counterrevolution*, 97.

80. Ramón "Mongo" Grau Alsina and Valerie Ridderhoff, *Cuba desde 1930* (Madrid: Agualarga Editores, 1997), 135, 141.

81. Luisa Yañez, "Ailing Hero behind Pedro Pan Mission an Inspiration to Exiles," *Sun Sentinel, South Florida*, 30 October 1998.

82. Grau and Ridderhoff, *Cuba desde 1930*, 137; and Msgr. Bryan Walsh, interview by author, Miami, 20 March 2000.

83. Msgr. Bryan Walsh, interview by author, Miami, 20 March 2000.

84. Geldof, *Cubans*, 228; "Men of Conscience," *Miami Herald*, 17 September 1986; see also Ramón Grau to Walsh, 31 October 1986, and Grau's letters written from prison to Walsh on 20 April 1978 and 15 May 1979, box 22, Walsh Papers.

85. Torres, *Lost Apple*, 82; Conde, *Operation Pedro Pan*, 62; Torreira and Buajasán, *Operación Peter Pan*, 249.

86. "Men of Conscience," *Miami Herald*, 17 September 1986; Buchsbaum, "Cuban 'Peter Pan' Honored." See also Triay, *Fleeing Castro*, 227–29.

87. #178 Memorandum from the Joint Chiefs of Staff to Secretary of Defense McNamara. Appendix D: Outline OPlan, 26 April 1961, in *FRUS, 1961–1962*, X, 377.

88. Torreira and Buajasán, *Operación Peter Pan*, 185, 200–205, 227–29. Their Cuban report included a reproduction of the declaration Leopoldina (Polita) Grau made on her arrest on 8 February 1965. See also Leopoldina Grau, interview by Triay in *Fleeing Castro*, 39–41.

89. The Cuban report suggested Penny Powers might have been an MI5 agent, but it stated her role in Operation Pedro Pan was only revealed to Cuban state security after the arrest of the Graus in 1965. She was mentioned in a state security report of 10 December 1964 as meeting with the British ambassador regularly but had no official diplomatic accreditation. See Torreira and Buajasán, *Operación Peter Pan*, 214n59.

90. Leopoldina Grau, interview by Triay in *Fleeing Castro*, 84–85 (my translation); see also Polita Grau, interview in Bravo and Gómez, *Operación Peter Pan*, 238.

91. Grau and Ridderhoff, *Cuba desde 1930*, 139.

92. James Baker, interview in Bravo, *Operación Peter Pan* (film).

93. Torres, *Lost Apple*, 4.

94. Msgr. Walsh, interview by author, Miami, 20 March 2000.

95. M.D.W. (Mike) McCann, British Embassy, Tokyo, letter to Reverend Bryan O. Walsh 26 March 1963, box 22, Walsh Papers.

96. Torreira and Buajasán, *Operación Peter Pan*, 120. Powers had also been actively involved in the *Kindertransport* that rescued Jewish children from Germany in World War II.

97. See Torres, *Lost Apple*, 72.

98. Jennifer Mathieu and María A. Morales, "Exiles He Aided," *Miami Herald*, 5 November 1998. The Cuban report included reproductions of the charges against Leopoldina (Polita) Grau (200–204) and Ramón Grau's declarations at his trial (389–98), but there is no mention of child smuggling in any of these documents.

99. See Triay, *Fleeing Castro*, 43; see also Torreira and Buajasán, *Operación Peter Pan*, 290–92.

100. Torreira and Buajasán provided detailed information about the CIA links of many of the underground activists in Cuba. See Torreira and Buajasán, *Operación Peter Pan*, 176–206.

101. #273 Paper Prepared in the Central Intelligence Agency: Types of Covert Action against the Castro Regime, 8 November 1961, in *FRUS, 1961–1962*, X, 675; see also Triay, *Fleeing Castro*, 43.

102. Memorandum from James Baker to Philip Bonsal, 7 February 1961, quoted by Torres, *Lost Apple*, 76.

103. Grau and Ridderhoff, *Cuba desde 1930*, 151, 137, 149. Grau named René Velíz, a former accountant on his farm, who had been involved in a sabotage activity at a Shell refinery, as using a Pedro Pan visa to leave Cuba, 151–52.

104. Torreira and Buajasán, *Operación Peter Pan*, 207.

105. Memorandum to Brother Maximiliano from Father Bryan O. Walsh, 16 August 1962. Pedro Pan Collection, Museum of South Florida (History/Miami), Miami.

106. The birth dates given for three of the four young Cubans indicate they were

between sixteen and eighteen years of age, for whom clearance from Washington was required.

107. #273 Paper Prepared in the Central Intelligence Agency: Types of Covert Action against the Castro Regime, 8 November 1961, in *FRUS, 1961–1962, X,* 676.

108. "A Prisoner for Freedom," *Miami Herald,* 7 May 1998, 30A. The *Miami Herald* article stated she "played a major role in getting hundreds of Cuban children out [of Cuba] ... resettling them in the United States under Operation Pedro Pan. She and her husband, Amador Odio, were jailed as a result."

109. Del Toro's own description of her arrest and imprisonment does not mention any charge related to assisting children flee Cuba. See Medrano, *Todo lo dieron,* 81–83.

110. Sara del Toro, interview by Triay, *Fleeing Castro,* 42. Triay confirmed that no one was convicted in Cuba of "any crimes directly associated with Operation Pedro Pan." Triay, *Fleeing Castro,* 43.

111. Josefina Leyva, *Operación Pedro Pan: El exodo de los niños Cubanos. Una novela histórica* (Coral Gables, FL: Editorial Ponce de León, 1993).

112. Torreira and Buajasán, *Operación Peter Pan,* 291–92.

113. See Margarita Oteiza, interview by Eloísa Echazábal and Carmen Romañach, Miami, Pedro Pan Exodus YouTube channel, 31 March 2010, https://www.youtube.com/watch?v=R2HxEExZdOA.

114. These "other activities" conducted by the counterrevolutionary movement, which included sabotage and terrorist attacks, are detailed by Torreira and Buajasán, *Operación Peter Pan,* 176–206. See also Encinosa, *Cuba en Guerra.*

115. Torres, "Open the Books," 5M; Elaine de Valle, "Professor Plans to Sue CIA over Cuba Airlift Papers," *Miami Herald,* 12 January 1998.

116. "CIA and Pedro Pan," *Miami Herald,* 14 January 1998, 8A.

117. López-Miró, "Dark Side"; letter from Martin Guillermo de Salazar in "Readers' Forum," *Miami Herald,* 5 December 1990. For more letters published in response to this editorial, see María Elena Morales Lacedonia, "There's No 'Dark Side' of Operation Peter Pan," and Evelyn and Ben Clein, "A Jewish Peter Pan," *Miami Herald,* 5 December 1990.

118. Ena Curnow, "Afirma Monseñor Walsh que Pedro Pan fue obra humanitaria," *Diario las Américas,* 16 January 1998 (my translation).

119. Walsh, interview in Bravo, *Operación Peter Pan* (film).

120. Donald P. Baker, "A Journey out of the Past for 'Pedro Pan' Project," *Washington Post,* 26 January 1998, A19.

121. See Torres v. Central Intelligence Agency (U.S. District Court), 12 March 1999, PedroPan.org, http://www.pedropan.org/images/courts_ruling_on_CIAs_role_in_OPP.jpg. See also 29 F. Supp. 2d 497: Torres v. CIA. Illinois Northern District Court–29 F. Supp. 2d 497. 15 December 1998, and 39F. Supp. 2d 960: Torres v. CIA. Illinois Northern District Court–39 F. Supp. 2d 960. 12 March 1999.

122. Torres, *Lost Apple,* 238.

123. Triay, *Fleeing Castro,* 39. Another minor incident occurred prior to the 1961 invasion, when two British embassy officials were briefly detained by Cuban security. See "Cuba Detains Britons: Secret Police Hold 2 Consuls Incommunicado for 2 Hours," *New York Times,* 23 March 1961.

124. Msgr. Bryan O. Walsh, "The Origins of Operation Pedro Pan," paper presented at the Pedro Pan Conference, Florida International University, Miami, 20–21 April 2001, box 44, Walsh Papers.

125. Cathy Areu Jones, "Operation Pedro Pan: The Untold Story of a Cold War Conspiracy," *Oye Magazine* (c2001), PedroPan.org, http://www.pedropan.org/sites/default/files/OyeMagazineCiaArticle[1]_0_0.pdf.

126. Jesús Arboleya, interview by author, Havana, 6 May 2016.

127. Torres, *Lost Apple*, 310n16, 78, 288n45. See also María de los Angeles Torres, interview by María Hinojosa in "The Lost Children of Cuba: Operation Pedro Pan," National Public Radio, 12 June 2015, https://soundcloud.com/latinousa/the-lost-children-of-cuba-operation-pedro-pan.

128. See National Security Archive, "CIA Successfully Conceals Bay of Pigs History," posted 21 May 2014, http://nsarchive.gwu.edu/news/20140521/; and "CIA Releases Controversial Bay of Pigs History," posted 31 October 2016, http://nsarchive.gwu.edu/NSAEBB/NSAEBB564-CIA-Releases-Controversial-Bay-of-Pigs-History/.

129. White, *Kennedys and Cuba*, 71. Gen. Lansdale is often considered to be the model for the character Alden Pyle in Graham Greene's 1955 novel, *The Quiet American*.

130. Quoted by Elliston, ed., *Psywar*, 104.

131. U.S. Senate, *Alleged Assassination Plots*, 142.

132. Propaganda was the largest expenditure item in the CIA's Cuba covert action budget proposed for Operation Mongoose for the 1962 financial year. See #251 Memorandum from the Deputy Under Secretary of State for Political Affairs (Johnson) to Secretary of State Rusk, 22 July 1961, in *FRUS, 1961–1962, X*, 633.

133. #208 Memorandum from the President's Special Assistant (Schlesinger) to the Political Warfare Subcommittee of the Cuban Task Force, 8 May 1961, *FRUS, 1961–1962, X*, 490.

134. #315 National Intelligence Estimate: The Situation and Prospects in Cuba, 21 March 1962, *FRUS, 1961–1962, X*, 775–76.

135. #258 Memorandum from the President's Special Counsel (Goodwin) to President Kennedy, 1 September 1961, *FRUS, 1961–1962, X*, 646–47. The Alliance for Progress was also part of the Kennedy administration's political strategy to head off other Latin American countries taking "the Cuban road."

136. On 3 May 1961, Schlesinger wrote to Kennedy saying the Bay of Pigs had "created ... a vague fear in people's minds that the Kennedy administration is bent on a course of subversion and paramilitary warfare." See #196 Memorandum from the President's Special Assistant (Schlesinger) to President Kennedy, 3 May 1961, *FRUS, 1961–1962, X*, 427.

137. #208 Memorandum from the President's Special Assistant (Schlesinger) to the Political Warfare Subcommittee of the Cuban Task Force, 8 May 1961, in *FRUS, 1961–1962, X*, 492 (my emphasis).

138. David Lawrence, "Let's Invade Cuba," in *U.S. News and World Report*, 6 November 1961.

139. In an e-mail to this researcher, a Tamiment archivist commented on the collection, saying, "it would have been entirely in character for someone at NL to send copies of these letters to the CIA." E-mail from Peter Meyer Filardo re Collection 39, Letters from

Cuba, 1961–1963, Tamiment Archive, New York University Library, New York, received 23 February 2000.

140. Letter from Havana, 6 May 1962, from Collection 39, Letters from Cuba, 1961–1963. Tamiment Archive, New York University Library, New York.

141. Letter #14, from "B," Havana 20 August 1962, from Collection 39, Letters from Cuba, 1961–1963. Tamiment Archive, New York University Library, New York. It is not clear what the exhortation to "get to work on this very soon" means. It could relate to his/her initial remark about an invasion being an "absolute must."

142. Memorandum for the Record by Brig. Gen. Lansdale. Subject: Meeting with President, 16 March 1962, 2–3. Operation Mongoose, Cuba Collection, National Security Archive, Washington, D.C.

143. "Plight of Cuba Today: Agony, Hunger, Fear," *Miami Herald*, 11 March 1962, 1–2.

144. #555 Memorandum from Gerard C. Smith, Assistant Secretary of State for Policy Planning, to the Secretary of State, 13 July 1960, *FRUS, 1958–1960, VI*, 1011.

145. Memorandum for Chief of Operations, Cuba Project, Subject: Justification for U.S. Military Intervention in Cuba (TS), Appendix to Enclosure A, 12 March 1962. Top Secret, JCS 1969/321 Declassified 25 November 1997. Operation Mongoose, Cuba Collection, National Security Archive, Washington, D.C.

146. Wendell Rollason testimony of 7 December 1961 to U.S. Senate Subcommittee hearings, *Cuban Refugee Problem*, 162.

147. #273 Paper Prepared in the Central Intelligence Agency: Types of Covert Action against the Castro Regime, 8 November 1961, *FRUS, 1961–1962, X*, 675.

148. Tab B, "Political Support Plan," in Program Review by Brig. Gen. Lansdale, The Cuba Project, 20 February 1962, in Elliston, ed., *Psywar*, 79. This part was redacted in #304 published in *FRUS, 1961–1962, X*, 745–47.

149. Jean Wardlow, "Fidel's Victim's Son Now Amigo Guide," *Miami Herald*, 26 April 1962.

150. Grupo Areíto, *Contra Viento y Marea*, 41; Dubinsky, *Babies without Borders*, 17.

151. *FYI—The Plight of Pepito: Cuba's Lost Generation*, WTVJ, 1961, narrated by Ralph Renick, https://www.floridamemory.com/items/show/245399.

152. Miguel A. De La Torre, *La Lucha for Cuba: Religion and Politics on the Streets of Miami* (Berkeley: University of California Press, 2003), 34.

153. #304 Program Review by the Chief of Operations, Operation Mongoose (Lansdale), 20 February 1962. Only part of this document is published in *FRUS, 1961–1962, X*, 745–47. Complete details of parts "B. Political Support Plan" and "D. Psychological Support Plan" of this document were reproduced in Elliston, ed, *Psywar*, 80–82.

154. For example, Wendell Rollason told the Senate Subcommittee that the "problem of the Cuban refugees, which the Miami area now faces, is one of quantity, not quality." He acknowledged tensions were developing, but he was skeptical about resettlement as a solution, however, because "for every one Cuban to leave Miami this week, four more will arrive." Wendell Rollason testimony of 7 December 1961 to U.S. Senate Subcommittee hearings, *Cuban Refugee Problem*, 153–57.

155. Excerpts from this documentary (*Crisis Amigo*) were included in the minutes of

13 December 1961 hearings of the U.S. Senate Subcommittee, *Cuban Refugee Problem*, 180–85.

156. Ibid.

157. The series of meetings held by the NSC after the Bay of Pigs decided that Cuban exiles should now be regarded as an immigrant group and "encouraged to locate in other areas." See #205 Record of Actions at the 483rd Meeting of the National Security Council, Washington, 5 May 1961, in *FRUS, 1961–1962, X*, 482–83; and #206 Memorandum for the Record, Debrief of NSC meeting, 5 May 1961, in *FRUS, 1961–1962, X*, 486.

158. Close, "Cuban Children away from Home," 3–10.

159. "Pedro Pan a Secret Long Kept," *Miami Herald*, 24 October 1998, 25A.

160. Fr. Bryan O. Walsh testimony of 13 December 1961 to U.S. Senate Subcommittee hearings, *Cuban Refugee Problem*, 229.

161. Torres, *Lost Apple*, 183–84.

162. Letter from Katherine B. Oettinger, 17 February 1961, Appendix 5, in Adessa, "Refugee Cuban Children," 180.

163. Walsh, "Cuban Refugee Children," 402–3.

164. Ibid., 410–11.

165. Msgr. Walsh, interview by author, Miami, 20 March 2000.

166. Jesús Díaz, dir., *55 Hermanos* (Havana, ICAIC, 1978).

167. Dubinsky, *Babies without Borders*, 32.

168. Walsh, "The Origins of Operation Pedro Pan."

169. "Miami—Refugee City" in *U.S. News and World Report*, 5 December 1960, 62. See also Marcie Ersoff, "When a Cuban Child Gets Here," in *Miami Herald*, 30 December 1960, 1; "The Agonizing Wait" in *Newsweek*, 28 August 1961, 23, reported that Dade County schools were making special arrangements to cope with the thousands of Cuban children in local schools. Another article, "Cuba: Hard New Life," in *Time*, 15 September 1961, 43, noted that the federal government had set aside several million dollars to aid the ten thousand Cuban children in Florida schools.

170. Walsh, "Cuban Refugee Children," 234.

171. Msgr. Walsh, interview by author, Miami, 20 March 2000.

172. Erwin Potts, "8,000 Cuba Children Saved from Castro Brainwashing in 'Operation Exodus,'" *Miami Herald*, 8 March 1962, 1; "8,000 Fidel Won't Get," *Miami News*, 8 March 1962, 2A; Erwin Potts, "Ribicoff Appeals for Foster Care," *Miami Herald*, 8 March 1962, 1; "Ribicoff Asks Open Door Policy for Homeless Cuban Children," *Washington Post*, 8 March 1962, C19. This last article mentioned was aimed at potential foster parents and published on the page "For and about Women." It reported on Ribicoff's speech at a dinner in Miami the previous night (7 March 1962) explaining how Cuban children were being sent by their parents to the United States "to thwart the Castro regime's efforts at Communist indoctrination."

173. Marjorie Fillyaw, "Priest's Program aids 8,000 Cuban Children; U.S. Agencies Assist," NCWC News Service, 5 March 1962; Marjorie Fillyaw, "Appeal Made by Government, Catholic Agency for Foster Homes for Cuban Refugee Children," 12 March 1962, box 32, Walsh Papers.

174. John Leacacos, "10–15 Cuban Children Go to Palmdale," Cleveland *Plain Dealer*, 22 February 1962, 1, 4.

175. Dom Bonafede, "Cuban Youths Find Snow Lots of Fun," in *Miami Herald*, 28 February 1962; Mary Hirschfield, "New Way of Life Begins Here for 85 Cuban Refugees," Cleveland *Plain Dealer*, 28 February 1962, 1.

176. Mary Hirschfeld, "Cuban Resettlement Group Denies Mayor Was Ignored," Cleveland *Plain Dealer*, 4 March 1962, 5A; "Florida Papers, Please Note," Cleveland *Plain Dealer*, 8 March 1962.

177. Close, "Cuban Children away from Home," 8.

178. "Ribicoff Appeals to All Cities: Accept Refugees: Pledges Exiles Aid Anywhere," in *Miami News*, 9 March 1962, 1C.

179. "Ribicoff Cites Need to Resettle Cubans," in *New York Times*, 10 March 1962, 8.

180. See Casavantes, *Revolution Is for the Children* (especially chapter 5, "Our Cuban Visitors"); and McNally, *Catholicism*.

181. "Cuban Children Helped in Florida," *New York Times*, 27 May 1962, 41.

182. Tab D: "Psychological Support Plan," in General Lansdale's review of Operation Mongoose of 20 February 1962, in Elliston, ed., *Psywar*, 81. This part of Lansdale's review was not published in #304, *FRUS, 1961–1962, X*, 745–47 (my emphasis).

183. John Leacacos, "10–15 Cuban Children Go to Palmdale," Cleveland *Plain Dealer*, 22 February 1962, 1.

184. "Refugee Cuban Children Need Homes," in *Christian Century* 14 no. 79 (April 4, 1962): 417.

185. Melissa Soldani Lemon provides an extraordinary sample of responses to the appeal for foster families for the Pedro Pans; Melissa Soldani Lemon, *Are They White? American Families Offer to Open Their Homes to (Some) Cuban Refugee Children* (Amazon Digital Services, 2014) Kindle edition.

186. DHEW, Children's Bureau, *Facts about the Unaccompanied Cuban Refugee Children's Program: How to Apply for a Cuban Child*, 15 January 1963, 3–4. File 514, Lourdes Casals Library, Center for Cuban Studies, New York.

187. Walsh, "Cuban Refugee Children," 379.

188. Msgr. Walsh, interview by author, Miami, 20 March 2000. This statement seems to be verified by the mention of Luis and María Dorticós (then living in North Bergen, New Jersey) in the *Second Annual Newsletter of the Spokane Diocese Cuban Children's Program*, January 1968, box 16, Walsh Papers.

189. Official Memorandum of Caribbean Survey group, 23 March 1962, quoted by Torres, *Lost Apple*, 180.

190. #356 Memorandum from the [USIA] Operations Officer for Operation Mongoose (Wilson) to the Chief of Operations, Operation Mongoose (Lansdale), 20 July 1962, re "Specific tasks assigned to USIA," *FRUS, 1961–1962, X*, 857–62. This document also mentions a comic book called "Los Secuestradores" (The Kidnappers) about the "brainwashing of children" and a film that will discuss the mistreatment of children in Cuba.

191. Cliff Solway, dir., *The Lost Apple* (Talent Associates–Paramount, 1963). Well-known movie director David Susskind is listed in the credits as executive producer of this

film. The USIA is not identified in the credits, which state the film was made by "Robert Crone Films." Correspondence from 1963 in Msgr. Walsh's archives, however, suggests that the English version was produced first and later released in Spanish; see box 32, "The Lost Apple, 1963–1966," Walsh Papers.

192. Solway, dir., *The Lost Apple*. There are various versions of this documentary now available, including on YouTube, and various dates are given for its release: 1962 and 1963. The copy this researcher has was obtained as a videocassette from the Library of Congress in September 2001. Fr. Walsh was obviously involved in this movie project, as his archive includes several draft scripts, including the final English-language version; see box 32, Walsh Papers.

193. Memorandum for General Lansdale from Lt. Col. Patchell, Subject: "Psychological Operations Group," 17 July 1962, in Elliston, ed., *Psywar*, 102–3.

194. This correspondence was quoted by Torres, *Lost Apple*, 303n78.

195. Memorandum for General Lansdale from Lt. Col. Patchell, Subject: "Psychological Operations Group," 24 July 1962, 2. Operation Mongoose, Cuba Collection, National Security Archive, Washington, D.C.

196. Laura A. Belmonte, *Selling the American Way: U.S. Propaganda and the Cold War* (Philadelphia: University of Pennsylvania Press, 2010), 63.

197. Walsh, "The Origins of Operation Pedro Pan."

198. Letter from Fred Wardenburg, Talent Associates-Paramount Ltd., 444 Madison Avenue, New York, to Miss Dorothy Sullivan, Catholic Welfare Bureau, 395 N.W. First St., Miami, 21 March 1963. See also Miss Dorothea F. Sullivan, ACSW, Director of Social Services, Cuban Children's Program, to Monsignor Gallagher, Cleveland, Ohio, 25 September 1963, wherein Sullivan offers the film to be shown at a conference in Cleveland, box 32, Walsh Papers.

199. Thomas, "U.S.A. as a Country of First Asylum," 10–11.

200. Solway, dir., *The Lost Apple*.

201. #28 Memorandum from the Joint Chiefs of Staff to Secretary of Defense McNamara, 27 January 1961, *FRUS, 1961–1962, X*, 57.

202. See Directorio Revolucionario Estudiantil, *Nuestro Plan de Liberación* (New York: DRE pamphlet, c1961–1962). Directorio Revolucionario Estudiantil en exilio, Cuban Heritage Collection, University of Miami Libraries, Coral Gables, Florida.

203. "Memorandum on Preparing Refugees to Contribute to Education for Democracy in Cuba," paper presented by James D. Baker to the Senate Subcommittee hearings, *Cuban Refugee Problem*, 6 December 1961, 35–38.

204. Ibid., 37.

205. Ibid.

206. Ibid.

207. Tracy S. Voorhees, *Report to the President of the United States on the Cuban Refugee Problem* (Washington: U.S. Government Printing Office, 18 January 1961), 5–6.

208. Strong, "Refugees from Castro's Cuba," 76–77.

209. Oettinger, "Services to Unaccompanied Cuban Refugee Children," 384.

210. Torres, *Lost Apple*, 67.

211. Memorandum from J. Edgar Hoover, 27 January 1961, quoted by Torres, *Lost Apple*, 77–78.

212. This program, "Inter-American Institute of Social Formation," was sponsored by the Diocese of Miami and trialed in 1964; see box 10, Walsh Papers.

213. Dubinsky, *Babies without Borders*, 36.

214. Torreira and Buajasán, *Operación Peter Pan*, 383, 256–58 (my translation).

215. #28 Memorandum from Chairman of the JCS Lemnitzer to Secretary of Defense McNamara, 10 April 1962, in White, *Kennedys and Cuba*, 118–19.

216. Penny Powers, letter to Ambassador Philip Bonsal, 3 April 1961, quoted by Torres, *Lost Apple*, 104.

217. Penny Powers, letter to W. L. Mitchell of DHEW, quoted by Torres, *Lost Apple*, 104–5.

218. See the cases of Tony Alvarez and Olga Chorens and others mentioned in Torreira and Buajasán, *Operación Peter Pan*, 121–22, 184–84, and 241–42.

219. See Nestor T. Carbonell, *And the Russians Stayed: The Sovietization of Cuba: A Personal Portrait* (New York: William Morrow, 1989).

220. Arboleya, *Cuban Counterrevolution*, 116–18.

221. Schoultz, *That Infernal Little Cuban Republic*, 188.

222. #304 Memorandum for the Record. Attachment: Memorandum Prepared by Director of Central Intelligence McCone: "Unauthorized Cuban Raids," 29 March 1963, *FRUS, 1962–1963*, XI, 746.

223. Encinosa, *Cuba en Guerra*, 149.

224. #262 Memorandum for the Record, from John A. McCone, Director of Central Intelligence, 7 January 1963, *FRUS, 1962–1963*, XI, 653.

225. #260 Memorandum: "Cuban Focal Point in the Miami Area," 29 December 1962, *FRUS, 1962–1963*, XI, 647; #298 Memorandum from Gordon Chase of the National Security Council Staff to the President's Special Assistant for National Security Affairs (Bundy), 23 March 1963, *FRUS, 1962–1963*, XI, 729.

226. U.S. Cuban Refugee Center, Press release (Freedom Tower, Miami, 5 April 1963), 3. File 514, Lourdes Casal Library, Center for Cuban Studies, New York.

227. Torres, *Lost Apple*, 212–13.

228. #282 Memorandum from Gordon Chase of the National Security Council . . . : "Isolation of Cuba," 14 February 1963, *FRUS, 1962–1963*, XI, 700.

229. DHEW Children's Bureau, *Cuba's Children in Exile*, 5.

230. Some of these activities were outlined in U.S. Senate, *Alleged Assassination Plots*. In 1999, the Cuban government initiated a $181 billion claim against the U.S. government for war crimes committed over several decades of covert action operations. Significantly, Operation Pedro Pan, however, was not included in this case.

231. López-Miró, "Dark Side."

232. Polita Grau, interview with Luis Báez, "Al líder de ustedes lo protege alguién más que el G-2," *Juventud Rebelde*, 28 November 1993, 6.

Chapter 6. The Pedro Pan Paradox

1. Msgr. Walsh, interview by author, Miami, 20 March 2000; see also Walsh, "Cuban Refugee Children," 402–3.

2. Quoted by Conde, *Operation Pedro Pan*, 193. Tony de la Guardia was tried and executed in 1989 on serious corruption charges.

3. See the testimonies of Robert Hale (director, Visa Section, State Department) and James Hennessy (executive assistant to the INS Commissioner) of 13 December 1961 to U.S. Senate Subcommittee hearings, *Cuban Refugee Problem*, 205–14.

4. Kessler, *Inside the CIA*, 44.

5. Walsh, "Cuban Refugee Children," 402.

6. Ibid.

7. Msgr. Bryan O. Walsh, "Recollection of Havana Trip," 25 March 1963, box 44, Walsh Papers.

8. At this time the CIA was looking to "encourage visits to Cuba by knowledgeable and friendly observers" to extract intelligence about the situation on the island. See #268 Memorandum from McGeorge Bundy to Director of Intelligence McCone, 18 January 1963, *FRUS, 1962–1963*, XI, 665.

9. Torreira and Buajasán, *Operación Peter Pan*, 290 (my translation).

10. Fabián Escalante, interview by author, Havana, 20 April 1999.

11. Carol Rosenberg, "Ramón Grau, Organizer of Cuban Kids' Flight, Dies," *Miami Herald*, 4 November 1998.

12. Ojito, "Ramón Grau Alsina."

13. Torres, *Lost Apple*, 101–2.

14. Torreira and Buajasán, *Operación Peter Pan*, 290–92.

15. Triay, *Fleeing Castro*, 38–39.

16. Wayne S. Smith, *The Closest of Enemies: A Personal and Diplomatic Account of U.S.-Cuban Relations since 1957* (New York: W.W. Norton, 1997), 61.

17. Torreira and Buajasán, *Operación Peter Pan*, 215, 214n59. A Cuban state security report of 10 December 1964 noted that Penny Powers visited the British embassy three times a week and frequently used an embassy car.

18. Msgr. Walsh, interview by author, Miami, 20 March 2000.

19. Torres, *Lost Apple*, 297n33.

20. For Powers's role in establishing the Hillside School in Havana, see http://www.ishavana.org/index.php/history.

21. Miss Phyllis Howison Powers was awarded the honor of Member of the British Empire (MBE) in the Queen's new year's honors list of 31 December 1981 "[F]or services to education in Cuba. https://www.thegazette.co.uk/London/issue/48837/data.pdf. See also Torres, *Lost Apple*, 72.

22. Wayne Smith, interview in Bravo and Gómez, *Operación Peter Pan*, 256–57 (my translation).

23. Triay, *Fleeing Castro*, 43; Torreira and Buajasán, *Operación Peter Pan*, 389. Torres also confirmed this fact after obtaining access to the arrest records of Ramón Grau and others from the Center for Alternative Policy Studies (CEAP) at the University of Havana; see *Lost Apple*, 130.

24. Concepción Adam, interview in Ochoa, *Never Ever Neverland* (my translation).

25. Torreira and Buajasán, *Operación Peter Pan*, 277–78 (my translation).

26. Phillips, *Cuban Dilemma*, 277, 304–5.

27. Richard Eder, "100 Priests Are Seized in Cuba; 6 More Castro Foes Executed," in *New York Times*, 17 September 1961, 41.

28. Torreira and Buajasán, *Operación Peter Pan*, 246–47. See also "Regulación de pasajes. Las tarjetas se darán solo a interesados," *Revolución*, 14 September 1961, 1; and "Aclaración a viajeros. Facilitan trámite en la Reforma Urbana," *Revolución*, 19 September 1961, 2. See also letter written by "Kingston" from Havana, 19 September 1961, which lists all the new requirements of departing citizens demanded by the Cuban government, Letters from Cuba, 1961–1963, Collection 39, Tamiment Archive, New York University Library, New York.

29. Two officials from both airlines were subsequently arrested and imprisoned: Francisco (Pancho) Finlay, president of KLM in Cuba, who recruited several other CIA agents, and José Luis Pelleya, a lawyer for Pan American Airlines, who was charged with espionage. See Torreira and Buajasán, *Operación Peter Pan*, 251–56 240–46.

30. Corn, *Blond Ghost*, 64.

31. "Refugees from Castro," *Economist*, 22 December 1962, 1205. See also Masud-Piloto, *From Welcomed Exiles*, 51.

32. Fidel Castro's speech of 19 September 1961, in *Obra Revolucionaria*, #33, 1961, 13–31 (my translation).

33. María de los Angeles Torres, interview in Cardona and de Varona, *Flight of Pedro Pan*.

34. Adessa, "Cuban Refugee Children," 4, 50–51.

35. Masud-Piloto, *From Welcomed Exiles*, 51–52.

36. See "Ley 940: Creación del Ministerio del Interior" in Bell et al., eds., *Documentos de la revolución cubana 1961* (Havana: Editorial de Ciencias Sociales, 2008), 250–51. See also Tad Szulc, "Castro Speeding Effort to Set Up Communist State," *New York Times*, 18 June 1961, 3.

37. Msgr. Walsh, interview by author, Miami, 20 March 2000.

38. Torreira and Buajasán, *Operación Peter Pan*, 289–90, 382–83.

39. *Fidel in Chile*, 168. It should be noted that in the early 1970s Washington was using similar tactics to undermine the government of Salvador Allende, again with the assistance of the talented psywar practitioner David Phillips. See Wolfgang Saxon, "David Atlee Phillips Dead at 65: Ex-Agent Was Advocate of CIA," *New York Times*, 10 July 1988. See also "Chile and the United States: Declassified Documents Relating to the Military Coup, September 11, 1973," http://nsarchive.gwu.edu/NSAEBB/NSAEBB8/nsaebb8i.htm.

40. Fidel Castro, "The Envy of Goebbels," http://www.cuba.cu/gobierno/reflexiones/2009/ing/f110609i.html, 11 June 2009; see also Luisa Yañez, "Statue of Late 'Father' of Pedro Pan Unveiled," *Miami Herald*, 6 June 2009.

41. Fidel Castro quoted in Betancourt, *¿Por Que Carlos?* 62–63 (my translation).

42. Ibid.

43. Navarro, "Return to Cuba," AR6.

44. Eduardo Machado, *Havana Is Waiting and Other Plays* (Kindle Locations 588–90). (New York: Theatre Communications Group, 2011).

45. Fabián Escalante, interview by author, Havana, 20 April 1999.

46. José Buajasán, interview by author, Havana, 19 April 1999.
47. Torres, *Lost Apple*, 268.
48. Torreira and Buajasán, *Operación Peter Pan*, 290, 384 (my translation).
49. Francisco Méndez, interview by Bravo and Gómez, *Operación Peter Pan*, 188 (my translation).
50. De la Campa, *Cuba on My Mind*, 41.
51. Wayne Smith, interview in Bravo, *Operación Peter Pan* (film).
52. Tom Raum, "Elián Fight Back before Congress," *Washington Post*, 1 March 2000.
53. De La Torre, *La Lucha for Cuba*, 3.
54. "What's Best for Elián González?" *Washington Post*, 9 December 1999.
55. Alejandra Matus, "Una cruzada individual en favor de Elián González," *El Nuevo Herald*, 24 May 2000; Johnson, "Elián González Case."
56. Fidel Castro, "Let Us Save Elián," *Granma*, 12 December 1999.
57. Fidel Castro, speaking at the closing function of the 2nd International Havana Cigar Festival, at PABEXPO, 4 March 2000, http://www.cuba.cu/gobierno/discursos/2000/ing/f040300i.html.
58. Anita Casavantes Bradford, "Remembering Pedro Pan: Childhood and Collective Memory Making in Havana and Miami, 1960–2000," *Cuban Studies* 44 (2016): 303–4.
59. Alina M. Lotti, "Sentimientos manoseados," *Trabajadores*, 20 December 1999. The U.S.–Cuban migration agreements of 1994–1995 were established to prevent such dangerous and illegal departures from the island. See Leogrande and Kornbluh, *Back Channel*, 295–300.
60. Dubinsky, *Babies without Borders*, 7.
61. Ofra Bikel, dir., *Saving Elián* (Frontline, PBS, February 2001); for transcript, see www.pbs.org/wgbh/pages/frontline/shows/elian/etc/script.html.
62. Silvia Pedraza, "La perspectiva desde la isla," *El Nuevo Herald*, 27 March 2000, quoted by Casavantes, "Remembering Pedro Pan," 302.
63. Quoted by LeoGrande and Kornbluh, *Back Channel*, 340.
64. Msgr. Walsh, interview by author, Miami, 20 March 2000.
65. Fidel Castro, speaking at the closing function of the 2nd International Havana Cigar Festival, at PABEXPO, 4 March 2000. http://www.cuba.cu/gobierno/discursos/2000/ing/f040300i.html.
66. Ana Riewerts, phone interview from New York by author, 16 May 2002. See also Max Castro, "Hidden Support for a Father," *Miami Herald*, 26 January 2000.
67. "Pedro Pan Exiles Finding Their Past," *Miami Herald*, 4 December 2000.
68. Eloísa Echazábal, interview in Bikel, *Saving Elián*.
69. Lillian Guerra, "Elián González and the 'Real Cuba' of Miami: Visions of Identity, Exceptionality, and Divinity," *Cuban Studies* 38 (2007): 14.
70. Betancourt, *¿Por Qué Carlos?* See also Jesús Arboleya Cervera, Raúl Alzaga Manresa, and Ricardo Fraga del Valle, *La Contrarrevolución Cubana en Puerto Rico y el Caso de Carlos Muñiz Varela* (San Juan: Ediciones Callejón, 2016).
71. See Díaz, *De la Patria y el Exilio*; and Betancourt, *¿Por Que Carlos?* 55. In an extraordinary historical coincidence, a young man named Elián was also part of this first

"Antonio Maceo Brigade," as they called themselves for the Cuban independence fighter in the struggle against Spain in the nineteenth century.

72. "Pledge of Thanksgiving" by "The Children of Pedro Pan," 23 November 1990, Miami, Florida, box 12, Walsh Papers; see also the first edition of *Joven Cuba*, February 1974; and "A la Juventud Cubana" (April 1974), reproduced in *Contra Viento y Marea*, 254–56, 251–53.

73. José Quiroga, "The Cuban Exile Wars, 1976–1981," in *American Quarterly* 66, no. 3 (September 2014): 830.

74. Silvia Wilhelm, interview by Albor Ruiz, "Operación Peter Pan: Volando de Vuelta a Cuba," *Progreso Semanal*, 16 April 2011, www.cubadebate.cu/opinion/2011/04/16/operacion-peter-pan-volando-de-vuelta.

75. Tina Griego, "They Risked Everything to Open a Door to Cuba: They Were Shunned for It," *Washington Post*, 5 January 2015. This article also mentions the assassination of Carlos Muñiz.

76. Rosa María Gil, "The Assimilation and Problems of Adjustment to the American Culture of One Hundred Cuban Refugee Adolescents Attending Catholic and Public High Schools in Union City and West New York, New Jersey, 1959–1966" (master's thesis, Fordham University, 1968), 215.

77. Pedraza, *Political Disaffection*, 139.

78. Maura Juampere Pérez, "Apuntes acerca del surgimiento de los grupos de izquierda en la comunidad cubana en los Estados Unidos," in *La emigración cubana: Anuario 1995* (Havana: Centro de Estudios Alternativas Políticas, 1995), 60–64.

79. Editorial in first issue of *Joven Cuba*, February 1974, reproduced in Grupo Areíto, *Contra Viento y Marea*, 254.

80. Casavantes, *Revolution Is for the Children*, 197.

81. Quoted by Luis Ortega, *Cubanos en Miami* (Havana: Editorial de Ciencias Sociales, 1998), 15.

82. María Emilia Castagliola, in O'Reilly, *ReMembering Cuba*, 66.

83. Ana Mendieta, in Bravo and Gómez, *Operación Peter Pan*, 146.

84. Ed Canler, interview in Bravo, *Operación Peter Pan* (film).

85. María de los Angeles ("Candi") Sosa, in Bravo and Gómez, *Operación Peter Pan*, 100 (my translation).

86. Ana Menéndez, interview in Bravo and Gómez, *Operación Peter Pan*, 104–9 (my translation).

87. "Pedro Pan Exiles Finding Their Past," *Miami Herald*, 4 December 2000.

Conclusion: Ambassadors, Soldiers, or Spies?

1. "Half a lifetime, empty inside . . . And why? Because of ignorance and lies. / Forty years, half a lifetime, spent, lost, with nothing inside." Poem by an anonymous Pedro Pan, http://www.teresita.org/LaMitadDeUnaVida.html (my translation), accessed 23 December 2001.

2. CIA, *Cuban Counter Revolutionary Handbook* (October 1962), Cuban Information Archives, https://cuban-exile.com/doc_351–375/doc0370.html, 351–75.

3. #282 Memorandum from Gordon Chase of the National Security Council: "Isolation of Cuba," 14 February 1963, *FRUS, 1962–1963, XI,* 700.

4. Ileana Fuentes, interview in Ochoa, *Never Ever Neverland*.

5. See, for example, Encinosa, *Cuba en Guerra,* 132.

6. Eusebio Leal interview in Bravo and Gómez, *Operación Peter Pan,* 299, 288 (my translation).

7. Quoted by Sutherland, *Youngest Revolution,* 24.

8. Grupo Areíto, *Contra Viento y Marea,* 40 (my translation).

9. Carmen Romañach, in *50 Años de la Operación Pedro Pan* (TVMarti, 2013), http://www.martinoticias.com/a/17797.html.

10. Elisa (Ely) Chovel, interview by Conde, *Operation Pedro Pan,* 213. See also Torres, *Lost Apple,* 251.

11. Griego, "They Risked Everything."

12. John Dorschner, "The Pedro Pan Generation," *Miami Herald,* 22 September 2003, http://www.cubanet.org/htdocs/CNews/y03/sep03/22e6.htm.

13. DeWayne Wickham, "Send the Border Children to Guantánamo Bay," *Miami Times,* 9–15 July 2014, 1. The U.S. base at Guantánamo had been used to hold Cubans and Haitians who had tried to reach the United States by boat in the mid-1990s.

14. Sonia Almazán, interview by author, Havana, 12 May 2016.

15. Teresa de Jesús Fernández, "From This Side of the Fish Tank," in Torres, *By Heart/De Memoria,* 75–77.

16. Berta Álvarez, interview by author, Havana, 5 May 1999.

17. "Secrets and Official Lies," *Miami Herald,* 14 May 1998, 20A.

18. See Torres v. Central Intelligence Agency (U.S. District Court), 15 December 1998, PedroPan.org, http://www.pedropan.org/sites/default/files/December%2015%20 1998%20US%20DISTRICT%20COURT%20RULING%20ON%20THE%20REDACTIVE%20PROCESS%20EMPLOYED%20BY%20THE%20CIA.pdf.

19. Masud-Piloto, *From Welcomed Exiles,* xvii–xviii.

20. Conde, *Operation Pedro Pan,* xiii–xiv.

21. Susan Maret and Lea Aschkenas, "Operation Pedro Pan: The Hidden History of 14,000 Cuban Children," *Government Secrecy: Research in Social Problems and Public Policy* 19 (2011): 174.

22. #360 Memorandum from the Chief of Operations, Operation Mongoose (Lansdale) to the Special Group (Augmented) 25 July 1962. This review of Operation Mongoose stated: "State is responsible for refugee political policy matters, assisted by CIA in daily liaison." *FRUS, 1961–1962, X,* 880.

23. Torres, *Lost Apple,* 238.

24. Alex López, interview by author, Washington, D.C., 10 September 2001.

25. Msgr. Walsh, conversation with author, LASA conference, Miami, 16 March 2000. When interviewed by Cuban filmmakers, Msgr. Walsh was reluctant to accept any responsibility for those children who had problems while in care. See Bravo, *Operación Peter Pan* (film).

26. Antonia Cereijido, "The Lost Children of Cuba: Operation Pedro Pan," *Latino USA*, NPR, 12 June 2015, http://latinousa.org/2015/06/12/the-lost-children-of-cuba-operation-pedro-pan.

27. Sergio López-Miró, interview in Ochoa, *Never Ever Neverland*.

28. Poem by an anonymous Pedro Pan, http://www.teresita.org/disconnected.html, accessed 23 December 2001.

29. Torreira and Buajasán, *Operación Peter Pan*, 370–79; and Torres, *Lost Apple*, 201.

30. Torres, *Lost Apple*, 192–93.

31. See Fabián Escalante, *JFK: The Cuba Files: The Untold Story of the Plot to Kill Kennedy* (Melbourne: Ocean Press, 2006).

32. Andrés Gómez, "Miles de niños Cubanos víctimas de la CIA. La 'Operación Peter Pan' es otro de los grandes ataques contra el pueblo de la Isla," *Resumen Latinamericano* (Argentina) 47 (May–June 2000): 4 (my translation). Andrés Gómez was one of the key founders of the Areíto group in Miami and the Antonio Maceo Brigade that organized the visits of young Cuban Americans to the island.

33. María Masud, interview by author, Dallas, 29 March 2003.

34. Lisandro Pérez, "Reflections on the Future of Cuba," *Cuban Studies* 39 (2008): 89.

35. "Memorandum on Preparing Cuban Refugees to Contribute to Education for Democracy in Cuba," paper presented by James D. Baker to the Senate Subcommittee hearings, *Cuban Refugee Problem*, 6 December 1961, 35–38.

BIBLIOGRAPHY

Primary Sources

ARCHIVES AND LIBRARIES

Biblioteca Nacional José Marti, Havana
Biblioteca del Arzobispado de la Habana, Havana
Centro de Investigaciones Históricas de la Seguridad del Estado (CIHSE) [Center for Historical Investigations on State Security/Ministry of the Interior Museum now called Memorial de la denuncia]
Cuban Heritage Collection, University of Miami Libraries, Coral Gables, Miami, FL
Florida International University, Special Collections Archives: Cuban Living History Project, 1990–1998, Oral histories. Interviews conducted by Miguel González-Pando.
General Records of the Department of State, U.S. Embassy Havana, Microfiche of Record Group 59. New York University Library, New York.
Historical Museum of South Florida (now called History/Miami Museum)
Lourdes Casals Library, Center for Cuban Studies, New York City.
Walsh, Monsignor Bryan O., Papers. Barry University Archives and Special Collections, Miami Shores, Florida
Museo de la Alfabetización, Havana
National Security Archive, Cuba Collection / Bay of Pigs, Washington, D.C.
Partido Comunista de Cuba Archives, Havana
Prensa Latina, photographic archive, Havana
Tamiment Archive, New York University Library, New York

INTERVIEWS BY THE AUTHOR

Sonia Almazán (former *brigadista*), 6 September 2007, Montreal, and 12 May 2016, Havana.
Berta Álvarez Martens (former *brigadista*), 5 May 1999, Havana.
Jesús Arboleya (literacy *brigadista*, former diplomat at the Cuban Interests Section in Washington, D.C., and the Cuban U.N. Mission in New York), 23 April 1999 and 6 May 2016, Havana.
Noel Betancourt, 19 April 1999, Havana. (Noel was sent with his younger brother as unaccompanied minors on student visas to Miami in November 1960.)

Col. (r.) José Buajasán (co-author of the Cuban report, *Operación Peter Pan*), 19 April 1999 and 11 May 2016, Havana.
Ramón Torreira (co-author of the Cuban report, *Operación Peter Pan*), 19 April 1999.
José Cabañas (former MINREX official responsible for Cubans abroad, later first Cuban ambassador in Washington, D.C., after diplomatic relations were restored in 2015), Havana, 4 May 1999.
Gen. (r.) Fabián Escalante (former head of Cuban State Security), 20 April 1999 and 13 May 2016, Havana.
Armando Hart (former Minister of Education), 17 January 2001, Havana.
Alex López (former Pedro Pan), 10 September 2001, Washington, D.C.
María Masud (former Pedro Pan), 29 March 2003, Dallas, TX.
José Miller (director of Havana *patronato* or synagogue), 26 April 1999, Havana.
Manuel Moro (acting director of the literacy campaign's publicity department), 3 May 1999 and 13 and 24 January 2001, Havana.
Mirta Muñiz (executive member of the literacy campaign's publicity department), April–May 1999, Havana. (Mirta Muñiz was the director of the Havana office of Ocean Press, 1992–2001.)
Ana Riewerts (former Pedro Pan), 16 May 2002 (taped telephone interview from New York).
Nicolás and Silvia Ríos (Cuban émigrés), 11 May 1999, Miami. (Silvia's brother was a Pedro Pan.)
Javier Salado (former *brigadista*), 25 April 1999, Havana.
Nelson Valdés (former Pedro Pan), 29 March 2003, Dallas, TX.
Dr. Antonio Villaverde (former dean of the Catholic Social University of La Salle), 28 April 1999, Havana.
Msgr. Bryan O. Walsh, 20 March 2000, Miami.

OTHER PRIMARY SOURCES

Báez, Luis. "Al líder de ustedes lo protege alguién más que el G-2" (interview with Leopoldina [Polita] Grau). *Juventud Rebelde* (28 November 1993).
Baker, James D. "The Beginning of the Pedro Pan Program in Cuba." Unpublished manuscript, box 26, Monsignor Bryan O. Walsh Papers, Barry University, Miami.
———. "Memorandum on Preparing Refugees to Contribute to Education for Democracy in Cuba." Presented to the hearings of the Senate Subcommittee, 6 December 1961. In *Cuban Refugee Problem*, 87th Congress, 1st sess., pp. 35–38.
———. *Ruston: From Dreams to Reality*. Ruston-Baker Educational Institution, 2007. www.rustonacademy.net/getbakerbook.html.
Bell, José, Delia Luisa López, and Tania Caram, eds. *Documentos de la revolución cubana 1959*. Havana: Editorial de Ciencias Sociales, 2008.
———. *Documentos de la revolución cubana 1960*. Havana: Editorial de Ciencias Sociales, 2008.
Bonachea, Rolando E., and Nelson P. Valdés. *Revolutionary Struggle, 1947–1958: Volume 1 of the Selected Works of Fidel Castro*. Cambridge, MA: MIT Press, 1972.

Bonsal, Philip W. *Cuba, Castro, and the United States*. Pittsburgh: University of Pittsburgh Press, 1971.
Bravo, Estela, and Olga Rosa Gómez Cortés, eds. *Operación Peter Pan: Cerrando el círculo en Cuba*. Havana: Casa de las Américas, 2013.
Caso Imprenta [Print Shop Case]. Cuban state security report, 18 September 1961. CIHSE Archives, Havana.
Castro, Fidel. *Educación y revolución*. Mexico, D.F.: Editorial Nuestro Tiempo, 1983.
———. *El pensamiento de Fidel Castro: Selección temática. Tomo 1/2. Enero 1959–abril 1961*. Havana: Editora Política, 1983.
———. *Fidel and Religion: Conversations with Frei Betto on Marxism and Liberation Theology*. Melbourne: Ocean Press, 2006.
———. *Fidel in Chile: Major Fidel Castro's Speeches during His Visit to Chile*. New York: International Publishers, 1972.
———. *La Fortaleza Conquistada*. Havana: Editorial Abril, 1987.
———. *La Revolución Cubana, 1953/1962*. Mexico, D.F.: Ediciones Era, 1972.
———. *My Life: A Spoken Autobiography with Ignacio Ramonet*. London: Penguin Books, 2007.
———. Press conference at the closing function of the second International Havana Cigar Festival, at PABEXPO, 4 March 2000. http://www.cuba.cu/gobierno/discursos/2000/ing/f040300i.html
———. "Report to the First Congress of the Cuban Communist Party." In *First Congress of the Communist Party of Cuba, Havana 17-22 December 1975*, pp. 15–260. Moscow: Progress Publishers.
Chang, Lawrence, and Peter Kornbluh, eds. *The Cuban Missile Crisis, 1962: A National Security Archive Documents Reader*. New York: The New Press, 1992.
Children of Pedro Pan. "Pledge of Thanksgiving," 23 November 1990, Miami, Florida. Box 12, Msgr. Bryan O. Walsh Papers, Barry University, Miami.
CIA. *Cuban Counter Revolutionary Handbook* (1962). Cuban Information Archives. http://cuban-exile.com/doc_351-375/doc0370.html.
Close, Kathryn. "Cuban Children away from Home." *Children* 10, no. 1 (January–February 1963): 3–10.
Comisión Nacional de Alfabetización de Ministerio de Educación. *Alfabeticemos!* Havana: Imprenta Nacional de Cuba, 1961.
———. *Cumpliremos! Temas sobre la Revolución para los Alfabetizadores*. Havana: Imprenta Nacional de Cuba, 1961.
———. *Venceremos!* Havana: Imprenta Nacional de Cuba, 1961.
Conferencia: "La nación y la emigración," Abril 1994, La Habana, Cuba. Havana: Editora Política, 1994.
Conferencia de Obispos Católicos de Cuba. *La Voz de la Iglesia en Cuba: 100 Documentos Episcopales*. Mexico, D.F.: Obra Nacional de la Buena Prensa, 1995.
Cortés, Carlos E., ed. *Cuban Exiles in the United States*. New York: Arno Press, 1980.
———. *Cuban Refugee Programs*. New York: Arno Press, 1980.
———. *The Cuban Experience in the United States*. New York: Arno Press, 1980.

Cuba y la Conferencia de Educación y Desarrollo Económico y Social. Havana: Editorial Nacional de Cuba, March 1962.
Cuba–Girón: La gran conjura. Cuadernos de Estudios. Havana: Centro de Investigaciones Operativas del MININT, April 1994.
de la Campa, Román. *Cuba on My Mind: Journeys to a Severed Nation.* London: Verso, 2000.
del Mar, Marcia. *A Cuban Story.* Winston-Salem, NC: John F. Blair Publisher, 1979.
Deutschmann, David, ed. *Che Guevara Reader: Writings on Politics and Revolution.* Melbourne: Ocean Press, 2003.
Deutschmann, David, and Deborah Shnookal, eds. *Fidel Castro Reader.* Melbourne: Ocean Press, 2017.
Directorio Revolucionario Estudiantil. *Nuestro Plan de Liberación.* DRE pamphlet, ca. 1961–1962. Directorio Revolucionario Estudiantil en exilio, Cuban Heritage Collection, University of Miami Libraries, Coral Gables, Florida.
———. *Ideario.* DRE pamphlet, n.d. Directorio Revolucionario Estudiantil en exilio, Cuban Heritage Collection, University of Miami Libraries, Coral Gables, Florida.
Dubelman, Abraham. "Cuba." In *American Jewish Year Book.* Vol. 63. Philadelphia: American Jewish Committee and Jewish Publication Society of America, 1962.
Echazábal, Eloísa. "Eloisa's Story." Pedro Pan Exodus, http://pedropanexodus.com/eloisas-story/.
"Educational Program of the Dade Country Schools for Cuban Refugee Children and Adults," 1 December 1961, Box 29, Monsignor Bryan O. Walsh Papers, Barry University, Miami.
Eire, Carlos. *Learning to Die in Miami: Confessions of a Refugee Boy.* New York: The Free Press, 2010.
———. *Waiting for Snow in Havana: Confessions of a Cuban Boy.* New York: The Free Press, 2003.
El Indio Naborí. *Cartilla y farol: Poemas militantes.* Havana, 1982.
Elliston, Jon, ed. *Psywar on Cuba: The Declassified History of U.S. Anti-Castro Propaganda.* Melbourne: Ocean Press, 1999.
¿En qué tiempo puede cambiare la mente de un niño? Mesa redonda sobre Elián González. Edición especial para la familia cubana. Havana: Editorial Abril, 1999.
Espín, Vilma. *La batalla de la igualdad no es solo de las mujeres, es de toda la sociedad.* Havana: Editorial de la mujer, 1988.
Fernández, Alina. *Castro's Daughter: An Exile's Memoir of Cuba.* New York: St. Martin's Press, 1998.
Ferrer, Raúl. "La ley de nacionalización de la enseñanza." In *Alfabetización, nacionalización de la enseñanza,* ed. Ministerio de Educación. Havana: Imprenta Nacional de Cuba, 1961.
Foreign Broadcast Information Service (FBIS) Daily Report (Cuba) 1959–1962.
FYI—The Plight of Pepito: Cuba's Lost Generation. WTVJ video, 1961. https://www.floridamemory.com/items/show/245399.
García Gallo, Gaspar J. "Educar: tarea decisiva de la Revolución." In *Escuela y Revolución en*

Cuba 1, no. 1. Havana: Ministerio de Educación y el Sindicato Nacional de Trabajadores de la Enseñanza y la Ciencia, December 1962–January 1963.
García Luis, Julio, ed. *Cuban Revolution Reader: A Documentary History of Fidel Castro's Revolution.* Melbourne: Ocean Press, 2008.
Gómez, Andrés. "Miles de niños Cubanos víctimas de la CIA. La 'Operación Peter Pan' es otro de los grandes ataques contra el pueblo de la Isla." *Resumen Latinoamericano* (Argentina) 47 (May–June 2000).
González, Flora. "I Was an 'Elián' of the Early 1960s." *Boston Globe* (3 February 2000).
González-Pando, Miguel. Cuban Living History Project of Florida International University. https://fiu.catalog.fcla.edu/fi.jsp?st=Gonz%C3%A1lez-Pando&ix=kw&fl=bo&fa=materialtypes_facet%3AVideo%5C+%5C%28all%5C+formats%5C%29&S=2031573004032314&fa=corpauthor_facet%3AFlorida%5C+International%5C+University%5C+Cuban%5C+Living%5C+History%5C+Project.
Grau Alsina, Ramón "Mongo," and Valerie Ridderhoff. *Cuba desde 1930.* Madrid: Agualarga Editores, S.L., 1997.
Grupo Areíto. *Contra el viento y marea.* Havana: Casa de las Américas, 1978.
Guevara, Ernesto Che. *Reminiscences of the Cuban Revolutionary War.* Melbourne: Ocean Press, 2006.
Hart, Armando. *Aldabonazo: Inside the Cuban Revolutionary Underground, 1952–1958.* New York: Pathfinder Press, 2004.
———. "Dos capítulos del mensaje educacional a la nación: Educación, sociedad y estado." *Nueva Revista Cubana* 2, no. 1 (January–May 1960): 162–71.
———. *Informe del Ministro de Educación de Cuba sobre la lucha contra el analfabetismo y tarea de la Sociedad y los estudiantes.* Havana: Ministerio de Educación, July 1961.
Huberman, Leo, and Paul M. Sweezy. *Cuba: Anatomy of a Revolution.* 2nd ed. New York: Monthly Review Press, 1961.
Hunt, Howard. *Give Us This Day.* New Rochelle, NY: Arlington House, 1973.
Kenner, Martin, and James Petras, eds. *Fidel Castro Speaks.* Harmondsworth, Middlesex: Penguin Books, 1972.
Kornbluh, Peter, ed. *The Bay of Pigs Declassified: The Secret CIA Report on the Invasion of Cuba.* New York: The New Press, 1998.
Lewis, Oscar, Ruth M. Lewis, and Susan M. Rigdon. *Four Men: Living the Revolution: An Oral History of Contemporary Cuba.* Urbana: University of Illinois Press, 1977.
———. *Four Women: Living the Revolution: An Oral History of Contemporary Cuba.* Urbana: University of Illinois Press, 1977.
———. *Neighbors: Living the Revolution: An Oral History of Contemporary Cuba.* Urbana: University of Illinois Press, 1978.
López, Alex. "Dos años en Matecumbe y Florida City." *Areíto* 5, no. 17 (1978).
Lorenzetto, Anna, and Karel Neys. *Methods and Means Utilized in Cuba to Eliminate Illiteracy. UNESCO Report.* Havana: Editora Pedagogica, 1965.
The Lost Apple. Directed by Cliff Solway, produced by David Susskind. Talent Associates–Paramount, 1963.
March, Aleida. *Remembering Che: My Life with Che Guevara.* Melbourne: Ocean Press, 2011.

Medina, Pablo. *Exiled Memories: A Cuban Childhood*. New York: Persea Books, 2002.
MINFAR. *Manual de Capacitación Cívica*. Havana: Ministerio de las Fuerzas Armadas Revolucionarias, 1960.
Ministerio de Educación. *Alfabetización, Nacionalización de la Enseñanza*. Havana: Imprenta Nacional de Cuba, April 1961.
———. *Congreso de Alfabetización, 2–5 Septiembre, Documentos*. Havana: Ministerio de Educación, 1961.
———. *Educación y Revolución: Universidad Popular. Sexto Ciclo*. Havana: Imprenta Nacional de Cuba, 1961.
Mitchell, William L. "The Cuban Refugee Program." *Social Security Bulletin* 25, no. 3 (1962): 3–8.
Movimiento Democrata Cristiano de Cuba. *Nuestra Postura*. Pamphlets Collection 26, c. 1962. Grupos Políticos Cubanos en el exilio, Cuban Heritage Collection, University of Miami Libraries, Coral Gables, Florida.
Movimiento Unidad Revolucionario. *Conozca lo que ocurrirá a usted y a su país*. Pamphlets Collection 2, ca. 1962. History and Politics in Cuba, Cuban Heritage Collection, University of Miami Libraries, Coral Gables, Florida.
Mujica, René J. "Some Recollections of My Experiences in the Cuban Literacy Campaign." *Journal of Reading* 25, no. 3 (December 1981).
Ochoa, Marina, dir. *Never Ever Neverland*. ICAIC, 2015.
Ochoa, Marina, and Guillermo Centeno, dirs. *Del Otro Lado del Cristal*. ICAIC, 1995.
Oettinger, Katherine Brownell. "Services to Unaccompanied Cuban Refugee Children in the United States." *Social Service Review* 36, no. 4 (1962): 377–84.
"La patria potestad pasarán a poder de estado todos los niños desde los tres años de edad." Chain letter to Cuban mothers. CIHSE Archives, Havana.
"Pedro Pan Exodus: Margarita Oteiza, Ruston Academy, Cuban Boys Home, Matecumbe Professor." Interview by Eloisa Echazábel and Carmen Romañach. 31 March 2010. YouTube video posted 3 December 2014.
Pérez Firmat, Gustavo. *Next Year in Cuba: A Cubano's Coming of Age in America*. New York: Anchor/Doubleday, 1996.
Phillips, David Atlee. *The Night Watch*. New York: Ballantine, 1977.
Phillips, R. Hart. *Cuba: Island of Paradox*. New York: An Oblonsky Book. Astor–Honor, 1959.
———. *The Cuban Dilemma*. New York: An Oblonsky Book. Astor–Honor, 1962.
"República de Cuba; Ministerio de Educación. Doctor Osvaldo Dorticós Torrado..." Ley No. 31 August 1961. Copy of false *patria potestad* law. CIHSE Archives, Havana.
Rodríguez-Nogués, Lourdes. "Psychological Effects of Premature Separation from Parents in Cuban Refugee Girls: A Retrospective Study." Ph.D. diss., Boston University School of Education, 1983.
Rodríguez Rodríguez, Inocencia, ed. *Asociación de Jóvenes Rebeldes, Documentos para una historia de future*. Havana: Editorial Abril, 1989.
Sartre, Jean-Paul. *Sartre on Cuba*. New York: Ballantine Books, 1961.
Soldani Lemon, Melissa. *Are They White? American Families Offer to Open Their Homes to (Some) Cuban Refugee Children*, Kindle edition. Amazon Digital Services LLC, 2014.

Spokane Diocese Cuban Children's Program. "Second Annual Newsletter," January 1968. Box 16, Monsignor Bryan O. Walsh Papers, Barry University, Miami.

Strong, Sr. Miriam. "Refugees from Castro's Cuba: 'Of Fish and Freedom': A Historical Account of the Cuban Refugees Received and Relieved by His Excellency Bishop Coleman F. Carroll in the Catholic Diocese of Miami, Florida, 1959–1964." Master's thesis, Fordham University, 1964.

Sutherland, Elizabeth. *The Youngest Revolution: A Personal Report on Cuba.* London: Pittman Publishing, 1970.

Taber, Robert. *M–26: Biography of a Revolution.* New York: Lyle Stuart, 1961.

Thomas, John F. "Cuban Refugee Program." *Welfare in Review* 1, no. 3 (1963): 1–20.

———. "Cuban Refugees in the U.S." *International Migration Review* 1/2 (1967): 46–57.

———. *The Cuban Refugee Program: Aiding Children and Youth.* Report prepared for the DHEW, 10 March 1964. Box 29, Monsignor Bryan O. Walsh Papers, Barry University, Miami.

———. "U.S.A. as a Country of First Asylum." *International Migration Review* 3, nos. 1 and 2 (1965): 5–14.

Torres, María de los Angeles, ed. *By Heart/De Memoria: Cuban Women's Journeys in and out of Exile.* Philadelphia: Temple University Press, 2003.

Torres v. Central Intelligence Agency. 39F. Supp. 2d 960: Torres v. CIA. Illinois Northern District Court–39 F. Supp. 2d 960. 12 March 1999. Decisions of the U.S. District Court, posted on www.pedropan.org 26 July 2014. http://www.pedropan.org/sites/default/files/March%2015%201999%20US%20DISTRICT%20COURT%20RULING%20ON%20THE%20ROLE%20OF%20THE%20CIA%20IN%20OPERATION%20PEDRO%20PAN.pdf

———. 29 F. Supp. 2d 497: Torres v. CIA. Illinois Northern District Court–29 F. Supp. 2d 497. 15 December 1998. http://www.pedropan.org/sites/default/files/December%2015%201998%20US%20DISTRICT%20COURT%20RULING%20ON%20THE%20REDACTIVE%20PROCESS%20EMPLOYED%20BY%20THE%20CIA.pdf

Universidad Popular. *Educación y Revolución.* Havana: Imprenta Nacional de Cuba, April 1961.

U.S. Department of Health, Education and Welfare (DHEW), Children's Bureau. *Cuba's Children in Exile: The Story of the Unaccompanied Cuban Refugee Children's Program.* Washington, D.C.: Government Printing Office, 1967, 1–14.

———. *Facts About the Unaccompanied Cuban Refugee Children's Program: How to Apply for a Cuban Child*, 15 January 1963, pp. 3–4. File 514, Lourdes Casals Library, Center for Cuban Studies, New York.

U.S. Department of State. Publication 7171, *Cuba.* Washington: Department of State, 1961.

———. *Foreign Relations of the United States: Cuba, 1958–1960*, VI. Washington, D.C.: Government Printing Office, 1991.

———. *Foreign Relations of the United States: Cuba, 1961–1962*, X. Washington, D.C.: Government Printing Office, 1997.

———. *Foreign Relations of the United States: Cuban Missile Crisis and Aftermath, 1961–1963*, XI. Washington, D.C.: Government Printing Office, 1996.

U.S. Senate, Committee on the Judiciary. *Cuban Refugee Problem.* Hearings before the Sub-

committee to investigate Problems connected with Refugees and Escapees, 87th Congress, 1st sess., 6, 7 and 13 December 1961, pp. 1–304. Washington, D.C.: Government Printing Office, 1962.

———. *Cuban Refugee Problem. Hearings before the Subcommittee to investigate Problems connected with Refugees and Escapees.* 87th Congress, 2d sess.: Part II, 3 and 4 December 1962, pp. 305–399. Washington, D.C.: Government Printing Office, 1963.

U.S. Senate Select Committee. *Alleged Assassination Plots involving Foreign Leaders. An Interim Report.* Washington, D.C.: Government Printing Office, 1975.

Veciana, Antonio, with Carlos Harrison. *Trained to Kill: The Inside Story of CIA Plots against Castro, Kennedy, and Che.* New York: Skyhorse Publishing, 2017.

Voorhees, Tracy S. *Interim Report on the Cuban Refugee Problem*, 19 December 1960, in *U.S. Department of State Bulletin.* Washington, D.C.: Government Printing Office, 9 January 1961.

———. *Report to the President of the United States on the Cuban Refugee Problem.* Washington, D.C.: U.S. Government Printing Office, 18 January 1961.

Walsh, Fr. Bryan O. Speech delivered at the Southeastern Regional Meeting of the National Conference of Catholic Charities, Richmond, Virginia, 26 March 1962. Box 45, Monsignor Bryan O. Walsh Papers, Barry University, Miami.

———. "The Community Looks at the Problem: The Church." Paper presented at the National Resettlement Conference for Cuban Refugees, Miami, Florida, 30 January 1961. Box 18, Monsignor Bryan O. Walsh Papers, Barry University, Miami.

Walsh, Msgr. Bryan O. "Cuban Refugee Children." *Journal of Inter-American Studies and World Affairs* 13: 3–4 (July–October, 1971): 378–415.

———. "Cubans in Miami." *America* 114, no. 9 (26 February 1966): 286–89.

———. "Operation Pedro Pan." Paper presented at Barry University Convocation, 40th Anniversary Convocation, 9 November 2001. Box 18, Monsignor Bryan O. Walsh Papers, Barry University, Miami.

———. "Recollection of Havana Trip," 25 March 1963. Box 44, Monsignor Bryan O. Walsh Papers, Barry University, Miami.

———. "The Origins of Operation Pedro Pan." Paper presented at the Pedro Pan Conference, Florida International University, Miami, FL., 20–21 April 2001. Box 44, Monsignor Bryan O. Walsh Papers, Barry University, Miami.

White, Mark J., ed. *The Kennedys and Cuba: The Declassified Documentary History.* Chicago: Ivan R. Dee, 1999.

Secondary Sources

50 Años de la Operación Pedro Pan. TV Martí special, 2013. http://www.martinoticias.com/a/17797.html.

Abendroth, Mark. *Rebel Literacy: Cuba's National Literacy Campaign and Critical Global Citizenship.* Duluth, MN: Litwin Books, 2009.

Adessa, Rev. Domenick Joseph. "Refugee Cuban Children: The Role of the Catholic Welfare Bureau of the Diocese of Miami, Florida, in Receiving, Caring for, and Placing Unaccompanied Cuban Refugee Children, 1960–1963." Master's thesis, Fordham University, 1964.

Alfabetización 50 Años. 1961–2011, Bohemia. Edición especial, 30 December 2011.
Alonso, Dora. *El Año 61*. Havana: Editorial Letras Cubanas, 1981.
Andrew, Christopher. *For the President's Eyes Only*. New York: HarperCollins, 1995.
Arboleya, Jesús. "La influencia de la cultura norteamericana en Cuba." *CubaDebate*, 1 August 2016. http://www.cubadebate.cu/opinion/2016/8/1/la-influencia-de-la-cultura-norteamericana-en-cuba.
———. *The Cuban Counterrevolution*. Athens, OH: Center for International Studies, Ohio University, 2000.
Arboleya Cervera, Jesús, Raúl Alzaga Manresa, and Ricardo Fraga del Valle. *La Contrarrevolución Cubana en Puerto Rico y el Caso de Carlos Muñiz Varela*. San Juan: Ediciones Callejón, 2016.
Arce, Sergio. *The Church and Socialism: Reflections from a Cuban Context*. New York: Circus Publications, 1985.
Ares, Guillermina. *Alfabetización en Cuba: Historia y testimonios*. Havana: Editora Política, 2000.
Arguelles, Lourdes. "The U.S. National Security State: The CIA and Cuban Émigré Terrorism." *Race and Class* 23, no. 4 (1982): 287–304.
Armengol Acierno, María. *Children of Flight Pedro Pan*. New York: Silver Moon Press, 1994.
Arnove, Robert F., and Harvey T. Graff, eds. *National Literacy Campaigns*. New York: Plenum Press, 1987.
Azicri, Max. *Cuba: Politics, Economics, and Society*. London: Pinter Publishers, 1988.
Baker, Donald P. "A Journey out of the Past for 'Pedro Pan' Project." *Washington Post*, 26 January 1998.
Bell, Maya. "Operation Pedro Pan." *Orlando Sentinel*, 10 December 1994.
Belmonte, Laura A. *Selling the American Way: U.S. Propaganda and the Cold War*. Philadelphia: University of Pennsylvania Press, 2008.
Bengelsdorf, Carollee, and Alice Hageman. "Emerging from Underdevelopment: Women and Work in Cuba." *Race and Class* 19, no. 4 (1978): 361–78.
Benson, Devyn Spence. *Antiracism in Cuba: The Unfinished Revolution*. Chapel Hill: University of North Carolina Press, 2016.
———. "Not Blacks, but Citizens! Racial Politics in Revolutionary Cuba, 1959–1961." Ph.D. diss., University of North Carolina at Chapel Hill, 2009.
Betancourt, Luis Adrián. *¿Por Qué Carlos?* Havana: Editorial Letras Cubanas, 1981.
Bikel, Ofra, dir. *Saving Elián*. Frontline, PBS, February 2001.
Bissell, Richard. *Reflections of a Cold Warrior: From Yalta to the Bay of Pigs*. New Haven: Yale University Press, 1996.
Blight, James G., and Peter Kornbluh, eds. *Politics of Illusion: The Bay of Pigs Invasion Reexamined*. Boulder, CO: Lynne Rienner Publishers, 1998.
Blum, Denise. "Cuban Youth and Revolutionary Values." Ph.D. diss., University of Texas, Austin, 2002.
Bohning, Don. *The Castro Obsession: U.S. Covert Operations against Cuba, 1959–1965*. Dulles, VA: Potomac Books, 2005.

Bonachea, Rolando E., and Nelson P. Valdés, eds. *Cuba in Revolution*. New York: Anchor Books, 1972.
Bowles, Samuel. "Cuban Education and the Revolutionary Ideology." *Harvard Educational Review* 41 no. 4 (1971): 472–500.
Bravo, Estela, dir. *Operación Peter Pan: Cerrando el círculo en Cuba*. BravoFilms, 2011.
Briggs, Laura. *Somebody's Children: The Politics of Transracial and Transnational Adoption*. Durham, NC: Duke University Press, 2012.
Brocklehurst, Helen. *Who's Afraid of Children: Children, Conflict, and International Relations*. Burlington, VT: Ashgate Publishing, 2006.
Buchsbaum, Herbert. "Cuban 'Peter Pan' Honored." *Miami Herald*, 2 October 1986.
Bunck, Julie Marie. *Fidel Castro and the Quest for a Revolutionary Culture in Cuba*. University Park: Pennsylvania State University Press, 1994.
Callan, Emily C. "Bringing Operation Pedro Pan Back from Never Never Land: Is INA 207(B) the President's Solution to the Humanitarian Crisis at the Border?" *St. Thomas Law Review* 27, no. 2 (2015): 166–85.
Calvo, Hernando, and Katlijn Declercq. *Cuban Exile Movement: Dissidents or Mercenaries?* Melbourne: Ocean Press, 1999.
Carbonell, Nestor T. *And The Russians Stayed: The Sovietization of Cuba: A Personal Portrait*. New York: William Morrow, 1989.
Cardona, Joe, and Mario de Varona, dirs. *The Flight of Pedro Pan: An Untold American Story*. WPBT Channel 2, 1999. Barry University Library, Miami, Florida.
Casavantes Bradford, Anita. "Remembering Pedro Pan: Childhood and Collective Memory Making in Havana and Miami, 1960–2000." *Cuban Studies* 44 (2016): 283–308.
———. *The Revolution Is for the Children: The Politics of Childhood in Havana and Miami, 1959–1962*. Chapel Hill: University of North Carolina Press, 2014.
———. "Understanding Elián: The Politics of Childhood in Miami and Havana, 1959–1962." Ph.D. diss., University of California, San Diego, 2011.
Cereijido, Antonia. "The Lost Children of Cuba: Operation Pedro Pan." Latino USA, NPR, 12 June 2015. http://latinousa.org/2015/06/12/the-lost-children-of-cuba-operation-pedro-pan.
Chase, Michelle. *Revolution within the Revolution: Women and Gender Politics in Cuba, 1952–1962*. Chapel Hill: University of North Carolina Press, 2015.
Chaviano, Hugo. "Cuban Parents' Fears Were Real." *Chicago Tribune*, 21 January 1998.
"CIA and Pedro Pan." *Miami Herald*, 14 January 1998.
Cimientos. Mundo Latino, 1995.
Clark, Juan M. "The Exodus from Revolutionary Cuba, 1959–1974: A Sociological Analysis." Ph.D. diss., University of Florida, 1975.
Conde, Yvonne M. *Operation Pedro Pan: The Untold Exodus of 14,048 Cuban Children*. New York: Routledge, 1999.
Corn, David. *Blond Ghost: Ted Shackley and the CIA's Crusades*. New York: Simon and Schuster, 1994.
Crahan, Margaret E. "Catholicism in Cuba." *Cuban Studies*, 19 (January 1989): 3–24.
Curnow, Ena. "Afirma Monseñor Walsh que Pedro Pan fue obra humanitaria." *Diario de Américas*, 16 January 1998.

de la Fuente, Alejandro. *A Nation for All: Race, Inequality, and Politics in Twentieth-Century Cuba*. Chapel Hill: University of North Carolina Press, 2001.
De La Torre, Miguel A. *La Lucha for Cuba: Religion and Politics on the Streets of Miami*. Berkeley: University of California Press, 2003.
de Valle, Elaine. "Professor Plans to Sue CIA over Cuba Airlift Papers." *Miami Herald*, 12 January 1998.
Dewart, Leslie. *Cuba, Church, and Crisis*. London: Sheed and Ward, 1964.
Díaz, Jesús, dir. *55 Hermanos*. Havana: ICAIC, 1978.
Díaz, Jesús. *De la Patria y el Exilio*. Havana: Ediciones Union, 1979.
Díaz González, Cristina. *The Red Umbrella*. New York: Alfred A. Knopf, 2010.
Didion, Joan. *Miami*. New York: Vintage Books, 1987.
Domínguez, Jorge I. *Cuba: Order and Revolution*. Cambridge, Mass: The Belnap Press, 1978.
———. *U.S.-Latin American Relations during the Cold War and Its Aftermath*. Cambridge: Harvard University Weatherhead Center for International Affairs, January 1999.
Donahue, Marjorie L. "Operation Pedro Pan: How Thousands of Children Shuffled under Castro's Nose." *Voice*, 3 March 1978.
Dorschner, John. "The Pedro Pan Generation." *Miami Herald*, 22 September 2003. http://www.cubanet.org/htdocs/CNews/y03/sep03/22e6.htm.
Dubinsky, Karen. *Babies without Borders: Adoption and Migration across the Americas*. New York: New York University Press, 2010.
Duharte Jiménez, Rafael. "The 19th Century Black Fear." In *AfroCuba: An Anthology of Cuban Writing on Race, Politics, and Culture*, ed. Pedro Pérez Sarduy and Jean Stubbs, 37–46. Melbourne: Ocean Press, 1993.
Edgette, Judith. "Domestic Collection on Cuba." In *Studies in Intelligence*, CIA, Fall 1963. NND #947003, 41–45. Cuba Collection, National Security Archive, Washington, D.C.
Eire, Carlos. "Operation Pedro Pan: The Untold Exodus of 14,048 Cuban Children." Review *Operation Pedro Pan: The Untold Exodus of 14,048 Cuban Children*, by Yvonne Conde. *Hispanic American Historical Review* 81, nos. 3–4 (August–November 2001): 820–23. https://muse.jhu.edu/article/12604.
Encinosa, Enrique. *Cuba en Guerra: Historia de la oposición anti-Castrista 1959–1993*. Miami: Cuban American National Foundation, 1994.
Escalante, Fabián. *JFK: The Cuba Files. The Untold Story of the Plot to Kill Kennedy*. Melbourne: Ocean Press, 2006.
———. *The Cuba Project: CIA Covert Operations Against Cuba 1959–1962*. Melbourne: Ocean Press, 2004.
Escape from Havana: An American Story. CNBC documentary, 2010. http://classic.cnbc.com/id/37151179.
Fagen, Richard R. *Cuba: The Political Content of Adult Education*. Stanford: Hoover Institute of Studies, Stanford University, 1964.
———. *The Transformation of Political Culture in Cuba*. Stanford, CA: Stanford University Press, 1969.
Fagen, Richard R., Richard A. Brody, and Thomas J. O'Leary. *Cubans in Exile: Disaffection and the Revolution*. Stanford, CA: Stanford University Press, 1968.

Fanon, Frantz. *The Wretched of the Earth*. London: Penguin Books, 1990.
Fass, Paula S. "Children in Global Migrations." *Journal of Social History* 38, no. 4 (summer 2005): 937–53.
———. "The Memoir Problem." *Reviews of American History* 34, no. 1 (2006): 107–23.
Fernández, Alvaro F. "Operation Pedro Pan: A Horribly Black Mark on (U.S.) History." *Progreso Weekly*, 9 April 2009.
———. "The Pedro Pans Attack, but Only the Women." *Progreso Weekly*, 23 June 2010.
Fernández, Damián J. *Cuba and the Politics of Passion*. Austin: University of Texas Press, 2000.
———. "Youth in Cuba: Resistance and Accommodation." In *Conflict and Change in Cuba*, ed. Enrique A. Baloyra and James A. Morris, 189–211. Albuquerque: University of New Mexico Press, 1993.
Fernández, Damián J., and Madeline Cámara Betancourt, eds. *Cuba, the Elusive Nation: Interpretations of National Identity*. Gainesville: University Press of Florida, 2000.
Fernández, Lourdes. "30 Years Later, Pedro Pan Children Recall, Give Thanks." *Miami Herald*, 24 November 1990.
Fernández Soneira, Teresa. *Cuba: Historia de la Educación Católica 1582–1961, Tomo II*. Miami, FL: Ediciones Universal, 1997.
Foner, Philip S., ed. *On Education by José Martí: Articles on Educational Theory and Pedagogy, and Writings for Children from* The Age of Gold. New York: Monthly Review Press, 1979.
———. *Our America: Writings on Latin America and the Struggle for Cuban Independence by José Martí*. New York: Monthly Review Press, 1977.
Forgacs, David, ed. *The Gramsci Reader: Selected Writings, 1916–1935*. New York: New York University Press, 2000.
Fox, Geoffrey E. "Cuban Workers in Exile." *Trans-Action* 8 (September 1971): 21–30.
———. "Honor, Shame, and Women's Liberation in Cuba: Views of Working-Class Émigré Men." In *Female and Male in Latin America*, ed. Ann Pescatello, 273–89. Pittsburgh: University of Pittsburgh Press, 1973.
Freire, Paolo. *The Pedagogy of the Oppressed*. 30th anniversary ed. New York: Continuum, 2002.
García, María Cristina. *Havana USA: Cuban Exiles and Cuban Americans in South Florida, 1959–1994*. Berkeley: University of California Press, 1996.
Gay, Kathlyn. *Leaving Cuba: From Operation Pedro Pan to Elián*. Brookfield, CT: Twenty-First Century Books, 2000.
Geldof, Lynn. *Cubans: Voices of Change*. New York: St. Martin's Press, 1991.
Gil, Rosa María. "The Assimilation and Problems of Adjustment to the American Culture of One Hundred Cuban Refugee Adolescents Attending Catholic and Public High Schools in Union City and West New York, New Jersey, 1959–1966." Master's thesis, Fordham University, 1968.
Gleijeses, Piero. *Shattered Hope: The Guatemalan Revolution and the United States*. Princeton, NJ: Princeton University Press, 1991.
———. "Ships in the Night: The CIA, the White House, and the Bay of Pigs." *Journal of Latin American Studies* 27 (1995): 1–42.

González-Levy, Sandra. "Church, Cuban Exiles Must Reaffirm Their Mutual Respect." *Miami Herald*, 11 December 1997.
González-Mandri, Flora. "Operation Pedro Pan: A Tale of Trauma and Remembrance." Review of *The Lost Apple*, by María de los Angeles Torres, and *Sonia Flew*, by Melinda López. *Latino Studies* 6 (2008): 252–67.
González-Pando, Miguel. *The Cuban Americans*. Santa Barbara, CA: Greenwood Press, 1998.
Gott, Richard. "The Plan Is to Send Haiti's Orphans to the U.S.: But History Tells Us to Beware." *Guardian*, 19 January 2010.
Grandin, Greg. *The Last Colonial Massacre: Latin America in the Cold War*. Chicago: University of Chicago Press, 2004.
Griego, Tina. "They Risked Everything to Open a Door to Cuba: They Were Shunned for It." *Washington Post*, 5 January 2015.
Guerra, Lillian. "Elián González and the 'Real Cuba' of Miami: Visions of Identity, Exceptionality, and Divinity." *Cuban Studies* 38 (2007): 1–25.
———. "To Condemn the Revolution Is to Condemn Christ." *Hispanic American Historical Review* 89, no. 1 (2009): 73–109.
———. *Visions of Power in Cuba: Revolution, Redemption, and Resistance, 1959–1971*. Chapel Hill: University of North Carolina Press, 2012.
Gutiérrez Alea, Tomás, dir. *Memorias del subdesarrollo*. ICAIC, 1968.
Hageman, Alice L., and Philip E. Wheaton, eds. *Religion in Cuba Today: A New Church in a New Society*. New York: Association Press, 1971.
Halbert-Brooks, Ann E. "Revolutionary Teachers: Women and Gender in the Cuban Literacy Campaign of 1961." Master's thesis, University of North Carolina, 2013.
Halebsky, Sandor, and John M. Kirk, eds. *Cuba: Twenty-Five Years of Revolution, 1959–1984*. New York: Praeger, 1985.
———. *Cuba in Transition: Crisis and Transformation*. Boulder, CO: Westview Press, 1992.
———. *Transformation and Struggle: Cuba Faces the 1990s*. New York: Praeger, 1990.
Hamilton, Carrie. *Sexual Revolutions in Cuba: Passion, Politics, and Memory*. Chapel Hill: University of North Carolina Press, 2014.
Harris, Mark Jonathan, and Deborah Oppenheimer. *Into the Arms of Strangers: Stories of the Kindertransport*. New York: Bloomsbury Publishing, 2000.
Hernández, Rafael. "'La lucha entre lo nuevo y lo viejo fue en todas partes.' Entrevista al General (r) Fabián Escalante." *Temas* 56 (October–December 2008): 16–28.
Hernández, Rafael, Haraldo Dilla, Jennifer Dugan Abbassi, and Jean Díaz. "Political Culture and Popular Participation in Cuba." *Latin American Perspectives* 18, no. 2 (spring 1991): 38–54.
Hinckle, Warren, and William Turner. *Deadly Secrets: The CIA–Mafia War against Castro and the Assassination of JFK*. New York: Thunders Mouth Press, 1992.
Hirschfield Davis, Julie. "White House to End Exemption for Cubans Who Arrive without Visas." *New York Times*, 12 January 2017.
Holbrook, Joseph. "Catholic Student Movements in Latin America, Cuba, and Brazil, 1920s to 1960s." Ph.D. diss., Florida International University, 2013.

Holst, John D. *Social Movements, Civil Society, and Radical Adult Education.* Westport, CT: Bergin and Garvey, 2002.
Huberman, Leo, and Paul M. Sweezy. *Socialism in Cuba.* New York: Monthly Review Press, 1969.
Hynson, Rachel. "'Count, Capture, and Reeducate': The Campaign to Rehabilitate Cuba's Female Sex Workers, 1959–1962." *Journal of the History of Sexuality* 24, no. 1 (January 2015): 125–53. DOI: 10.1353/sex.2015.0005.
———. "Sex and State Making in Revolutionary Cuba, 1959–1968." Ph.D. diss., University of North Carolina, Chapel Hill, 2014.
Jeffreys-Jones, Rhodri. *The CIA and American Democracy.* New Haven: Yale University Press, 1989.
Jenkins, John, ed. *Travelers' Tales of Old Cuba.* Melbourne: Ocean Press, 2000.
Johnson, Candace. "Framing for Change: Social Policy, the State, and the Federación de Mujeres." *Cuban Studies* 42 (2011): 35–51.
Johnson, Dirk. "The Elián González Case: The Refugees; Children of 'Operation Pedro Pan' Recall Painful Separations from Parents." *New York Times*, 22 April 2000.
Johnson, Haynes. *The Bay of Pigs: The Leaders' Story of Brigade 2506.* New York: W.W. Norton, 1964.
Jolly, Richard. "Education." In *Cuba: Economic and Social Revolution*, ed. Dudley Seers, 160–255. Chapel Hill: University of North Carolina Press, 1964.
Jones, Cathy Areu. "Operation Pedro Pan: The Untold Story of a Cold War Conspiracy." *Oye Magazine* (ca. 2001). http://www.pedropan.org/sites/default/files/OyeMagazineCiaArticle[1]_0_0.pdf.
Judson, C. Fred. *Cuba and the Revolutionary Myth: The Political Education of the Cuban Rebel Army, 1953–1963.* Boulder, CO: Westview Press, 1984.
Kahl, Joseph. "The Moral Economy of a Revolutionary Society." *Trans-Action* 6, no. 6 (April 1969). http://link.springer.com/article/10.1007%2FBF02804735.
Kapcia, Antoni. *Cuba: Island of Dreams.* Oxford: Berg, 2000.
———. "Educational Revolution and the Revolutionary Morality in Cuba: The 'New Man,' Youth, and the New 'Battle of Ideas.'" *Journal of Moral Education* 34, no. 4 (December 2005): 399–412.
Kaplan, Dana Evan. "Fleeing the Revolution: The Exodus of Cuban Jewry in the Early 1960s." *Cuban Studies* 36 (2005): 129–54.
Kirk, John M. *Between God and the Party: Religion and Politics in Revolutionary Cuba.* Tampa: University of South Florida Press, 1989.
———. *José Martí: Mentor of the Cuban Nation.* Tampa: University of South Florida, 1983.
Kozol, Jonathan. "A New Look at the Literacy Campaign in Cuba." *Harvard Educational Review* 18, no. 3 (1978): 341–77.
———. *Children of the Revolution: A Yankee Teacher in the Cuban Schools.* New York: Dell Publishing, 1978.
Lanier, Alfred. "Operation Pedro Pan's Code of Silence." *Chicago Tribune*, 15 January 1998.
Legarreta, Dorothy. *The Guernica Generation: Basque Refugee Children of the Spanish Civil War.* Reno: University of Nevada Press, 1984.

Leiner, Marvin. *Children Are the Revolution: Day Care in Cuba*. Harmondsworth: Penguin Books, 1978.
———. *Sexual Politics in Cuba: Machismo, Homosexuality and AIDS*. Boulder: Westview Press, 1994.
———. "The 1961 National Cuban Literacy Campaign." In *National Literacy Campaigns*, ed. Robert F. Arnove and Harvey T. Graff, 173–96. New York: Plenum Press, 1987.
LeoGrande, William M., and Peter Kornbluh. *Back Channel to Cuba: The Hidden History of Negotiations between Washington and Havana*. Chapel Hill: University of North Carolina Press, 2014.
Leyva, Josefina. *Operación Pedro Pan: El éxodo de los niños Cubanos*. Coral Gables, FL: Editorial Ponce de León, 1993.
López, Melinda. *Sonia Flew*. New York: Dramatists Play Service, 2009.
López-Miró, Sergio. "The Dark Side of Peter Pan." *Miami Herald*, 29 November 1990.
López Vigil, María. *Cuba: Neither Heaven Nor Hell*. Washington, D.C.: EPICA, 1999.
Lora, Margarita E. "Peter Pan Wasn't Political." Letter to the editor. *Washington Post*, 21 February 1998.
Lotti, Alina M. "Sentimientos manoseados." *Trabajadores*, 20 December 1999.
Luke, Anne. "Youth Culture and the Politics of Youth in 1960s Cuba." Ph.D. diss., University of Wolverhampton, U.K., 2007.
Lutjens, Sheryl L. "Restructuring Childhood in Cuba: The State as Family." In *Children on the Streets of the Americas: Homelessness, Education, and Globalization in the United States, Brazil, and Cuba*, ed. Roslyn Arlin Mickelson, 149–58. New York: Routledge, 2000.
MacDonald, Theodore. *Making a New People: Education in Revolutionary Cuba*. Vancouver: New Star Books, 1985.
Machado, Eduardo. *Havana Is Waiting and Other Plays*. Kindle edition. New York: Theatre Communications Group, 2011.
Maret, Susan, and Lea Aschkenas. "Operation Pedro Pan: The Hidden History of 14,000 Cuban Children." In *Government Secrecy: Research in Social Problems and Public Policy* 19: 171–84. Bingley, West Yorkshire: Emerald Group Publishing, 2011.
Masud-Piloto, Felix Roberto. *From Welcomed Exiles to Illegal Immigrants: Cuban Migration to the U.S., 1959–1995*. Lanham, MD: Rowman and Littlefield, 1996.
Mathieu, Jennifer, and María A. Morales. "Exiles He Aided Bid Grau Farewell." *Miami Herald*, 5 November 1998.
Matthews, Herbert L. *Revolution in Cuba*. New York: Charles Scribner's Sons, 1975.
———. *The Cuban Story*. New York: George Braziller, 1961.
Matus, Alejandra. "Una cruzada individual en favor de Elián González." *El Nuevo Herald*, 24 May 2000.
May, Elaine Tyler. *Homeward Bound: American Families in the Cold War Era*. New York: Basic Books, 1988.
McNally, Michael. *Catholicism in South Florida*. Gainesville: University Presses of Florida, 1982.
Medin, Tzvi. *The Shaping of Revolutionary Consciousness*. Boulder, CO: Lynne Rienner Publishers, 1990.

Medrano, Mignon. *Todo lo dieron por Cuba*. Miami: Cuban American National Foundation, 1995.
Mencía, Mario, ed. *Time Was on Our Side*. Havana: Editora Política, 1982.
Mesa-Lago, Carmelo. *Revolutionary Change in Cuba*. Pittsburgh: University of Pittsburgh Press, 1971.
Miller, Warren. *90 Miles From Home: The Face of Cuba Today*. New York: Crest Books, 1961.
Moncarz Percal, Raúl. "The Golden Cage: Cubans in Miami." *International Migration* 16, nos. 3–4 (1978): 160–72.
Montalvo, Tina. "Operation Pedro Pan Flew Kids to Freedom." *Miami Herald*, 15 June 1986.
Moreno, José A. "From Traditional to Modern Values." In *Revolutionary Change in Cuba*, ed. Carmelo Mesa-Lago, 471–500. Pittsburgh: University of Pittsburgh Press, 1971.
Morley, Morris H. *Imperial State and Revolution: The United States and Cuba, 1952–1986*. Cambridge: Cambridge University Press, 1987.
Muñiz, Mirta, and Deborah Shnookal, eds. *José Martí Reader: Writings on the Americas*. Melbourne: Ocean Press, 1999.
Navarro, Mireya. "A Return to Cuba: A Search for Himself." *New York Times*, 21 October 2001.
———. "Miami's Exile: Side by Side Yet Worlds Apart." *New York Times*, 11 February 1999.
Nelson, Lowry. *Rural Cuba*. New York: Octagon Books, 1970.
Nuñez Machín, Ana. *La Epopeya: Historia de la Campaña de Alfabetización*. Havana: Editorial de Ciencias Sociales, 1983.
Ojito, Mirta. "Ramón Grau Alsina, 75, Cuban Who Aided Children's Escape." *New York Times*, 6 November 1998.
O'Reilly Herrera, Andrea, ed. *ReMembering Cuba: Legacy of a Diaspora*. Austin: University of Texas Press, 2001.
Ortega, Luis. *Cubanos en Miami*. Havana: Editorial de Ciencias Sociales, 1998.
Otero, Lisandro. "Utopia Revisited." In *Bridging Enigma: Cubans on Cuba*, ed. Ambrosio Fornet, 17–30. *South Atlantic Quarterly* vol. 96. Durham, NC: Duke University Press, 1997.
Padula, Alfred L., Jr. "The Fall of the Bourgeoisie: Cuba, 1959–1961." Ph.D. diss., University of New Mexico, 1974.
Padula, Alfred, and Lois M. Smith. "Women in Socialist Cuba, 1959–1984." In *Cuba: Twenty-Five Years of Revolution*, ed. Sandor Halebsky and John M. Kirk, 79–92. New York: Praeger, 1985.
Paulston, Rolland G. "Education." In *Revolutionary Change in Cuba*, ed. Carmelo Mesa-Lago, 375–97.
Pedraza, Silvia. *Political Disaffection in Cuba's Revolution and Exodus*. New York: Cambridge University Press, 2007.
Pérez, Lisandro. "Reflections on the Future of Cuba." *Cuban Studies* 39 (2008): 85–91.
Pérez, Louis A., Jr. *Cuba and the United States: Ties of Singular Intimacy*. Athens, GA: University of Georgia Press, 1980.
———. *Cuba: Between Reform and Revolution*. New York: Oxford University Press, 1988.

———. *Cuba in the American Imagination: Metaphor and the Imperial Ethos.* Chapel Hill: University of North Carolina Press, 2008.
———. *Essays on Cuban History: Historiography and Research.* Gainesville: University Press of Florida, 1995.
———. *On Becoming Cuban: Identity, Nationality, and Culture.* Chapel Hill: University of North Carolina Press, 1999.
Pérez, Maura Juampere. "Apuntes acerca del surgimiento de los grupos de izquierda en la comunidad cubana en los Estados Unidos." In *La emigración cubana: Anuario 1995,* 60–64. Havana: Centro de Estudios Alternativas Políticas, 1995.
Pérez Cruz, Felipe de J. *La Alfabetización en Cuba: Lectura histórica para pensar el presente.* Havana: Editorial de Ciencias Sociales, 2001.
———. *Las coordenadas de la Alfabetización.* Havana: Editorial de Ciencias Sociales, 1988.
Pérez-Stable, Marifeli. "Politics and Conciencia in Revolutionary Cuba." Ph.D. diss., State University of New York, Stony Brook, 1985.
———. *The Cuban Revolution: Origins, Course, and Legacy.* New York: Oxford University Press, 1993.
———. *The United States and Cuba: Intimate Enemies.* New York: Routledge, 2011.
Powers, Thomas. *The Man Who Kept the Secrets: Richard Helms and the CIA.* New York: Alfred Knopf, 1979.
Poyo, Gerald E. *Cuban Catholics in the United States, 1960–1980: Exile and Integration.* Notre Dame, IN: University of Notre Dame Press, 2007.
Prados, John. *Presidents' Secret Wars: CIA and Pentagon Covert Operations from World War II.* Chicago: Ivan R. Dee, 1996.
Prieto, Abel. "Cuba's National Literacy Campaign." *Journal of Reading* 25, no. 3 (December 1981): 215–21.
Prohias, Rafael J., and Lourdes Casal. *The Cuban Minority in the U.S.* Vol. 1. New York: Arno Press, 1980.
Provenzo, Eugene F., Jr., and Concepción García. "Exiled Teachers and the Cuban Revolution." *Cuban Studies* 13, no. 1 (winter 1983): 1–15.
Quintanales, Mirtha Natacha. "The Political Radicalization of Cuban Youth in Exile: A study of Identity Change in a Bicultural Context." Ph.D. diss., Ohio State University, 1987.
Rabe, Stephen. *The Most Dangerous Area in the World: John F. Kennedy Confronts the Communist Revolution in Latin America.* Chapel Hill: University of North Carolina Press, 1999.
Randall, Margaret. *Cuban Women Now: Interviews with Cuban Women.* Toronto: Women's Press, 1974.
———. *Women in Cuba: Twenty Years Later.* New York: Smyrna Press, 1981.
Raum, Tom. "Elián Fights Back before Congress." *Washington Post,* 1 March 2000.
Reed, Gail. "Flight of Fear." In *Cuba Update,* 7–8. New York: Center for Cuban Studies, 1994.
Regalado Someillan, Yamile. "The Cartooned Revolution: Images and the Revolutionary Citizen in Cuba, 1959–1963." Ph.D. diss., University of Maryland, 2009.
Rego, Oscar. "La nacionalización de la enseñanza." *Bohemia,* 8 June 1973.

Ressler, Everett M., Neil Boothby, and Daniel J. Steinbock. *Unaccompanied Children: Care and Protection in Wars, Natural Disasters, and Refugee Movements*. Oxford: Oxford University Press, 1988.
Rey Díaz, Ana Angélica. *Conrado Benítez: Primer maestro mártir*. Havana: Editora Política, 1987.
Roccena Ortiz, Karol. "Accounts of Desperate Times: Six Refugee Life Histories." Ph.D. diss., University of California, Irvine, 1983.
Rodríguez, Juan Carlos. *The Bay of Pigs and the CIA*. Melbourne: Ocean Press, 1999.
Rosenberg, Carol. "Ramón Grau, Organizer of Cuban Kids' Flight, Dies." *Miami Herald*, 4 November 1998.
Rosenthal, Marguerite G. "The Problems of Single Motherhood in Cuba." In *Cuba in Transition*, ed. Sandor Halebsky and John M. Kirk, 161–75.
Rositzke, Harry. *The CIA's Secret Operations: Espionage, Counterespionage, and Covert Action*. Boulder, CO: Westview Encore, 1988.
Ruiz, Albor. "Operación Peter Pan: Volando de vuelta a Cuba." *Progreso Semanal*, 16 April 2011. www.cubadebate.cu/opinion/2011/04/16/operacion-peter-pan-volando-de-vuelta.
Safa, Helen. "Hierarchies and Household Change in Postrevolutionary Cuba." *Latin American Perspectives* 36, no. 1 (January 2009): 42–52.
Saxon, Wolfgang. "David Atlee Phillips Dead at 65: Ex-Agent Was Advocate of CIA." *New York Times*, 10 July 1988.
Scheer, Robert, and Maurice Zeitlin. *Cuba: An American Tragedy*. Harmondsworth, Middlesex, U.K.: Penguin Books, 1964.
Schlesinger, Stephen, and Stephen Kinzer. *Bitter Fruit: The Untold Story of the American Coup in Guatemala*. Garden City, NY: Anchor Books, 1983.
Schoultz, Lars. "Benevolent Domination: The Ideology of U.S. Policy toward Cuba." *Cuban Studies* 41 (2010): 1–19.
———. *That Infernal Little Cuban Republic: The United States and the Cuban Revolution*. Chapel Hill: University of North Carolina Press, 2009.
Schrecker, Ellen. *Many Are the Crimes: McCarthyism in America*. Princeton: Princeton University Press, 1998.
Seers, Dudley, ed. *Cuba: Economic and Social Revolution*. Chapel Hill: University of North Carolina Press, 1964.
Serra, Ana. *The "New Man" in Cuba: Culture and Identity in the Revolution*. Gainesville: University Press of Florida, 2007.
Serra Robledo, Matilde, et al., eds. *El pueblo dice . . . Vivencias de la Campaña de Alfabetización en Cuba*. Havana: n.p., 1999.
Smith, Lois M. "Sexuality and Socialism in Cuba." In *Cuba in Transition*, ed. Sandor Halebsky and John M. Kirk, 177–91. Boulder, CO: Westview Press, 1992.
Smith, Lois M., and Alfred Padula. "The Cuban Family in the 1980s." In *Transformation and Struggle: Cuba Faces the 1990s* ed. Sandor Halebsky and John M. Kirk, 175–88. New York: Praeger, 1990.
———. *Sex and Revolution: Women in Socialist Cuba*. New York: Oxford University Press, 1996.

Smith, Wayne S. *The Closest of Enemies: A Personal and Diplomatic Account of U.S.-Cuban Relations since 1957*. New York: W.W. Norton, 1997.
Soley, Lawrence. *Radio Warfare: OSS and CIA Subversive Propaganda*. New York: Praeger, 1989.
Stanley, Frances. *The New World Refugee . . . The Cuban Exodus*. USA: Church World Service, ca. 1966.
Stone, Elizabeth, ed. *Women and the Cuban Revolution*. New York: Pathfinder Press, 1981.
Stout, Nancy. *One Day in December: Celia Sánchez and the Cuban Revolution*. New York: Monthly Review Press, 2013.
Suárez, Andrés. *Cuba: Castro and Communism*. Cambridge, MA: MIT Press, 1967.
Suchlicki, Jaime. *University Students and Revolution in Cuba, 1920–1968*. Coral Gables, FL: University of Miami Press, 1969.
Sweig, Julia. *Inside the Cuban Revolution: Fidel Castro and the Urban Underground*. Cambridge: Harvard University Press, 2002.
Thomas, Hugh. *Cuba or the Pursuit of Freedom*. New York: Da Capo Press, 1998.
Thomas-Woodard, Tiffany A. "Toward the Gates of Eternity: Celia Sánchez Manduley and the Creation of Cuba's New Woman." *Cuban Studies* 34 (2003): 154–80.
Torreira Crespo, Ramón, and José Buajasán Marrawi. *Operación Peter Pan: Un caso de guerra psicológica contra Cuba*. Havana: Editora Política, 2000.
Torres, María de los Angeles. "Cuban Diaspora: Children Lost in Political Conflict." *Chicago Tribune*, 20 October 2002.
———. "Elián and the Tale of Pedro Pan." *Nation*, 27 March 2000.
———. "Immigration Policies Aimed Exclusively at Youth Undermine Their Families." *La Prensa* (San Diego), 14 December 2012.
———. "The Lost Children of Cuba: Operation Pedro Pan." Interview by María Hinojosa, *An Interview With* podcast, National Public Radio, 12 June 2015. https://soundcloud.com/latinousa/the-lost-children-of-cuba-operation-pedro-pan.
———. *In the Land of Mirrors: Cuban Exile Politics in the United States*. Ann Arbor: University of Michigan Press, 2001.
———. "Open the Books on Operation Pedro Pan." *Miami Herald*, 18 December 1994.
———. *The Lost Apple: Operation Pedro Pan, Cuban Children in the United States, and the Promise of a Better Future*. Boston: Beacon Press, 2003.
Triay, Victor Andres. *Bay of Pigs: An Oral History of Brigade 2506*. Gainesville: University Press of Florida, 2001.
———. *Fleeing Castro: Operation Pedro Pan and the Cuban Children's Program*. Gainesville: University Press of Florida, 1998.
Urcelay-Maragnes, Denise. *La Leyenda Roja. Los voluntarios cubanos en la guerra civil española*. León: Editorial Lobo Sapiens, 2011.
Valdés, Nelson. "Let Elián González Go Home: Hypocrisy and Family Values." Cuba-L Direct Service, 3 December 1999.
———. "The Radical Transformation of Education." In *Cuba in Revolution*, ed. Rolando E. Bonachea and Nelson P. Valdés, 422–55. New York: Anchor Books, 1972.
Veciana-Suárez, Ana. *Vuelo a la libertad*. New York: Scholastic, 2004. (Also published in English as *Flight to Freedom*. New York: Orchard Books, 2002.)

Wald, Karen. *Children of Che: Childcare and Education in Cuba.* Palo Alto, CA: Ramparts Press, 1978.

Wall, Richard H., Jr. "Operation Pedro Pan: An Examination of the Factors That Resulted in 14,048 Cuban Children Being Sent to the United States." Master's thesis, California State University, Long Beach, 2011.

Wenski, Bishop Thomas G. "Ties between the Cuban Catholic Church and the Archdiocese of Miami." Paper presented at LASA, Miami, 16–18 March 2000. Monsignor Bryan O. Walsh Papers, Barry University, Miami.

Wise, David, and Thomas B. Ross. *The Invisible Government.* New York: Random House, 1964.

Wyden, Peter. *The Bay of Pigs: The Untold Story.* New York: Touchstone/Simon and Schuster, 1979.

Yañez, Luisa. "Ailing Hero behind Pedro Pan Mission an Inspiration to Exiles." *Sun Sentinel, South Florida,* 30 October 1998.

———. "Base de datos sobre el histórico éxodo de la Operación Pedro Pan." *El Nuevo Herald,* 12 May 2009.

———. "Cubans Reconnect with Past through Pedro Pan Database." *Miami Herald,* 17 May 2009.

———. "El éxodo de 14,048 menores cubanos." *El Nuevo Herald,* 16 May 2009.

———. "Pedro Pan was Born of Fear, Human Instinct to Protect Children." *Miami Herald,* 16 May 2009.

———. "Ramón Grau Alsina, Anti-Castro Activist." *Sun Sentinel, South Florida,* 4 November 1998.

———. "Statue of Late 'Father' of Pedro Pan Unveiled." *Miami Herald,* 6 June 2009.

Yepe, Manuel E. "Cómo calificar aquel crimen." *Cubadebate,* 4 November 2010. www.cubadebate.cu/opinion/2010/11/04/como-calificar-aquel-crimen . . .

Zeitlin, Maurice. *Revolutionary Politics and the Cuban Working Class.* Princeton, NJ: Princeton University Press, 1967.

INDEX

Afro-Cubans, 34, 39–40, 72; desegregation and, 39, 61; discrimination against, 10, 36. *See also* Racism
Agrarian reform, 21, 32, 45, 46, 64, 67, 75, 194, 227n4; Catholic hierarchy and, 46; U.S. government response to, 46
Agrupación Católica Universitaria (ACU). *See* Catholic University Association
Alfabeticemos, 92
Allende, Salvador, 22, 255n120, 279n39
Alliance for Progress, 163, 166, 272n135
Almazán, Sonia, 154, 216, 248n214
Almeida, Juan, 40
Álvarez, Berta, 144, 217
Álvarez, Tony, 136
Ana Betancourt schools, Anitas, 36, 41, 90–91
Anti-Americanism, 54, 75
Anti-Batista movement, 21, 26, 30; Catholics and, 30, 45; violent repression of, 25, 31; women and, 35, 123; youth involvement in, 25–26, 144. *See also* Batista regime
Anti-Castro movement, 13, 24, 59, 72, 135, 156, 178; assassination plots against Fidel Castro, 125; Bay of Pigs, 83, 141; Catholics and, 48, 49, 83, 114, 120, 150–52; CIA and, 116; decline of, 194, 213; literacy campaign, 81, 98; *patria potestad* hoax and, 105–6, 113, 126, 161; Pedro Pans and, 30, 143–45, 147, 158, 168, 215. *See also* Bay of Pigs; Counterrevolution
Anticommunism, 47, 179, 220; Cold War and, 54, 130; Catholic church and, 30, 47–48, 50, 117, 126; family and, 105, 108–12, 177
Antonio Maceo brigade, 11, 209, 216, 225n51, 280n71, 283n32
Aquino, Vivian and Sixto, 148
Árbenz, Jacobo, 118–19; agrarian reform, 119
Arboleya, Jesús, 90, 93, 101

Areíto group, 210, 283n32
Arteaga Betancourt, Cardinal, 153, 198
Artime, Manuel, 143, 151, 166
Association of Rebel Youth (Asociación de Jóvenes Rebeldes, AJR), 28, 29, 72, 77, 82
Asunce, Manuel, 81, 248n218
Auerbach, Frank, 140

Baker, James, 38, 52, 63, 261n88; links with counterrevolution, 157, 169, 171; Operation Pedro Pan and, 133, 134, 137–39, 140, 169, 170, 190–91, 193. *See also* Ruston Academy
Banks, 75, 125, 231
Batista, General Fulgencio, 21, 25, 26, 30, 33, 34
Batista regime, 33, 34, 64; Catholic church and, 45; corruption under, 51, 54, 64, 73; opposition to, 21, 25–26, 30, 31, 35, 144
Bay of Pigs: invasion at, 31, 34, 61–62, 116–17, 163, 177, 199, 253; aftermath of, 56, 141, 156–57, 160–62, 165, 169, 176, 194; build up to, 29, 31, 34, 119–22, 126; Catholics and, 151; CIA and, 80, 119, 121, 137, 162, 193; Cuban émigrés and, 165–66, 194; failure of, 76, 156, 180, 194; literacy campaign and, 7, 50, 60, 63, 73, 76, 80, 81; Operation Pedro Pan and, 4, 137–38, 160, 169–70, 193; Pedro Pans and, 143–44, 164, 170, 193, 215; prisoners, 136, 142, 195. *See also* Anti-Castro movement; Central Intelligence Agency; Counterrevolution
Becas. *See* Scholarships
Belén College, 47, 55, 143
Benítez, Conrado, 72
Betancourt, Noel, 131–32, 158, 257n28
Bissell, Richard, 121, 161
Boarding schools, 1, 32, 33, 133
Bohemia, 26, 56, 95, 114, 116, 146
Bonsal, Philip, 135, 171, 193

Boy scouts, 61
Brainwashing, 1, 24, 110, 118, 191. *See also* Indoctrination
Brigade 2506, 142, 144, 156, 164; captured members of, 142, 195. *See also* Bay of Pigs
Brigadistas, 3, 7, 15, 23, 27, *102*; age of, 81; experiences of, 92–101; gender of, 8, 38, 81, 145; motives of, 70, 73, 74, 82–86; parents and, 38, 82, 86, 103, 146; recruitment of, 65, 77–79, 84, 87, 88; training of, 70–71, 73, 76, 80, 82, 84–85, 87, 91, 95
British embassy, 139, 140, 169, 170, 174, 199, 200, 271n123, 278n17
Buajasán, José, 47, 204

Cabañas, José, 249
Camp Columbia, 64
Caravan of Sorrow, 122–23
Carroll, Coleman, 129, 141, 152, 198
Caso imprenta. *See* Print shop case
Castro, Fidel, 2, 4, 5, 7, 21, 22; assassination plots against, 125, 162; death of, 18; on Cubanization of Cuba, 7, 221; on emigration, 202, 203; on Operation Pedro Pan, 113–14, 203; on racism, 39; U.S. obsession with, 161; Walsh and, 203, 208
Castro, Fidelito, 58, 123
Castro, Raúl, 27, 28, 35
Catholic Charities, 152, 155. *See also* Catholic Welfare Bureau
Catholic church, 119, 155, 214; anticommunism and, 30, 47–48, 50, 117, 126, 179; counterrevolution and, 30, 150–52, 161; Cubanization of, 46; Operation Pedro Pan and, 1, 17, 19, 150–55, 171, 182, 199, 203, 219; *patria potestad* hoax and, 113, 114, 121, 126, 158; revolution and, 43, 45–51, 55, 113–14, 151–53, 161, 198
Catholic clergy, 46, 47, 49, 114, 122; anti-Castro movement and, 48, 57, 150–51, 154; departure from Cuba of, 50–51, 124, 153, 155; Operation Pedro Pan and, 152, 199. *See also* Catholic church
Catholic hierarchy, 28, 48, 154, 169; attitude to Batista regime, 45; response to the revolution, 31, 45, 49, 55, 105; revolutionary government and, 153, 161, 198. *See also* Catholic church
Catholic Hispanic Center Miami (Centro Hispano Católico, CHC), 111, 129, 145, 191
Catholic schools, 55–57, 60, 145, 263; anti-Castro movement and, 49, 77; literacy campaign and, 56, 59; nationalization of, 51, 54, 110, 124; U.S. Catholic schools, 130, 155. *See also* Education reform; Private schools
Catholic students, 30–31, 48–49, 143
Catholic University Association (ACU), 48, 143, 151
Catholic Welfare Bureau (CWB), 16, 127, 132, 149, 168, 175, 188–89; Cuban Children's Program and, 152–56; Operation Pedro Pan and, 133, 138, 140, 143, 147–48, 150, 152, 155, 160, 184, 218; Walsh and, 1, 5, 128–29, 132, 141, 150, 155. *See also* Catholic Charities
Catholic youth, 30, 45, 48, 60, 143, 153
Center for Historical Investigations on State Security (Centro de Investigaciones Históricas de la Seguridad del Estado, CIHSE), 12, 141, 251nn54, 252n61
Central America: refugee families from, 5, 18, 216
Central Intelligence Agency (CIA), 8, 15, 28, 38, 116–18, 123, 125–26, 140, 167, 192; Bay of Pigs invasion and, 80, 119, 121, 137, 162, 193; counterrevolution and, 12, 17, 120, 135, 136, 152, 161–63, 165, 168, 197, 213; Operation Pedro Pan and, 144, 160, 164, 170–75, 183, 193–94, 203, 217, 220; propaganda of, 9, 16, 17, 114, 120–22, 126, 158, 175–79, 183, 187, 188; sponsored speaking tours, 123, 166, 179, 268n60, 269n71. *See also* Anti-Castro movement; Counterrevolution; Psychological warfare
Child abuse: institutional, 218; Pedro Pans and, 3, 218
Child-care centers (círculos *infantiles*), 17, 24, 35, 36, 89, 110–11, 113, 114. *See also* Day-care program
Childhood: concepts of, 14, 32–33, 210, 226n63
Child refugees: from Central America, 5, 18, 216; other cases of, 108, 130. *See also* Hungarian refugees; Jewish children; Kindertransport; Spanish Civil War
Children: Cuban revolution and, 7–9, 26–29, 31, 40, 70, 101, 231n85; exodus of, 1–2, 4; revolutionary government policy on, 17, 24–25, 28, 31–35, 41, 105–6, 111–12, 114, 202, 214. *See also* Education reform; Families; Literacy campaign; Operation Pedro Pan; Youth
Children's Bureau, U.S. Department of Health, Education, and Welfare, 139, 182, 186, 192, 195
Chile, 22, 61, 153, 203

Chorens, Olga, 136
Chovel Vilano, Ely, 16, 158, 208, 212
Christians. *See* Religion
Christmas, 43. *See also* Three Kings Day
CIA. *See* Central Intelligence Agency
Círculos infantiles. *See also* Child-care centers; Day-care program
Civil Rights movement, 28, 210
Cleveland, 184, 185
Cold War, 6, 198, 217; anticommunism and, 53, 54, 60, 108, 128, 193, 215, 220; Catholic church and, 30, 40–48, 50, 117, 126, 158, 179; Operation Pedro Pan and, 4, 8–9, 15, 19–20, 190, 134, 198, 215, 220–21; propaganda, 4, 24, 60, 108–9, 113, 118
Colombia, 166, 185
Comellas, Tony, 169
Committees for the Defense of the Revolution (CDR), 28, 77
Communism, 23, 35, 158, 167, 181, 190, 193; Catholic church and, 47–49, 119, 126; Cuba and, 35, 48, 50, 53, 58–59, 67, 73, 110, 132, 142, 157; family and, 4, 17, 49, 60, 106, 109–10, 123; fear of, 120, 123, 132, 154, 157, 191; struggle against, 30, 120, 130, 134–35, 150, 154, 166–67, 179, 186. *See also* Anticommunism; Cold War; Socialism
Conciencia, 22–24, 28, 43, 61, 69, 74, 221–22; definition of, 228n17. *See also* Literacy campaign; Nationalism; New Cuban; New Man; New society
Conde, Yvonne, 13, 58, 72, 217, 218, 230n57, 261n104
Conrado Benítez brigades. *See Brigadistas*; Literacy campaign
Coral Gables High School, 138
Costa Rica, 123
Counterrevolution, 135, 137, 141, 178; Bay of Pigs invasion and, 117, 170; *patria potestad* hoax and, 126; propaganda and, 118, 120, 126, 129, 204; Operation Pedro Pan and, 117, 129, 133, 135, 137, 170, 172, 174–75, 183, 193, 195–96, 214; students and, 190; terrorist activities of, 34, 123, 172, 194, 209; U.S. government support for, 135–36, 163, 187. *See also* Anti-Castro movement; Bay of Pigs; Central Intelligence Agency; Cuba Project; Operation Mongoose
Crisis Amigo: U.S. documentary, 180
Cuban Adjustment Act, 142, 224n25

Cuban-American community, 17, 186, 206, 208; Bay of Pigs and, 119, 137; CIA and, 162, 190; resentment against, 180–81, 180–85; Operation Pedro Pan and, 3, 5, 16, 17, 134, 152, 173, 208, 216. *See also* Cuban refugees; Cuban Refugee Program; González, Elián
Cuban Children's Program, 19, 130–31, 139, 148–50, 161, 181–82, 218; benefit to Catholic Church of, 155–56; "magnet effect" of, 4, 127, 128, 138, 146–50, 158, 214; Operation Pedro Pan and, 15, 128, 133, 138, 152, 220. *See also* Operation Pedro Pan
Cuban Communist Party (PCC), 67, 109
Cuban constitution of 1940, 52, 54
Cuban Exiles. *See* Cuban-American community
Cubanidad. *See* Cuban identity
Cuban identity (*cubanidad*), 12, 22, 43, 210, 221. *See also* Nationalism; New Cuba; New Cuban
Cubanization, of Cuba, 7, 20, 43
Cuban Missile Crisis, 2, 15, 142, 160, 165, 186, 188, 194, 197, 213
Cuban Refugee Center, 166, 167, 179, 195
Cuban Refugee Committee, Miami, 132
Cuban Refugee Program, 5, 148, 166, 185, 195. *See also* Cuban refugees
Cuban refugees, 6, 106, 129, 141–42, 155, 164, 181, 197, 217, 273n154; propaganda value of, 178–79, 185, 215; resentment against, 180–82, 184; resettlement of, 129, 134, 184, 195; U.S. policy on, 7, 108, 130, 143, 165–68, 216. *See also* Cuban-American community; Cuban Children's Program; Cuban Refugee Program; Propaganda war
Cuban revolution, 22, 24, 42; Afro-Cubans and, 39–40; audacity of, 6, 9–10, 27, 221; Catholic church and, 43, 45–51, 55, 113–14, 151–53, 161, 198, 221; children and, 7–9, 26–29, 31, 40, 70, 101, 231n85; consolidation of, 63, 156, 202, 221; families and, 9, 28, 30, 43, 61, 103, 217; leadership of, 22, 24, 26, 27, 42, 53, 67; socialism and, 3, 23, 33, 48, 50, 83, 101, 126, 157, 201; U.S. response to, 108, 128, 159, 176, 215; women and, 26, 33, 34–39, 81, 111; youth and, 8–9, 17, 20–21, 24–30, 48, 65, 70, 77, 80, 82, 101–3, 143–44, 157, 221; *See also* New Cuba; New Cuban; Social revolution
Cuban Revolutionary Council (CRC), 120, 122, 163, 164, 166, 259n59

308 · Index

Cuba Project, The, 116–19, 129, 141, 161–63, 167–68, 178–79, 185, 186, 215; Operation Pedro Pan and, 170, 193, 217. *See also* Bay of Pigs; Central Intelligence Agency; Operation Mongoose; Propaganda war; Psychological Warfare
Cuba socialista, 45
Cuervo, María Teresa (Teté), 199
Currency exchange, 147, 220
Cushing, Cardinal, 45

Day-care program (*círculos infantiles*), 35, 111, 113. *See also* Child-care centers
De la Campa, Román, 206
Democratic Christian Movement (MDC), 98, 150
Department of Health, Education, and Welfare (DHEW), 139, 148, 161, 165–66, 184, 186–87, 192, 197. *See also* Children's Bureau; Cuban Children's Program
Department of State Security (DSE) Cuban. *See* State Security
Díaz, Mario, 65, 70, 73, 89, 90
Díaz, Sergio, 137
Díaz, Valentín, 145
Díaz Lanz, Pedro, 45
Directorio Revolucionario Estudiantil (DRE). *See* Revolutionary Student Directorate
Doctors, 64, 67, 68, 201. *See also* Public health campaign
Dorticós, Osvaldo, 29, 47, 112, 113, 120, 186
DRE. *See* Revolutionary Student Directorate
Dubinsky, Karen, 192

Education reform, 8, 43, 51–57, 59, 110, 127; priority of, 54, 59, 64. *See also* Catholic schools; Private schools; Religion; Teachers; Textbooks
Eire, Carlos, 40, 58, 146
Eisenhower, Dwight D., 6, 117
El Encanto department store, 34, 172
El Mundo, 28, 29, 106, 111
Emigration, 128, 158; as a political weapon, 13, 128, 215, 217; Cuban families and, 6, 17, 141, 142, 147; Cuban government attitude to, 142, 201–2, 207. *See also* Cuban refugees
English language, 42, 56, 60
Escalante, Fabián, 204
Espín, Vilma, 35–36, 91. *See also* Federation of Cuban Women

Fagen, Richard, 92
Fair Play for Cuba Committees, 177
Families: anticommunism and, 105, 108–12, 177; impact of separation on, 3, 14, 76, 193, 206, 212, 218; literacy campaign and, 8, 27, 38, 61, 70, 76, 77, 86–90, 103; religion and, 39, 48, 105; revolution and, 9, 28, 30, 43, 61, 103, 217; revolutionary government policy and, 17, 24–25, 28, 31–35, 41, 105–6, 111–12, 114, 202, 214; reunification of, 3, 10–11, 141–42, 181, 195; separation of, 5, 76, 101, 142, 158, 161, 147. *See also Patria potestad*; Patriarchal family; Women
Fanon, Frantz, 42
Federación de Mujeres Cubanas (FMC). *See* Federation of Cuban Women
Federal Bureau of Investigation (FBI), 192
Federation of Cuban Women (FMC), 35–36, 77, 82, 90, 91, 94, 99, 111, 239n272
Federation of University Students (FEU). *See* Students
Feminine Crusade (*Cruzada feminina*), 166
Fernández, Damián J., 23
Ferrer, Raúl, 68, 69, 74, 75, 92
Ficha escolar, 110
Finlay, Berta de la Portilla, 148
Finlay, Francisco (Pancho), 148, 169, 279n29
Flogar department store, 29
Foster care, 130, 132–34, 149, 213; appeals for foster parents, 184, 186, 187; Pedro Pans' experience in, 145, 146, 210, 211, 218; program for Pedro Pans, 15–16, 19, 127, 149, 184, 224n21. *See also* Cuban Children's Program; Operation Pedro Pan
Freedom Flights, 142
Freire, Paolo, 68, 74, 75, 80, 92
Fuentes, Ileana, 30

Germany, 61
Giquel, Sergio, 138
González, Elián, 3, 12, 17, 18, 73, 186, 187, 204–8, 211, 212
Gramsci, Antonio, 43, 102
Grau, San Martín, Ramón, 168
Grau Alsina, María Leopoldina (Polita), 12, 125, 161, 168, 169, 170, 199–200, 270n89, 270n98
Grau Alsina, Ramón (Mongo), 12, 125, 136, 154, 168–69, 170, 171, 192, 199–200, 270n89, 270n98
Guarch, Jorge (George), 16

Guatemala, 118–20, 121, 137
Guevara, Ernesto Che, 22, 23, 27, 33, 35, 43, 66, 119, 157; concept of "New Man," 22, 74; on Marxism, 100

Hale, Robert, 138, 140, 142
Hart, Armando, 27, 122; on education reform, 51, 53, 54, 110; on family, 32, 116; on literacy campaign, 65, 67–68, 81, 101, 103; on Operation Pedro Pan, 183
Hart Phillips, Ruby, 25, 49, 72, 100, 121, 201
Hebrew Immigrant Aid Society (HIAS), 57
Hoover, J. Edgar, 192
Housing reform, 32, 39
Huddleston, Vicki, 208
Humanism, 20, 63, 67, 73, 77; literacy campaign and, 101, 103, 104
Hungarian refugees, 58, 128, 258n36

Illiteracy, 51, 64–66, 68, 74, 77, 216
Illiterates, 59, 64, 65, 67–69, 73, 75, 78–79, 85, 92, 95
Immigration and Naturalization Service (INS), 138, 140, 167, 171, 217
Imperialism, 113, 72; fight against, 73, 82, 87, 95, 100
Indigenous children: removal of, 11
Indoctrination, 24, 114, 130–31, 156, 157, 208, 222; education reform and, 28, 53–54, 59, 110, 149; fear of communist, 2, 19, 58, 105–6, 108, 133–34, 139; literacy campaign and, 9, 61, 63, 72–74, 124, 161; Pedro Pans and, 143; plan to counteract, 190–92; U.S. "educational mission," in Cuba, 52–53. *See also* Brainwashing; Education reform
Integrated Revolutionary Organizations (ORI), 113

Jamaica plan, 139, 197–98
Jewish children, 9, 130, 132, 157; Operation Pedro Pan and, 57. *See also* Hebrew Immigrant Aid Society (HIAS)
Jewish school, 57
Jews, 61
Johnson, Lyndon B., 156
Joven Cuba, 210
July 26, celebration of, 34
July 26 Movement, 25, 29, 40, 124, 183
Junior Patrols (*Patrolles Juveniles*), 28, 29
Juventud Católica Obrera (JOC), 143

Kapcia, Antoni, 30, 69
Kendall: Cuban refugee children's camp in Miami, 144, 150, 215
Kennedy, Jacqueline, 185
Kennedy, John F., 6, 24, 119, 128, 178; Bay of Pigs and, 120, 161, 163, 253; Cuba policy of, 117, 135, 161–62, 176, 180; Cuban refugee policy of, 130, 141, 148, 163, 166, 178
Kennedy, Robert, 162, 163, 194, 266n28
Key West incident, 133
Kindertransport, 9, 270
KLM (Royal Dutch airlines), 140, 148, 169, 201, 279n29
Kozol, Jonathan, 69, 73, 74, 79, 80, 89, 101

La Epoca department store, 172
Lansdale, Edward, 129, 162, 167, 168, 175, 178–80, 185–88, 194, 272n129
Lantigua, Pedro, 81, 248n218
La Salle College, 31, 55, 154; relocation of, 155
La Salle University, 63
Latin America, 49, 55, 163; Cold War in, 6, 118, 166, 179, 187; Cuban revolution and, 3, 49, 64, 82, 118, 123, 176, 215; refugees from, 134, 216
Lewis, Oscar, 32, 33, 37, 50
Literacy, 43, 51, 64, 66–67, 68, 74, 92; José Marti and, 67–68. *See also* Education reform; Literacy campaign
Literacy campaign: as a nation-building project, 40, 43, 63, 66, 73; assessment of, 74–75, 79, 92, 123–24; Bay of Pigs and, 7, 50, 60, 63, 73, 76, 80–81; families and, 8, 27, 38, 61, 70, 76, 77, 86–90, 103; legacy of, 11–12, 93, 95, 101–4, 222; mass organizations and, 68, 82; mythologization of, 77, 81; Operation Pedro Pan and, 3, 8–9, 13, 17, 62, 63, 73, 101; opposition to, 96, 97, 98, 161; political nature of, 9, 23, 65–66, 70, 72–73, 82, 91–92, 104; propaganda about, 77–80; public health campaign and, 76, 91, 96, 246; religion and, 49–50, 83; revolutionary consciousness and, 28, 61, 69; schools and, 56, 59, 90, 157, 161; teaching materials of, 36, 74–75; women and, 8, 63, 82, 94, 95, 97–99, 111; *See also* Ana Betancourt schools; *Brigadistas*; Education reform; Literacy
López, Alex, 1, 152, 218
López, Sergio, 125
López Vigil, María, 50
Lost Apple, The, 187–88, 190

Machado, Eduardo, 158
Maids, 35, 210
Marinello, Juan, 49
Martí, José, 26, 27, 35, 43, 64, 103, 192, 211; on children, 113, 116; on education and literacy, 67–68, 96, 100; on national sovereignty, 22; on race, 40; on youth, 27
Marx, Karl, 103
Marxism, 111, 114, 158, 190
Masud, María, 87
Matecumbe: Cuban refugee children's camp, 210
Matthews, Herbert, 65
May Day celebration, 41, 151
Medina, Pablo, 26
Memorias de subdesarrollo, 41
Mendieta, Ana, 31, 145, 210
Mendieta, Raquel, 31, 145
Menéndez, Pedro, 132, 258n31
Mexico, 108, 195, 219
Miami Herald, 1, 16, 58, 59, 105, 110, 139, 173, 178, 179, 217
Middle class, 5, 14, 100, 145, 157, 210, 216; religion and, 8, 110; revolution and, 27, 33–35, 38, 41–43, 59, 61, 109–11, 158, 173, 216; tradition of sending kids to U.S., 4, 5, 132; values of, 9, 10, 103. *See also* Families; Patriarchal family; Religion
Mikoyan, Anastas, 30, 48
Military service, 164, 201
Militias, 80, 46, 50, 90, 97; women and, 35, 36; youth and, 28, 55, 84
Mind control, 118. *See also* Brainwashing; Indoctrination
Ministry of Education, Cuban (MINED), 51, 54, 55. *See also* Education reform
Ministry of the Interior, Cuban (MININT), 197, 201, 204
Miró Cardona, José, 55, 120, 136, 163, 164
Missile Crisis, Cuban, 3, 142, 160, 165, 186, 188, 194, 197, 213
Monroe Doctrine, 221
Motherhood: Cuban view of, 26, 36, 110, 114
Movement for the Recovery of the Revolution (MRR), 135
Movimiento Democrático Cristiano (MDC). *See* Democratic Christian Movement
Muñiz, Carlos, 150, 209
Muñiz, Mirta, 34, 79

Nationalism: Cuban, 7, 53, 54, 74, 75, 221. *See also Conciencia*; New Cuba
Nationalization: of education, 40, 51, 54–57, 110, 154–55, 200. *See also* Catholic schools; Education reform; Private schools
National Security Council, U.S. (NSC), 116, 117 141, 163, 166, 168
Native American children: removal of, 11
Nazi-occupied Europe, 9, 157; refugees from, 257n17
New Cuba, 9, 21–22, 39, 41, 43, 45, 53, 60, 214, 222; literacy campaign and, 62, 63; youth and, 24, 28, 103. *See also* Nationalism
New Cuban, 22, 24, 26, 34, 38, 45, 60, 62, 111, 190, 227n7. *See also Conciencia*; Youth
New Man. *See* New Cuban
New society, 23–24, 34, 43, 190. *See also* Social revolution; Socialism
Newsweek, 49, 61, 72, 110, 167
New York Times, 25, 65, 73, 120, 121, 130, 136, 165, 185, 199, 201

October Missile Crisis. *See* Cuban Missile Crisis
Odio, Amador, 172, 271n108
Odio, Sara del Toro, 172, 271n108
Oettinger, Katherine Brownell, 139, 182, 187, 192
Office of Strategic Services (OSS), 118
Omega 7, 209
Opa Locka center, 146, 165, 167, 206
Operation Family (*Operación Familia*), 32. *See also* Families
Operation Mongoose, 161–64, 167, 175, 180, 187, 194, 202, 255n128; Operation Pedro Pan and, 168–72. *See also* Cuba Project; Propaganda war; Psychological warfare
Operation Pedro Pan, 127, 160–61; airfares and, 4, 127, 133, 199; airlines and, 201; Catholic church and, 150–56, 171, 182, 199, 203, 219; CIA and, 144, 160, 164, 170–75, 183, 193–94, 203, 217, 220; counterrevolution and, 117, 129, 133–38, 170, 172, 174–75, 183, 193–96, 214; Cuban government and, 147, 201–6, 214; driving factors of, 4, 52, 55, 127, 128, 138, 146–50, 214; family emigration and, 141–42, 166, 195, 202; legacy of, 2, 11, 18, 216; literacy campaign and, 3, 8–9, 13, 17, 38, 62–63, 73, 101; mythologization of, 3, 5, 17, 132, 135, 173, 216; origins of, 4, 117, 129, 132–34, 137–38, 140, 148–49; parents

and, 2, 7, 9, 139, 150, 212; politics of, 3, 17, 186, 217; psychological warfare and, 214, 217; secrecy of, 139, 181–83, 186, 188, 197; U.S. media reports of, 1, 132, 139, 183; Walsh and, 8, 15, 19, 135, 147–50, 155, 181–85, 198–99, 202. *See also* Catholic Welfare Bureau; Cuban Children's Program; Families; Operation Mongoose; Parents; *Patria potestad*; Patriarchal family; Pedro Pans; Visa waivers; Walsh, Bryan O.

Operation Pedro Pan Group, Inc., 16, 134, 152, 174, 208

Organizaciones Revolucionarias Integradas (ORI). *See* Integrated Revolutionary Organizations

Oteiza, Margarita, 172, 238n250

Padula, Alfred, 42, 111

Pan American Airlines, 120, 136, 140, 167, 169, 201, 279n29

Parents, 9, 13–14, 145, 157–58, 161, 204, 206, 210; anti-Castro movement and, 5, 133–34, 137–38, 143, 164, 172, 199, 215; anxieties of, 38, 43, 77, 87, 126, 161; Operation Pedro Pan and, 1, 4–5, 31, 40, 43, 58, 106, 110, 137, 139, 145, 150, 206; emigration of, 18, 114, 141, 142, 150; rights of, 8, 19, 32, 49, 55, 105, 124, 127, 207–8. *See also* Families; *Patria potestad*; Patriarchal family

Partido Socialista Popular (PSP). *See* Popular Socialist Party

Patria potestad, 226; Catholic church and, 113, 114, 121, 126, 158; CIA and, 16, 118, 121, 124–25, 193; Cuban government on, 32, 106, 107, 109–11, 114, 200–201, 203–7; definition of, 226n72; Elián González case and, 206–8; fake law of, 112–16, 123–24, 126, 127, 157, 170, 182; Fidel Castro on, 202–4, 208; Operation Pedro Pan and, 128, 146, 158, 203, 215, 220; scare campaign about, 17, 18, 32, 72, 105–8, 128, 161, 176, 214–15, 220; U.S. media reports and, 105, 177; Walsh on, 208. *See also* Anticommunism; Families; Print shop case; Women

Patriarchal family, 9, 24, 30, 32, 34, 38, 43, 48, 59, 61. *See also* Families; Women

Pedro Pans, 135, 139; abuse of, 3, 210–11, 218; accelerated maturity of, 15, 103, 210; adjustment of, 145–46, 189, 210; age of, 9, 14, 30, 144–45; arrivals of, 5, 130, 148, 160, 183, 184, 268n65; class background of, 5, 8, 14, 27, 59, 100, 145–46; definition of, 16, 257n28; gender of, 16, 145, 164; gratitude of, 3, 173, 207, 209, 216; "king-size," 171, 194; political activism of, 5, 14–15, 30–31, 143–45, 168, 171; relocation of, 181, 195; propaganda value of, 49, 179, 186, 188, 215; separation of siblings, 193, 212; stranding of, 3, 18, 186, 195, 213; success stories of, 101, 216; U.S. "investment" in, 52, 179, 189–93, 215–16; Walsh and, 30, 59, 143–44, 146, 186. *See also* Families; Operation Pedro Pan; Parents

Pérez, Louis A., Jr., 42

Pérez Serantes, Enrique, 45, 46, 48, 49, 51, 153, 198

Peter Pan, 6, 15, 16, 173, 212

Phillips, David Atlee, 118–19, 120, 121, 122, 141, 255n120, 262n88, 279n39

Pioneers (*pioneros*), 28, 72

Plain Dealer, Cleveland, 184–85

Plan asistencial, 90, 111, 239, 251

"Plausible denial": U.S. government's use of, 116, 154, 173

Political culture: transformation of, 42, 68, 74, 104; revolution and, 18, 20, 34

Popular Socialist Party (PSP), 47, 49, 113

Powers, Penny (Phyllis Howison), 148, 199; Operation Pedro Pan and, 169–70, 174, 192–93, 199–200, 270n89, 277n216, 278n17, 278n21. *See also* Ruston Academy

Print shop case (*caso imprenta*), 112–15, 200

Private schools, 26, 31, 55–57, 110, 131, 154; anti-Castro movement and, 56; nationalization of, 40, 54–55, 59, 133, 161; Pedro Pans and, 59; racial segregation and, 39–40; relocation of, 55. *See also* Catholic schools; Education reform

Propaganda war: against Cuba, 175–80, 188, 213, 215. *See also* Cuba Project; Operation Mongoose; Psychological warfare; United States Information Agency

Prostitution, 35, 90

Psychological warfare (psywar), 118–20, 159, 162, 175–76, 180, 185, 187, 203, 255n118, 269n71; children and, 7, 19, 119, 176, 187, 203; definition of, 118; Operation Pedro Pan and, 214, 217; *patria potestad* hoax and, 19, 203, 204. *See also* Central Intelligence Agency; Cuba Project; Operation Mongoose; *Patria potestad*; Propaganda war; Radio Swan

Public health campaign, 76, 91, 96, 246n175
Puerto Rico, 132, 209

Racism, 38; racial segregation, 39–40
Radio Swan, 119, 120–21, 193, 250n16
Ray, Manuel (Manolo), 172, 177
Refugees. *See* Cuban refugees
Religion: religious belief, 39, 45, 47, 60, 114; religious education, 47, 235n161; repression of, 50; revolution and, 39, 49–50, 57, 113, 122. *See also* Catholic church
Renick, Ralph, 15, 180, 225n70
Rescate, 114
Rescate: anti-Castro group, 125, 161, 169, 256n144
Revolución, 87, 114, 115, 124
Revolutionary consciousness. See *Conciencia*
Revolutionary Democratic Front (FRD), 135, 259n59
Revolutionary Movement of the People (MRP), 113, 172, 177
Revolutionary National Militias (MNR), 28, 35, 55, 80, 84, 97
Revolutionary Recovery Movement (MRR), 135
Revolutionary Student Directorate (DRE), 30, 48, 144, 151, 153, 165, 190
Revolutionary Unity (UR), 98, 120
Ribicoff, Abraham, 148, 166, 184, 185, 197, 274n172
Ríos, Nicolás, 41, 114, 157
Ríos, Silvia, 31, 144, 157
Rollason, Wendell, 106, 130, 136, 166, 167, 179, 268n70, 273n154
Russia. *See* Soviet Union
Russian revolution, 113
Ruston Academy, 31, 40, 52, 56, 133, 148, 169, 199, 200, 258n31, 261n88; Baker and, 38, 52, 55, 133, 171; Operation Pedro Pan and, 171–72, 190, 192. *See also* Baker, James; Powers, Penny

Salado, Javier, 87
Sánchez, Celia, 33, 35
Santamaría, Haydée, 81
Sartre, Jean-Paul, 25, 27
Schlesinger, Arthur, 121, 161, 163, 176
Scholarships (*becas*), 41, 56, 90, 156, 239n264; awarded to *brigadistas*, 83, 85–86, 102, 245n140; Operation Pedro Pan and, 4, 146, 199, 214, 220; Soviet, 58, 239n264; U.S. scholarships, 55, 56, 58, 146–47, 214, 220, 245n140
Sex: *brigadistas* and, 38, 63, 97–98; youth and, 38
Smith, Wayne, 200, 206
Socialism, 45, 67, 97; Cuban revolution and, 3, 23, 33, 48, 50, 83, 101, 126, 157, 201; family and, 38, 111, 113; religion and, 45, 50, 83
Socialist bloc, 50, 123, 201; Cuba's trade with, 109; refugees from, 128, 201; student exchanges with, 57–58
Social revolution, 2, 10, 21, 43, 126, 158, 176, 215; education and, 51; traditional values and, 9, 10, 24, 34, 36–37, 91, 109; youth and, 20, 193, 215. *See also* Families; New Cuba; Racism; Patriarchal family; Women; Youth
Sosa, María de los Angeles (Candi), 58, 211–12, 218
Soviet Union, 108, 112, 118, 222; children and, 58, 106, 107, 108, 110, 112, 123, 222; Cuba's alignment with, 30, 48, 58, 109, 117, 176; family in, 112, 113, 116
Spain, 46, 49, 50, 108, 151, 195, 219; Cuba's independence struggle from, 74
Spanish Civil War, 46, 108, 154
State Department, U.S., 5, 138, 147, 166, 171, 175, 182; Cuban revolution and, 124, 164, 166, 176; response to Cuban refugee crisis, 6, 129, 135, 167, 217; Walsh and, 140–42, 167, 198
State Security, Cuban, 13, 112, 114, 116, 141, 168, 197, 199, 200, 204
Stolen Generation, 11
St. Raphael's, 156
Street children, 19, 33, 113, 132, 149, 186
Strong, Miriam, 47, 145, 191
Students, 56, 58, 85, 110, 111, 147; political activism of, 25, 30–31, 165, 179; high school students, 26, 27, 81; literacy campaign and, 65–66, 70, 79, 80, 161; speaking tours of, 179, 268n60. *See also* Catholic schools; Catholic students; Pedro Pans; Private schools; Youth
Student strike, 26, 31
Student visas, 131, 138–39, 140, 147, 160, 260n80
Sutherland, Elizabeth, 22, 42

Teachers, 31, 54, 56, 64, 86, 92, 103; corruption of, 54; departure of, 53, 64, 68, 155; José Martí's concept of, 68; literacy campaign and, 65, 68, 69–70, 72, 79, 161; education reform and, 57, 110; reeducation program (U.S.)

for, 191; volunteer, 8, 23. *See also Brigadistas;* Catholic schools; Private schools

Textbooks, 52, 53, 54, 55, 75. *See also* Education reform; Literacy campaign

Thomas, John, 195

Three Kings Day, 28, 230n50. *See also* Christmas

Time, 105, 107

Torres, María de los Angeles, 3, 14, 142, 170, 199, 206, 218; FOIA case against the CIA, 172–75, 193, 217

Trump, Donald J., 2, 5, 18

Unaccompanied minors. *See* Pedro Pans

UNESCO: Report on the Cuban literacy campaign, 74–75, 79, 92

Unidad Revolucionaria (UR). *See* Revolutionary Unity

United States: Cuban dependence on, 22, 42, 52, 162; cultural influence of, 7, 9–10, 42, 43, 56; historical relationship with Cuba, 6, 9, 11, 18, 22, 190, 220

United States embassy, Havana, 31, 40, 54, 199, 121; closure of, 137–38, 140, 197, 199; support for counterrevolution, 135

United States Information Agency (USIA), 175, 185, 187–89, 217

United States visas, 18, 128, 135–37, 140–41, 143, 165–66, 194, 198; children and, 4, 18, 105, 108, 128. *See also* Student visas; Visa waivers

University of Havana, 25, 48

University reform movement, 25

Urban reform, 40, 41, 51, 121, 201. *See also* Housing reform

U.S. News and World Report, 58, 177

Valdés, Nelson, 139, 144, 146, 165, 168

Varadero *brigadista* training camp, 70–71, 73, 76, 80, 82, 84–85, 87, 91, 95. *See also Brigadistas*

Varona, Manuel Antonio (Tony) de, 135, 164

Veciana, Antonio (Tony), 125

Verde Olivo, 116

Villanueva University, 49, 57, 147

Villaverde, Antonio, 63, 99

Villaverde, Bishop Alberto, 46

Visa waivers, 136, 149, 152, 154, 166–67, 169, 172, 182, 195, 198, 199, 201–2, 219–20; distribution of, 127, 152, 263n154; Operation Pedro Pan and, 5, 128, 138–42, 260n83; use by adults, 171, 194; Walsh and, 5, 13, 139–43, 154, 167, 182, 195, 198, 219

Vorhees, Tracy, 129, 130, 132

Walsh, Bryan O., 8, 13, 107, 123, 156, 169, 218; anti-Castro movement and, 169, 172; Catholic Welfare Bureau and, 1, 5, 128–29, 132, 141, 150, 155; CIA and, 141, 167, 173–74; Cuban Children's Program and, 131, 150, 152, 155; Elián González and, 208; Fidel Castro and, 203, 208; on day care, 111; on origins of Operation Pedro Pan, 117, 129, 132–34, 137–38, 140, 148–49; on parents' rights, 124, 127; Operation Pedro Pan and, 8, 15, 19, 135, 147–50, 155, 181–85, 198–99, 202; Pedro Pans and, 30, 59, 143–44, 146, 186; *The Lost Apple* and, 187–88, 197; trip to Cuba (1963), 153, 198; view of literacy campaign, 8, 63, 127; visa waiver authority of, 5, 139–43, 154, 167, 182, 195, 198, 219; U.S. State Department and, 140–42, 167, 198

Washington Post, 174, 207

Welfare Planning Council (Dade County), 132

Women, 35, 49, 101, 146; CIA propaganda and, 112, 114, 121–23, 166; liberation of, 35–36; revolution and, 26, 33, 34–39, 81, 111. *See also* Families; *Patria potestad*; Patriarchal family

Youth, 27, 45, 95, 102; anti-Batista movement and, 25–26; communism and, 157, 190, 192; Cuban revolution and, 8–9, 17, 20–21, 24–30, 48, 65, 70, 77, 80, 82, 101–3, 143–44, 157, 221; culture of, 28, 30; ideological battle for, 9, 17, 45, 47, 62, 102; opposition to Castro government, 31, 143, 179, 190; reeducation of, 190–93. *See also Brigadistas*; Catholic students; Catholic youth; Literacy campaign; Pedro Pans; Social revolution; Students; Youth revolt

Youth revolt, 1960s, 10–11, 27, 28, 30, 60, 210

DEBORAH SHNOOKAL is a historian, writer, and editor with a Ph.D. in history. She is cofounder of Ocean Press, an independent publisher with a list focusing on books from and about Latin America in English and Spanish. She coedited the *José Martí Reader: Writings on the Americas* and the *Fidel Castro Reader*. She is currently a research fellow at the Institute of Latin American Studies, Melbourne, Australia.

www.ingramcontent.com/pod-product-compliance
Lightning Source LLC
Chambersburg PA
CBHW030734250426
43671CB00035B/322